KNOWLEDGE:
ITS CREATION, DISTRIBUTION, AND
ECONOMIC SIGNIFICANCE

VOLUME I

KNOWLEDGE
AND KNOWLEDGE
PRODUCTION

KNOWLEDGE:
ITS CREATION, DISTRIBUTION, AND
ECONOMIC SIGNIFICANCE

VOLUME I

KNOWLEDGE
AND KNOWLEDGE
PRODUCTION

BY FRITZ MACHLUP

PRINCETON UNIVERSITY PRESS

Copyright © 1980 by Princeton University Press

Published by Princeton University Press, Princeton, New Jersey
In the United Kingdom: Princeton University Press, Guildford, Surrey

All Rights Reserved

Library of Congress Cataloging in Publication Data will be
found on the last printed page of this book

This book has been composed in VIP Melior

Clothbound editions of Princeton University Press books
are printed on acid-free paper, and binding materials are
chosen for strength and durability

Printed in the United States of America by Princeton
University Press, Princeton, New Jersey

Designed by Laury A. Egan

CONTENTS

ANALYTICAL TABLE OF CONTENTS   vii

PREFACE   xiii

THE STORY OF THIS WORK   xv

1   Introduction   3

PART ONE: TYPES OF KNOWLEDGE

2   The Known and the Knowing   27

3   Mundane, Scientific, Humanistic, Artistic, and Other Classes of Knowledge   59

4   Alternative Classifications of Knowledge   101

PART TWO: QUALITIES OF KNOWLEDGE

5   Truth, Beauty, and Goodness   113

6   Other Standards of Quality   125

7   Notions of Negative Knowledge   144

PART THREE: KNOWLEDGE AS A PRODUCT

8   Choosers and Users of Knowledge   155

9   Stocks and Flows of Knowledge   161

10   The Economic Cost of Knowledge   178

11   Transmission and Reception   186

12   Consumption, Investment, Intermediate Product   193

13   Uses, Value, and Benefits of Knowledge   202

14   Knowledge Industries and Knowledge Occupations   225

LIST OF PAGES WITH LINES OF TEXT RETAINED FROM THE 1962 VOLUME   242

INDEX   245

ANALYTICAL TABLE
OF CONTENTS

1 INTRODUCTION   3

THE ECONOMIST AS A STUDENT OF KNOWLEDGE PRODUCTION   3
Knowledge as a Datum in Economic Analysis   3
Knowledge as a Product, a Function of
   Resource Allocation   5

TERMINOLOGICAL PROPOSALS   7
"Production and Distribution"   7
"Knowledge and Information"   8

THE PROGRAM FOR THIS WORK   9
Some of the Reasons for Our Curiosity   9
In Quest of Light or Fruit?   11
A Preview of the Eight Volumes   13
A Preview of Volume I   17
Scope of the Expanding Work   20

TWO CHARGES AND APOLOGIES   20
Going Too Far Afield   21
Valuing the Invaluable   23

PART ONE: TYPES OF KNOWLEDGE

2 THE KNOWN AND THE KNOWING   27

THE DOUBLE MEANING OF KNOWLEDGE   27

MEANINGS OF KNOWING   29
Knowledge-Of and Knowledge-About   29
To Know That versus to Know How   30
To Know What, to Know That, and to Know How   33
The Special Status of Knowing That   36
An Assortment of Knowns and Knowings   38
Arrangement by Interrogative Pronoun   41
Further Comments on Knowing That and Knowing How   44

ELEMENTS AND MODES OF KNOWING   46
The Examples Surveyed for Different Modes of Knowing   46
The Elements of Knowing   47
Modes as Combinations of Elements   52

DEGREES OF KNOWING 52
Elements, Modes, and Degrees 53
More Details, More Accuracy, More Confidence 55

INFORMATION AND KNOWLEDGE 56
To Know and to Inform 56
Enduring Knowledge and Timely Information 57

3 MUNDANE, SCIENTIFIC, HUMANISTIC, ARTISTIC,
AND OTHER CLASSES OF KNOWLEDGE 59

MUNDANE KNOWLEDGE 59
Persuasive Definitions 59
Mundane Knowledge, Intentional Learning, and Erudition 60
The Proportions among Types of Knowledge 61

SCIENTIFIC KNOWLEDGE 62
Science Excluding Empirical Knowledge 62
Admitting Empirical Sciences 64
Expelling All but the Natural Sciences 65
Science in Other Languages 67
A Definition Reflecting a Polyglot Consensus 68

HUMANISTIC KNOWLEDGE 70
Traditional Meanings 71
The Humanists' Identity Crisis 73
Legal and Institutional Definitions 74
The Antiscientistic Humanist 75
The Two Cultures 79
The Characteristics of the Humanities 81

SOCIAL-SCIENCE KNOWLEDGE 84
Historical Development 85
Methodological Controversies 85
An Academic Subject Group 87
The Sense of It All 89

ARTISTIC KNOWLEDGE 90
Liberal, Professional, Mechanical, and Fine Arts 90
Performance versus Precepts for Performance 91
Creation and Communication 92

KNOWLEDGE WITHOUT WORDS 92
Verbal and Nonverbal Arts 93
Visual Arts 94

Performing Arts   94
Mundane Experiences   96
Knowing a Tune and Knowing a Feeling   98
Knowledge as a Mere Euphemism   100

4   ALTERNATIVE CLASSIFICATIONS OF KNOWLEDGE   101

    VARIOUS ASPECTS AND DISTINCTIONS   101
    Basic and Applied Knowledge   101
    Theoretical and Historical; General-Abstract and
        Particular-Concrete; Analytical and Empirical   102
    Knowledge of Enduring and of Transitory Interest   103
    Knowledge for Many and Knowledge for Only a Few   105
    Instrumental, Intellectual, and Spiritual Knowledge   106

    THE CHOSEN CLASSES   107
    Five Classes of Knowledge   108
    Subjective Sorting and Operational Criteria   108

            PART TWO: QUALITIES OF KNOWLEDGE

5   TRUTH, BEAUTY, AND GOODNESS   113

    KNOWLEDGE VERSUS BELIEF   113

    KNOWLEDGE AND TRUTH   114
    Facts and Propositions   115
    Verifiability, Confirmability, Falsifiability   115
    Relevance for the Purposes of this Study   117
    The Wrong Fifty Per Cent   118
    Pastime and Artistic Knowledge   118
    Practical Knowledge Had Better Be True   119

    KNOWLEDGE AND BEAUTY   120
    The Object and the Form   120
    Performing Arts   121
    Beautiful Theories, Beautiful Exposition   121

    KNOWLEDGE AND GOODNESS   122
    Ethics   122
    Normative and Empirical Statements   123
    Moral Education   123
    A Special Class of Knowledge?   124

6   OTHER STANDARDS OF QUALITY   125

HIGH-GRADE AND LOW-GRADE KNOWLEDGE   125
Serious versus Lightweight Knowledge   125
Workmanlike versus Shoddy Knowledge   128

UNWANTED KNOWLEDGE   129
Wanted by Some, Unwanted by Others   130
Nuisance Commercials as the Price of Desired Gifts   131

NONCOMPREHENDED KNOWLEDGE   132

RESTRICTED OR FORBIDDEN KNOWLEDGE   133
The Victims of Dangerous Knowledge   133
Unwholesome Knowledge   134
Obscene Knowledge and Pornography   136
Erotic Knowledge and Intellectual Freedom   138
Inflammatory or Explosive Knowledge   141

7   NOTIONS OF NEGATIVE KNOWLEDGE   144

Accepted Knowledge Negated by New Knowledge   144
Disproved and Suspended Knowledge   145
Knowledge Losing Relevance   145
Alternative Knowledge: Acceptance Pending   146
Demoted Sciences   146
Controversial Knowledge Claims   147
Questionable Knowledge   148
Vague Knowledge   148
Superstitions   149
Illusive Knowledge   150
Confusing Knowledge   150
Excluded Possibilities and Negative Predictions   151
Conclusion   152

PART THREE: KNOWLEDGE AS A PRODUCT

8   CHOOSERS AND USERS OF KNOWLEDGE   155

Consumers' Choice, Entrepreneurial Initiative,
   Political Decision   155
Subjectively New and Socially New Knowledge   158
Knowledge as an Intermediate or a Final Product   159

9 STOCKS AND FLOWS OF KNOWLEDGE 161

The Stock of Recorded Knowledge 162
A Collection of Scientific Journals 163
The Role of Books 165
The Stock of Knowledge in Human Minds 167
The Flow of Knowledge 170
Generation, Dissemination, and Use of Information 173
Accumulation, Replacement, Current Input,
    Consumption, and Waste 176

10 THE ECONOMIC COST OF KNOWLEDGE 178

The Private and Social Cost of Acquiring Knowledge 178
Knowledge at No Cost 178
The Scarcity Value of Alertness 180
The Intentions of the Recipient of Knowledge 181
The Initiative to Produce Knowledge 183

11 TRANSMISSION AND RECEPTION 186

Techniques and Intents of Knowledge Production 186
Types of Individual Knowledge Transmitters: Eight Levels 187
Knowledge Receiving as Knowledge Production 190

12 CONSUMPTION, INVESTMENT, INTERMEDIATE PRODUCT 193

Production: The Use of Valuable Input for
    Valuable Output 193
Investment in Knowledge and Investment for Knowledge 195
Knowledge as Intermediate Product 196
Knowledge-Producing Personnel in Business Firms 198
Instruments for the Production of Knowledge 198
Who Pays for It and How? 199
Chatting and Other Knowledge Production by Amateurs 200

13 USES, VALUE, AND BENEFITS OF KNOWLEDGE 202

USES OF KNOWLEDGE 202
Information Service and Knowledge Acquired 203
Pastime Knowledge and Practical Knowledge 204
Process versus Contents of Information 205
Some More Examples of Use 205

THE VALUE OF KNOWLEDGE   207

Value of Information   208
Value of Knowledge to Individual Would-Be Knowers   208
Practical and Intellectual Knowledge   209
The Private and Social Value of Education   211
Higher Earnings for Longer Schooling   212
An Alternative Notion of the Value of Schooling   213
The Private and Social Value of Scientific Journals   215

BENEFITS FROM KNOWLEDGE   217

Benefit-and-Cost Analysis   218
Five Types of Benefit-and-Cost Comparisons   219
Eager Ophelimetricians   220
Who Pays? Who Benefits?   222

14 KNOWLEDGE INDUSTRIES AND KNOWLEDGE OCCUPATIONS   225

KNOWLEDGE INDUSTRIES   225

What We Don't Know about Some Knowledge Industries   225
The Type of Product or the Type of Labor   226

INDUSTRIES AND OCCUPATIONS   227

Knowledge Industry   227
Knowledge Occupation   228
Degrees of Arbitrariness   229
A Heuristic Fiction: "Complete" Division of Labor   230
Production for Interindustry Trade and Intraindustry Use   231
The Major Knowledge Industries and Branches   232

FIRMS, INDUSTRIES, AND THE WHOLE ECONOMY   235

The Occupational Structure of Single Firms   235
A Different Model of the "Information Economy"   237
Strategies and Tactics in Quantitative Analysis   241

PREFACE

BIBLIOMETRICIANS have presented impressive evidence of the knowledge explosion that has occurred in our time. The publication of the work of which this volume is the first installment may be seen as a flagrant instance of the knowledge explosion: a single book of mine—*The Production and Distribution of Knowledge in the United States*, published by the Princeton University Press in 1962—has octupled within eighteen years, expanded into a series of eight volumes. The reasons for this expansion are discussed in "The Story of This Work," which follows this preface and tells about the origin and development of my research. One point, however, should be clarified right now: my concepts of knowing and knowledge are unusually wide. I do not confine myself to scientific or technological or verified or practical or intellectual knowledge. Anything that people think they know I include in the universe of knowledge.

The breadth of my concept of knowledge can be judged from the fact that a rendition in German would require three words: *wissen*, *kennen*, and *können*. The questions "Do you know France and do you know French?" would call for answers in German: "*ja, ich kenne Frankreich und ich kann Französisch*." A Frenchman, asked for his knowledge of England and English, has to distinguish between two verbs when he admits to *connaître l'Angleterre* and *savoir l'Anglais*. To know what, to know about, and to know how— all are encompassed in the wide concept of knowledge employed in the present work.

The extent to which the first volume of this serial work draws on what was contained in my 1962 book can be seen from the List of Pages with Lines of Text Retained from the 1962 Volume (below, p. 242). Only slightly more than forty pages of the earlier book, or 15 per cent of the present volume, have been retained.

Three chapters of this volume were prepublished, partly or in full: Chapter 9 appeared with some cuts in *Kyklos*, vol. 32, nos. 1-2; Chapter 10 in *Wandlungen in Wirtschaft und Gesellschaft— Festschrift für Walter Adolf Jöhr*, ed. by Emil Küng (Tübingen: Mohr-Siebeck, 1980); and Chapter 13 in *Knowledge: Creation, Diffusion, Utilization*, vol. 1, no. 1. I appreciate the publishers' permission to reprint.

Several grants in aid of my research have been received over the years, but in listing some of the sponsors it is necessary to stress that different sources of funds supported different stages and phases of the project. Much of the research for the 1962 volume will be used in Volumes III to VIII of the new work; most of the grants received since 1971 have been for research to be used for Volumes III to VI. Only a minute fraction of the financial support received for the entire project was used for preparing the material for the present volume. It is for this reason that I should begin my list of sponsors with the two who financed most of the reference work and typing of Volume I: The Ford Foundation and the Earhart Foundation. Yet, since I have done the writing of this volume simultaneously with the research on later volumes, I should not defer naming the chief supporters of the project as a whole: The National Science Foundation, The National Endowment for the Humanities, the National Institute of Education, the Alfred P. Sloan Foundation, and the John and Mary Markle Foundation.

Over the years, 1971 to 1980, my research team has varied in size, from between six to twenty-four persons, mainly graduate students working part-time as research assistants. Most of them were economists, but anthropologists, psychologists, historians, educationists, engineers, literature majors, information scientists, computer scientists, and other specialists were among them. The total number up to now exceeds sixty. I shall name them in the prefaces of the volumes in which I report on their research. For this volume I have to thank only two of them: Mary Taylor Huber, who supplied materials and documentation for Chapter 3, and Jessica Kennedy, who helped me with the Index. Two friends of mine have influenced my thinking in essential ways: Professor Donna Kerr, philosopher and educationist, had much to do with Chapter 2, "The Known and the Knowing," and Professor Kenneth Boulding, economist and social philosopher, made many helpful suggestions for almost all chapters. Finally, I want to thank three good spirits of the Princeton University Press: Herbert Bailey, director, for his encouragement, counsel, and confidence in me and my longevity; Sanford Thatcher, assistant director, for his skill in steering my ambitious projects through the dangerous waters of editorial policy; and Peggy Riccardi, the editor in charge of my manuscripts, for her understanding, literary taste, and exquisite feeling for language.

Princeton University and   FRITZ MACHLUP
New York University

THE STORY of this work is, I think, worth telling. This should imply that it is also worth reading. I have tried it out on a few patient victims, and they said it had made no demands on their patience and they felt in no way victimized. Boldly generalizing from their flattering reactions, I offer my story to any reader who is not averse to browsing through authors' self-advertisements.

My first thought was to include this story in the Introduction. Sanford Thatcher, of the Princeton University Press, wisely advised against it: such intimate matters about the author and his work were, he said, more suitable for the Preface. However, I do not like long prefaces. So I decided to stick this story between preface and introduction; it would no longer be prefatory, but still proemial or preludial, still a part of the preliminary material of the book.

How One Thing Led to Another

How did I ever come to think of inquiring into the production of knowledge as an economic activity of the nation and to estimate size and growth of this sector of the economy? It was not a sudden flash, a brainstorm out of the blue; nor was it an idea suggested by conversation or by reading a particular book or article. Instead, it was a case of intellectual chain reactions, taking place gradually over a period of twenty-five years. It was a case of "how one thing led to another." Each linkage is plausible, but the beginning and the end are so unlike each other that no one could have foreseen this evolution.

It began with an interest in monopolistic or imperfect competition, aroused in 1933 by reading the well-known books on this subject and by discussions at Harvard with a group of fine economists. I was soon writing on monopoly and competition, first only on pure theory. Later I turned my attention to the institutions promoting restrictions on competition, among them the system of patents of invention. I spent a few years studying the economics of patent protection and intended to do a book on this subject. Such a book has to be focused on the analysis of benefits and costs. If the patent system succeeds in diverting material and human resources into research, development, patenting, litigation, and whatever is connected with inventing, the cost of these resources has to be estimated. Was it possible to divide R and D activities into those that were and those that were not induced by the patent incentive? Even if such a separation were feasible, would it not be essential to compare the patent-induced investments in (or expenditures for) R and D with the total?

Having recognized that R and D was an essential part of my theoretical and empirical research, it became clear to me that these activities were closely linked with education. R and D was complementary with higher education in some aspects and competitive in others. Quality education was surely a precondition of quality research. I became interested in the total effort the nation had been making, at conspicuously increasing costs and decreasing benefits, to create and disseminate scientific and technological knowledge. It was apparent that trained personnel was required for R and D and that education, especially higher education, had to prepare it. Thus, to be systematic in my work, I had to inquire into the educational system at all levels. If I wanted to find out how the nation produced knowledge, I could not confine such an inquiry to what the R and D people liked to call "S and T information"—scientific and technological information. All schooling, all college work, all graduate education had to be included in a comprehensive study of the production of knowledge in the United States.

From the inclusion of education, it was only a small step to the inclusion of books and journals, magazines and newspapers. Reading, as a matter of fact, is a significant part of education, but the question arose whether there is a way to separate intellectual from pastime reading, absorption of knowledge of enduring relevance from "getting informed" about current news items, and receiving messages useful for immediate action, but of strictly transitory relevance. There may indeed be a way to make such separations, to estimate the proportions between quasi-permanent and merely ephemeral knowledge, but it would be of even greater interest to include both in the total to be captured in any quantitative research. The next annexation, after that of information through the printed word, was information through the electronic media of communication, radio and television broadcasting. And there are also several other channels over which information and knowledge of all sorts is transmitted. I regarded it as imperative to include artistic creation and communication and, on a more mundane level, the roles of telegraph, telephone, and the postal services.

Two final steps remained, and they proved to be of strategic importance: the inclusion of information services and information machines. The information-machine industry, especially, had a well-nigh spectacular growth in the 1950s, led by the development of the computer and electronic data processing. The growth rates observed in this and other "knowledge industries" and "knowledge occupations" seemed to me so extraordinary that I became convinced of the need for a quantitative study that would show the share of each knowledge industry in the gross national product of the United States. I had never in my past work engaged in statistical investigations. Now it seemed imperative that I should.

Returning to the theme "How One Thing Led to Another," I may say that the chain from the theory of competition and monopoly to a statistical investigation of knowledge production in the United States is long and tangled. From link to link, however, the connection is relatively easy to see.

Public Lectures and Sponsored Research

Apart from the chain of ideas, there is a chain of events from an idea for a research project to its execution, and eventually its completion. The execution required financial support, and I shall presently speak about the sponsors of my research. But it also required encouragement and moral incentives. The research climates at the Johns Hopkins University and at Princeton University and some invitations to endowed lectures elsewhere provided both.

Endowed lectures have often been responsible for publications of pamphlets or slim books. This time a heavy tome grew out of five lectures. The first of these was the John L. Senior Lecture in American Studies which I gave in March 1959 at Cornell University; the other four were the Moorhouse I. X. Millar Lectures which I gave in October 1960 at Fordham University. Had it not been for the persuasive powers of Father William T. Hogan, S.J., of Fordham University, I doubt that I would have been enterprising enough to embark on the research for this ambitious project. I grossly underestimated the immense amount of work when I gave in to Father Hogan's persuasion. Of course, after I had seriously started the research, I never thought of turning back.

The task I had set for myself was not a one-man job; I needed research assistance. Fortunately, I had a group of able graduate students at Hopkins, and in 1959 I secured grants from three sources: the National Science Foundation, the Ford Foundation, and a large corporation. These grants were chiefly in support of research on some of the earlier links in the chain of ideas, namely, "The Economic Aspects of Patent Protection, Technological Inventions, and Their Development." As a matter of fact, most of the work financed by these grants was on projects fully consistent with the title of the sponsored research. Still, I was able to get some portion of the assistants' time for the statistical research needed for the comprehensive investigation of knowledge production.

The three grants continued when I moved to Princeton; some of my research assistants came with me. During my first year at Princeton University, I had a group of seven collaborators, two post-doctoral and five working towards their Ph.D. degrees. That I was freed from teaching duties during my first term at Princeton was of great help in completing my book.

The Publication of the 1962 Volume

The book, under the title *The Production and Distribution of Knowledge in the United States*, had been promised to the Fordham University Press as an issue of the Millar Lecture series. When I delivered the manuscript of 600 typed pages and 84 statistical tables, I found that this was far more than Father Quain, the director of the Press, had expected. Arranging the complicated multicolumn tables in a form suitable for printing in a format of normal octavo size appeared to raise serious problems. I turned to Herbert Bailey of the Princeton University Press for advice. He saw no forbidding problems in the composition of my tables and asked me to let him read the manuscript. He liked what he saw and undertook to talk to Father Quain. The results of the discussions between the directors of the two university presses were that the Fordham University Press kindly released me from my commitment, and the Princeton University Press put my manuscript through the customary refereeing process.

The referees reported that this was a "pioneering" work. Instead of the customary request or condition that the author cut or prune the manuscript to "acceptable size," I was praised for my inclusion of some rather controversial comments and digressions and encouraged to extend critique and recommendations of this kind to several chapters of the book. I appreciated the wisdom of the editorial board in allowing me additional space to add more of my personal value judgments to the factual statistical estimates. The book, no doubt, became far more readable: after all, it is not easy to present masses of statistical series in a good prose style with occasional humor to lighten the serious disquisition.

The Outline of the 1962 Book

The book was published in December 1962. In the first chapter, "Introduction," the outline of the book was described as follows:

"Our first task . . . will be to develop the conceptual framework for an analysis of 'knowledge production.' This will involve discussions of the meanings of the term 'knowledge' and of the various ways in which scholars—philosophers, sociologists, and others—have classified knowledge. It will further require an analysis of the various methods of producing knowledge, with appropriate distinctions between technical and economic points of view. Finally, it will call for the formulation of criteria for deciding under what conditions knowledge is a 'final' product, or only an 'intermediate' one, and, if it is a final product, whether it is investment or a service to consumers. All this is on the program for Chapter II.

"Chapter III is a brief essay on the significant difference between an 'industry approach' and an 'occupation approach' to the study of knowledge production. The industry approach will be followed in the subsequent six chapters, and only the last chapter of the book will return to the problem of the secular increase in the share of 'knowledge-producing occupations' in the total labor force.

"Chapter IV, the longest in the volume, is devoted to Education, the largest of the knowledge industries. After brief discussions of education outside the schools—in the home, on the job, in the church, in the armed services—historical statistics and expenditure analyses are presented, first, for elementary and secondary schools and, then, for institutions of higher education. The problems of the productivity—social rate of return—and of the efficiency of education are examined, and, finally, a proposal for school reform is submitted. Earnest consideration of this proposal is requested.

"Another long chapter, V, deals with Research and Development and the enormously rapid growth rate in this activity, largely financed with government funds. The various subdivisions—basic research, applied research, and development—are treated separately as well as jointly; the inventive process and the role of the patent system in the promotion of inventive effort are analyzed. After an examination of the competitiveness between industrial research and secondary and higher education and the essential complementarity between basic research and education, a warning is sounded against the widely favored expansion of industrial research and development, because it may lead to a fatal curtailment in the training of research scientists. Too rapid growth of applied research and development work may conceivably dry up the supply of research personnel and, thus, force cutbacks of research in the future.

"The Media of Communication are to be treated in Chapter VI, which will include historical and statistical surveys of printing and publishing—books, periodicals, newspapers—of the stage and the cinema, of radio and television, telephone and telegraph, the postal service, and of a few other media. Though each of these discussions is relatively brief, they add up to a considerable compendium.

"Chapter VII is devoted to a survey of Information Machines. Here the replacement of men by machines in the processing of information and the prompt availability of information needed for more rational decision-making are discussed. Some basic facts about electronic computers and automatic control systems are presented, and the spectacular growth of this industry is shown by means of statistical data furnished by some of the larger firms.

"Information Services will be discussed in Chapter VIII, in a somewhat groping fashion because of the awkward conceptual and statistical problems involved. Several information services are rendered jointly with other services at joint costs and, in view of the arbitrariness of statistical separation, no satisfactory treatment seems possible.

"A summary statement of the expenditures for the products of the various knowledge industries is to be presented in Chapter IX. Although the growth rate of knowledge production as a whole is naturally less sensational than the growth rates in some of its parts, it still is impressive. An ever-increasing part of the actual and potential gross national product has been taken by the production of knowledge. The causal connections are complex and undoubtedly go in both directions: an increase in the production of certain kinds of knowledge, in the nature of investment, leading to increased productivity in the use of resources and to higher national incomes; the increase in total income, in turn, leading to greater consumption of other kinds of knowledge and also providing ampler funds for investment in more knowledge of the productive types.

"The last chapter, X, will treat of the gradual, but distinct, change in the occupational composition of the labor force that has been going on at least since 1900 and has become even more conspicuous in recent years. This change involves a continuous increase in 'knowledge-producing' workers and a relative decline in what used to be called 'productive labor.' The changing employment pattern now shows such a rapid trend towards the use of more brainpower relative to the use of physical strength or physical skills that a serious problem of employability of less-educated members of the labor force arises.

"The plan of this book shows, I submit, a unity of conception which sharply distinguishes it from a collection of essays. Yet the author's effort to make each chapter as self-contained as possible will be apparent. This is attempted for the sake of specialists who may be interested in some chapters but not in others. It is quite likely that many 'educators' will want to read only Chapter IV, and many 'research scientists' only Chapter V. Although I cannot say that they would not miss anything if they chose to neglect the rest of the book, at least they would never know that they have."

How the Book Was Received

The book was reviewed in professional journals, general-interest magazines, and several daily papers. The most widely used attribute reviewers bestowed on my work was "pioneering." Featured in most notices was my discovery of the unexpectedly high total dollar value of production by knowledge industries (for 1958), its large share in the national product, and its rapid growth (in the previous decade). Learned and professional journals emphasized, as one should expect, issues of particular interest to their special fields.

The most perceptive and commendatory of the reviews in economic journals was by Kenneth Boulding. He offered several useful suggestions, and also a few criticisms which were intended to "underline the great importance and the pioneering nature of this study, ... That it could easily be mistaken for a simple exercise in national-income arithmetic should not blind the reader to its revolutionary potential. The very concept of a knowledge industry contains enough dynamite to blast traditional economics into orbit."[1]

One of Boulding's criticisms was leveled against my recommendations for school reform; he quite rightly held that my plan for shortening primary and secondary schooling from twelve to nine or ten years was based on arguments for which I had merely casual evidence, if any. The same criticism was made by Mary Jean Bowman.[2] Yet, she substituted for the "Machlup Plan" a "Bowman Plan," which included, among other desirable features, an abolition of junior high school, with a reduction of primary plus secondary education to eleven years. Her major criticism of my approach towards measuring the total annual value of knowledge production related to my technique of using opportunity costs—the value of alternative outputs, that is, of outputs not produced but foregone for the sake of the actually chosen use of resources. She questioned my combining these opportunity costs, to the extent that they were mere estimates, with statistical data from the national-income-and-product accounts.

Robert Lekachman was most complimentary of what he considered "perhaps the finest portion of this volume . . . the long virtuosic

[1] Kenneth E. Boulding, "The Knowledge Industry," *Challenge*, May 1963, p. 38.

[2] Mary Jean Bowman, "Professor Machlup on Knowledge and Reform," *The School Review*, vol. 71, no. 2 (1963), pp. 235-245.

chapter on education, which displays the talents of interpretation and advocacy for which the author is equally famous among his fellows." Of the work as a whole he found that "seldom has a pioneer investigation of so complex a topic as a freshly defined industry received so elegant and so fascinating an initial treatment. The book deserves attention for the incisiveness of the argument, the novelty of the definitions, and the freshness of the information which is gathered, sorted, and interpreted."[3]

Especially gratifying was the review by Theodore Schultz. He commented favorably on my inclusion of opportunity costs in my estimates of the value of knowledge produced by education: "[Machlup] is every inch an economist in facing up to the analytical issues implicit in earnings foregone and other opportunity costs of schooling, and the vexing issues underlying the benefits from schooling whether they are 'consumption' or 'investment' and whether they accrue to students or to others. . . . Machlup's treatment of earnings foregone and of other neglected opportunity costs is not only formally correct but refreshingly clear and remarkably all-inclusive."[4]

Schultz mentioned "the special merit of the . . . chapter on 'Research and Development.' " He found that "the concise section on inventive effort and patent protection is a classic, and so is the treatment of the complementarity between basic research and higher education." Several of Schultz's comments on various parts of my work were challenging and will cause me to give careful attention to the issues in question in the respective chapters of this new work. It may be worth noting where Schultz saw the chief strength of my book: "Without any fanfare or claim that this book is about economic growth, Professor Machlup has made a major contribution to this branch of economics."[5]

This may or may not agree with the judgment expressed by Shane Hunt, who wrote that "basically this is a book on economic structure. In place of the conventional division of an economy into primary, secondary, and tertiary industries, Professor Machlup proposes an entirely different division into those economic activities which have as their product some form of knowledge, and those which do not."[6]

---

[3] Robert Lekachman, Review, *Political Science Quarterly*, vol. 78 (September 1963), pp. 468-469.

[4] Theodore W. Schultz, Book review, *The American Economic Review*, vol. 53 (September 1963), p. 837.

[5] Ibid., p. 836.

[6] Shane Hunt, Review, *Journal of Political Economy*, vol. 73 (June 1965), p. 311.

If secular changes in the structure of the economy—in the composition of output and labor force, and in the functional distribution of income—are important criteria of development and growth, Hunt's and Schultz's descriptions of the implications of my findings are consistent.

The Multiversity and the Knowledge Industry

In his Godkin Lectures at Harvard University in April 1963, Clark Kerr, then President of the University of California, discussed "The Uses of the University." He sketched the historical development of the university from its medieval beginnings to the present and showed how ideals and reality had changed; how Cardinal Newman's "Idea of a University," favoring liberal over useful knowledge, and Abraham Flexner's "Idea of a Modern University," favoring elitist research over service stations for the general public, had both given place to the "Idea of a Multiversity," trying to be everything to everybody. This evolution was part of a major transformation that had taken place in the United States: "Basic to this transformation is the growth of the 'knowledge industry,' which is coming to permeate government and business and to draw into it more and more people raised to higher and higher levels of skill."[7]

Quoting my findings concerning the relative share of "knowledge production" in the United States and its rate of growth, he remarked that "knowledge has certainly never in history been so central to the conduct of an entire society," that the "knowledge industry" may well "serve as the focal point for national growth" in the second half of this century, and that "the university is at the center of the knowledge process."[8]

The acceptance of my findings, but especially of my terms, made Clark Kerr the butt of vehement attacks by revolting students, discontented professors, and well-meaning philosophers. The leader of the students charged Kerr with having called the large university a "knowledge factory." Two professors, without checking, repeated that "knowledge factory" was one of Kerr's phrases.[9] The philosopher, having learned from Kerr's reply to the professors[10] that Kerr had not spoken of a "knowledge factory" but rather of the growth of

---

[7] Clark Kerr, The Uses of the University (Cambridge, Mass.: Harvard University Press, 1963), p. 88.

[8] Ibid.

[9] Sheldon S. Wolin and John H. Schaar, "Berkeley and the Fate of the Multiversity," New York Review, vol. 4, no. 3 (March 11, 1965), p. 15.

[10] Clark Kerr, "An Exchange on Berkeley," New York Review, vol. 4, no. 5, Special Spring Issue (April 8, 1965), p. 35.

the "knowledge industry," and that this term was not Kerr's but quoted from my book, was still distressed by the thought of a university as "an 'industry' whose business . . . is knowledge."[11] That an institution of higher learning should be regarded as a part of an "industry" offended the high-minded lover of wisdom. He believed that Kerr's acceptance of that term reflected some dehumanizing attitudes of the new managers of our educational enterprises.[12] The difference between Kerr and his antimaterialistic critics was not the absence of idealism in Kerr's lectures but his critics' failure to look into my book to see that neither industry nor occupation—the words I used in designating my two approaches—were in any sense demeaning intellectual and humanistic knowledge.

I have included this little comedy of errors regarding my innocent word coinage partly because of its entertainment value, but chiefly because of its implied lesson that we check our references not only superficially but by reading enough to understand from the context what the author meant by his words. "Knowledge industry" has certainly become an accepted term in discussions of economic and social change and involves no slur on whatever type of knowledge is created or communicated—cognitive or affective, practical or esoteric.

Interdisciplinary and International Reactions

The interdisciplinary character of my book was reflected in the variety of special professional groups that published reviews or com-

[11] Henry David Aiken, Predicament of the University (Bloomington: University of Indiana Press, 1971), p. 114.

[12] ". . . if one treats the production of knowledge as an industry and the university as its center, one has defined the university's institutional function in industrial terms." Ibid., p. 388.—One may forgive a philosopher his unawareness of economic terms in the official language of the United States Government, the "Standard Industrial Classification," which includes agriculture, amusement, recreation, professional services, and government itself among the "major industry groups." The U.S. Census of 1890 distinguishes "mechanical and manufacturing industries" from other industries. The dictionary definitions of industry include, besides "diligence in any task" and "systematic work," "a particular branch of productive labor," stated as going back to 1566, long before the industrial revolution.—The sociologist Everett Hughes, in an article first published in 1952, commented on the supposedly current "extension of the term 'industry' to include so much more than manufacturing" and considered it "an interesting datum," probably reflecting the higher prestige of that efficient form of organization. After mentioning the "advertising industry" and the "amusement industry" as examples, he added: "No one has yet, so far as I know, talked of the medical, educational, and labor-union industries, but I suppose someone will." Everett C. Hughes, "The Sociological Study of Work: An Editorial Foreword," The American Journal of Sociology, vol. 57 (March 1952), reprinted in his The Sociological Eye (Chicago: Aldine-Atherton, 1971), p. 298.

ments in their periodicals. Apart from journals on education and research, the magazines and newsletters of publishers, librarians, journalists, radio and television broadcasters, accountants, advertising professionals, and public-relations specialists were among those that took notice of the book. Among the learned societies—besides those of economists—that considered the volume as relevant to the research interests of their members were the sociologists, the anthropologists, the political scientists, and the information scientists.

International interest in the book showed itself first through lengthy reviews in foreign-language journals, and later through frequent citations and comments in journal articles and books. But only two translations into foreign languages have been published: Russian and Japanese.

The Russian edition appeared in 1966 under the title *Proizvodstvo i rasprostranenie zanii v SShA*.[13] A preface, twenty-six pages long, was written by G. V. Poluninoi. It raised the question why a work by a "bourgeois" apologist from an "imperialist country" should merit a translation into Russian. He gave several reasons for it, chief among which were the novelty of the conception and the mass of valuable data that resulted from an attempt to compute magnitudes "hitherto not computed by anyone." He regarded the material as of "unquestioned interest to Marxist investigators of the economics of capitalist countries," particularly to investigators of the rapidly expanding "nonproductive sphere." He concluded that it is "necessary to insist on a genuinely scientific Marxist investigation of this sphere."

The Japanese edition appeared in 1969 under the title *Chishiki Sangyō*.[14] The translation was made by a team of researchers under the supervision of Tatsuo Takahashi and Hiroshi Kida. The title means literally "Knowledge Industry"; this term, evidently, has caught on in Japanese discussion. The book had surprisingly large sales and became the topic of private and public discussion groups. In Japan the interest in the growth of knowledge production has remained intense. One research institute undertook to replicate my statistical investigation with Japanese data and published its findings in a separate book. Another organization invited me several times for lecture series on further developments in this area and published three small books of my papers in Japanese translation.

[13] Translated by I. I. Diumulen, U. I. Kozlov, and M. Z. Shterngarts; edited by E. I. Rosental (Moscow: Progress, 1966), xxx and 462 pp.

[14] *Chishiki Sangyō* (Tokyo: Sangyō Nohritsu Tanki Daigaku, 1969), xxxv, 447, and 16 pp.

Demands for a New Edition with Updated Statistics

The discovery of the relatively large size and enormous growth of knowledge production gave a jolt to many observers and interpreters of economic development. No one had expected the production of knowledge in the United States to be of the order of magnitude that I had calculated for 1958. I myself had never suspected this result of my calculations. I had finished writing most of the chapters of the book before I came to the summary chapter in which I totaled the figures I had estimated for each of the various knowledge industries. I could not believe my eyes, and still less my arithmetic (done with pencil and paper), when I saw that aggregate knowledge production was 29 per cent of (adjusted) gross national product. And I was startled when I saw the growth rates of the various knowledge industries and the growth rate of the aggregate. If that growth were proceeding at the rate I had found for the decade before 1958—2½ times the average rate of growth of other components of total GNP—the share of knowledge production in total activity would soon reach 50 per cent.

I had made similar calculations for the share of knowledge *occupations* in total activities. I had found that the ratio of workers in the labor force who were engaged in knowledge-producing activities to the total civilian labor force was 31.6 per cent in 1959, and had grown by 30 per cent in nine years. When I added the number of full-time students of working age to both magnitudes, so that the persons engaged in knowledge work included those who produce knowledge in their own heads, and this number is then compared with the "potential labor force"—the full-time students of working age being added to both the numerator and the denominator—the share of knowledge workers in the potential labor force was 42.8 per cent. That these ratios would reach and surpass 50 per cent within a few years was a relatively safe guess.

Was growth in knowledge production continuing at the rates I had calculated? When would the output of the knowledge industries reach the 50 per cent mark? These questions were on the minds of many of my readers. I received dozens of inquiries every year. Had I updated my statistical series? Had I made some projections? Had I heard of anyone else doing a project of this sort? For years my answers to all these questions had to be negative.

Fortune Magazine did not take my "no" for an acceptable answer. Mr. Gilbert Burck, a member of its board of editors, assigned a researcher to the task of updating, partly by means of rough projections, my aggregate and some of the larger subaggregates for the year 1963. Burck's article was very interesting but did not reveal the methods of computation.[15] Even the total dollar amount of knowledge production was not clearly stated, though it could be read off a bar diagram or calculated from the statement that from 1958 to 1963 it had grown by 43 per cent. Although the article conveyed the impression that this was an extraordinary rate of growth, it failed to explain that it was actually a declining rate. During the same five years, the gross national product had increased by 32.5 per cent and the portion constituted by non-knowledge production by 28 per cent. Thus the growth rate of knowledge production was only 1½ times that of the other components of GNP, much less than the 2½ times I had calculated for an earlier period. Burck's article realized that knowledge production "could approach the 50 percent mark," but it wisely withheld a prediction of when this might happen.

In 1967 Jacob Marschak delivered a lecture on the "Economics of Inquiring, Communicating, and Deciding," which was published in May 1968. He began with a reference to the "informational revolution," and to the "rapid growth of the knowledge industry." On the basis of my estimates of the share of knowledge production in the gross national product of 1958 and on its growth rate of about ten per cent per year, he made a projection according to which the share of the knowledge output would by then (1967) "appear to straddle the 40 per cent mark."[16]

In 1968 Peter Drucker wrote a book titled *The Age of Discontinuity*. Part IV of it was on "The Knowledge Society" and Chapter 12, on "The Knowledge Economy." Based evidently on my estimates and his own projections, Drucker stated that the "knowledge industries . . . accounted in 1955 for one-quarter of the U.S. gross national product" and that, "by 1965, . . . the knowledge sector was taking one-third of a much bigger national product." He gave no basis for this projection but he projected even further and stated that "in the late 1970s it [the knowledge sector] will account for one-half of the total national product."[17]

In 1977 Marc Uri Porat completed a doctoral dissertation at Stanford University on "The Information Economy." An expanded version was published by the Office of Telecommunications of the U.S.

[15] Gilbert Burck, "Knowledge: The Biggest Growth Industry of Them All," *Fortune*, November 1964, pp. 128-131, 267-268, 270.

[16] Jacob Marschak, "Economics of Inquiring, Communicating, and Deciding," *American Economic Review*, Papers and Proceedings, vol. 58 (May 1968), p. 1.

[17] Peter F. Drucker, *The Age of Discontinuity* (New York: Harper & Row, 1968), p. 263.

Department of Commerce in a set of nine volumes under the same title, with appropriate subtitles for each volume.[18] It presented a detailed analysis of the statistical data for 1967 of the national-income-and-product accounts, developed by the Bureau of Economic Analysis. Using techniques different from those I had employed for my 1958 estimates, Porat's numerical findings on the share of "information activities" are not easily comparable with mine. His major procedural innovation was to divide the "information economy" into a "primary information sector," comprising "those firms which supply the bundle of information goods and services exchanged in a market context," and a "secondary information sector," which "includes all the information services produced for internal consumption by government and noninformation firms."[19] In 1967 the "value added" originating in the primary information sector amounted to 25.1 per cent of GNP, and that of the secondary sector to 21.1 per cent, together, 46.2 per cent. This is a larger share than that projected by Marschak for the same year. Nevertheless, Porat held that my total for 1958 may have been too high.[20]

Research for a Second Edition or a New Work

I knew nothing about Porat's research when I decided in 1972 that I had a moral obligation to undertake myself the job of updating the statistical analysis, provided I could secure the necessary financial support. The National Science Foundation and the National Endowment for the Humanities agreed to sponsor my research. I chose 1970 as the terminal year for the update of the statistics and assembled a research staff of twelve graduate students, chiefly part-time, for the statistical work.

In the third year of our effort, I allowed myself to take on an addi-

---

[18] Marc Uri Porat, The Information Economy (Washington: U.S. Department of Commerce, Office of Telecommunications, 1977). Volumes 3-8 were written with the assistance of Michael R. Rubin, who signed as sole author for volume 9.

[19] These definitions should not be taken literally. For example, "the wages of workers employed in public education" were included in the primary sector, because education "has direct analogs in the primary information sector." Ibid., vol. 1, p. 51.

[20] Porat was not critical of my statistical efforts: "The omission of value-added estimates from earlier work undoubtedly reflected the state of data processing facilities available at the time. Without fast computers and, more importantly, very extensive interlocked machine readable data bases, it is doubtful whether a more comprehensive report could have been prepared. In the 15 years since Machlup's research, a wealth of information became available and accessible." (Ibid., vol. 1, p. 47) Porat's emphasis on "value-added estimates" reflects constructs and operational concepts of the knowledge industries rather different from mine; but this will be discussed in a later volume.

tional task, an ambitious inquiry into the economics of scholarly publishing, a project also sponsored by the National Science Foundation and the National Endowment for the Humanities. This inquiry seemed to promise a rich harvest of new data on book publishing, journal publishing, abstracting and indexing services, and libraries; very little was known about these sectors of knowledge production, and I thought that this expansion of the scope of my data base was worth the delay in completing my second edition or new work. Now that I have completed the four volumes on *Information through the Printed Word*,[21] I am not sure that the new material enriches the particular parts—probably in Volume V of this work—sufficiently to justify the long delay and the renewed effort of another updating of all my statistical series from 1970 to, say, 1978. On the other hand, I must admit that it is more helpful to have the series brought forward by several years. All statistical series in this work will go to the latest available year, and the grand total will be calculated for 1975 or the latest year for which it can be done.

[21] Fritz Machlup, Kenneth Leeson, and Associates, *Information through the Printed Word: The Dissemination of Scholarly, Scientific, and Intellectual Knowledge*. Vol. 1, *Book Publishing*, vol. 2, *Journals*, vol. 3, *Libraries* (New York: Praeger Publishers, 1978), vol. 4, *Books, Journals, and Bibliographic Services* (New York: Praeger Publishers, 1980).

VOLUME I

KNOWLEDGE
AND KNOWLEDGE
PRODUCTION

CHAPTER 1

INTRODUCTION

EVERY BRANCH of learning takes a good many things for granted. If these things *have* to be explained, "Let George do it." George is always someone in another discipline. Hence, the analysis of the production and distribution of knowledge falls into George's field.

George has always been a popular fellow. People were inclined to rely upon him even if they did not know whether he really existed. In recent years, however, Georges have actually appeared on the scene in increasing numbers. Many of them are called "interdisciplinary research workers."

THE ECONOMIST AS A STUDENT OF KNOWLEDGE PRODUCTION

Anything that goes under the name of "production and distribution" sounds as if it clearly fell into the economist's domain. An analysis of "knowledge," on the other hand, seems to be the philosopher's task, though some aspects of it are claimed by the sociologist. But, if one speaks of the "communication of knowledge in the United States," the specialist in education may feel that this is in his bailiwick; also, the mathematician or operations researcher specializing in communication theory and information systems may prick up his ears. In fact, some of the knowledge to be discussed here is technological, and thus the engineer may properly be interested. When I tried out the title of this study on representatives of various disciplines, many were rather surprised that an economist would find himself qualified to undertake this kind of research. Of course, they did not really know what kind of research I was planning under that intriguing title.

Knowledge as a Datum in Economic Analysis

Knowledge has always played a part in economic analysis, or at least certain kinds of knowledge have. There has always been the basic assumption that sellers and buyers have knowledge of the markets, that is, of their selling and buying opportunities. The theories of supply and demand, of competition and monopoly, of relative prices, interdependence, and all the rest, all have been based on the assumption that sellers know the highest prices at which they can sell and buyers know the lowest prices at which they can buy. In addition, it has always been assumed that producers have *knowledge of the technology of the time*, that is, of their production opportunities. In other words, the assumption has been that they know the lowest cost at which they can produce. The usual supposition has been that all producers in an industry are familiar with the "state of the technical arts."

This does not mean that economic theorists have regarded technological knowledge as unchanging. But to most economists and for most problems of economics the state of knowledge and its distribution in society are among the data assumed as given. There is nothing wrong with this. When an economist analyzes the effects of new taxes, of changes in interest rates or wage rates, it would be unreasonable for him *not* to assume a given state of technology. And, even when he analyzes problems of growth and development, he will often find it expedient to assume either a given state of the arts or a given rate of progress, whatever this may mean.

An increasing number of economists these days concern themselves with the prospective growth of the economy during the next twenty or thirty years. Needless to say, they cannot take the state of technical knowledge as given and constant. On the other hand, they do not want to burden their models with more stuff than is absolutely necessary for their task and, therefore, they choose to assume a given rate of advance of productivity, to project the past rate of advance into the future. In other words, the progress of technical knowledge is made an exogenous variable, or a simple trend function, a function of time.

Incidentally, the same practice prevails concerning other important variables in growth economics—for example, population and labor force. There was a time when economists regarded the explanation of population growth as their business. Later they got out of this job and assigned it to George—this time a specialist, the demographer. Only very exceptional economists today concern themselves with the economic determination of population changes and would include population as a dependent variable in their growth model. The choice between taking a variable as exogenous or making it an endogenous one, a variable determined by the system of functions, is a matter of relevance and convenience. No economist, for example, would refuse to recognize the explanation of capital formation as a part of his job. He constructs elaborate models in which investment functions and saving functions, together with several other equations, are supposed to serve this task. Yet, there are problems—for example, projections of national-income figures into the future—for which a rate of accumulation will expediently be assumed as given, and the underlying functions be left aside.

Now, the growth of technical knowledge and the growth of productivity that may result from it are certainly important factors in the analysis of economic growth and other economic problems. But with one very minor exception—namely, the theory of patent protection—the stock of knowledge and especially the state of technology have customarily been treated as exogenous variables or as trend functions in economic models. Yet we have implicitly recognized that the stock of knowledge can be increased by special efforts; that the allocation of resources to education and to research and development is an important economic variable which can significantly alter the rate of increase of knowledge, both basic and applied. In recent years economic statisticians have given a good deal of attention to the appropriations made by society for the creation and communication of knowledge. The economics of education and the economics of research and development are new areas of specialization which have rapidly developed, partly with the generous aid of research foundations.

Knowledge as a Product, a Function of Resource Allocation

The "promotion" of knowledge from the rank of an exogenous independent variable to that of an endogenous variable dependent on input, on the allocation of resources, is an important step. Not that this idea is a novel one. Adam Smith in 1776 wrote that "man educated at the expense of much labor and time . . . may be compared to one of those expensive machines,"[1] and the notion of the "capital concept applied to man"[2] has never completely disappeared from the economic treatises. It was especially emphasized by writers, such as Friedrich List, who gave much prominence to the development of the productive powers of man. In connection with several policy issues, the differences between the private and social benefits from such investment in knowledge were discussed with great intensity—for example, in the arguments for infant-industry protection. But never before our time was the interest of economic writers so closely concentrated upon the analysis of economic growth and development, and thus it is not surprising that there is now such a burst of activity in studying the productivity of investment in knowledge.

---

[1] Adam Smith, *An Inquiry into the Nature and Causes of the Wealth of Nations* (London: George Routledge and Sons, 1903 [1st ed., 1776]), pp. 78-79.

[2] Raymond J. Walsh, "Capital Concept Applied to Man," *Quarterly Journal of Economics*, vol. 49 (1935), pp. 255ff.

The focus of these studies is upon education, basic research, and applied technical research and development, thus, upon the production of such types of knowledge as may be regarded as investments in the sense that they will pay off in the future through increased productivity. A few economists aim their analytical weapons at a somewhat different target: market research. Recognizing that the assumption of full knowledge of selling and buying opportunities cannot be maintained for all problems, and that increased effort in market research may lower the costs and raise the revenues of the firm, economists have started to analyze the marginal efficiency of investment in market research. All these kinds of knowledge have in common that they are instrumental in increasing the efficiency of the economy.

There are, however, many other types of knowledge besides those designed to pay off in the future; there are, for example, types of knowledge that give immediate pleasure to the recipients, and society is allocating ample resources to the dissemination of such knowledge. Although it would, of course, be possible to confine a study of the production and distribution of knowledge to types of knowledge that are expected to yield a future return in terms of increased productivity, such a limitation would not satisfy a transcendent intellectual curiosity. Moreover, whether an investigator's interests be wide or narrow, he could not study "productive" knowledge without paying considerable attention to "unproductive" knowledge because ever so often they are joint products. What is taught at school, printed in books, magazines and newspapers, broadcast over the radio, or produced on television is knowledge of many sorts—and to study one is to analyze all.

An even further expansion of the scope of the study seems promising. As an economy develops and as society becomes more complex, efficient organization of production, trade, and government seems to require an increasing degree of division of labor between knowledge production and physical production. A quite remarkable increase in the division of labor between pure "brain work" and largely physical performance has occurred in all sectors of our economic and social organization. This increase can be observed in the growing role, measured in terms of manpower, of the government of most political bodies as well as of the management of business firms; it can also be observed in the ratios of "nonproductive" to "productive" labor in many industries. The so-called nonproductive workers are those who shuffle papers and give signals, who see to it that others "know" what to do. To include this sort of "knowledge production" may look strange to most readers at first blush but will become more understandable and look more sensible at later stages of the discussion. Thus, besides the researchers, designers, and planners, quite naturally, the executives, the secretaries, and all the intermediary transmitters of knowledge in the economy will eventually come into the focus of our analysis of the production and distribution of knowledge.

If society devotes considerable amounts of its resources to any particular activity, economists will want to look into this allocation and get an idea of the magnitude of the activity, its major breakdown, and its relation to other activities.

TERMINOLOGICAL PROPOSALS

The economist undertaking this study will have to prepare himself for it by developing a conceptual framework for an analysis for which he does not find ready-made tools. He will have to use terms that have established meanings in other fields of discourse and may not find these meanings suitable for his task. The problems arising from these needs will be taken up for careful scrutiny later in this volume. At this point, however, we propose a time-saving terminological agreement.

"Production and Distribution"

So far in this introduction we have always referred to pairs of economic activities, such as "production and distribution," "acquisition and transmission," "creation and communication" of knowledge. We can save words and drop the twin phrase as soon as we realize that we may designate as "knowledge" anything that is known by somebody and as "production of knowledge" any activity by which someone learns of something he or she has not known before, even if others have.

In this sense, disclosure, dissemination, transmission, and communication become parts of a wider concept of "production of knowledge." Of course, we shall then have to distinguish a special kind of "socially new knowledge"—that which no one has had before—but since we shall have much more to say about the production of old knowledge in new minds—"subjectively new knowledge," if you like—the proposal will on balance save words.

Thus, if I tell you something that you have not known, or have only vaguely known, or have forgotten, I am producing knowledge, although I must have had this knowledge, and probably several others have too. In other words, "producing" knowledge will mean, in this book, not only discovering, inventing, designing, and planning but also disseminating and communicating. This applies to *how-to* knowledge as well as to knowledge *of* something and knowledge *about* something. To know *what* and to know *that* are neither less nor more important than to know *how*. (See below, Chapter 2.)

"Knowledge and Information"

By the same token, I prefer that we get rid of the duplication "knowledge and information" when we refer to *what* people know or are informed about. One may, with good reasons, insist on distinguishing "information" from "knowledge" by having "information" refer to the *act* or *process* by which knowledge (or a signal, a message) is transmitted. Even when the word is not used for the act of communicating but for the contents of the communication, one may want information to refer to the knowledge currently conveyed by that act in contrast to the knowledge previously accumulated in the knower's mind or records. This would be analogous to the economist's indispensable distinction between flows and stocks, where the flows may constitute current additions to the stocks. One may liken the flow of incoming knowledge to income that can be added to the existing stock of knowledge, capital.[3]

To others, however, the pair of words suggests different dichotomies. By "information," for example, some mean to refer to disconnected events or facts and by "knowledge," they allude to an interrelated system (though others want to confer upon systematic or ordered knowledge the nobler title "science"). One author, for example, proposes to contrast "knowledge," or "contextual knowledge," which "illuminates the basic causal structure of some field of operations," with "information," which "provides current data on the variables in that field."[4] In the same vein, another author says that "Information . . . is essentially raw data, Knowledge . . . is interpreted data."[5]

The specialist in "information theory" uses the word, as he

---

[3] "It is certainly tempting to think of knowledge as a capital stock of information, knowledge being to information what capital is to income. . . ." Kenneth E. Boulding, "The Economics of Knowledge and the Knowledge of Economics," *American Economic Review*, vol. 56, Papers and Proceedings (May 1966), p. 3.

[4] The same author, however, decides later to treat both as "information," yet he continues to oscillate between talking about "bits of knowledge" and "bits of information." Anthony Downs, *An Economic Theory of Democracy* (New York: Harper and Row, 1957), pp. 81, 208, 215, 219.

[5] Charles West Churchman, "Problem and Representation in Problem-Solving and Inquiry," in M. Mesarovic, ed., *Formal Models and Non-Numerical Problem-Solving by Computers*, Proceedings of Fourth Systems Symposium (Cleveland: Case Western Reserve University, 1969).

frankly admits, in a "rather strange way," in "a special sense which
. . . must not be confused at all with meaning." To him, "information
is a measure of your freedom of choice when you select a message.
. . . Thus greater freedom of choice, greater uncertainty, and greater
information all go hand in hand."[6] This concept serves a significant
purpose in an important field, but it is not what is commonly meant
by "information." Perhaps the fact that the special use of the word is
becoming increasingly current should make it more desirable to use,
whenever possible, the word "knowledge" for the ordinary meaning
of "information." *Webster's Dictionary* defines "information" as
"knowledge communicated by others or obtained by personal study
and investigation," or, alternatively, as "knowledge of a special
event, situation, or the like." Hence, in these ordinary uses of the
word, all information is knowledge. I shall, in certain contexts, give
in to common usage and refer to particular kinds of knowledge as
information, but I shall try to avoid the redundant phrase "knowledge *and* information" when both are meant to signify contents. On
the other hand, I shall not mind saying "knowledge and information" when the first refers to the contents and the second to the
process.

THE PROGRAM FOR THIS WORK

Perhaps more should be said about the desirability of my undertaking: an economist investigating the production and distribution of
knowledge.

The production of knowledge is an economic activity, an industry,
if you like. Economists have analyzed agriculture, mining, iron and
steel production, the paper industry, transportation, retailing, the
production of all sorts of goods and services, but they have neglected
to analyze the production of knowledge. This is surprising because
there are a good many reasons why an economic analysis of the production of knowledge seems to be particularly interesting and promising of new insights. Some of the reasons refer to observed facts,
others to probable relations to economically significant developments, still others to novel hypotheses that call for investigation.

Some of the Reasons for Our Curiosity

(1) It is a fact that increasing shares of the nation's budget have
been allocated to the production of knowledge.

---

[6] Warren Weaver, "The Mathematics of Information," in *Automatic Control* (New
York: Simon and Schuster, for *The Scientific American*, 1955), pp. 100, 104.

(2) It can also be shown that a large portion of the nation's expenditures on knowledge has been financed by government, so that much of the production of knowledge depends on governmental appropriations.

(3) One may strongly support the judgment that the production of some kinds of knowledge yields social benefits in excess of the private benefits accruing to the recipients of that knowledge.

(4) It is probable that the production of certain kinds of knowledge is limited by inelasticities in the supply of qualified people, which raises questions of policy, especially concerning the allocation of public funds.

(5) The facts that the production of knowledge of several types is paid for by others than the users of the knowledge and that these types of knowledge have no market prices raise questions of their valuation for national-income accounting as well as for welfare-economic considerations.

(6) The production of one type of knowledge—namely, technology—results in continuing changes in the conditions of production of many goods and services.

(7) One may advance the hypothesis that new technological knowledge tends to result in shifts of demand from physical labor to "brain workers."

(8) There is evidence of a change in the composition of the labor force employed in the United States, in particular of an increase in the share of "knowledge-producing" labor in total employment.

(9) There is ground for suspicion that some branches of the production of knowledge—formal education, in particular—are quite inefficient, although it is difficult to ascertain input-output ratios and to make valid comparisons, especially since the very wastefulness is held to be productive of psychic incomes and social benefits.

(10) It has been suggested that some of the growth in the production of knowledge may be an instance of "Parkinson's Law," which implies that administrators tend to create more work for more administrators.

(11) There is probably more validity in the hypothesis that the increase in the ratio of knowledge-producing labor to physical labor is strongly associated with the increase in productivity and thus with the rate of economic growth, though one may suspect that only a small fraction of all currently produced knowledge is a cause of enhanced productivity, whereas a much larger part is the consequence of the increased incomes derived from gains in productivity.

These and a good many other points indicate some of the reasons why it may be said that an economic analysis of the production of knowledge is not only justified but overdue. What I shall have to offer may be only prolegomena to the subject. And, to repeat, it will not be possible for me in this attempt to stay within the confines of economics. Indeed, I shall linger with particular pleasure in some outlying fields, and I trust that the representatives of these fields of learning will be hospitable to the ingressions of a friendly outsider. This kind of benevolence and indulgence may be needed especially for those parts of my work that lie in territories over which philosophers, historians, sociologists, and educationists claim sovereignty. They might regard my incursions into their fields as not necessary for my scholarly objectives—and I would have no other defense than my unbounded intellectual curiosity. If I write a work on knowledge, I simply cannot restrain myself and "stick to my last" as a professional economist.

In Quest of Light or Fruit?

The stated observations, suggestions, hypotheses, and problems are, I submit, sufficient reasons for being curious about the economics of knowledge production. Is it purely intellectual curiosity or is it an anticipation of pragmatic insights that motivates our inquiry? For those who accept the generalization advanced by Pigou, a great British economist, social studies are to be justified chiefly by the expectation of an attractive pay-off:

> When a man sets out upon any course of inquiry, the object of his search may be either light or fruit—either knowledge for its own sake or knowledge for the sake of the good things to which it leads. . . . there will, I think, be general agreement that in the sciences of human society, be their appeal as bearers of light ever so high, it is the promise of fruit and not of light that chiefly merits our regard.[7]

I must confess that I am less mission-oriented than Pigou wanted social scientists to be. I would undertake my inquiry even if it promised nothing but light; but I believe that fruit can grow and ripen only where there is enough light, and that most inquiries that shed light on problems, societal or not, eventually prove useful to society. I fear, however, that a requirement to justify each research project in the social sciences by its "promise of fruit" can become a stultifying constraint. I do not insist, on the other hand, on keeping this inquiry "pure" and "basic." On the contrary, I shall unashamedly indulge in

[7] Arthur Cecil Pigou, *The Economics of Welfare* (London: Macmillan, 1920), pp. 3, 4.

value judgments and policy recommendations wherever I think that they are reasonable. Thus, I embark on this investigation primarily in a quest for light, but I shall gladly pluck every fruit that it may bear.

Another utilitarian advocacy of the production and widest possible distribution of knowledge may be quoted here, though the promised fruit was intangible, in the realm of nonmaterial values. It stressed the importance of "the diffusion of knowledge among the people. No other sure foundation can be devised, for the preservation of freedom and happiness."[8] In making this statement, Jefferson no doubt was thinking of the types of knowledge that may qualify for "nice" adjectives, such as intellectual, useful, truthful, broadening, deepening, uplifting, and similar terms of approbation. How strange that for most liberal thinkers—academics as well as statesmen— knowledge is almost always "good" and worthy of wide diffusion, although history is full of attempts by governors—political, moral, and religious leaders, and well-meaning parents—to discourage the spread of "dangerous" or "unwholesome" knowledge. There has been in the past, as there is at present, "forbidden knowledge," and production and distribution of particular kinds of knowledge is discouraged by governmental proscription or public disapproval. Although most respecters of human freedom oppose any and all restrictions on the dissemination of knowledge, many parents hope to postpone the acquisition of pornographic knowledge (and even the most innocent sex information) by their young children; most social workers wish that the knowledge of where to obtain harmful drugs were less widely diffused; and workers for the cause of internal and international peace want to prevent the spread of the knowledge of how to make bombs, both of the primitive Molotov type and of the highly developed nuclear type. Many high-spirited statements about the blessings of unlimited diffusion of knowledge are sensible only if one is aware of the exceptions and exclusions which the speaker or writer would surely propose were he more cautious in his pronouncements.

What I shall have to say, in the next and in subsequent chapters, on various types of knowledge may make it clear that unspecified and unqualified pronouncements are rarely valid even on such matters as human knowledge, including "more knowledge about knowledge."

[8] Thomas Jefferson, in a letter of August 13, 1786 to George Wythe, his most admired "mentor and friend," a cosigner of the Declaration of Independence. Reprinted in *The Writings of Thomas Jefferson* (Washington: The Thomas Jefferson Memorial Association, 1903), vol. 5, p. 396.

A Preview of the Eight Volumes

At the end of "The Story of This Work"—which preceded this Introduction—I explained why a large expansion of my original 1962 book was not merely justified but well-nigh imperative. Expansion of the scope was dictated by the extension of the statistical series by at least seventeen years (1959 to 1975), and possibly twenty years (to 1978); by changes in institutions (governmental, legal, technological) and in social priorities; and by the explosion of the literature. Beyond these imperatives, there was substantial expansion imposed by my personal intellectual curiosity: I had been reading with increasing fascination in the areas of philosophy and intellectual history of knowledge. No one, I hope, will deny that more extensive discussions of issues in these areas are pertinent to the subject of my work. They account for expansions and additions in what will now be presented in Parts One and Two in Volume I, and for the development of entirely new themes in Volume II.

The new work is planned to take the form of a series of eight volumes. The present outline envisages thirty-three parts, some short enough to share a volume with up to seven other parts, some long enough to claim the space of half a volume. The titles of some of the parts are still subject to change, as is also their sequence. The subtitles of the eight volumes, however, seem to be more nearly definitive—though I shrink from making a firm commitment even on this score. It may turn out, as the writing proceeds, that an oversupply of material for one volume forces me or the editors of the press to rearrange the contents and to retitle the volumes accordingly. The present plan provides for the following sequence of volumes:

Volume I: Knowledge and Knowledge Production
Volume II: The Branches of Learning, Information
    Sciences, and Human Capital
Volume III: Education
Volume IV: Research and New Knowledge, Cognitive
    and Artistic
Volume V: Media of Communication
Volume VI: Information Services and Information
    Machines
Volume VII: Knowledge Production: Its Size and Growth
Volume VIII: Knowledge Occupations and the Knowledge-
    able Society

The proposed sequence is the result of several rearrangements; it is in fact the seventh version of my draft outline. Let me explain some of the considerations and reconsiderations that have led me to the present outline. I had no difficulties finding the "best" solution for Volume I; I shall later explain it in detail. Volume II, however, still gives me headaches. My present plans for it envisage five parts: "The Branches of Learning," chiefly an intellectual history of the classification of disciplines; "The Departments of Erudition," mainly an institutional history of the classification systems used in academies of sciences, universities, and libraries; "The Information Sciences," largely a descriptive and methodological survey of recently developed, and still developing, disciplines dealing with information and communication; "The Economics of Knowledge and Information," for the most part a survey of specialties of economics, but concerned with such problems as incomplete and uncertain knowledge, the demand for better information and its cost, incentives for the search for new knowledge, and many other topics that have occupied increasing space in the economic journals; and finally, "Knowledge as Human Capital," an old but recently revitalized theme of economic analysis with side-glances to educational, psychological, and sociological issues.

To devote a part in Volume II to information science has been an afterthought, after most of the other parts of Volume II had been completed or drafted. It occurred to me that a comprehensive work on knowledge production could not reasonably disregard the existence and rapid growth of several relatively young disciplines that concern themselves with systems of information and communication. Attempts to integrate or unify them under the name "information science" have not been successful, partly because some of the disciplines are jealously guarding their autonomy. Researchers in library science and information systems analysis seem to be prepared to accept a merger under the broader name "information science." This cannot be said, however, of the specialists in communication theory and, still less, of those in computer science and engineering. Cyberneticists and students of human communication, artificial intelligence, and living systems are still debating whether they represent constituent fields or only cognate fields of information science. Certain aspects of psychology on the one hand, and of semiotics, on the other, are also closely concerned with processes of transmission and reception of information. The interrelationships among the mentioned area of inquiry, and perhaps a few that I have omitted, should be explored. I propose to invite statements from several representatives of these fields or subfields, each setting forth his or her views on the lines that connect them systematically or just tangentially with one another. My task then will be to analyze the congruences, similarities, differences, and contradictions among the solicited papers, and to report the findings in Part Three of Volume II under the title "Information Sciences: Its Constituent, Complementary, and Cognate Disciplines."

Volume III will be entirely devoted to Education. The present outline provides for eight parts. I may have to add chapters or rearrange the sequence of the thirty-eight chapters now planned, but I foresee no serious complications in the general organization of the contents.

Volume IV has been a great problem. Its proposed title, "Research and New Knowledge, Cognitive and Artistic," may not be sufficiently explicit to convey that the volume will combine two major subjects of rather different nature: Research and Development, and Artistic Creation and Communication. I have long pondered the question of the most appropriate sequence. At one time I considered having R and D followed by my discussion of libraries; then I thought that Print Media of Communication, with an emphasis on books and journals, would make a better sequel to R and D and a better antecedent to a discussion of libraries. I concluded, however, that the print media and the electronic media of communication ought not to be separated into different volumes, chiefly because they have several problems in common—for example, copyright protection and competition for, and income from, advertising. My decision to couple in the fourth volume R and D with Artistic Creation and Communication raises a few awkward problems because of the frequent communication of fine arts through print media and of performing arts through electronic media. On the other hand, the linking of chapters on research in natural and social sciences and in the humanities with discussions of artistic creation will allow me to reflect on the issue of "the two cultures," the alleged chasm between mathematical-minded and humanistic-historical-minded scholars. In announcing this plan, I do not want to commit myself to its execution. When I eventually put things together, I may find a different sequence preferable in some significant respects.[9]

[9] To indicate some of my present misgivings I may point to some problems of the demarcation between creation and communication of knowledge, scientific and artistic. The generation of new scientific knowledge in basic or applied research can be separated from its subsequent communication through discussions with fellow researchers, papers delivered at conferences or conventions, letters and articles in journals, or monographs and other books. In the fine arts, the demarcation line is still sharp enough: in painting and sculpture the creation by the artist is quite separate from the communication of his work through its exhibition in the art gallery or reproduction in print. In the performing arts, however, creation and communication in art may be inseparably linked. In theater arts we have to distinguish the creative work of the playwright, the director, the stage designer, and the costume designer from their intercommunications in cooperative planning and rehearsing and from the work of

Volume V, "Media of Communication," will, if the present plan remains intact, treat of the Print Media of Communication, the Electronic Media of Communication, Problems of Copyright, Advertising and Public Relations, Conventions and Conferences, and Media of Addressed Communication (by which I mean telecommunications and postal services).

Volume VI, "Information Services and Information Machines," is to contain parts on Libraries, Specialized Information Services, Management as Information System and Communication Process, Government as a Knowledge Industry, and Information Machines.

Volume VII, titled "Knowledge Production: Its Size and Growth," will be the summary volume with the findings obtained by the industry approach followed in Volumes III to VI. The two main parts will be on Total Production of Knowledge and the National Product, and Differences in Growth Rates in the Knowledge Industries.

The eighth and last volume, carrying the title "Knowledge Occupations and the Knowledgeable Society," will present new findings from the occupations approach towards estimating the relative share and growth of knowledge production. It will carry out an idea first proposed in the preface to my 1962 book, where I had said:

> Producers of knowledge may, however, work on very different levels: they may be transporters, transformers, processors, interpreters, or analyzers of messages as well as

---

the actor; but some element of artistic creation may be present not only in the process of rehearsing the play but actually in each performance. In the production of motion pictures, creative and communicative activities are conjoined in the work of the scriptwriter, the editor, the rewrite man, the director, the cameraman and the actors, but their joint creation and temporary intercommunication is quite separate from the ultimate process of communication through the showing of the film in cinemas or on television. In symphonic music we note the "division of artistic labor" among composer, conductor, and instrumentalists in the different processes of composing, rehearsing, and performing. If it is the performance to which we assign the function of communication, it undoubtedly includes also more than a little artistic creation. In the case of dance, say, classical ballet, we find a combination of the problems cited for the theater arts and for symphonic music, made even more complex by the creative work of the choreographer. The point is that each and every performance is both artistic creation and communication.

If I may add another sentence in order to point to the blurred lines of demarcation between generation and communication of knowledge, on the one hand, and between scientific and artistic creation, on the other, let me remind the reader of the fact that the scientist and scholar becomes an artist in communicating his findings to the public—as lucid expositor, brilliant orator, writer of elegant prose—and that the production manager in book publishing may be an artistic creator in designing the book that is to communicate the scholar's findings.

original creators. What I have failed to do in this volume, and would do if I had time for it, is to attempt a statistical separation of knowledge-producing activity by these different levels. Perhaps I shall undertake this task as a sequel to the present book; or perhaps someone else will want to do it, especially with reference to the changes in the occupational structure, discussed in the last chapter of this volume.

I have made a preliminary study of changes in the structure of the knowledge-producing labor force in the United States from 1940 to 1970 and may be able to bring it forward to 1980. If the data permit, the proposed disaggregation should be not only in numbers of persons in the active labor force, but also in incomes earned and in years of schooling completed. I do not expect any spectacular results from these studies; on the contrary, I fear that they will merely disconfirm some hypotheses long entertained by many of us. The last part of the work will be called "A Knowledgeable Society: Sociological and Political Aspects." There I plan to discuss issues raised by writers on political science and sociology when they were confronted with my discoveries: the large size and fast growth of knowledge production in the United States. A structural development of these dimensions is, according to their argument, liable to alter the social and political makeup of our society.

The present outline of the thirty-three parts planned for the entire work provides for more than 150 chapters. This outline, however, is the result of six revisions, and I see no good reason for assuming that it will not be revised further as the writing proceeds. I therefore find it wiser to withhold the detailed table of contents of the seven subsequent volumes; I neither want to promise the reader that I shall deliver all the now envisaged chapters with exactly the titles that look good to me at the present moment, nor do I want to feel obliged to stick to an announced plan if I should prefer to change it.

A Preview of Volume I

The present volume can be previewed in detail without fear or chance of change; it is all down, black on white. It offers, besides the preliminary materials and this Introduction, Part One, "Types of Knowledge," Part Two, "Qualities of Knowledge," and Part Three, "Knowledge as a Product." (Readers interested in a comparison with my 1962 book may note that these three parts treat in depth what I tried to discuss briefly—in only forty-seven pages—in Chapters II and III of the old book.)

Chapter 2, on The Known and the Knowing, begins as a simple exercise in semantics but soon transgresses into the domains of more complex language analysis and theory of knowledge. I am probably vulnerable to the philosophers' charge that I lack the credentials for a serious study of the problems tackled. Chapter 3, on Mundane, Scientific, Humanistic, Artistic, and Other Classes of Knowledge, may expose me to a charge that, as an immigrant from continental Europe, I show a nostalgia for traditional meanings of science and humanistic scholarship which have long been abandoned by English-speaking scientists and humanists. I expect less resistance to my discussions of Knowledge Without Words. Chapter 4, on Alternative Classifications of Knowledge, retains most of what I proposed in my 1962 book.

Chapter 5, on Truth, Beauty, and Goodness as qualities of knowledge, is again an incursion into the domain of philosophy. In view of the strong disagreements among different schools of philosophy, I cannot hope for general approbation of my discussion, but neither need I fear general rejection. Chapter 6, on Other Standards of Quality, though containing plenty of controversial issues, particularly regarding pornography and other forbidden knowledge dissemination, may be acceptable to a majority of readers. Chapter 7, on Notions of Negative Knowledge, is a relatively brief essay on thirteen possible meanings of negative knowledge; it comes to the conclusion that we had better avoid the equivocal term.

In the seven chapters of Part Three, I am back in my home territory as a professional economist. Some of these chapters are useful preparation for the analyses in Volumes III to VIII. Chapter 9, on Stocks and Flows of Knowledge, and Chapter 10, on The Economic Cost of Knowledge, may be helpful to noneconomists as well as economists. Chapter 11, on Transmission and Reception, is rather exceptional in that it retains, without alteration, several pages from my 1962 book. Chapter 12, on Consumption, Investment, Intermediate Product, makes distinctions which are essential for the entire study of knowledge production as an economic activity. Chapter 13, on Uses, Value, and Benefits of Knowledge, was written chiefly for the enlightenment of noneconomists who, probably by exposure to unsound economic analysis, have become snared in serious fallacies. Chapter 14, on Knowledge Industries and Knowledge Occupations, explains the alternative approaches towards estimating the relative size and growth of knowledge production: the occupations approach will be used only in Volume VIII, whereas the industry approach will be pursued in Volumes III to VII; the difference between the two techniques of estimation has to be understood if the findings are to make much sense.

The explosion of the literature occurred both in the general area of information science and in several special fields of communication. An entire part of this work (Volume II, Part Four) will be devoted to the survey of the literature; in addition, many references to individual publications will be made in the discussions of various substantive issues in the parts on education, research and development, mass media of communication, and all the rest. The number of references to books and articles will probably be ten times that of my earlier work, not because in 1962 I was oblivious to the literature, but because most of the literature has come into existence since then.

Some readers of the first book have been impressed chiefly by the estimates of the total of knowledge production—its share in the national product and its rate of growth relative to the production of goods and services not related to knowledge production—whereas many others have been more interested in the composition of the total and in the changes of the composition over time. Has the cost of education increased its share in the national product? How have the proportions between primary, secondary, and tertiary education been changed over the years? How have research and development fared, and how have the relative allocations to basic research, applied R and D, humanistic studies, and the arts been altered? What has happened to book production, to scholarly journals, general-interest magazines, specialized newsletters, local newspapers? How have the electronic mass media—radio, television—developed in recent years? Has the role of advertising in all mass media been maintained or changed? These are only a few of an enormous array of questions to be answered in this new work.

It is an incidental benefit of the delay in the publication of this work that it gives me an opportunity to compare the techniques used by Porat with my own. In the nine volumes produced by the U.S. Department of Commerce, he presented data for a larger number of knowledge industries than I had in my tabulations for 1958, partly because, for 1967, statistical information was available that did not exist nine years earlier, but also because Porat included among the "quasi-information industries" in his "secondary sector" some industries to which I had not given this status and which I still prefer to exclude. In a sense, Porat's statistics constitute a partial merger of my two approaches, giving some knowledge occupations the status of quasi industries. It will be interesting to ascertain the magnitude of the resulting discrepancies.

The research for the new work continues while these lines are being written, and it will continue for several years, to supply the material for use in later volumes of the work. The research is carried out with a staff of varying size—between five and fifteen associates and assistants—under grants from various foundations and agencies: the National Science Foundation (two different divisions sponsoring research on different aspects of the study), the Ford Foundation, the Earhart Foundation, the Sloan Foundation, and the National Institute of Education.

Scope of the Expanding Work

Statistical curiosity, comparisons of relative shares, and fascination with comparative growth rates have not been the only reasons behind the demand for an expanded and updated edition of my work. At least three developments since 1958, besides the statistical records, have called for attention: changes in several knowledge-industry sectors (new kinds of information services, new types of information machines, new laws and regulations, new social and political concerns), changes in the socio-economic climate (expansion of the public sector, stronger egalitarian pressures, more drastic youth unemployment, acceleration of price inflation), and a veritable explosion of the literature on information. This literature has to be surveyed and the implications of the economic, social, and institutional changes have to be examined.

All these and hundreds of similar questions can be answered only on the basis of statistical estimates, and to produce these estimates is one of my assignments. But it would be a grave misunderstanding if my undertaking were regarded as just a statistical inquiry. Although quantitative analyses are indispensable for my work, my own inclination is to emphasize its qualitative aspects. Every branch of every knowledge industry has its economic, political, and social problems. To present and examine these problems is my ultimate concern, although there is a risk involved in such a broad interest: it implies transgressions from so-called positive and "objective" statistical data into the realms of theoretical speculation and "subjective" value judgments. That such transgressions add to the social significance of my work, rather than detract from it, is my sincere hope.

TWO CHARGES AND APOLOGIES

In discussions of my plans for this work, two charges have been leveled against its design: excessive expansionism—too many un-

necessary excursions into extraneous domains—and vulgar materialism—putting money values on things where only moral and cultural values ought to count. I think I should answer these charges.

Going Too Far Afield

I may be forgiven for trying to answer by raising a question. Does a
work which, beginning from its first paragraph, dedicates itself to an
interdisciplinary and transdisciplinary approach need an apology
for its meandering through several fields of inquiry? I intended this
question to be purely rhetorical, to be answered with a convinced
and convincing "of course not." Yet, a good many specialists in various fields have asked me why I had to go into this or that area, why
it was necessary for a work "essentially" interested in historical
statistics pertaining to the changing structure of the economy to take
up problems of language philosophy, epistemology, intellectual
history, political philosophy, ethics, aesthetics, and what not. Admittedly, I did not have to and it is not necessary. The admirable
nine-volume work on *The Information Economy* by Marc Porat is sufficient proof that one may confine oneself to economic statistics.
However, if I do not want to stay within such limits, do I—because
my training was in economics—need passport and visas to enter
fields usually cultivated only by specialists duly certified by academic authorities? Perhaps those who question my interdisciplinary
peregrinations do not mean to deny me free entry into other territories but merely doubt the wisdom of extending an economic investigation of information services and other knowledge-producing
activities into a work of encyclopaedic format or into a work on "Everything you always wanted to know about knowledge, and even
more." Thus it seems that I do have to say a few more words about
the wide scope of this work.

    The work of which this is the first volume does not purport to be a
treatise on the economics of knowledge and information. One of its
thirty-three parts is, in fact, to deal with this relatively new specialty
of economic science (Part Four, Volume II); but there it will be
shown that my work deals with only a fraction of the topics included
in that specialty. I have deliberately chosen to call my work *Knowledge: Its Creation, Distribution, and Economic Significance*, because
I wanted to convey to the reader that the discussion of "economic
significance" is only a part of my objective. Thus, although the scope of
my concern with knowledge is much wider than a discussion of its
economic significance, it is much narrower than that of the various
problems now treated under the heading "economics of information." This explains why economists may accuse me of doing too lit-

tle of what they regard as important with regard to knowledge and information, whereas noneconomists may fault me for doing too much of what they deem irrelevant for my (supposed) purposes.

Parochialism in academic disciplines may not have existed in earlier centuries, but nowadays it characterizes many representatives of various university departments. When one of my professorial colleagues from a natural-science department learned of the title of my work, he had no doubt that I was writing about "science" in the narrowest sense—the physical sciences. A colleague from the economics department assumed that I was writing about the effects of imperfect and uncertain knowledge on markets with various degrees of competition, and on the demand for information on the part of suppliers or users of goods and services. Professors in graduate schools of business expected me to write about management science and information systems. A professor of electrical engineering was sure I was dealing chiefly with communication theory and computer science. My friends in the library thought that I was working on library science and perhaps information science. The philosophers were less parochial, but some of them took it for granted that I would confine myself to "true" knowledge, since they had proclaimed that one can know only what was, subjectively as well as objectively, true. These are only a few of my experiences of scholarly expectations on the part of my academic colleagues, experiences which convinced me that I had to say why all these conceptions of knowledge were far too narrow for my purposes.

Take the case of the philosopher who wants to reserve the word "knowledge" for propositions with absolute truth value or almost perfect probability value. Propositional knowledge—"knowing that this is so"—is only a small part of the knowledge disseminated in schools at all levels. At lower levels, teaching to "know how to do," especially the basic skills, is the chief objective of the educational system and absorbs a substantial portion of the nation's expenditures for dissemination of knowledge. Knowing how to read and to write has little to do with knowing that something is true. On the other hand, educational theorists and psychologists have in recent years produced very interesting findings about teaching and learning, both know-*how* and know-*that*. If these findings prove acceptable in many situations and for many people, they may lead to the adoption of new teaching techniques. I mention this only because it explains why learning theory has to be included in my agenda for Volume III.

The charge of expansionism may also be interpreted as a charge of imperialism. As empires expand, annexing new territories and extending their political and economic influence over foreign lands, they become "imperialist" powers. Economists have been accused of imperialist propensities as they expand into domains of other disciplines, not only to look, see, and learn, but also to advise, influence, and take over. This is not my design. I am not trying, for example, to tell philosophers what they ought to mean by knowing and knowledge. I am trying, instead, to reconcile what some of them have been saying with what I regard as helpful when I talk about creating and disseminating knowledge and about the economic significance of such activities. I may add that economists who read the chapters in question may suffer no harm if they become acquainted with the problems which philosophers find pertinent when they ponder the ways of knowing.

None of this explains why I deal in Volume II with the history of ideas about the branches of learning. The answer is simply that it fascinates me, and I think that others may be interested too. Moreover, this intellectual history is closely connected with the institutional history of higher learning—academies, libraries, and universities—and can explain some of the systems of classification and departmentalization at present. Useless knowledge? Perhaps. But knowing for fun is a respectable human activity; and having fun need not be judged useless.

Valuing the Invaluable

Having tried, successfully or not, to defend myself against the charge of intellectual immodesty and academic expansionism, I should now attempt to clear myself of the accusation of crass materialism, a charge wholehearted noneconomists are wont to level at those who put money valuations on such intrinsically valuable, or invaluable, things as knowledge.

By devoting many chapters in this work to assess the economic significance of knowledge-producing activities, I openly admit my endeavor to put dollar tags on such things as education, research, and art. To do so is sometimes regarded as an attempt to confuse, confound, or lump economic values with cultural values, which many of my friends in academe see as a serious error, if not a heresy, a sacrilege. Using economic calculation in valuing cultural pursuits? Vulgar commercialism, insensitive grossness!

This charge is based on a misunderstanding. To find out how much, in terms of dollars or as a fraction of the gross national product, the nation spends on education, research, art, advertising, and so forth, neither involves a normative judgment—for example, that the relative allocation of resources to various types of education, research, art, and advertising is "just right," or that it reflects this or that bias—nor does it presuppose that the dollar amounts spent on various knowledge-producing activities indicate, let alone measure, the values of the benefits they bestow upon society. There is nothing that demeans the fine arts if we record how much, or how little, was spent for any particular cultural activity in 1978 or any other year. And, if we record the amounts of public and private expenditures for basic research in a certain year or over a longer period, this is not to deny that the eventual benefits from the investment may be worth a multiple of the outlays.

Some sensitive critics take offence at the very thought of having dollar values or dollar costs attached to various cultural activities which they deem intrinsically valuable. In the discussions on the productivity of education, for example, philosophers, psychologists, and sociologists have been irritated with attempts to calculate rates of return to private and social investments in schooling. They reject benefit-and-cost analyses that disregard nonassessable benefits and may therefore give misleading cues for public policy. In actual fact, those who decide on the appropriations of public funds do not, as a rule, disregard nonpecuniary benefits when they consider whether additional millions or billions of dollars should be appropriated to education, research, public health, transportation, environmental programs, social security, national defense, aid to agriculture or sugar refining, and so forth. One may take exception to the implied valuations of the alternative nonpecuniary benefits expected from the competing objectives; one may question the system of preferences revealed by choices made by elected representatives of the people, but one cannot reasonably claim that they are guided only by calculations based on pecuniary returns.

None of these considerations, however, could possibly support a position of know-nothingism. No matter whether we like or dislike the way our public and private decision-makers have decided to spend the funds at their disposal, it is interesting and may even be helpful to know how much is being spent for what: the charge that a study of the recorded or estimated money values constitutes vulgar materialism or insensitiveness to moral and cultural values is unfounded.

PART ONE

TYPES OF KNOWLEDGE

THE WORD KNOWLEDGE has fifteen dictionary meanings, but for our purposes two or three will do. One of these, however, calls for distinctions and classifications. The three chapters of Part One will be given to conceptual, semantic, and classificatory problems, some of them essential for the understanding of the arguments in the entire work.

Chapter 2   The Known and the Knowing

Chapter 3   Mundane, Scientific, Humanistic, Artistic, and Other Classes of Knowledge

Chapter 4   Alternative Classifications of Knowledge

The Known and the Knowing

SOME PEOPLE have firm convictions regarding the virtue or vice of beginning a discussion with definitions. Even nationalistic prejudices have been appealed to in this cause. I have heard references to Teutonic authoritarianism and its propensity at the very outset to impose definitions upon the helpless reader; to English pragmatism and its propensity to defer definitions until it has become clear what is called for in the setting of problems and issues; to French orthology and its propensity to proscribe discourse on undefined subjects. I have no convictions on this question. In the present instance, however, it would be impossible to begin with a definition, because we shall see that "knowledge" does not have just one meaning, which one can delineate and demarcate with a definition. It has several meanings, and two of them will be needed throughout this book. Although they are different, they are logically correlated and neither of them is dispensable in our discussion. The one is knowledge as *that which is known*; the other is knowledge as *the state of knowing*.

The two essential meanings of the word "knowledge" are usually not kept apart. Many philosophers of science, when they distinguish among different kinds of knowledge, mean different kinds of subjects, different kinds of things known. Yet, in epistemology different ways of knowing are examined: in order to study the relation between the knower and the known, one has to inquire into the ways of knowing, the ways of getting to know, as well as the classes into which to sort that which has been or is becoming known.

The Double Meaning of Knowledge

In everyday language we use the word "knowledge" just as often in the one as in the other of its meanings. We speak of having acquired "much knowledge," and we also speak of "having knowledge" of this or that. But if "knowledge" means both what we know and our state of knowing it, we might have to say that we "have knowledge of much knowledge."

The same kind of equivocation has developed with other words.

"Possession" means both that which we possess and the state of our possessing it, from which one might conclude that we have possession of our possessions. "Property" means both that which belongs to me and my right to it, which would imply that I have property of my property.

With the double meaning of "knowledge," we shall find the terminological proposal made in Chapter 1 even more justified. Knowledge as a state of knowing is produced by activities such as talking plus listening, writing plus reading, but also by activities such as discovering, inventing, intuiting. In the first group of activities at least two persons are involved, a transmitter and a receiver, and the state of knowledge produced in the consciousness of the recipient refers to things or thoughts already known, at least to the transmitter. Only one person is engaged in the second group of activities. The state of knowing that he or she produces may be of things or thoughts not known to anybody else.

Knowledge in the sense of "that which is known" exists as soon as one single person "has" it and, hence, it is first produced by the kind of processes mentioned above with the second group of activities producing a "state of knowing"—discovering, inventing, etc. Of course, if only one person has a particular piece of knowledge and does not share it with anybody, it may be that no one knows of it. We do not ordinarily take notice of knowledge possessed by only one knower. Only when he discloses what had been a one-man secret and thus does his part in producing in other minds a state of knowing what he alone has known will we speak of "socially new knowledge." When does such knowledge stop being socially "new"? How much time must have passed since its first acquisition or since its first disclosure? There is no need to answer this question, for little, if anything, depends on how it is answered. But it is important to bear in mind that from several points of view, and particularly from an economic point of view, the transmission of the knowledge from the first knower to at least a few others is essential. This implies that the production of new knowledge—in the sense of that which is known—is not really complete until it has been transmitted to some others, so that it is no longer one person's knowledge only.

In this context we may recall that Bertrand Russell distinguished between "social knowledge" and "individual knowledge," though with reference to rather different aspects. He meant by social knowledge what "the community knows . . . in its collective capacity, all the contents of the encyclopedia and all the contributions to the proceedings of learned bodies," and by individual knowledge, what an individual knows, "through his experience, . . . knowledge not possessed by those whose experience has been different."[1] One may assume that the production of individual knowledge in this narrow sense will rarely ever be a deliberate activity, let alone an economic activity. But this is a question for consideration at a later point.

MEANINGS OF KNOWING

If it is admitted that knowledge in the sense of *knowing* and knowledge in the sense of *what is known* are different things, it will not be surprising if I choose to separate the discussion as far as I can. In this section and the two subsequent ones, I shall focus on the meanings, modes, and degrees of knowing. Yet, despite the attempt to focus on knowing, the vision field will always include some of the things known. Indeed, significant differences in the meanings, modes, and degrees of knowing cannot be explored and explained without illustrative references to the contents of the knowledge.

Knowledge-Of and Knowledge-About

Philologists, philosophers, and sociologists have made much fuss about the "poverty" of the English language relative to other civilized languages, which have two words for the one English word "knowing." The French can distinguish between *connaître* and *savoir*, the Germans between *kennen* and *wissen*, whereas the users of English are limited to the one "knowing." William James, the American psychologist and philosopher, proposed to distinguish between "knowledge-of" and "knowledge-about," or ("mere dumb") knowledge by acquaintance and knowledge by systematic study and reflection.[2]

Although this distinction may be significant in many contexts, it is not consistently carried out in the French and German use of the pairs of words, either in their verb form or in the equivalent nouns.

---

[1] Bertrand Russell, *Human Knowledge: Its Scope and Limits* (New York: Simon and Schuster, 1948), p. 3.

[2] William James, "On the Function of Cognition," *Mind*, vol. 10 (1885), pp. 27-44, reprinted in his book *The Meaning of Truth: A Sequel to 'Pragmatism'* (London: Longmans, Green, 1910), chap. 1, pp. 1-42. The distinction goes back, as James recognized by extensive quotation, to John Grote, *Exploratio Philosophica: Rough Notes on Modern Intellectual Science*, part 1 (Cambridge: Deighton, Bell, 1865), p. 60. Grote distinguished between knowledge as "acquaintance or familiarity with what is known"—a "phenomenal" matter, a "presentation to the senses," or a "representation of it in picture . . . or imagination"—and knowledge as what is "embodied in concepts," expressed "in judgments or propositions," a "more intellectual notion of knowledge."

Many very learned definitions of the French *savoir* and *science* and of the German *wissen* and *Wissenschaft* run in terms of *connaissances* and *Kenntnisse*, respectively; that is, one member of the pair is defined and explained by the other, which thus is either equivalent or only of different extension. Likewise, many colloquial expressions in these two languages are quite inconsistent, using, for example, *connaître* and *kennen* for highly developed systems of thought, and *savoir* and *wissen* for matters of casual, personal experience. Thus, the idioms do not take advantage of the distinctions which the availability of the linguistic options would permit. In these circumstances, we need not feel cheated if we have to do with one word instead of two. As a matter of fact, we may save a good deal of trouble by being spared some specious hairsplitting. The only regret that I have is on behalf of any one who has to translate my book, or any of its parts, into another language. It happens that translators into French prefer to render "knowledge" as *connaissance*, whereas translators into German render it as *Wissen*, thus making contrary linguistic choices.

This simple comment, however, was only a short introduction to a discussion—which can be neither simple nor short—of more searching questions regarding the meaning of knowing. I must not avoid embarking on an exercise in language analysis, partly because it has an important bearing on the "wide concept of knowing" that I regard as pertinent to an inquiry into the economics of knowledge-producing activities, partly because the existence of a large literature on the ways of knowing makes it morally intolerable to ignore it. It would be parochial narrow-mindedness if I were to write a long treatise on the creation and distribution of knowledge but were to pay no attention to a discourse on the meaning of knowing that has been going on for at least 2,500 years and has in recent decades become increasingly excited and exciting.

To Know That versus to Know How

Classical philosophers were chiefly interested in the meaning of knowing *that* (something is the case), so-called propositional knowing. A good many philosophers and anthropologists engaged in language analysis have argued against the onesidedness and examined the meaning of knowing *how*. The philosopher Gilbert Ryle, for example, wrote a long chapter on "Knowing How and Knowing That" and provided many instructive illustrations for these two types of knowing.[3] That knowing *how* has a directly pragmatic connotation does not mean that propositions of the knowing-*that* type

[3] Gilbert Ryle, *The Concept of Mind* (London: Hutchinson, 1949), pp. 25-61. Ryle

are without pragmatic significance; indeed, such knowledge may have a clear and strong influence on the knowers' actions. On the other hand, some knowing *that* may merely satisfy the knowers' curiosity.

Many cross-connections exist between knowing *that* and knowing *how*, but the difference in essential meaning is categorical. I know *that* means that I confidently believe that something is so and not otherwise; I know *how* means that I am capable of doing something. Consider the following examples of knowledge claims or instances of propositional knowing. We know that the square root of 64 is 8; we know that, in French, *connaissance* was once spelled *connoissance*; we know that diphtheria is a highly infectious disease; we know that Avogadro's number is 6.02×10^{23}; we know that there have never been long-lasting price inflations without increases in the quantity of money; and we know that Alexander the Great, King of Macedonia from 336 to 323 B.C., extended his realm to include Persia and the Middle East of Asia and also Egypt in North Africa. These are examples of very different kinds of knowledge (formal, empirical, linguistic, historical, etc.), but all in the nature of knowing *that*, or propositional knowing. Some of the stated propositions may express "basic" knowledge underlying some how-to knowledge; for example, knowing Avogadro's number may inform practical actions in the application of physical chemistry, and knowing the association between monetary expansion and price inflation may inform political decisions regarding the economy. Still, all these propositions are in the nature of the know-*that* type. Knowledge of the know-*how* type, though often *related* to knowledge of the know-*that* type, is, or can be, *immediately* practical, since it is a skill or ability to *do* something, a capacity to perform.

The difference between knowing *that* and knowing *how* is most clearly manifest when exclusively practical capacities to perform are so far removed from conscious mental acts or states that they approach semiautomatic muscle movements without the actor's attention—subconscious motoric activity. Thus, I know how to swim, but I can swim also without thinking about it: my mind may be on other matters, so much so that I am not aware of my swimming. Not all kinds of knowing *how* are of this routine character. I shall later find it helpful to differentiate among various types of knowing *how* by

---

complained that "theorists have been so preoccupied with the task of investigating the nature, the source and the credentials of the theories that we adopt that they have for the most part ignored the question what it is for someone to know how to perform tasks" (p. 28).

the degree of attention they require in their exercise, in their actual performance.

We have to guard against a snag in the interpretation of knowing *how*; some ambiguities seem to have escaped the semanticists' eagle-eyes: (1) We may know how something looks. (2) We may know how something has happened. (3) We may know how something (an antecedent, a cause) is generally or universally connected with something else (a subsequent, an effect). (4) We may know how to perform a certain task. All these four kinds of knowing are knowing *how*, but only the fourth is meant by the philosophers who have expounded on the features and problems of knowing *how*. The first member of the set is *descriptive* knowledge; the second, *historical* knowledge (of a course of events); the third, *theoretical* knowledge (usually regarded as knowing *why*). The fourth, know-how in the usual sense, has been called *procedural* knowledge, but this is a poorly chosen adjective, which can give rise to other confusions.[4] The use of the adjective "procedural" has been preempted by methodologists interpreting the use of fundamental hypotheses in scientific theorizing as "procedural rules," which are neither analytic nor synthetic, neither true nor false, but only heuristic or not heuristic.[5] One may, perhaps, argue that the ability to present and sustain a theoretical argument—to reason from postulates, fundamental hypotheses, and factual assumptions to inferences regarding lower-level generalizations—is a skill, requiring "procedural know-how." Still, the designation of some hypotheses as procedural rules is not designed to point to the procedural knowing of how to use these rules.

The words "practice" and "practical," commonly used in connection with knowing *how*, can easily mislead us. As I have said, knowing *that* may be no less important for practical application than knowing *how*. To know a city and its streets, to know that traffic will be heavy between 8 and 9 in the morning, and to know how to drive

[4] Procedural knowing as a synonym for "knowing how" and antonym of propositional knowing was proposed by Israel Scheffler, *Conditions of Knowledge* (Chicago: Scott, Foresman, 1965), p. 14. Scheffler points to important differences between propositional and what he calls procedural knowledge. For example, in a propositional-knowledge claim it is meaningful to replace "knowing that" by "believing that," whereas in a claim of know-how such a substitution would be meaningless. You can say "I know how to perform" (swim, calculate, etc.), but you cannot reasonably say "I believe how to perform" (p. 19).

[5] Felix Kaufmann, *Methodology of the Social Sciences* (New York: Oxford University Press, 1944), pp. 77ff, especially pp. 87-88. The expression was used also by Henry Margenau, *The Nature of Physical Reality: A Philosophy of Modern Physics* (New York: McGraw-Hill, 1950), p. 13. Sir Karl Popper has also occasionally employed the term.

an automobile are three different kinds of knowing; all three are practical to one who has to make an appearance at 9 a.m. at a specified building in that city. Yet, only the capacity to drive the car is counted as knowing *how*. On the other hand, in acquiring that capacity—knowing how to drive—a learner is greatly helped by precepts, directives, and other statements of a knowing-*that* character.

Since the author of this book happens to be a professional economist, readers not close to that discipline may suspect that an economist's concern will be chiefly with practical knowledge. Having been told that knowing *that* need not be any less practical than knowing *how*, these readers may still suspect that practical knowledge (in the wider sense) would be in the center of the statistical, descriptive, and analytical inquiries in these volumes. One might think that business firms, households, and governments would be averse to spending money for any but practical knowledge; such a preconception, however, would be mistaken. Consumers spend large sums for information, or flows of knowledge, that merely satisfy their curiosity, their desire for entertainment, their cultural aspirations. Businessmen pay for television programs which add nothing to the practical know-how of anybody, viewers, customers, or insiders. Governments spend huge sums for the production and distribution of knowledge of all sorts, including, of course, a fair portion for teaching immediately practical knowledge, the basic skills.

This does not mean that the economic role of how-to knowledge is small. "Economic role" is an ambiguous phrase. How much of all knowledge-producing activity in the nation is designed to generate or disseminate knowledge for use in practical action? How much does the generation and dissemination of practical knowledge contribute to the growth of productivity and national income? These are, clearly, two entirely different questions. What portion of national income is spent for obtaining practical knowledge is something else than what portion of an increase in national income is attributable to the generation, dissemination, and use of practical knowledge. The first fraction may be small, the second large. Both, however, are worth investigating.

We shall return to the notion of "practicality" of knowledge. But there is much to do—or rather to talk about—before we get there for a more definitive analysis.

To Know What, to Know That, and to Know How

I find it necessary to add a third kind of knowing, namely, knowing *what*. At first blush it looks as if knowing *what* and knowing *that* are the same; it can be shown, however, that knowing *what* is much wider, in that it may contain many knowing *thats* and may have more cross-connections with knowing *how*. As a matter of fact, there is more than one kind of knowing *what*, but I shall talk first about the one which is densely populated with knowing *thats*, or propositional knowing.[6]

If I claim to know a city, a language, a literature, a work of art, a discipline or field of study, or any other complex of knowable things, I cannot possibly formulate what I know about these subjects in a single proposition. Each of these complex subjects may contain thousands or millions of things knowable, many, perhaps all, statable in propositions in the form of "I know that. . . ." Yet, nobody, or hardly anybody, will claim knowledge of almost all of them; most people who claim to know a complex subject will in fact know only a fraction of the propositional knowledge that makes up the total. Knowing *what* means knowing an undetermined portion of all possible knowing-*that* claims about the subject.

Do you know Paris? Yes, I have been there, but what do I know about it? According to a guidebook, Paris has approximately 5,500 streets, 75 theaters (not counting cabarets and cinemas), 175 churches, over 50 university buildings, over 50 hospitals, 57 museums, 14 parks, some 120 bus lines, 23 cemeteries. How many streets do I have to know, to know Paris? As many as a taxi driver? or perhaps only the major boulevards and a few streets around my hotel? How many churches should I have visited and in what detail should I have studied them? All the stained-glass windows and the gargoyles? How well do I have to know the Louvre, the Tuileries, the Eiffel Tower, the Panthéon; how well the railroad stations, the lines of the Metro? Do I have to know that the rue de la Paix runs from the Boulevard des Capucines to the Place de l'Opéra? (Only the last of all these potential knowings was here formulated in the form of a know-*that* proposition, but all the others could equally well be expressed in such a form.) The connection between knowing *what* and knowing *how* is rather simple in this case: I know how to get by the shortest route (or in the shortest time) from the Étoile to the Sorbonne. (If I drive a car, I have to know that this or that is a one-way street.)

As a second example of knowing *what*, I propose a foreign language, French. To say honestly "I know French," how many of the many thousands of French words do I have to know? How much of

[6] My concept of knowing *what* is not the same as Broudy's. See Harry S. Broudy, "Mastery," chap. 5 in B. Othaniel Smith and Robert H. Ennis, eds., *Language and Concepts in Education* (Chicago: Rand McNally, 1961), p. 77.

its grammar and syntax, how many idioms and colloquialisms? I suppose that most of the things knowable about the French language can be stated in the form of appropriate propositions, though this may be difficult for matters of pronunciation and intonation. In any case, hundreds of thousands of items of knowing *that* may add up to complete knowledge of French, but a fraction of the total will commonly be accepted in support of the claim that "I know French." The connection between knowing French as a subject and knowing how to read French, how to speak French, how to write French, and how to understand spoken French is too evident to require elaboration. There will hardly be a dispute about the fact that the degrees of knowing may be different, and that the degrees may be measured in different ways: regarding knowing French as a subject, perhaps by the ratio of individual items of knowing *that* to the total complex of knowing *what*, and regarding knowing how to converse in French, perhaps by the fluency, accuracy, intelligibility, and elegance of expression in speaking, and by the ease and correctness in the understanding of the partners' utterances.

For my last example of knowing *what*, I choose economics, a complex of thousands of definitions, assumptions, facts, observed regularities, and models. How many of the special fields, apart from micro- and macroeconomics, does one have to "know" to justify a claim of knowing economics? The classifiers have distinguished welfare economics, doctrinal history, economic history, comparative systems, economic growth and development, economic fluctuations and stabilization, economic statistics, econometrics, national-income accounting, monetary and fiscal theory, public finance, international economics, business finance and management, industrial organization, industry studies, agricultural and natural resources, manpower and labor economics, demographic economics, consumer economics, urban economics, regional economics—to mention only the major headings. Would familiarity with or mastery of three or four of these fields be sufficient to legitimize the claim "I know economics"? What minimum number of single items of knowing *that* would be required for a warranted claim to know even one of the special fields? This may be the proper place to point to the difference between knowing and demonstrating that one knows.[7] What you demonstrate that you know is at best a portion of what you know. And the ability to demonstrate your knowing is a know-how not necessarily proportional to the amount of your propositional

---

[7] I want to acknowledge my indebtedness to Donna H. Kerr, whose pointed questions and blunt comments in discussion were immensely helpful to me in developing this section.

knowing. The knowing *how* that is related to the knowledge of economics, or any other field of study, manifests itself in the knower's ability to convince, to advise, to teach, and to pass examinations.

Summarizing my exposition of this meaning of knowing *what*, I may emphasize again that it relates to large complexes of propositional knowing—and knowing *what* can be resolved (decomposed, broken down) into large numbers of single knowing-*that* propositions. Perhaps I may refer to this concept of knowing *what* as the particle theory of knowing, where the whole complex consists of masses of single propositions in the form of knowing *that*. The latter can be judged as true or false—or undecided, if one is prepared to admit this into one's scheme of logic. The former, however, the knowing *what*, can be judged only in terms of the relative numbers of relevant knowing-*that* propositions which the knower can affirm.

As a transition to a second kind of knowing *what*, I may return for a moment to my knowing Paris. Does it consist only of thousands of particles of propositional knowing, or does it perhaps include also some sentimental, emotional "knowing"? I can well imagine a lover of Paris saying that no one knows Paris who has not felt the elation and awe inspired by seeing the architectural grandeur of the cathedral of Notre Dame, or the loveliness and enchantment of seeing and smelling the blooming chestnut trees on the banks of the Seine in early spring. If these are parts of knowing *what*, they cannot be properly expressed in propositional knowing.

This statement captures the second meaning of knowing *what*: feelings which can be known only by experience, not described in words of prose. I might call it ineffable knowledge were it not for the poets who sometimes can convey in words of poetry what cannot be expressed in declarative propositions. Feelings of pleasure and of pain, of love and of hate, of awe, sympathy, fear, pity, envy, guilt, remorse, and many others, can be known by personal experience. They are included in the category of knowing *what*, since they are nonpropositional contents or components of *what* is known.

The Special Status of Knowing That

I have mentioned the differences among knowing *what*, knowing *that*, and knowing *how*, as if these were all there is. There are some more, for example, knowing *whom*, knowing *who*, and knowing *why*. Before I introduce the newcomers and tell about their roles, I want to talk about the special status accorded to knowing *that*. This status is not the result of everyday discourse among ordinary people but, instead, a philosopher's convention that began with Plato. Persons seeking, claiming, and achieving "superior knowledge" don't just talk as common folk; instead, they make declarative statements, formulate propositions, categorical assertions, hypothetical syllogisms, and all the rest. To many learned people, or scientists, knowledge seems to be almost exclusively propositional knowing. (I may feel compelled several times in these volumes to repeat this reference to one-sided interpretations of the meaning of knowledge.)

The school of analytic or linguistic philosophers has made the analysis of the meaning of knowing one of its major tasks—not from the point of view of traditional epistemology, not from a psychological point of view, not from an anthropological point of view, not from points of view of historical semantics, but from their special procedures of language analysis: words must mean what they ought to mean in the most logical of all logical discourses. The linguistic philosophers on the ultra-fussy wing, insisting on the "strong" meaning of knowing, have stipulated conditions for the right use of the word so strict that few can ever meet them; moreover, the conditions are stricter for the third person ("he or she knows") than for the first person ("I know"). The analysts want "I know" to mean, first, that what I claim to know is really true, second, that I am sure of it, and, third, that I have a right to be sure of it.[8] Two further conditions are imposed on the meaning of "He knows," namely, that I am sure that he knows that what he claims to know is really true, and that I am sure that he has a right to be sure of it.[9]

If I, speaking for myself, were to claim to be sure and to have a right to be sure of the truth of my propositions, I would betray a lack of scientific modesty and of the proper attitude of always conceding the possibility that I may be wrong. If I were to claim that a third

[8] Alfred J. Ayer, The Problem of Knowledge (Harmondsworth: Penguin Books, 1956), p. 35.

[9] Some expositors, for example, Israel Scheffler, try to simplify this statement of conditions by reducing it to three steps also for "He knows"; this works, however, only if the third person's acceptance of the adequacy of the evidence is the same as that of the first person. See Scheffler, Conditions of Knowledge, pp. 16 and 21. "The point is that when we assert that a person X knows that Q, we are not only (in effect) affirming the truth of our whole assertion, but we are committing ourselves also to the truth of the embedded substantive statement 'Q' " (p. 22).—My point, that there may be five conditions imposed on the strong meaning of knowing, rests on the possibility that I do not accept the same evidence that satisfies the third person as giving him the right to be sure about the truth of the proposition he averts. Disagreement on the adequacy of evidence is not rare. Michael Polanyi wrote on the "personal" judgment involved: "Things are not labelled 'evidence' in nature, but are evidence only to the extent to which they are accepted as such by us as observers. . . . Indeed, no scientist can forego selecting his evidence in the light of heuristic expectations." Michael Polanyi, Personal Knowledge, 2d ed. (London: Routledge and Kegan Paul, 1962 [1st ed., 1958]), p. 30.

person had such unquestionable assuredness of the truth, I would appear to be rather prejudiced. If we took this rigmarole (of several sureness piled on one another) at its face value, the word "knowing," or at least the expression "propositional knowing," would have to be banished from our vocabulary.

Having undertaken to write about knowledge, I am not joining the fussy JTB fanatics—"Justified True Belief" zealots.[10] I incline more towards historical semantics, trying to find out what people mean (or meant) when they say (or said) something, not what they ought to mean (or ought to have meant). I shall not dodge further discussion of the relationship between knowledge and truth, but I shall defer it to the first chapter of Part Two. For the moment, I want to look into a whole string of meanings of knowing, as people of all kinds, classes, and professions use the word in less formal, less artful speech.

An Assortment of Knowns and Knowings

The variety of meanings reasonably attached to the word "knowing" is far greater than most of us realize before looking into this business. I have formulated many questions beginning with "Do you know . . . ?" and have tried to give an honest answer beginning with "Yes, ..." and proceeding either to some reservations and limitations or to justifications of my affirmative reply. (It was not vanity that made me omit questions about my knowledge which I would have to answer in the negative, but just the thought that I wanted to examine the meanings of knowing, not the meanings of not knowing. As a matter of fact, the "conditions" imposed on "significant propositions" are the same for affirmative and negative sentences.)

After I had experimented with many questions and answers, I found it helpful to arrange the questions according to a set of interrogative pronouns or particles such as what, who, whom, when, where, and how. This would not lead to an omission of knowing that, partly because most of the questions allow for answers in the form of that clauses. Thus, there are many questions which I would place into combined categories because "I know that. . . ." would answer questions about what, who, whom, when, and where.

For some of the categories I formulated several questions, because I wanted a variety of subjects to be represented, ranging from the most mundane personal matters to sophisticated scientific problems. I shall have questions and answers appear in juxtaposition, num-

---

[10] Again I want to say how much I owe to the stimulating discussions with Donna H. Kerr. She gave me courage as well as advice.

bered from 1 to 33, in order to facilitate references to them in the subsequent discussion.

QUESTIONS	ANSWERS
1. Do you know European economic history?	Yes, enough for my present needs in research, but not enough to teach it on a graduate level.
2. Do you know the Phlogiston theory?	Yes, it was the (now rejected) theory of an invisible substance contained in combustible bodies and disengaged in the process of combustion.
3. Do you know Paris?	Yes, I have been there many times, but never for very long. I could not draw you a map from memory.
4. Do you know the Sixth Symphony by Beethoven?	Yes, the *Pastoral*; I've heard it often and might be able to hum a few themes.
5. Do you know Rembrandt's *Nightwatch*?	Yes, I saw it in Amsterdam, and of course in reproductions.
6. Do you know Thomas Mann's *Buddenbrooks*?	Yes, I have read it, but the book is so long, and I read it so long ago, that I cannot remember it very well.
7. Do you know migraine headaches?	Yes, I've suffered from them for many years, though lately less frequently.
8. Do you know that you ought not to say that you know unless you are sure of your evidence?	Yes, but I do not accept this pedantic restriction on ordinary speech.
9. Do you know that the unemployment rate increased in June from 5.6 to 5.7 per cent?	Yes, but such figures mean little; there are different ways to define the term, to get the data, to treat them, and to obtain a measurement.
10. Do you know that the annual rate of price inflation	Yes, but the question is who expects, and on the basis of

is expected to be much lower in 1980 than in 1979?

what assumptions regarding unknown future policies does he expect?

11. Do you know that your trousers are torn in the back?

Yes, someone else has told me, but I don't know how I tore them.

12. Do you know that this is your wife's birthday?

Yes, but only now that you have reminded me of it: I might not have thought of it.

13. Do you know that it is long past dinnertime?

Yes, you have just made me aware of it.

14. Do you know the capital of California?

Yes, [I know that it is] Sacramento.

15. Do you know the second law of thermodynamics?

Yes, it is the law of entropy. [I know that] in irreversible processes, such as the mixing of hot and cold gases or the change of a solid to a liquid, disorder will increase. I ought to learn more about this law to be sure that I comprehend all that is implied.

16. Do you know the program for the concert tonight?

Yes, [I know], if I was told correctly, that they would play Mozart, Debussy, and Bartók.

17. Do you know what the weather forecast is?

Yes, I have heard it: [I know there is] a 40 per cent chance of showers in the afternoon.

18. Do you know what time it is?

Yes, if my watch is correct, [I know that it is] ten minutes past twelve.

19. Do you know the meaning of knowledge ?

Yes, to me it means [or I know that it comprises] all the things that can be connected with the verb to know.

20. Do you know the years when the Thirty Years War was fought?

Yes, [I know that they were] 1618 to 1648.

21. Do you know where my briefcase is?

Yes, [I know that it is] on my secretary's desk; I saw it there this morning.

22. Do you know who killed J. F. Kennedy?	Yes, [I know that it was] Lee Harvey Oswald, if the Warren Commission was right, which seems to be the case.
23. Do you know who is President of Austria?	Yes, [I know that it is] Dr. Kirchschläger; I have actually met him a few times.
24. Do you know your neighbor?	Yes, but not socially; it is only a nodding acquaintance.
25. Do you know calculus?	Yes, both differential and integral, but I have forgotten how to do differential equations.
26. Do you know French?	Yes, I read it fluently, but my speaking knowledge is only fair.
27. Do you know any nursery rhymes?	Yes, I have heard many, but can recite only one or two by heart.
28. Do you know the fairy tale of Snow White and the Seven Dwarfs?	Yes, I had to tell it sometimes to my grandchildren.
29. Do you know regression analysis?	Yes, but only in principle; I use my assistants for such work.
30. Do you know the backstroke?	Yes, it is my favorite stroke in swimming.
31. Do you know how to ski?	Yes, I have been a downhill skier for sixty years and can still do it well.
32. Do you know how to play chess?	Yes, I was not bad at it as a young man but have not played in years.
33. Do you know how to distinguish different tastes and aromas of imported wines?	Yes, but only superficially; I am not a connoisseur and cannot identify them.

Arrangement by Interrogative Pronoun

We may arrange the 33 examples of knowing into nine groups according to the interrogative pronouns to which the answers reply.

Items 1 to 7 refer to questions about knowing *what* (that is, knowing countless relevant items of knowing *that*); items 8 to 13 are of the more traditional and respectable type of knowing *that*; items 14 to 19 combine the preceding two categories and thus are in the nature of knowing *what* and *that*; item 20 represents knowing *when* and *that*; item 21, *where* and *that*; items 22 and 23, *who* and *that*; item 24 answers the question *whom*; items 25 to 29 combine *what* and *how*; and items 30 to 33 are typical instances of knowing *how*.

Trying to justify these distinctions, I will occasionally have to strain my vision and discernment of subtle nuances. Perhaps I should begin with the distinctions between knowing *what*, knowing *what* and *how*, and knowing *how*. All my examples of knowing *what* (items 1 to 7) refer to definite subjects ranging from an area of study to a specific obsolete theory, to a large city, to several works of art, and to a feeling of pain. Although I called them instances of knowing *what*, I tried to indicate that there could usually be connections with knowing *how*, as, for example, when I said that I might be able to hum themes from the *Pastoral* Symphony. Likewise I mentioned, in the very first item, that my knowledge of the subject was not adequate to enable me to teach it on a graduate level. Again, when I spoke about my knowing Paris, I mentioned the potential of knowing how to draw a map. Still, I left these implied references to knowing *how* at the side and was satisfied to characterize all seven as illustrations of knowing *what*.

I have regarded the last four items, 30 to 33, as illustrations of knowing *how*. Two of them were physical abilities, where perhaps a fair amount of knowing *that* was involved in the process of learning, but little, if any, was involved in the actual exercise of the skill.[11] Incidentally, I might use this occasion to distinguish the extent to which mental alertness and attention is needed in swimming, on the one hand, and downhill skiing, on the other. Swimming may be semiautomatic movements, whereas downhill skiing requires constant attention to stationary and moving obstacles. Chess playing (item 32) is an exercise of know-how acquired after a learning process that involves the understanding of rules in the nature of knowing *that*. The actual playing of chess involves a continuing mental strain requiring abilities—know-how—of various sorts. The know-how of the winetaster (item 33) is of a particular type in that its acquisition is hardly based on any kind of knowing *that*. This know-how is ac-

---

[11] Ryle, *The Concept of Mind*, p. 41. "We learn *how* by practice, schooled indeed by criticism and example, but often quite unaided by any lessons in the theory."

quired only by practice and it is not clear whether its development is reserved to people with special talents.

Both knowing *what* and knowing *how* are needed in items 25 to 29. The point is that the abilities calling for the know-how in question may be kept in reserve, so to speak. All five illustrations may be cases of latent knowing *what*—calculus, regression analysis, French, nursery rhymes, and fairy tales. In all these instances the knowledge may be partial or complete, superficial or profound, unconsciously remembered or actually recalled, potentially usable or actually exercised. Some of these differences were pointed out in my answers. Knowing French may be a knowledge to understand, to read, to speak, and to write, and the levels of achievement may be very different. The combination of knowing *what* and knowing *how* was also clearly indicated in my claimed knowledge of regression analysis. Since I understand it, it is a case of knowing *what*, but since I let my assistants do the actual work, it is a knowing *how* for them but not for me.

Taking up the six examples of knowing-*that* statements, items 8 to 13, I confess that I have indulged in being sarcastic by choosing exclusively such knowledge claims as could never pass the JTB test prescribed by the fussy wing of the analytic philosophers. Indeed, a critical referee may call a foul on the first of my knowledge claims, item 8, where I in effect state merely my knowledge of, or acquaintance with, the categorical imperative of the language analysts (telling us what we ought to do or not to do) and proceed to a statement rejecting their commandment. The referee may also point out that imperatives are not propositions and, therefore, not subject to a truth test. I concede that I was mischievous, but I do not repent, because I think the problems involved are worth thinking about.

In order to exhibit the knowing-*that* character of the six claims, I made sure that the *that* was already contained in the question: I said not just "do you know" but "do you know that. . . ." None of the knowledge claims in my answers, however, allow any claims of being sure of the truth of, or even a firm belief in, the "known" proposition. In the examples about the past rate of unemployment (item 9) and the future rate of price increase (item 10), I went out of my way to show that these are at the same time examples of knowing *that* and examples of knowing *that we can never be sure* of knowing *that*. Two others of my examples of knowing *that* lack the supposedly essential condition of certification: I had no evidence to justify my knowing that my trousers were really torn (item 11), I simply, perhaps naively, believed the two friends who told me so (perhaps as a practical joke); and whether it was really past dinnertime (item 13) is just a matter of custom and convention.

Having reviewed seven examples of knowing *what* (items 1-7) and six examples of knowing *that* (items 8-13), it should not be too difficult to comprehend the combined category of statements about knowing *what and that*, illustrated by items 14 to 19 of my list of questions and answers. The *what* refers to the general subject known, the *that* to the proposition stated about it. The questions name the subject about which knowledge may be claimed, the answers are in the form of propositions, preceded by the claim "I know that . . ." placed within brackets. The examples seem ill-chosen in that they do not bring out the major difference, discussed earlier, between knowing *what* and knowing *that*, in which the *what* refers to a complex entity or collective of many parts, decomposable into many single propositions, and the *that* refers to a single proposition. It should not really surprise us that this difference vanishes if the two contraries are combined in hybrid forms, simply because the *what* is reduced to a single entity, stripped from the context of a larger subject.

Similar combinations of the questions when, where, who, and whom with the propositional knowing *that*, as shown in items 20 to 24, require no commentaries. All these questions could be answered in the form of knowing *that*.

Further Comments on Knowing That and Knowing How

Some additional comments on the contrast between knowing *that* and knowing *how* may be helpful in view of differences in the interpretations by different philosophers. One question that has occupied a good many writers relates to the definition of knowing *how*: is it an art, an ability, a disposition, a state of mind, a set of rules, observance of rules or canons, the application of criteria, a sequence of actions, a practice, a performance, a skill? I shall not join this argument; if we know what we are talking about, we need not spend time trying to formulate the most appropriate definition. The illustrations furnished above—knowing how to swim, knowing how to ski, knowing how to play chess, knowing how to identify vintages of wines, knowing how to draw a map of Paris, knowing how to solve differential equations, knowing how to converse in French, knowing how to recite nursery rhymes, knowing how to do regression analysis, knowing how to demonstrate one's understanding of difficult arguments—should be ample exemplification, pinpointing the essentials of what is meant. The common denominator of all the know-hows enumerated is the ability to perform a certain kind of activity or task.

Gilbert Ryle proposed a sharp distinction: "We build up habits by drill, but we build up intelligent capacities by training." He concluded that "drill dispenses with intelligence, training develops it."[12] Although the distinction is valid in principle, it may be difficult, I submit, to draw a clear line in a spectrum of learning activities which may begin as conscious training and gradually submerge into more mechanical drill.

Michael Polanyi emphasized a similar, yet sufficiently different, distinction, not related to the acquisition but rather to the exercise of know-how, or, as he calls it, "subsidiary or instrumental knowledge." The distinction is between "connoisseurship" as the art of knowing and "skills" as the art of doing.[13] Accepting this dichotomy, I would say that the winetaster applies his connoisseurship, and the downhill skier his skill. Polanyi also stresses the fact that the performer may have either a merely "subsidiary awareness" of using his know-how or a "focal awareness"; and he finds them "mutually exclusive." Thus, if a pianist in performance were to give his attention to his fingerwork—of which he ought to be only "subsidiarily aware"—his focal attention to the music would thereby be arrested.[14]

In Ryle's view, "Understanding is a part of knowing *how*." He justifies this dictum by arguing that "the knowledge that is acquired for understanding intelligent performance of a specific kind is some degree of competence in performances of that kind."[15] This is undoubtedly true for some kinds of knowing *how*, for example, for understanding a speech in a foreign language, and perhaps an argument presented with mathematical derivations. It will hardly be accepted, however, that the understanding of new scientific theories is "a part of knowing *how*" and that understanding of a musical or artistic performance requires "competence in performances of that kind."[16] A music critic (and musicologist) need not be a composer or musician, an art critic (and art historian) need not be a painter or sculptor, and a medical doctor may understand surgery even if he is not a surgeon.

There is a strange difference between Ryle and Polanyi regarding

[12] Ibid., pp. 42-43.

[13] Polanyi, *Personal Knowledge*, p. 88.

[14] Ibid., pp. 55-56.

[15] Ryle, *The Concept of Mind*, p. 54.

[16] For Ryle, "Roughly, execution and understanding are merely different exercises of knowledge of the tricks of the same trade." Ibid., p. 55. I submit that understanding may require a comprehension of underlying theories.

the time it takes to acquire basic theoretical knowledge, on the one hand, and know-how in performance, on the other. Says Ryle, "Learning *how* or improving in ability is not like learning *that* or acquiring information. Truths can be imparted, procedures can only be inculcated, and, whereas inculcation is a gradual process, imparting is relatively sudden."[17] Says Polanyi: "Years of study may not suffice to master the theory [of relativity] and see the facts [accounted for by relativity] in its context."[18] The contradiction, or conflict of opinions, is easily resolved if we understand the human propensity to generalize. In this instance, both authors have overgeneralized. Some propositional knowing is easily imparted, with a sudden flash of light, whereas other pieces or complexes of knowing may take years to acquire or may remain entirely inaccessible to many students; similarly, some performing know-how may be learned by the gifted in no time at all, whereas other abilities to perform can be acquired only in years of hard training or perhaps never. The time it takes to learn, to acquire knowledge, is not among the characteristics either of knowing *that* or of knowing *how*.

ELEMENTS AND MODES OF KNOWING

A substantial carry-over from the previous section can be drawn upon for an analysis of the elements and modes of knowing. One fundamental dichotomy in meaning can be seen also as a difference in the mode of knowing: knowing *that* versus knowing *how*. Another distinction, less fundamental but still significant, calls for further examination: knowing *of* and knowing *about*. It will soon become clear, however, that binary divisions will not suffice in an examination of the elements of knowing; a considerable number of such elements are differentiated only by subtle nuances, shading gradually into one another, like the colors in a spectrum. A spectrum cannot meaningfully be divided into just two kinds or categories.

The Examples Surveyed for Different Modes of Knowing

I went again through the list of 33 examples that I had compiled for use in the previous section; this time, however, my concern was not with the type of question answered by the knowledge claims, but rather with the type of mental state or activity that was involved in the various examples of knowing. Although I learned a great deal from this analysis, and although I am convinced that many readers

[17] Ibid., p. 59.   [18] Polanyi, *Personal Knowledge*, p. 16.

would profit if I shared with them my detailed findings or conclusions regarding each of the 33 items, I am afraid that other readers might be bored if they were invited to go through such a lengthy exercise. The Germans have a somewhat ungracious expression to register impatience with overly detailed and tedious reporting: "I did not really want to know it all with such exactitude." ("So genau wollt' ich's gar nicht wissen.") I am anxious not to bore and, hence, I will forego presenting my tabulation. A brief summary of my conclusions may do.

I found that between two and seven elements may be present in any one instance of knowing, and I identified a total of thirteen elements in the whole lot of 33 examples. Two or more instances of knowing will be said to represent the same mode of knowing if they contain the same set of elements. Needless to say, my attempt to break down the mental states or activities was influenced by similar work done by philosophers, psychologists, and language analysts.

The Elements of Knowing

The following thirteen elements may possibly be present, though not all in the same instance, in the state or act of knowing: (1) being acquainted, (2) being familiar, (3) being aware, (4) remembering, (5) recollecting, (6) recognizing, (7) distinguishing, (8) understanding, (9) interpreting, (10) being able to explain, (11) being able to demonstrate, (12) being able to talk about, and (13) being able to perform.

Some of these elements of knowing are mutually exclusive in the same instance of knowing, because they are alternatives, either in kind or in degree. The first two, acquaintance and familiarity, represent differences in degree, though it will be quite arbitrary to draw a hard and fast line between the two. It should be clear, however, that I am either "merely acquainted" or "quite familiar" with something (or someone) knowable. Of course, the alternative becomes really disjunctive by the terms being modified by "merely" and "quite," respectively. Otherwise one might reasonably say "I am not only acquainted but even familiar with it (or him or her);" in this case acquaintance would be the wider concept and include familiarity.

Being acquainted or being familiar with, as elements of knowing, were probably suggested by William James' distinction between "knowledge of" and "knowledge about," which he described as "knowledge by acquaintance" and "knowledge by systematic study and reflection." The two pairs of opposites are not equivalent or analogous, since James referred to the origin of the knowledge acquired, whereas being acquainted or being familiar refer to qualities of knowing or, from another point of view, to elements of knowing.[19] One may, of course, hold that familiarity can be only the result of study and reflection, but this is too rigid a definition.

Being aware of is an element of knowing incompatible with either being acquainted or being familiar with. I can be aware of a certain situation, say, that it is long past dinnertime, that the weatherman has predicted rain, or that this is my wife's birthday, but in none of these instances can I reasonably say that I am acquainted or familiar with the facts in question. Obversely, I can be acquainted with Rembrandt's *Nightwatch* and familiar with Beethoven's *Pastoral* Symphony, but I cannot be aware of them. I conclude that only one of the first three elements can be present in any one instance of knowing (unless familiarity is treated as a high degree of acquaintance).

Elements 4 and 5 both have to do with memory: remembering is used here to refer to stored knowledge, recollecting, to retrieved knowledge.[20] Remembering (in this narrow sense) is not a conscious state of mind: the thing known has been stored away in the knower's inactive memory files. This has been called latent knowledge; perhaps "dormant" knowledge would be the most telling metaphor. Recollecting stands for bringing what has been latently known from the inactive memory to active consciousness; it is thus being reactivated. Remembering and recollecting are of course closely interrelated: only what is remembered, or has been retained, can be recollected. We might have spoken, instead, of dormant and active remembering; needless to say, what has been recollected for a brief moment, or for a short period of time, can again be sent back to the inactive files. Thus, although dormant and active remembering cannot happen at the same time, all dormant knowledge can with the right stimulus become active. Remembering, therefore, implies potential recollecting.

Remembering and potential recollecting are elements of knowing in all but five or six of the instances described on my list; they seem inconsistent only with being aware. If I am aware of this or that situation or presence, it usually would make no sense to say that I remember or recollect it. All instances of knowing possibly characterized as being either acquainted or familiar with the thing known also include remembering and potential recollecting.

[19] John Grote, from whom James derived his distinction, had contrasted "acquaintance or familiarity" with knowledge expressed in "judgments or propositions." (See above, footnote 2 of this chapter.)

[20] This distinction is Ryle's, who used remembering for not having forgotten, and recalling or recollecting for an occurrence at a moment, "sometimes deliberately and sometimes involuntarily." *The Concept of Mind*, pp. 272ff.

The next two elements possibly present in instances of knowing are recognizing and distinguishing. They are not nearly as ubiquitous as being acquainted or familiar with the thing known, or as remembering and potentially recollecting it. A difference between recognizing and distinguishing should be mentioned: almost anything that can be recognized by the knower can also be distinguished by him from similar things, people, or ideas; that is, he will not confuse it with them. On the other hand, certain things, people, or ideas can be distinguished in theory, in mental models or constructs, although the knower may not be able to recognize them on sight or hearing. For example, I may be able to distinguish a major from a minor scale or chord in theory but not on hearing them produced on a piano or by an orchestra. In order to bring out this difference, I say "distinguishing" when I want to include or emphasize the intellectual or propositional knowing of knowables and "recognizing" when I want to emphasize sense perceptions—seeing, hearing, touching, smelling, and tasting—as the basis for recognizing.

It may go without saying but, nevertheless, we should not fail to note that there is an element of knowing *how* involved in recognizing anything. Recognizing is a performance which presupposes knowing, but it is not clear whether and how the ability to recognize a thing, a person, an idea, a musical theme, or what not, depends on a talent, on a skill acquired by training, or entirely on the degree of knowing. It happens that I personally have always had great difficulties recognizing the faces of acquaintances, friends, even close relatives. Many people are able to recognize men and women whom they have met only once and for only the shortest time, whereas I am embarrassed by my failure to recognize colleagues and associates I have known for years and have met almost a hundred times. When I finally figure out who they are, or when they kindly reveal their identity, I can recollect so much about our joint experiences and of their past achievements that no one can doubt my knowing them, or my knowing of them and about them.

Although the ability to recognize is undoubtedly an element of knowing, it is probably neither a measure nor a sure test of knowing. As a mountain climber, I have found some who would recognize all the mountains in all the ranges visible from a peak, whereas some of their fellow climbers, who had been there far more often, were unable to match or even approach their feats of recognition. Similar differences can be observed when photographs of mountains and mountain ranges are shown to mountaineers who had been equally well acquainted with the regions in question. Analogous observations can be made in recognition tests of quotations from well-known literary works and of musical themes. I have witnessed such tests administered to musicians—instrumentalists and conductors —who failed to recognize passages of symphonies, chamber music, or operas which they, by their own admission, "knew" perfectly well. They would say, "oh sure, I know this well, but right now I cannot place it."

Recognizing is regularly combined with being acquainted or familiar with, but not with being aware of; it goes well with knowing *what*, but not with knowing *that*. Although it is itself a kind of knowing *how*, it is often combined with observing the execution of other performing skills. For example, recognizing a good chess player or expert skier, and distinguishing them from mediocre performers, presupposes *some* knowledge of the same arts, though perhaps long ago and more in theory than in action. A former singer, now without voice, may be a good judge of singing; also, a conductor or piano accompanist, who never could sing, may recognize a good singer.

Let us proceed to the next two elements of knowing: "understanding" and "interpreting." These are ambiguous words, and it may be a mistake to allow without warning the confounding of different meanings of each. To understand a symphony, to understand a novel, to understand economics, to understand the second law of thermodynamics, to understand French, to understand regression analysis, and to understand the game of chess, are rather different cognitive, or in some instances affective, processes. (I have deliberately omitted the most complex concept of understanding: the *Verstehen* of other persons' thoughts and actions, so fundamental for all social sciences and humanities.)

There are surely different levels of understanding even where this word applies to different objects or subjects. As I have said before, understanding French may be limited to understanding spoken or written French, but may extend to understanding French grammar and philological peculiarities. In some contexts, understanding may be almost congruent with knowing, but, in this case, one clearly would have to distinguish several levels of knowing. In other instances, one may have to keep understanding down to its role as an element of knowing. Many people, for example, who know regression analysis may know very well how to perform it and, yet, have poor understanding of its meaning and, especially, of the meanings and the limits to the conclusiveness of the results obtained. With regard to some types of knowing *how*, understanding or interpreting do not come in at all. Knowing how to swim or ski requires no understanding of the performances in question.

I proceed to what I have called the tenth and eleventh elements of knowing: being able to explain and being able to demonstrate. Both these come definitely under the rubric of knowing *how*. Both performances are often regarded as the best possible tests of the claimed abilities. It should be obvious that the ability to explain is strongly correlated with the element of understanding, but I would deny that conceptually the two are the same. I admit that operationally it would be hard to test understanding independently of the ability to explain. My personal experience emboldens me to say that sometimes I am convinced that I understand although I feel unable to explain; and in other instances my attempt to explain, in spoken or written words, often increases or reinforces my understanding. These observations refer chiefly to cognitive knowing, but they may well have a bearing also on emotional and affective knowing.

Demonstrating may often consist of explaining, but in many instances it does not; for example, where it requires merely placing check marks in the right boxes on a form, or where demonstrating refers to the know-how of doing something physically. I repeat an earlier remark to the effect that what you demonstrate that you know is at best a portion of what you know. This applies much more to cognitive knowing than to abilities to perform.

Being able to talk about what you know was listed as the twelfth element of knowing. It overlaps with explaining and demonstrating but will be different in many instances. The knower may often be able to talk about *what* he knows, *that* he knows, and his knowing *how*, without being able either to explain or to demonstrate. Being able to talk about is probably the most ubiquitous of all elements of knowing. Talking about what one knows is surely the most frequent way of making one's knowledge explicit.

The last element on my list was *being able to perform*, by which I meant to refer to specific kinds of doing, going beyond the various abilities inherent in previously discussed elements. The ability to perform was exemplified in items 25 to 33 of the long list. It does not take much analysis to conclude that this element of knowing is always combined with such other elements as remembering, recollecting, recognizing, and talking about, and is often combined with being acquainted or familiar with. It is never combined with being aware of.

A distinction ought to be made between activities described in intransitive verbs and others described in verbs that may have an object. He who knows how to sing may not be able to sing everything, not only because he may be unfamiliar with certain songs or arias, but because his ability to sing may be limited to music of a specific type. One who knows how to play the piano may possibly be able to play "Chopsticks" or simple tunes but may not be able to play Mozart or Brahms. Similar qualifications may have to be made regarding dancing, painting, and so on. There is much less need for similar qualifications in instances of knowing how to exercise physical skills.

Modes as Combinations of Elements

My enumeration of thirteen elements of knowing is of no great importance: I could have compressed my list or could have expanded it. Other analysts may find that some of the elements should be broken down further, or they may wish to have some fused into one; again others may wish to eliminate some of my elements as supererogatory or may wish to add one or two that I have disregarded. My intention has been merely to aid in the comprehension of the modes of knowing.

This brings me back to my statement that different combinations of elements make for different modes of knowing. I have not, however, bothered to discuss these combinations in detail. Although I have indicated which of the elements are frequently combined with one another and which of them resist combination in the same mode of knowing, my conception is not sufficiently thought out to justify a more elaborate discussion of details. What I have said is more than enough to show the complexity of the modes of knowing and quite enough for us to proceed with an exposition of what I believe to be involved in the state or process of knowing.

DEGREES OF KNOWING

In the preceding section I have probably several times crossed the border between analysis of modes of knowing and a discussion of degrees of knowing—provided such a border exists. If so, is it a clear and undisputed frontier? I submit, and propose to show, that differences in degrees of knowing of any type (what, that, how, etc.) are not correlated with the modes of knowing; hence, modes and degrees are different things, and there is a border between inquiries into each. This does not imply that the border is clear, firm, and undisputed, but for our purposes it does not matter. I have a few observations to make about the degrees of knowing.

The reader who remembers and recollects that this book is chiefly concerned with the creation and dissemination of knowledge and its economic significance may wonder whether an examination of the degrees of knowing is really necessary for our purposes. Necessary?

surely not. Illuminating? probably. Indeed, few questions are more important in the economics of knowledge than those concerning the incremental benefits and incremental costs of achieving higher degrees of knowing. Having said this, I shall promptly try to forget it. In scholarly work one should not always be confined by pragmatic considerations.

Elements, Modes, and Degrees

There is no way of avoiding an overlap in examining elements, modes, and degrees of knowing. This has become manifest in the previous discussions of understanding, explaining, and demonstrating. I spoke of levels of understanding, but I would be hard put to "explain" the difference between levels and degrees—though I feel strongly that there may be discernible degrees of knowing on each of the different levels.

To speak of degrees is to suggest quantification, at least relative ordering where cardinal measuring is not feasible. The developers of tests of cognitive achievements have come forth with scores expressed in numbers with three digits. This apparent exactness does not imply a measurement of well-defined quantities of knowledge demonstrated in the test; it may still constitute relative ordering even if it is based on counting the numbers of correct and incorrect answers to questions assigned equal weights by the testers. (A chapter in Volume III will be devoted to educational testing.) Tests of this type can never establish the degree of knowing particular *thats*, *whats*, and *hows*; at best they establish the degree to which the knower has *demonstrated* this knowledge. To say this is not to downgrade the validity of test scores for various purposes. (For many purposes one may not be interested in the degree of the tacit knowledge possessed by the knowers but only in the degree to which they can express it or demonstrate it through some other type of performance.)

One of the difficulties of establishing and defining degrees of knowing in any internally consistent fashion is that different elements combined in any one of the modes of knowing may be "gradable" independently from one another, and there is no unique way to combine (aggregate, average) the separate grades or degrees. Assume that a particular mode of knowing includes being familiar with, remembering and recollecting, recognizing, understanding, and being able to talk about. An example of this mode would be the knowing of a novel, say, *Buddenbrooks*. With how many details of its plot am I familiar? How accurately do I remember them and how easily (readily) can I recollect them? If I am shown selected paragraphs of this and other novels, how well can I recognize and correctly identify the ones selected from *Buddenbrooks*? How well do I understand the plot, the characters and their actions, the relations with German culture in general and with business ethics and commercial practices of the period? How well, in talking about the book, can I hit its highlights and convey to others some of the essential things that are worth singling out? Assume we could assign a numerical rating to each of these elements of knowing, how can we arrive at a degree of my knowing the book? I might get a poor rating in recollecting, a high rating in recognizing, and a mixed rating in the various aspects of understanding, but these ratings could be aggregated or averaged only in arbitrary fashion.

In the next chapter, in my discussion of artistic knowledge, I distinguish degrees of knowing a tune, a musical theme. Six degrees are arranged in a plausible way, giving the appearance of an ascending order of the degree of knowing, each degree clearly higher than the preceding and lower than the subsequent. Yet, the selection of the elements of knowing is purely arbitrary, and it can be shown that a different combination of elements may well lead to a different ranking. For example, I may recognize a melody just in the sense that it sounds familiar and I conclude I must have heard it before. I may, and this is clearly a higher degree of knowing, recollect when and where I have heard it. I may recollect, and this is even better, of what composition it is a part. But now come three elements of knowing which are not comparable on any rating schedule: I may know, recollect, and state details about the entire composition, its form, structure, key, etc., and also about its relationship to other compositions by the same and other composers. Alternatively, I may be able to hum the melody, either approximately or perfectly accurately. Or I may be able to reproduce it on the piano, with or without the accompanying voices of the score. Which of these three achievements should get highest rating? I must conclude that degrees of knowing cannot be determined, except in arbitrary ways, when various elements of knowing can be judged separately.

In many competitions, especially where artistic skills are being compared, performance is judged on the basis of averaging of the subjective ratings by selected referees, and of aggregation of the average ratings on different parts of the test, or of altogether different tests. I have often wondered about the judging of national and international competitions in figure skating and ice dancing; and I have concluded that the final ranking of the competitors cannot help being highly subjective. I am afraid that the determination of degrees of knowing, even of entirely cognitive matters, involves large doses of subjective value judgments.

More Details, More Accuracy, More Confidence

Since the previous examples in this section were of artistic knowledge and of cognitive knowledge of the arts, I want to conclude the discussion of degrees of knowing with examples concerning cognitive knowing of things from the world of public, objectively observable facts. In order to eliminate one of the largest obstacles on the way towards determining degrees of knowing, I propose to exclude instances involving various levels and degrees of understanding. The list of 33 items does not offer a good example of purely factual knowledge, free from ingredients of personal experience, from the exercise of skills, and from the requirement of understanding on various levels. Good examples may be taken from the areas of military and political intelligence, business management information, and other factual reports serving governmental, commercial, or financial decision-makers. For knowledge of this sort, can one determine degrees of knowing without running into problems of arbitrary weighting of different elements of knowing?

At least three attributes may be significant in appraising the degree of knowing matters of this sort: knowledge of details, accuracy, and confidence in the reliability of the knowledge. No report can be perfect on all these scores. Assume a certain appropriation of funds is available for the improvement of the present state of knowing. One may choose to allocate these funds to obtaining knowledge (1) in greater detail, (2) of greater accuracy, or (3) of greater reliability. In concrete instances and under specified conditions, a decision-maker may be able to optimize his search by going after what would help him most; but, in general, it is not possible to say whether the degree of knowing would be increased more decisively by more details, more accuracy, or more confidence in the reliability of one's knowledge.

The third attribute, confidence in the reliability of one's knowing, has objective as well as subjective aspects. The objective aspects relate to the experts' consensus about the adequacy of evidence; the subjective aspects relate to the knower's and decision-maker's own confidence in whatever evidence may support the specific knowledge claims in question. Many economists and some other social scientists prefer to speak of "uncertainty of information" when they discuss what I call confidence in its reliability. I distinguish estimates of the *probabilities* of specified occurrences (and of the prob-

abilities of confirmation of propositions regarding these occurrences) from my *confidence* in the reliability of these estimates. That
all knowledge is uncertain and, at best, probable is one thing; that I
am uncertain about whether the probability estimates available to
me are sufficiently reliable is another thing. This second type of uncertainty is more clearly expressed by the word confidence, which
also has the advantage that it reminds us of its subjective aspects.

This is not the only insertion of subjectivity into the notion of
degrees of knowing. The assignment of weights to the three attributes—knowledge of details, and accuracy, besides confidence—is
also a subjective matter. We shall have to live with this realization,
whether we like it or not. I am not disturbed by it.

INFORMATION AND KNOWLEDGE

In Chapter 1, I touched on the meaning of "information" and decided to prefer the word "knowledge" whenever possible in lieu of
the word "information." It may not be out of place, however, to add
here a few words concerning the relation between the two terms as
they are used in everyday speech and in professional parlance.

To Know and to Inform

Linguistically, the difference between "knowledge" and "information" lies chiefly in the verb form: to *inform* is an activity by which
knowledge is conveyed; to *know* may be the result of having been
informed. "Information" as the act of informing is designed to produce a state of knowing in someone's mind. "Information" as that
which is being communicated becomes identical with "knowledge"
in the sense of that which is known. Thus, strictly speaking, the difference lies not in the nouns when they refer to *what* one knows or is
informed about; it lies in the nouns only when they are to refer to the
act of informing and the *state* of knowing, respectively.

The semantic relationships expressed so bluntly merit a reformu-
lation with greater care and some qualifications. We must first distinguish between mental acts and states, on the one hand, and the
contents to which these acts or states apply, on the other. With regard to the former—the acts and states—there is a clear and significant difference between information and knowledge. Information is
the *activity* or *process* of informing and getting informed; knowledge is the *state* of knowing. The act or process of informing may
create (produce) a state of knowing. This connection, however, is not
true by definition. A process of information is neither necessary nor

sufficient to produce a state of knowing. It is not necessary, since it is possible for a state of knowing to emerge from creative thinking, observing, experimenting, intuiting, speculating, theorizing, inventing, discovering, etc. Nor is it sufficient, since it is possible for information to be abortive in several respects; for example, it may not penetrate the recipient's mind or consciousness, it may not be understood, it may not be retained for even the shortest time span, etc.

Now we turn to the contents. By getting *informed* about something, the recipient may reach a *state of knowing the contents* of the information. The contents of the information received may be the same as the contents of what is known as a result, but not necessarily so, because the merging of the new inflow with the preexisting stock of knowledge may result in a reordering, restructuring, or revised understanding of the latter. It may not be possible to compare the "changed" and the "added" knowledge, because it is not the addition that counts: that which I know after the reception of the new information may be different from what I had known before, not in quantity but in kind or structure. As a matter of fact, the contents of the new information may have negated, disconfirmed, refuted some of what I had known before; thus the stock of knowledge in my mind may not be *larger* than it was; it may not even be *better* than the previous one, since the new information may eventually prove to have been false, inaccurate, misleading, deceptive; the new knowledge may simply be *different* from the old, and the difference need not be the same as the contents of the new information received.

Apart from such instances, where the contents of the received information changes the contents of the knowledge previously in the recipient's mind, there will be many instances where the contents of the information and the contents of the knowledge transmitted and received by the process of information *are* the same. In these instances, information and transmitted knowledge are the same *as far as their contents are concerned*. Yet, some people prefer to use these two nouns in a discriminating fashion even when they refer to contents: they call some pieces of knowledge "knowledge," others "information." Is there any tradition or any philosophically sound reason for such a linguistic discrimination?

Enduring Knowledge and Timely Information

There are indeed different usages. In denying that there is a difference between knowledge and information when both refer to what one knows or is informed about, I may have offended against common usage in some respects. If our stock of knowledge includes the multiplication table, one may object to calling it "information." If we know the law of supply and demand and also know that certain prices have just gone down, it may be preferable to speak of the actual price change as a piece of information, and of the usual consequences of a price change as a piece of knowledge. One may object to referring to the law of supply and demand as a piece of information, but there should be no serious difficulty in referring to the report of the price change as having become part of our knowledge.

In compound nouns such as "information science," "information system," or "information services" the first member of the pair, modifying the second, refers to information as a process, or sequence of actions. When the word "information" is used for the contents of the transmitted messages, such contents will regularly be secondary, never original, knowledge: a disseminator conveys what he knows to a recipient, who thereby learns what the former had known.

The fact that information, in the sense of contents conveyed, refers to secondary (not original) and concrete (not abstract, general or universal) pieces of intelligence has suggested to many a hierarchical ranking, giving knowledge a superior status and information an inferior one. We may recall the nostalgic questions asked by T. S. Eliot: "Where is the *wisdom* we have lost in *knowledge*? Where is the *knowledge* we have lost in *information*?"[21] In the inquiries on which I embark in this book I shall not indulge in prejudgments, however high-minded. And, although I have to accept linguistic usage in referring to certain subjects of communication as information, I shall not deny it the status of knowledge. All information, in the sense of the contents conveyed, is knowledge, although not all knowledge may properly be called information.

[21] T[homas] S[tearns] Eliot, *The Rock: A Pageant Play* (New York: Harcourt, Brace, 1934), p. 7. (Emphasis supplied.)

CHAPTER 3

Mundane, Scientific, Humanistic, Artistic, and Other Classes of Knowledge

ATTEMPTS to classify knowledge (in the sense of that which is known) are often more enlightening than attempts to define it. Classifications are said to make little sense unless it is stated what purposes they are to serve. Sometimes, however, the purpose may be merely to give an impression of the range and variety of things that are there to think about. An exhaustive classification may suggest a definition; a merely illustrative classification would leave the definition open but may still suggest most of what is meant by the term in question.

MUNDANE KNOWLEDGE

Just because so may writers on knowledge have such very lofty views about its meaning and want us to think immediately of science and truth and higher learning, I want to begin at the low end of the pole, the everyday knowledge of the common people.

Persuasive Definitions

I have seen a good many "persuasive definitions" of knowledge—with the defining scholar trying by his definition to restrict the designation "knowledge" to what he considers worth knowing. Now, if he wants to show his respect or contempt for one kind of knowledge or another, he has every right to do so. But what he needs for this purpose is a set of distinctions of different types of knowledge, not a definition; he need not exclude some of the things some people know (or believe they know) from the concept of "knowledge." It may well be less important to know baseball scores than symphony scores; less important to know all makes of cars than to know how an engine works; less important to know the plots of Hollywood movies than the works of Shakespeare. But these value judgments do not suggest any dividing lines between knowledge and nonknowledge;

at best they suggest distinctions and classifications of types of knowledge.

There are those who seem to identify knowledge with the things taught in schools, colleges, and universities, so that their classifications often cover not much more than academic learning. Their customary division of academic learning into natural sciences, social sciences, and humanities, plus various professional disciplines such as medicine, law, and engineering, helps to perpetuate a tradition in organizing the faculties of institutions of higher education. Since this tradition is strong—and is reflected in all sorts of governmental activities, acts of legislatures, and charters of learned societies—we shall not disregard the classes of knowledge (or rather branches of learning and research) which it distinguishes. But we shall have to bear in mind that "higher learning" and knowledge acquired by systematic research must not be granted a monopoly right to the designation "knowledge." If knowledge is what people know, it encompasses far more than what professors teach or what can be read in the encyclopaedias, old and new.

Mundane Knowledge, Intentional Learning, and Erudition

If we overcome the persuasive definitions of knowledge by which some philosophers of science have tried to appropriate the term for the purposes of their own preoccupations, and if we thus understand that knowledge may refer to millions of thought objects that have nothing to do with research, scholarship, higher learning, and professional qualification, our conception of knowledge is radically changed.

Perhaps, in the simplest possible dichotomy, one may divide the total stock of knowledge into (1) plain, everyday, mundane knowledge and (2) school learning. In a more structured division of the stock of knowledge present in the people's memories, one may perhaps distinguish (a) what people have unintentionally absorbed and distilled from their private, personal experiences; (b) what people have "picked up," without much effort, through exposure to talk and chatter of other persons in their surroundings, or through reading newspapers and magazines, listening to the radio, watching television, etc.; (c) what people have learned in school or at home, paying attention to what teachers, parents, siblings, and friends have tried to teach them in a process of consciously developing fundamental learning and basic skills; and (d) what people have learned in painstaking study from teachers in higher education, from books and journals, and in systematic research.

Most of the "private" knowledge and the "picked up" knowledge may be what I have called mundane, everyday knowledge; and much of the knowledge acquired through intentional learning, study, and research may be what I have called school learning. We should not expect, however, that the *a* and *b* categories of the second partition will be equivalent to mundane knowledge and that the *c* and *d* categories will completely overlap with school and book learning. One learns at school many more things than "academic subjects"; and it is by no means clear how to characterize the basic skills that one acquires in elementary education. Are the language skills—reading and writing—to be included in one's acquired "knowledge"? To come back to an earlier distinction, if these skills are accepted as coming under the designation of knowledge, they are surely of the know-*how* type, not of the know-*that* type. The knowledge of reading and the knowledge of writing in our own language are hardly items stored in and retrieved from our memories; acquired and retained by practice, these basic skills are more analogous to knowing how to jump, to dance, to ride a bicycle.[1]

The Proportions among Types of Knowledge

It is tempting to speculate about the inventory of knowledge in human memories. To be sure, its composition would depend on the state of the intellectual development in the society in question. The proportions between knowledge acquired in everyday experiences and knowledge acquired through intentional learning experiences surely depend on the society's (or community's) educational system. Unfortunately, such speculations about the relative quantities of different kinds of knowledge in our memories are moot: we have not (yet) discovered how to take inventory of the cognitive contents of our brains. I shall later in this volume suggest that certain estimates, which are impossible regarding stocks of knowledge, are not entirely out of the question regarding flows of knowledge received. But let us not jump ahead in our argument; let us, instead, proceed methodically with our discussion of the classes of knowledge which have been distinguished in the literature. These distinctions, as I

[1] I have just come across a very similar formulation by the philosopher Walter Kaufmann in his *What is Man* (New York: Reader's Digest Press—McGraw-Hill, 1978) p. 56: "We think of 'know-how' as a skill or aptitude that is acquired by *doing* something, and not by the kind of study associated with the humanities. This is true enough of swimming or riding a bicycle. But the knowledge of how to compose a quartet or a symphony is acquired by studying music written by one's predecessors; and the way to learn to write poems, plays, novels, or philosophy, or to paint or sculpt is to study the works of past masters."

have said, have largely disregarded mundane knowledge and confined themselves to the "higher" levels of learning. Top-level standing is usually accorded to so-called scientific knowledge.

Scientific Knowledge

I regard it as unhelpful to single out a class of knowledge under the
heading "scientific knowledge" or "science." This nonconformist
view may strike most readers as exotic, to put it mildly, and I must
beg them to have the patience to consider the reasons for my position.

The reasons are basically semantic and linguistic, but in effect
pragmatic. The point is that the meaning of the word "science" has
changed over time and is different today in different disciplines, in
different countries, and in different languages. Some of the changes
seem bewildering, and some of the differences are utterly confusing.
If "science" means one thing to a physicist, another thing to a philosopher of science, a third thing to an historian, a fourth to an
economist, a fifth to a Frenchman, a German, or a Russian, the word is
an obstacle to successful communication, an instance of semantic
noise. In addition, the artificial methodological restrictions that have
been built into some of the concepts of science have given rise, and
continue to give rise, to pseudo problems and pseudo conflicts wasting the valuable time of writers, teachers, and students, time that
could fruitfully be spent on substantive research and less obscuran-
tist teaching. It is a fair conclusion that a brief survey of historical
semantics and of linguistic and geographic inconsistencies of "science" should be well worth while.

Science Excluding Empirical Knowledge

Let us begin with the semantic changes over the centuries. From the
philosophers of antiquity to those of the eighteenth century, science
stood for knowledge of things that "cannot be otherwise," because
they relate to "the necessary and the eternal." For Aristotle, science
was concerned with absolute certainties, logically demonstrable
truths. Aristotle's position was thus described by William David
Ross:

> In his logic Aristotle lays it down that science should start
> with axioms, definitions, and hypotheses of the existence of
> the fundamental objects of the science. There is, I suppose,
> no science but mathematics in which this will take us very
> far. It was certainly not by this method that he reached the

success he did in biology. But probably he did not think of biology as a science. By a science he meant just a body of research in which this method *does* work, i.e., a mathematical science, and he never, I think, applies the name science quite deliberately to anything else. Biology, psychology, ethics, politics, were rather inquiries than sciences.[2]

Even for Francis Bacon, the champion of empiricism, science was—at least at one point—"the image of the essentials" (*essentiae imago*). Descartes held that "any knowledge that can be questioned ought not to be called science"; and Christian Wolff, German philosopher in the eighteenth century, defined science as absolutely certain knowledge, logically deduced from unchanging principles.[3] Ephraim Chambers' *Cyclopaedia* confirms that "Science, in philosophy, [is] a clear and certain knowledge of any thing, founded on self-evident principles, or demonstration."[4]

The English logician William Duncan proposed a set of distinctions according to the type of mental operations employed in discovering and ordering knowledge, especially regarding the kind of judgment and the method of reasoning: for "*scientific* knowledge," judgment rests on "intuition," and the manner of reasoning is syllogistic "demonstration"; for "*natural* knowledge," judgment rests on "experience," and reasoning is by "induction and analogy"; and for "*historical* knowledge," judgment rests on "testimony," and reasoning is by "criticism and probable conjecture."[5] This restrictive use of "science" to mean only "perfect knowledge which permits no doubt" was in evidence as late as the first half of the nineteenth century. For example, Sir John Herschel, the eminent British astronomer, defined scientific knowledge as abstract knowledge or knowledge "demonstrable" with mathematical certainty.[6]

[2] William David Ross, ed., *Aristotle Selections* (New York: Charles Scribner's Sons, 1927), p. xiii.

[3] These quotations and paraphrases of Bacon, Descartes, and Wolff are from the article "Science" in André Lalande, *Vocabulaire technique et critique de la philosophie*, 5th ed. (Paris: Presses Universitaires de France, 1947), pp. 933-937.

[4] Ephraim Chambers, *Cyclopaedia or Universal Dictionary of Arts and Sciences*, 2d ed. (London, 1738). However, a broader definition also is offered in the same article: "Science, is more particularly used for a formed system of any branch of knowledge; comprehending the doctrine, reason and theory of a thing, *without any immediate application thereof to any uses or offices of life.*" (Emphasis supplied.)

[5] William Duncan, *Elements of Logick*, 4th ed. (London: R. and J. Dodley, 1759), pp. 145-155. (I am indebted to Professor Wilbur Samuel Howell for this reference.) For Duncan, mathematics was the paradigm of purely scientific knowledge.

[6] Sir John Herschel, *Preliminary Discourse to Natural Philosophy* (London: Longman, Rees, Orme, Brown and Green, 1831), quoted from Joseph Agassi, "Imper-

From the point of view of present-day semantics, the refusal to recognize empirical knowledge of nature as "scientific" seems quite stubborn and unreasonable. Yet, it was nothing but a terminological convention:[7] "science" was a system of definitions, axioms, and syllogistic deductions, whereas systems of knowledge based on observation of and generalizations about natural phenomena were regarded as "natural philosophy." Astronomers and physicists did not feel degraded by being called natural philosophers rather than scientists; nor did historians, political economists and other students of human society take offense at being called moral philosophers. This was the way language had developed in the universe of academic discourse over almost 2,500 years.

Admitting Empirical Sciences

Language did change, however. Francis Bacon, Denis Diderot, and Immanuel Kant had much to do with the expansion of the concept of science. Kant's concept still included "science proper," which dealt with propositions of apodictic certainty,[8] that is, with purely analytic propositions; but his definition was more general and comprised any well-ordered body of knowledge systematized according to specified principles.[9] On this definition, the three classes of

fect Knowledge," *Philosophy and Phenomenological Research*, vol. 32 (June 1972), p. 467.

[7] ". . . what is to be called a 'science' and who is to be called a 'scientist' must always remain a matter of convention. . . ." Karl R. Popper, *The Logic of Scientific Discovery* (London: Hutchinson, 1959), p. 52.—The question, however, is how general the agreement among different "scientists" and "philosophers" has to be before one may reasonably regard it as a convention.

[8] The notion of apodictic certainty received a severe shock with the announcement, in 1931, of Gödel's "undecidability theorem." Kurt Gödel, Viennese mathematical logician, proved that all axiomatic systems, except very simple ones, must contain assertions that can be neither demonstrated nor refuted by logical deduction from the given axioms. There are whole classes of mathematical claims that will remain undemonstrable.

[9] Immanuel Kant, *Critick of Pure Reason* (London: William Pickering, 1848), pp. 574-587. This is the section on "The Architectonics of Pure Reason" of the "Transcendental Methodology." German 2d ed. (Riga: Hartknoch, 1787), pp. 860-879.—In conformance with this wide concept of science, Kant defined metaphysics as "the science of the first principles of human cognition" (1848, p. 581). With this definition Kant did not depart from earlier views; for example, d'Alembert, the French encyclopaedist, said about the position taken by John Locke in his *Essay Concerning Human Understanding* that Locke "reduced metaphysics to what as a matter of fact it must be, the experimental science of the soul. . . ." Jean LeRond d'Alembert, "Discours préliminaire des éditeurs," in *Encyclopédie, ou Dictionnaire Raisonné des Sciences, des Arts, et des Métiers* (Paris: Briasson, David, Le Breton, and Durand, 1751), vol. 1, p. xxvii.—The mental experiments alluded to in d'Alembert's statement do not, of course, make metaphysics an *empirical* science.

higher learning which earlier logicians and philosophers had distinguished—mathematics and formal logic, natural philosophy, and
moral philosophy—became three divisions of *science* or, alternatively, different sciences.

Expelling All but the Natural Sciences

After this expansion of "scientific" knowledge to include empirical
as well as analytic systems, a new exclusion from the concept of science was proposed in mid-nineteenth century England. The meaning of science and scientific knowledge was narrowed to what previously had been natural philosophy, whereas the previous domain
of science (knowledge *a priori*) and the previous domain of moral
philosophy were to be refused the designation of "scientific" knowledge. In other words, a new definition of science was to restrict it to
the study of natural phenomena.

Historians of science do not agree on precisely when and how this
change in the meaning of the word came about.[10] The semantic
change was not accepted anywhere but in English-speaking countries, and even there, not without protest. Understandably, social
scientists and historians were protesting more vigorously, but even
some natural scientists resisted.[11] They saw no reason for a concept
of science that excluded studies of man and human society.

[10] The *Oxford English Dictionary* gives 1867 as the earliest use of the term in this
restrictive meaning; *Murray's New English Dictionary* gives 1864. John Theodore
Merz, *History of European Thought in the Nineteenth Century* (London: W.
Blackwood, 1896), vol. 1, p. 89, assumes that the use of "science" for "natural science" goes back to the establishment of the British Association for the Advancement
of Science in 1831. My own research leads me to believe that the French reorganization of the Institut de France in 1803 set a precedent by having an Académie des Sciences (without specifying "Naturelles") and a separate Académie des Sciences
Morales et Politiques. As far as the United States is concerned, it is not easy to pin-
point any dates for the transition to the restrictive meaning of science. One source has
this to say: "In the United States shortly after the middle of the nineteenth century,
the meaning of the word 'science' began significantly to change. Before, any well-
organized body of knowledge or speculation had been called a science. Science con-
noted orderliness and system, in ethics no less than in geology." Lawrence R. Veysey,
The Emergence of the American University (Chicago: University of Chicago Press,
1965), p. 133.—When the National Academy of Science (singular) was set up in 1863,
it had a section for Ethnology; and a later plan for reorganization, in 1892, proposed a
section for "Anthropology, including Sociology, Economic Science, etc." This seems
to indicate that the semantic restriction of science to refer only to natural and mathematical sciences came in the United States much later than in England.

[11] "Science is not wrapped up with any particular body of facts; it is characterized
as an intellectual attitude. It is not tied down to any peculiar methods of inquiry; it is
simply sincere critical thought, which admits conclusions only when these are based
on evidence." John Arthur Thomson, *Introduction to Science* (New York: Holt, 1911),
p. 57.—"There is a slang usage, like that for which 'hall' means a music hall or 'pic-

Philosophers had little or no use for the restrictive definition. Continental European philosophers hardly took notice of it. Some even stuck to the classical primacy of formal over empirical sciences.[12] But, in general, they continued to distinguish between formal and empirical sciences and to include among the latter the social and the cultural sciences along with the natural sciences.[13] Some philosophers proposed other kinds of exclusion—for example, of all propositions not deducible from fundamental hypotheses.[14] Most customary have been the exclusions of normative, evaluative, or other nonfalsifiable propositions or systems of knowledge. This issue has

---

tures' moving pictures, according to which 'science' means natural science. Whether history is a science in that sense of the word, however, need not be asked; for in the tradition of European speech, going back to the time when Latin speakers translated the Greek *episteme* by their own word *scientia*, and continuing unbroken down to the present day, 'science' means any organized body of knowledge." Robin G. Collingwood, *The Idea of History* (Oxford: Clarendon Press, 1946), p. 249.—"... the 'natural' has been dropped, and only the 'science' retained, partly by mere abbreviation (just as 'omnibus' has been changed into 'bus'), and partly because students of science were by no means averse from hearing their study called 'science' without any qualification; ... the implication ... flattered their vanity." Norman R. Campbell, *What is Science?*, reprinted (New York: Dover Publications, 1952 [1st ed., London: Methuen, 1921]), p. 9.

[12] Benedetto Croce is an example of a protagonist of this view: "But we cannot rest satisfied with asserting the right of Logic to be recognized as a science; we must make the further demand that Philosophy alone—and not the empirical sciences—be admitted as science in the strict sense of the word." Benedetto Croce, "The Task of Logic," in *Encyclopaedia of the Philosophical Sciences*, vol. 1, *Logic* (London: Macmillan, 1913), p. 201.

[13] Carnap took science to comprise "all theoretical knowledge, no matter whether in the field of natural sciences or in the field of the social sciences and the so-called humanities, and no matter whether it is knowledge found by the application of special scientific procedures, or knowledge based on common sense in everyday life." Rudolf Carnap, "Logical Foundations of the Unity of Science," in Otto Neurath, Rudolf Carnap, and Charles Morris, eds., *Foundations of the Unity of Science: Toward an International Encyclopedia of Unified Science*, bound ed. (Chicago: University of Chicago Press, 1969 [1st ed., 1939]), vol. 1, p. 45.—"We cannot refuse the name *science* to logic or to the non-quantitative branches of mathematics such as analysis situs, projective geometry, etc. Nor is there good reason for refusing the adjective *scientific* to such works as Aristotle's *Politics* or Spinoza's *Ethics* and applying it to statistical 'investigations' or 'researches' that do not advance the understanding of anything." Morris R. Cohen, *Reason and Nature: An Essay on the Meaning of Scientific Method* (New York: Harcourt, Brace, 1931), p. 89.

[14] "We reserve the term 'science' for knowledge which is general and systematic, that is, in which specific propositions are all deduced from a few general principles." Morris R. Cohen and Ernest Nagel, *An Introduction to Logic and Scientific Method* (New York: Harcourt, Brace, 1934), p. 191. This definition excludes history and thus does not accommodate the historical sciences, which in all other languages are unquestioned members of the universe of scientific knowledge.

remained controversial; expressions like "normative science" are frequently encountered. The meaning of "scientific method" is also in dispute,[15] and, incidentally, not translatable into foreign languages.

Science in Other Languages

The restrictive meanings of "science," limiting the term to empirical, positive (nonnormative), operational, falsifiable propositions, or even to systematic study of natural (nonsocietal, noncultural) phenomena, are confined to Anglo-American parlance. In French, German, Italian, Russian, Japanese, and most other languages, the words for "science" stand for *systems of knowledge acquired by sustained study*.[16] If one wishes to refer to natural sciences, the word "science" will not do; one has to use a qualifying adjective or compound noun. There is no difference in these languages between scientists and scholars; the French *savant* and the German *Gelehrte* or *Wissenschaftler* may be a natural scientist, social scientist, historian, archaeologist, philosopher, literary critic, or writer on jurisprudence or on any learned discipline.[17] This is reflected in the organization of

[15] "... the attempt to define scientific method or to analyze science is a search for a *persuasive* definition. I hold this to be true because I believe that the term 'science' has no definite and unambiguous application." Max Black, "The Definition of Scientific Method," in Robert C. Stauffer, ed., *Science and Civilization* (Madison: University of Wisconsin Press, 1949), p. 69.—Black supports this statement as follows: "Neither observation, nor generalization, nor the hypothetic-deductive use of assumptions, nor measurement, nor the use of instruments, nor mathematical construction—nor all of them together—can be regarded as essential to science. For branches of science can easily be found where any of these criteria is either absent or has so little influence as to be negligible. ... I propose that we treat 'scientific method' as a historical expression meaning, among other things, 'those procedures which, as a matter of historical fact, have proved most fruitful in the acquisition of systematic and comprehensive knowledge' " (pp. 80-81).

[16] Economists may be interested in Schumpeter's definitions of science. He supplied several, which he regards as largely equivalent: (1) "A science is any kind of knowledge that has been the object of conscious efforts to improve it." (2) "A science is any field of knowledge that has developed specialized techniques of fact-finding and of interpretation or inference (analysis)." (3) "A science is any field of knowledge in which there are people, so-called research workers or scientists or scholars, who engage in the task of improving upon the existing stock of facts and methods and who, in the process of doing so, acquire a command of both that differentiates them from the 'layman' and eventually also from the mere 'practitioner'." Joseph A. Schumpeter, *History of Economic Analysis* (New York: Oxford University Press, 1959), p. 7.

[17] In French, *science* is defined as "knowledge in depth" [*connaissance approfondie*] and as "the totality of well-organized knowledge pertaining to certain categories of facts and phenomena, . . . such as the moral sciences, the historical sciences, the physical sciences, the mathematical sciences," etc. Also as the "*ensemble of objective*

the academies of sciences in many countries: they are divided into classes, categories, and sections, but even the names of these divisions reflect the comprehensive meaning of the word "science." For example, the oldest of the existing academies, the Italian Accademia Nazionale dei Lincei has a class of "Moral, Historical, and Philosophical Sciences" divided into seven categories, including "philosophical sciences," "juridical sciences," and "social and political sciences."

A Definition Reflecting a Polyglot Consensus

Taking account of the characteristics of science specified in the most authoritative dictionaries, encyclopaedias, and philosophic treatises

---

(exact or approximate) knowledge [connaissances objectives (justes ou approchées)] of nature, society, man and his thoughts." Grand Larousse encyclopédique (Paris: Larousse, 1964), vol. 9, p. 680.

In German, Wissenschaft is defined as "the totality of knowledge [Erkenntnisse] in all fields (natural sciences, legal sciences, historical sciences, philological sciences and many others) or . . . also their systematic extension (research), exposition and explanation." Der grosse Brockhaus, 16th ed. (Wiesbaden: Brockhaus, 1957), vol. 12, p. 556.

In Italian, scienza "in a broad sense" is defined as "knowledge, in a special conception of knowing," analyzed and systematically treated "in various disciplines (philosophy, gnoseology, logic, etc.). In a narrower and more modern sense, however, science is distinguished from philosophy . . . , although the differentiation is extremely complex and controversial." One may "distinguish three kinds of knowledge: popular [volgare] or not unified; scientific or partially unified; and philosophical or totally unified." Enciclopedia Italiana (Rome: Istituto delle Enciclopedia Italiana, 1936), vol. 31, p. 154.

In Russian, naúka is defined as "the sphere of human activity the function of which is the elaboration and theoretical systematization of objective knowledge of reality; one of the forms of social consciousness. . . ." Bolshaiâ Sovetskaiâ Entsiklopedeiâ [Great Soviet Encyclopaedia], vol. 17, p. 323.—The Russian-English Dictionary (edited by Smirnitsky) gives "science, study, knowledge" as the English equivalents of naúka, but the comprehensive meaning of the word is clear from composite terms such as lyudi naúki [men of science, scholars], tochniye naúki [exact sciences] and gumanitarniye naúki [humanities, though the literal translation would be "humanistic sciences"].

In Japanese, the basic character of all words relating to science is gaku, which stands for "learning," "study," though gakumon is more often used when "studies" are referred to, and ka gaku as the equivalent of "science." The entire family of terms refers to schooling; for example, gakko means school; gakusei, student; gakusha, learned man, scholar. A Japanese vocabulary for some of the disciplines may be of interest: shizen ka gaku, natural science; shakai ka gaku, social science; keizai gaku, economic science; jin bun ka gaku, cultural science; bun gaku, literature; butsuri gaku, physical science. It is clear that gaku and ka gaku are meant to refer to all branches of learning, that is, to all "sciences" in the most comprehensive sense—as in all languages except present-day English and American English. Kenkyusha, Japanese-English Dictionary (Tokyo: Kenkyusha, 1976); Sanseido, English-Japanese Dictionary (Tokyo: Sanseido, 1975).

in languages other than English, I have formulated a definition of science that reflects the broadest international consensus: science is a body of coherent, systematic knowledge of any subject, formal or empirical, natural or cultural, arrived at by any method whatever, provided it (1) is based on hard, honest and serious study and research and reaches insights not available to laymen or superficial observers and (2) is designed for either intellectual or general-pragmatic purposes, but not for immediate practical application in a concrete case or situation.

This cosmopolitan definition of science stresses the status of the *scientist's* systematic knowledge by contrasting it with the naive or unsystematic knowledge of the *layman* and the applied knowledge of the *practitioner*. It is presented here to inform or remind the English-American teacher-scientist-scholar of the disparity between the meaning of "science" to which he has become accustomed and the international meaning of the word or its foreign "equivalents." No one, to be sure, can reasonably expect English or American educators and writers to become cosmopolitan and renounce their accustomed word usage. But it would be desirable if they at least appreciated that the restrictive sense in which they use "science" and "scientific" is not translatable into foreign languages except by awkward circumlocution.[18]

What conclusions should I draw for myself from these linguistic differences over time and among nations? The most sensible conclusion would be that the phrase "scientific knowledge" should be ruled out from this study, because its meaning would not be clear (it would, as we have seen, convey different ideas to members of different disciplines) and because it would not be translatable into foreign languages. In some contexts, however, the phrase will be unavoidable. For example, when we classify subjects taught in academic in-

[18] A few examples may illustrate the awkward situation. A Swedish writer on the theory of science, in an article published in English, cautiously supplies a footnote at the beginning of his paper, warning his readers that "Science is here taken in the broad sense of 'Wissenschaft,' 'scienza,' 'naúka,' etc." Gerard Radnitzky, "Ways of Looking at Science," *Scientia* (*Rivista di Scienza*, Milan), vol. 104 (1969), p. 49. Other authors are less specific and simply speak of "science in the broad sense of the word" or "science in the wide sense." One way to get around the difficulty is to avoid using the word as a singular without article—"science"—and use it instead with the indefinite article, "a science" or "a particular science," or in the plural, "the sciences." Still, how should one translate the title of a paper delivered in 1975 at the Colloquium on Semiotics in Berlin on "Semiotik in der Kunstwissenschaft" (semiotics in the science of the fine arts)? Max Weber's famous essay "Wissenschaft als Beruf" has been rendered as "Science as a Vocation," which misleads readers unaccustomed to the wide meaning of science. For them the title should have referred to "Research and Higher Learning" or to "Science and Scholarship."

stitutions or research projects supported by federal agencies (such as the National Science Foundation or the National Endowment for the Humanities), we may not always be able to avoid references to "scientific" subjects as contrasted with "humanistic" ones.

HUMANISTIC KNOWLEDGE

In conformance with the cosmopolitan definition of science, I should not talk of humanistic knowledge but, instead, of the cultural sciences.[19] I could try to define the cultural sciences, or (waiving the linguistic reservation) the humanities, as the systems of integrated knowledge that concern themselves with human culture, studying artifacts and historical materials and using them as foundation and framework for the presentation of the languages, literatures, philosophies, religions, values, arts, and customs of the civilizations which have contributed to the shaping of the contemporary outlook in life. By direct contact with the creations of philosophers, poets, and artists, those professing humanistic disciplines make an effort to stimulate the senses, emotions, and imaginations of the student while developing his critical judgment and refining his taste.[20] That I use cultural sciences and humanistic studies as synonyms will be, I hope, pardoned by most humanists, especially if I add that my emphasis on *human* culture does not imply a denial of the existence of animal cultures. It may be pretentious, however, to begin by suggesting new terms and definitions; it is more appropriate to examine traditional ones.

[19] The English term "humanities," standing, according to the *Oxford English Dictionary*, for "learning or literature concerned with human culture, as grammar, rhetoric, poetry, and especially the ancient Latin and Greek classics," has no single-word equivalent in other languages. In French, *les humanités* are strictly delimited as study of Latin and Greek in secondary schools; the term is derived from the Latin *humaniora*, a word used also by German educators for study of the classical languages in the *humanistischen Gymnasium*, one of three or four types of secondary school. *Les humanités* are not even mentioned in André Lalande's *Vocabulaire technique et critique de la philosophie*. In German, the nearest equivalent to the English-American humanities is *Geisteswissenschaften* (intellectual sciences), a term coined as a translation of moral sciences, but sometimes replaced by *Kulturwissenschaften*, with literature and history as chief constituents. In Russian, *Gumanitarniye naúki* (humanistic sciences) comes closest to the English, but requires the noun "sciences."

[20] In formulating this statement I have greatly profited from the descriptions in *Announcement of the University of Chicago. The College Number for the Sessions 1932-33*, May 25, 1932, p. 21.

Traditional Meanings

Most of us who have become used to seeing the humanities as a cluster of academic disciplines often united as one of three (or sometimes four) major divisions of American colleges and universities will be surprised to learn that this use of the term is of rather recent origin. The eleventh edition of the *Encyclopaedia Britannica*, published in 1910-11, had no separate entry "humanities," but only one on "humanism." This was defined as "any system of thought or action which assigns a predominant interest to the affairs of men as compared [i.e., contrasted] with the supernatural or the abstract." Thus, humanism was interpreted as a break with "the medieval traditions of scholastic theology and philosophy," as a dedication to "the rediscovery and direct study of the ancient classics," and "essentially a revolt against . . . ecclesiastical authority." The article mentioned also that Oxford University had a curriculum "*Litterae Humaniores*," consisting of "Latin and Greek literature and philosophy"; that at Scottish universities the professor of Latin held the title Professor of Humanity; and finally, that "the plural 'humanities' is a generic term for the classics."[21]

The 1960 edition of the *Britannica* at last offered an entry on the humanities as a term applied "in the 20th century . . . in universities and colleges to a group of disciplines distinguished in content and method from the physical and biological sciences and, if less decisively, from the social sciences. . . . "[22] The qualification "in the 20th century" is quite accurate, for this meaning of the humanities did not yet exist in the nineteenth century, at least not in the organization charts of academic institutions.

Here are a few examples: The University of California (Berkeley) in 1868 was organized into two major divisions, the College of Arts and the College of Letters. The College of Arts was split in 1893 into a College of Social Sciences and a College of Natural Sciences. In 1915 these two were recombined with the College of Letters into a single College of Letters and Science. There was no reference to

[21] *Encyclopaedia Britannica*, 11th ed., vol. 13, p. 872. Two major suits of the "humanists" from the sixteenth to the nineteenth century were to replace the crude Latin texts chosen and prescribed by the Christian divines with the elegant classical writings of pagan authors (such as Terence, Virgil, Horace, Cicero, Caesar, and Sallust) and to add the study of Greek grammar and literature (Aristotle in the original rather than in Latin translation, and also Hippocrates, and the Greek version of the New Testament). See Martin L. Clarke, *Classical Education in Britain: 1500-1900* (Cambridge: at the University Press, 1959), pp. 3-22.

[22] *Encyclopaedia Britannica*, 1960 ed., vol. 11, p. 876.

"humanities." At present, the Berkeley catalogue mentions the humanities only in connection with undergraduates' breadth requirements and with representation of the faculties on their legislative bodies.—The Johns Hopkins University had from its inception in 1876 a Faculty of Philosophy, which comprised all nonprofessional academic departments. College courses were divided into seven groups, of which the first was "Classical" and the seventh "Modern Languages." Later, there were schools, colleges, and divisions, but none bore the name "humanities." It was only in the 1950s that a program in the humanities was proposed.—In the first third of this century, Yale University had a division of Language, Literature, and the Arts. The first reference to humanities in the Yale catalogue was in 1946-47, when they were mentioned as one of four groups for purposes of distribution requirements; in 1948-49 the humanities became one of five faculties of the University, apart from its professional schools.—The timing was very similar at Harvard. The first reference to humanities in its annual catalogues was in 1946-47, when it appeared as one of the triad of subject groups in the General Education course. As one of the "three areas" of distribution requirements, the humanities replaced "Arts, Letters, and Philosophy" in 1955-56.—Princeton University, at the beginning of the twentieth century, had departments of Philosophy and of Language and Literature, which were later called divisions. By 1921 it had a Division of Philosophy, Literature, and Art. In the catalogue of 1941 a "Divisional Program in the Humanities" was listed, and it still exists. A "Council of the Humanities" was established in 1953.— The institution that had started this taxonomic trend was, it seems, the University of Chicago, which in an academic reorganization in 1930 established, in place of what had been the Faculties of Arts and Literature, a Division of the Humanities. If my perfunctory survey is correct, 1930 is the beginning of the humanities as a recognized academic division under this nowadays generally used designation.

Not only is the term "humanities" a recent addition to the official language of academe, it seems to be used far more in the United States than in British universities. Thus, in the debate about the "wide gulf" between the *Two Cultures*, started in 1959 by Sir Charles Snow, of Cambridge University, it was not the "humanist" who was pictured as the "scientist's" foe but rather the "literary intellectual." Perhaps we can assume that a humanistic scholar in the United States would be a literary intellectual if he resided in England.

I shall return to the Two-Culture controversy after some exploration of just what branches of learning are supposed to make up the humanities. Even those few who agree that there are essential characteristics which distinguish the humanities from other disciplines have found it difficult to obtain a consensus on just which areas of inquiry should be included under the heading of humanistic studies.

The Humanists' Identity Crisis

Absence of consensus would be too mild an expression to describe the failure of academic humanists to agree on the question of the delimitation of the humanities—at least if we go back some twenty years, before the U.S. Congress took it upon itself to decide the question.

In the view of many highly respected humanists, the arts— "music, the fine arts, the decorative arts, the arts of the theatre," in the listing by Howard Mumford Jones—were not only admitted to the humanities but were regarded as paradigmatic of them. In the view of some, certain branches of philosophy—logic and analytic philosophy—were considered alien to the humanistic spirit. The sociologist George Caspar Homans held that "between the social sciences and many of the so-called humanities no intellectual line can be drawn: all are social sciences (or, if you like, all are humanities)." To those who emphasized the humanities' basic concern with human values, Homans replied with a rhetoric question: "In what sense is the study of Romance philology a study of human values rather than a study of the way men have behaved?" With regard to the place of history, the classicist Paul L. MacKendrick suggested that Gibbons' *Decline and Fall of the Roman Empire* was "a humanistic work, because it was written with a profound sense of individuation," but the *Cambridge Ancient History*, "because it was written by a team, is not: it is social science." The historian Hugh R. Trevor-Roper found the distinguishing criterion of "humane subjects" in the fact that they have "no direct scientific use; they owe their title to existence to the interest and comprehension of the laity; they exist primarily not for the training of professionals but for the education of laymen." Carl J. Friedrich, the political scientist, held that "the focus of the humanities is upon critical examination and evaluation of the *products* of man in cultural affairs . . . , whereas the focus of the social sciences is upon the *way* men live together, including their creative activities."

All these quotations are taken from a report of the American Council of Learned Societies on a symposium on "The Relationship between the Humanities and the Social Sciences" (*ACLS Newsletter*, March 1961). One of the participants of the session contributed a "frivolous story," a statement attributed to Erwin Panofsky, the great art historian: "Those who think and get somewhere are mathematicians. Those who think and don't get anywhere are philosophers. Those who don't think and get somewhere are the natural scientists. Those who don't think and don't get anywhere are the humanists." Neither this witty statement nor any of the others would have enabled me to provide appropriately labeled boxes into which to sort various branches of intellectual knowledge, let alone to attempt statistical estimates of the costs incurred by society in the production and distribution of the particular kinds of knowledge.

Legal and Institutional Definitions

In matters of science and scholarship, no vote, no ballotting process can decide questions on which the scientists and scholars differ. But where nothing more than a classification for purposes of financial support is concerned, a vote of the legislators can settle an argument. Thus, in the United States, the Act that established in 1965 the National Endowment for the Humanities should, in listing the constituent disciplines (and creating separate National Foundations for the Arts and the Humanities), enable us to make separate boxes or columns for scientific, artistic, and humanistic knowledge. (This does not assure a solution to the problem of compiling statistical data for the cost of creating and disseminating these categories of knowledge, because the primary sources may have used breakdowns different from those written into the acts of Congress.)

An earlier description of the constituency of the humanities was given by the American Council of Learned Societies. It continues to describe itself as "a federation of national organizations concerned with the humanities—the languages and literatures, philosophies and religions, history and the arts, and the associated techniques— and with the humanistic elements in the social sciences."[23] This program includes the arts among the humanities—although the lawmakers want them separated—and it includes history—although many historians see themselves as social scientists. But it also divides the social sciences into humanistic and "nonhumanistic" elements, leaving us in doubt whether the latter are "scientific" in some mysterious sense. For a continental European—or, as a matter of fact, for anyone who did not go to school in an English-speaking country—this makes no sense, since all humanistic disciplines are sciences, though of course not natural sciences. In practice, the national and private foundations in the United States have tried to

---

[23] This statement appears on the inside cover of the *ACLS Newsletter*.

draw a line by looking at the printed or typed pages: algebraic equations and statistical tables suggest something "scientific" whereas a purely narrative exposition, especially of a philosophical or historical nature, gives the impression of a "humanistic" study.[24]

The Antiscientistic Humanist

Many statements in recent years reveal an antagonism on the part of representatives of humanistic disciplines towards the natural sciences, or rather towards the "scientific" departments of the universities and certain claims of superiority frequently heard from those professing the "hard sciences." Sometimes the antagonism degenerates into downright hostility. Whereas the traditional "enemy" of the classical humanists had been the theologian—the divine, engaged in "divine" studies, to be countered by humane or humanistic studies—in recent times Enemy No. 1 has been the "scientist." In the words of a respected scholar, "humanistic studies have been faced with a much more formidable rival in the form of the scientific method."[25] And another eminent humanistic scholar complained that the word "scientific" sometimes "degenerates into a vague honorific, synonymous with the advertiser's 'reliable' or 'guaranteed.' "[26]

Many plausible explanations can be found for the widespread antiscientism among representatives of the humanities. Foremost, one may suspect, has been the resentment of being on the losing side in a battle for money, prestige, and good students; but I shall discuss also

[24] I wonder where this distinction leaves me and my work? Up to this point, I have been philosophizing to such an extent that I ought to qualify as a humanist writing a thoroughly humanistic study. This is apt to change, however, when, beginning in Volume III, I shall present scores of statistical tables, showing dollar expenditures, inviting numerical comparisons, and pointing to all sorts of quantitative relationships. The humanistic elements of my work will on many a page be pushed aside by the "nonhumanist" ones, even where my statistical efforts will be directed to the task of showing how much has been spent for the production and distribution of humanistic knowledge.

The answer, perhaps, is simply that this study, with all its interdisciplinary ambitions, is patently "social science," and the difficulties in labeling it are due only to an odd legal situation: the legislature, the U.S. Congress, has created agencies to sponsor education, research, and other activities in "science," "technology," "medicine," "education," "humanities," and "the arts," but not in the social sciences. As a result, funds for social sciences have to come out of the budgetary appropriations of the other agencies, and this forces staff and reviewing panels to look for "humanistic" and "scientific" elements in social-science projects.

[25] Lord [Alan] Bullock, "The Future of Humanistic Studies," Lecture presented at the Aspen Institute, Summer 1978. (Lord Bullock was Vice Chancellor of Oxford University from 1969 to 1973.)

[26] Jacques Barzun, Science, the Glorious Entertainment (New York: Harper and Row, 1964), p. 14.

other, intellectually more respectable reasons. The jealousy of liberal financial support for natural sciences and technology, while only small alms are being given for research in the humanities, should not be mistaken for sheer greed for money; several perquisites go with research grants: research assistants, secretaries, typists, release from teaching duties, and often extra summer salaries for research—benefits rarely available to humanistic scholars. Closely related are the gains in the prestige that come to the recipients of large outside grants. To the extent that this prestige impresses the administrative officers of the universities as well as the members of committees on appointments and promotion, it translates again into pecuniary advantages. But even as a nonpecuniary benefit, public or professional recognition of the grantees' standing in the academic world is much coveted. Competition for good students is also effective; it is a fact, if one may assume test scores to be valid, that physics and mathematics have been attracting the best students. Professors in the humanities have resented being left with the less talented or less ambitious students.

A strong reason for the humanists' resentment of the natural sciences lies in the loss of dominance over the curriculum. In the seventeenth and eighteenth centuries the classicists had virtually a monopoly of the students' time. Originally it had been a duopoly, a sharing of the curriculum with theology, but it developed into a monopoly. In Volume II, in the chapter on Universities, I shall show how in Europe, as later also in the American colonies, the curriculum had been based almost entirely on classical languages and classical literature. Change came only slowly, partly with the ascendency of the natural sciences, partly with the defection of modern from classical "liberal culture." In the United States the change was accelerated, at the end of the nineteenth century, when the elective system allowed students to devote more time to the natural sciences.[27] Professors in the classical humanities fought a defensive battle, and lost it at most institutions. The old arguments employed in the eternal battle over the curriculum are still being repeated in many academic committees and in the writings of dedicated humanists.

The antiscientism of the humanists, incidentally, is rather different from the occasional attacks on scientism made in the writings on the methodology of the social sciences. What social scientists mean

[27] "The elective system, which, following the decline of general education is once more resurgent, came increasingly to serve the interest of the professional entrepreneur rather than the student for whom it was intended. In short, educational policy . . . simply disappeared." Henry David Aiken, *Predicament of the University* (Bloomington: Indiana University Press, 1971), p. 115.

by scientism is the "slavish imitation of the method and language" of the natural sciences for research in the social sciences, and the "very prejudiced approach which, before it has considered its subject, claims to know what is the most appropriate way of investigating it."[28] The adjective "scientistic," in contradistinction to "scientific," was coined to characterize this unfortunate methodological prejudice. Such criticisms were properly raised by social scientists protesting against attempts to impose on them and their fellow researchers in the social sciences methods which may have been productive in physical research but are not appropriate to studies of man and society. Natural scientists have never prescribed their methods, research techniques, or technical language for use in *humanistic* studies; after all, they denied the term "scientific" to all studies in the humanities. Thus, humanists have had no occasion to protest against prescriptions or impositions from natural scientists.

On the other hand, humanistic scholars have had a good reason for their antiscientism if they meant by scientism the presumption of natural scientists in excluding the humanities from the category of scientific knowledge and scientific research. As I showed in the section on Scientific Knowledge, the takeover of the term "science" by natural scientists in English-speaking countries was an appropriation of a designation previously shared by students of culture.[29] Humanists could, not unreasonably, feel dispossessed, especially when the natural scientists began to claim superiority of scientific over "nonscientific" knowledge. Since this arrogation of superiority followed the appropriation of the term only after some time and only gradually, the humanists did not immediately protest against the semantic conversion. When they finally noticed the degradation involved, they resented their having become second-class or third-class academic citizens but did nothing to restore their right to the designation as (cultural) scientists. Instead, they began attacking "science" and "scientists" for all sorts of misdeeds, actual or presumed.

Thus, Lord Bullock complains that "the superiority of scientific

---

[28] Friedrich A. Hayek, "Scientism and the Study of Society," *Economica*, Part 1, n.s., vol. 9 (1942), p. 269. Reprinted in Hayek, *The Counter-Revolution of Science* (Glencoe, Ill.: Free Press, 1952), pp. 15-16.

[29] "It is an interesting reflex of the British situation that the Royal Society, early this century, deliberately excluded from its scope the social sciences and other fields of learning which, in other countries, would be regarded as part of 'science' in its universal sense." C[harles] P. Snow, *The Two Cultures: And a Second Look* (Cambridge: at the University Press, 1964), p. 105, note 37. (The story of the decision of the Royal Society and the subsequent establishment of the British Academy will be told in the chapter on Academies of Sciences in Volume II.)

over humanistic studies was . . . asserted" on the basis of two criteria, namely, "the *understanding* of nature . . . and the practical *application* of scientific knowledge in the transformation of human life by technology." Of course, *natural* sciences deal only with natural, not with cultural phenomena; and knowledge of physics and chemistry is useful in technological development. This can hardly be a criticism of the natural sciences; it would be a criticism of *science* for its disregard of man, society, culture, values, and of any knowledge useful chiefly through the pleasure it gives to those who appreciate it.[30]

Jacques Barzun blames "scientists" for their "searching for the 'really real' . . . ," an ambition which he regards as responsible for the loss of the "balance of mind" achieved, according to Alfred North Whitehead, through the union of "passionate interest in the detailed facts with equal devotion to abstract generalization."[31] Barzun is probably correct in stating that many natural scientists have lost this precious balance of mind. Yet, his attacks on "science" cannot help striking us as somewhat pointless if they are based on the single-mindedness and often rather narrow interests of devotees of laboratory sciences. At some places in his tract Barzun seems to be a sincere admirer of the "glory" of the achievements in some of the natural sciences, but most of the time he is quite sarcastic in his characterization of the entertainment of the experimentalist, the playful man (*homo ludens*) with his toys, ranging "from the ludic to the ludicrous."[32] Barzun is especially acerbic regarding the blessings of modern technology. To reproach natural scientists for playing with gadgets and machinery is no more reasonable than it would be for a natural scientist to reproach a humanistic scholar for playing with words and abstract ideas.

One more antiscientistic argument of humanists deserves to be mentioned: natural scientists have, as a rule, regarded "reductivism" as one of their guiding precepts, though their opinions differ as to just what their theoretical propositions should be reduced—to "the familiar," to physical phenomena, physicalist explanations, physicalist language, reproduceable physical sense perceptions, or what not. Humanistic scholars object to demands that any of these

[30] Cardinal Newman's statement is often quoted with approval by humanists: "Knowledge is capable of being its own end. Such is the constitution of the human mind that any kind of knowledge, if it really be such, is its own reward." Quoted from Aiken, *Predicament of the University*, p. 119.

[31] This statement from Alfred North Whitehead, *Science and the Modern World* is quoted in Barzun, *Science*, p. 5.

[32] Barzun, *Science*, pp. 111, 113.

"reductions" be performed regarding inner experiences or emotions—human experiences of their own or other minds. This divergence in procedural rules led a philosopher to the statement (not easy to understand for an uninitiated and very difficult to translate into any foreign language) that a "theme in the humanistic critique of science is the reductive tendency of science."[33] Incidentally, reductivism is now rejected and discredited by the newest generation of philosophers of science;[34] but it is true that most natural scientists trained in old-fashioned "scientific method" still believe in it religiously.

The main source of the humanists' antiscientism is their own feeling of being under attack from the scientific establishment. "We should be deceiving ourselves if we underestimated the antihumanistic thrust of so much recent writing."[35] This was said in 1968. Sixty years earlier the warning had been: "The humanities need to be defended today against the encroachment of physical science, as they once needed to be against the encroachments of theology."[36]

The Two Cultures

The antiscientism of many writers on the humanities is, I submit, best explained as a reaction to the disrespect many natural scientists express for the humanists' work. The superiority complex of many representatives of the natural sciences manifests itself in their philosophical-position statements. They look down on any type of knowledge other than that generated by what they call their scientific method. It is understandable if those who are said to be seekers and disseminators of an "inferior" type of knowledge resent this attitude and become hostile to the scientific supermen.

In his Rede lecture of 1959 on "The Two Cultures and the Scientific Revolution" and its sequel in 1963 on "The Two Cultures: A Second Look," C. P. Snow, now Lord Snow, examined the mutual incomprehension and dislike of the representatives of natural science and literary scholarship: "Literary intellectuals at one pole—at

[33] John Compton, "Science, Anti-Science and Human Values," *The Key Reporter*, vol. 44 (Winter, 1978-1979), p. 2.

[34] For example, Rudolf Carnap, Herbert Feigl, Richard Braithwaite, Sir Karl Popper, Carl Hempel, to mention only a few. Brief references to their writings can be found in the chapter on "What is Meant by Methodology?" in my *Methodology of Economics and Other Social Sciences* (New York: Academic Press, 1978).

[35] Harry Levin, "The Modern Humanities in Historical Perspective," in J. C. Laidlaw, ed., *The Future of the Modern Humanities* (Cambridge: The Modern Humanities Research Association, 1969), p. 16.

[36] Irving Babbitt, *Literature and the American College: Essays in Defense of the Humanities* (Boston: Houghton, Mifflin, 1908), p. 31.

the other scientists, and as the most representative, the physical scientists. Between the two a gulf of mutual incomprehension—
sometimes (particularly among the young) hostility and dislike, but
most of all lack of understanding."[37] Snow regards the two groups as
two cultures "in an intellectual but also in an anthropological
sense," in that the members of each culture share "common attitudes, common standards and patterns of behaviour, common approaches and assumptions."[38]

Snow's sympathies seem to be more on the side of the natural scientists, whose arguments he finds "usually much more rigorous, and
almost always at a higher conceptual level, than literary persons' arguments."[39] His main point, however, is the lack of intercommunication and mutual understanding, a result of overspecialized education at all levels of schooling and research. Those trained in literary
scholarship "couldn't cope with the simplest concepts of pure science; . . . [and] would be even less happy with applied science."[40]
On the other side, the natural scientists, though often interested in
music or color photography, think little or nothing of books: "of the
books which to most literary persons are bread and butter, novels,
history, poetry, plays, almost nothing at all."[41] These blank spots in
the vision fields of the people in the two camps may be deplorable
and may well explain some of the mutual contempt or derision. If I
may satirize the conflict, I propose these pronouncements: The humanistic scholars say "we are thinkers, they are tinkers; we read
great books, they play with gadgets." And the physical scientists say
"we are rigorous, objective, and exact in measurement and argument, they speculate about subjective impressions; we test all
hypotheses in our laboratories, they bury themselves in dusty
books."

I submit that Lord Snow gets two things mixed up: mutual comprehension and mutual appreciation. As far as comprehension is
concerned, the gulf between the "two cultures" is not any wider
than the many gulfs are between the different disciplines within
each culture. The mutual incomprehension between an entomolo-
gist and a nuclear physicist is not less than that between either of the
two and a structural linguist, a social historian, or an analytic philosopher. (Snow does consider this point; he even discusses the possibility of "two thousand and two cultures," but he decides in favor
of the "dialectic.") I have found that my own specialty, economics,

[37] C[harles] P. Snow, *The Two Cultures: And a Second Look* (Cambridge: at the
University Press, 1964), p. 4
[38] Ibid., p. 9.   [39] Ibid., p. 12.
[40] Ibid., p. 30.   [41] Ibid., p. 13.

is equally far removed from the ready grasp of most molecular biologists as it is from the ready grasp of most Romance philologists. Lord Snow emphasizes the shocking ignorance of literary intellectuals of such things as the second law of thermodynamics or the structure of DNA. I know of no comprehension tests on these pieces of knowledge administered to random samples of geologists or meteorologists, on the one hand, and of musicologists or historians, on the other, but I wonder whether their test scores would be significantly different. To be sure, it would be nice if more people were better educated and if their interests were broader. And, perhaps, broader education could lead to greater appreciation of what the other fellow is doing. But the mutual antipathy between the members of the "two cultures" is not due to mutual incomprehension but to a cultivation of snobbish snubbing.

The antagonism described and deplored by Lord Snow is, as I like to put it, between "literary intellectuals" who consider themselves as the *only* intellectuals, and "natural scientists" who consider themselves as the *only* scientists. There is no good reason why students of nature and students of human culture should disrespect or dislike each other. However, if the former call the research of the latter nonscientific, and the latter call the work of the former nonintellectual, one cannot expect much mutual appreciation.

Lord Snow had an afterthought: there was still another "body of intellectual opinion," consisting of students of "social history, sociology, demography, political science, economics, . . . psychology . . . , all of them concerned with how human beings are living or have lived. . . ." This he recognizes as "becoming something like a third culture."[42] Snow found that "such a culture has . . . to be on speaking terms with the scientific one." Yet he never commented on the fact that his two or three cultures together comprise only a small minority of society, perhaps less than 10 per cent. He took no account of the semieducated counterculture and none of the overwhelming majority of people who are entirely uninterested in scientific or intellectual knowledge of any sort.

The Characteristics of the Humanities

I still have to examine what criteria or features have been found to serve as unifying characteristics of the disciplines corralled under the term "humanities." I may begin with a very negative pronouncement on this task, expressed on the occasion of the fiftieth anniversary of the Modern Humanities Research Association. The

[42] Ibid., p. 70.

pronouncement holds that "modern humanities" is no more than a slogan, invented partly for purposes of propaganda after "the classical humanities . . . [had] lost their basic characteristics and their prestige . . . ," and that the term "somehow survived as a convenient one in curricular classification."

> We have lived . . . with its paradoxes and ambiguities, trying in vain to give it connotative definition and meaningful reality. . . . As a term, . . . it has done far more harm than good, and should be abandoned.
> The truth . . . is that there is no combination of from three to (as the Congress of the United States was recently led to believe) nine or more academic disciplines with common subject matters, methods, attitudes, objectives, and results that set them apart from the sciences and social sciences. This notion is sheer nonsense. . . ."[43]

We might just as well give up our search for common characteristics; or we might follow one of Parker's suggestions and use the term "humanities" as a substitute for some category such as miscellaneous subjects not elsewhere classified. Let other academic divisions collect the disciplines which they think qualify as mathematical, physical, biological, or social sciences and assign any that do not fit, but are worth being taught and researched, to the miscellaneous category, euphoniously called "the humanities." This may be the honest way out of the conceptual dilemma, but I doubt that it will appeal to dedicated humanists, or to students of the sciences of human culture. Thus, we continue to search for common characteristics of the miscellaneous disciplines.

A study of the Report of the Commission on the Humanities, which provided the rationale for the establishment of the National Endowment for the Humanities in 1965, does not contribute much to our search.[44] It enumerates the subjects that should be included and it indulges in purple prose to plead the cause. If learned men wish to persuade legislators that financial support to the humanities will be an urgent task of government, eminently in the national interest, they will find the right line and the right words for the task—but we should not expect a piece of closely reasoned analysis. We learn that

[43] William Riley Parker, "The Future of the 'Modern Humanities'," in Laidlaw, *The Future of the Modern Humanities*, p. 107. Parker had compiled over forty statements attempting to define humanities (apart from dictionary definitions) and found all of them unenlightening (p. 114).

[44] *Report of the Commission on the Humanities* (New York: American Council of Learned Societies, 1964).

"the humanities may be regarded as a body of knowledge and insight, as modes of expression, as a program for education, as an underlying attitude toward life." The sales pitch is that the humanities are capable of "humanizing" technology; of instilling individuals with "intellectual humility, sensitivity to beauty, and emotional discipline"; and of helping society sustain a healthy "social, moral, and aesthetic development."[45] A few years after the establishment of the National Endowment for the Humanities, its chairman found it appropriate to explain why the humanities had so little influence on the nation's "practical affairs." He suggested that one of the reasons may be that the humanities lacked a "conceptual framework that brings together the great bag of subjects, from art to linguistics, that are" included.[46]

Lord Bullock, in an attempt to show that humanistic studies are "capable of offering something *distinctive*," lists "five characteristics . . . to identify humanistic studies": (1) Humanistic studies, contrary to the social and behavioral sciences, "move . . . from generalization towards the particular, from abstraction towards the concrete," because "human experience . . . is always experienced in a particular context." (2) "A central concern . . . is the discussion of values, historical judgments, questions of purpose and . . . meaning. . . ." (3) Essential for humanistic studies are the "possibility and the necessity to look at human actions, beliefs and creations . . . from within . . . seen and felt from the inside." (4) Although "exacting in their standards of scholarship," the humanists' evidence does not "exclude . . . constructive interpretation . . ." and may combine "elements of fact, speculation and judgment, the objective and the subjective." (5) Humanistic studies refuse "to repudiate the past as irrelevant"; in fact, "on all questions of value, purpose and meaning . . . —whether moral, political, religious, aesthetic, or philosophical—the argument is never concluded . . . because such questions are not settled by the accumulation of new knowledge, only debated in a different context."[47]

Lord Bullock's list of characteristics is lucidly formulated and is in conformance with the best thinking on the problem. The trouble is that, as with all ideal types, there is no perfect fit between "the real thing" and the mental construct. None of the disciplines commonly counted among the humanities has all five characteristics, and some

[45] Ibid., pp. 2, 3.

[46] Barnaby C. Keeney, "Foreword," in *National Endowment for the Humanities, Third Annual Report* (Washington: National Endowment for the Humanities, 1969), p. 1.

[47] Bullock, "The Future of Humanistic Studies."

have at best one or two of them. Try them out, for example, on linguistics, and you find that most of them are quite out of place.

One of the finest statements on programs for humanistic education
was made in 1957 in a report on the humanities to the president of
The Johns Hopkins University by a team of four scholars.[48] The
summary of the purposes of humanistic education stresses *history*—knowledge of the past, with emphasis on the particular, the
unique; *value*—with emphasis on the categorical imperative; and
taste joined with imagination—a rare quality to be cultivated and
protected. All three are strongly tied to tradition and refer to human
action and judgment. But although the programmatic role of this
conception is of great significance—understand the past! act respon-
sibly! cultivate good taste!—it is by no means certain that the three
precepts would do as criteria in a definition of humanistic disciplines.

It is probably no coincidence that most statements by scholars
dedicated to the humanities have a strongly lyrical quality: they are
formulated in a flowery style and are laden with emotion. Charles
Frankel, for example, observes that "the humanities are a curious
combination of involvement and detachment; of the search for scientific objectivity and irrepressible personal idiosyncrasy; of piety towards the past and the critique of the past; of private passion and
public commitment. Some humanistic disciplines display one or
another of these tensions more conspiciously than others, but the
tensions are characteristic of all humanistic enterprises".[49]

SOCIAL-SCIENCE KNOWLEDGE

Adjectives were available to specify the types of knowledge discussed in the preceding sections: mundane, scientific, humanistic. If
we proceed to the social sciences, we are forced to press a noun into
service as an adjective: "social-scientific knowledge" sounds awkward (just as "natural-scientific knowledge" would jar our ears); the
expression "social knowledge" has a different connotation; and
"societal knowledge" does not seem right either. Thus, we arrive at
"social-science knowledge."

[48] Don Cameron Allen (English Literature), Clifton Cherpack (Romance Languages),
Henry Rowell (Classics), and C. Vann Woodward (American History), Report on the
Humanities to President Milton S. Eisenhower, Johns Hopkins University, February
1957 (mimeographed). Excerpts in *Johns Hopkins Magazine*, April 1979, pp. 4-5.

[49] Charles Frankel, "Why the Humanities?" *Ideas* (A Publication of the National
Humanities Center), vol. 1, no. 1 (Winter 1979), pp. 2-3 and 13-14.

Historical Development

We are spared, with regard to the social sciences, the lengthy explorations in historical semantics of the kind required for scientific knowledge and humanistic knowledge. The only essential piece of terminological information is that in the eighteenth and early nineteenth centuries the designation "moral philosophy" was generally used for what now is called social sciences. Moral need not have the connotation of ethical, but may refer to the *mores*, the customs, of society; and philosophy was simply a synonym for science in the present (international) sense, namely, systematic inquiry, as contrasted with the layman's or practitioner's knowledge. Moral philosophy was juxtaposed to natural philosophy; it became social sciences at about the same time natural philosophy became natural sciences.[50]

The historical development was not quite so smooth as the preceding paragraph makes it appear: there have been occasional deviations and aberrations in terms and concepts. For example, Comte in his *Positive Philosophy* proposed "social physics" as a synonym for "social philosophy" or "social science." Ampère preferred "political sciences" in lieu of "social sciences." Cournot spread the various social sciences among the columns and rows of a matrix of sciences, including theoretical sciences, historical sciences, and technical sciences; anthropology and ethnology were regarded as biological sciences, history was among the political sciences, and chrematology (the theory of wealth, or economics) was an entirely theoretical science. For Pearson, most of the social sciences belonged in the division of biological sciences. For details on these and other taxonomic peculiarities, and for full documentation, the reader may be referred to Part One, "The Branches of Learning," in Volume II of this work. The deviations fortunately did not give rise to the chains of confusions and controversies that have been so notorious in the discussions of "scientific" and "humanistic" knowledge.

Methodological Controversies

Things have been different, and far less peaceful, with regard to the discussions of the "proper methods" for the study of society. There has been plenty of methodological controversy about a variety of questions. Are the social sciences fundamentally different from the natural sciences? If so, just what is the essential difference in method of inquiry? What are the similarities and differences be-

[50] Francis Bacon, in the early seventeenth century, used the terms "science," "philosophy," and "doctrine" as equivalents.

tween studies of human action—man in society—and humanistic studies? Are the same methods of inquiry helpful in all the different social sciences, or are different methods appropriate to different areas or types of problems? These questions are stated here to indicate the scope of methodological conflict, not to promise any answers. Perhaps a few particularly important points of view, taken and defended by influential methodologists, may be worth describing, chiefly to give an idea of how knowledge of social sciences may differ from the types of knowledge treated in the preceding sections.

John Stuart Mill saw a striking "contradistinction" between *physical* science and *moral* (or psychological) science. The difference between "these two departments of our knowledge does not reside in the subject-matter with which they are conversant," because "everything which can possibly happen in which man and external things are jointly concerned, results from the joint operation of a law or laws of matter, and a law or laws of the human mind . . . . Any compound effect or phenomenon which depends both on the properties of matter and on those of mind, may thus become the subject of two completely distinct sciences, or branches of science." Mill proceeded to show that "there are no phenomena which depend exclusively upon the laws of mind," and that most social sciences, therefore, "presuppose all the physical sciences." (This should not be confused with reductivism.) He also distinguished among different social sciences, some concerned with "man as a mere individual," others with man's feelings towards, and relations with, "other individual human or intelligent beings," and again others with man "living in a state of society, . . . union or aggregation of human beings for a common purpose or purposes." He pointed to important differences between studies that are based on fictitious hypotheses of isolated, idealized motives, abstracting from all other motives, and studies that "embrace every part of man's nature, insofar as influencing the conduct or condition of man in society."[51]

I have offered these few snatches from an essay first published almost 150 years ago—in 1836, to be exact—because they, and the rest of that essay, provide more insights into the foundations of social sciences than can be gained from most writings of our day. They are silent only on the relationships between social sciences and humanities, and understandably so since, as we have seen, the agglomeration of cultural studies under the heading "humanities" is an

[51] John Stuart Mill, "On the Definition of Political Economy; and on the Method of Investigation Proper to It," *London and Westminster Review*, October 1836; reprinted in *Essays on Some Unsettled Questions of Political Economy* (London: John W. Parker, 1844), pp. 129-137.

idea of this century and has gained academic recognition only over the last fifty years.

The social sciences share with the cultural sciences (humanities) the concern with human action, and with the artifacts and other consequences of human conduct. The most significant differences relate to the relative roles of the universal and the unique, the cognitive and the affective, the categorical and the symbolic, but these differences are not equally significant in the various disciplines, and, where they matter little, it is hard to decide whether the area in question is a social science or belongs to the humanities. Such conflicts of jurisdiction have arisen most frequently in historical studies. Intellectual history has regularly been assigned to the humanities, economic history to the social sciences. The assignment of social and political history, however, has remained controversial, and in some academies and universities a compromise has been made to the effect that history before the year 1400 or 1500 has been given to the humanists, and modern history to the social scientists.

One of the perennial bones of contention has been the billetting of psychology. It has sometimes been seen as a part of philosophy, assigned to what are now the humanities; sometimes it has been regarded as a natural science, especially in its physiological and experimental aspects; and it is, of course, a mental science par excellence—and thus, by virtue of at least one definition, a social science. The shuffling back and forth of psychology from one subject group to another may have been rather unsettling for the methodologists of this ancient field of study. In the process, it has had to undergo a sequence of name changes, including such outlandish names as pneumatics, pneumatology, phenomenology, aplopathoscopic pneumatology, and other aliases. Again I refer the reader to things to come in Volume II.

An Academic Subject Group

Courses in particular social sciences appeared relatively early in the offerings of American colleges and universities. A professorship in Moral Philosophy and Political Economy was established in 1819 at Columbia College. The combination of subjects professed by the same teacher was sometimes less congruous, as, for example, the professorship in Chemistry and Political Economy at South Carolina College in 1826, and the chair in Political Economy, History, and Metaphysics at William and Mary in 1827. Only in the 1870s were separate professorships in Political Economy created at Harvard, Yale, and Johns Hopkins. Courses in anthropology came in during the 1880s, but this subject was often linked with philosophy, psychology, sociology, and (probably stressing physical anthropology) with geology and zoology. Yale had in the 1880s a Department of Political and Social Sciences.

One of the earliest recognitions of the social sciences as a university division was—as I mentioned in my discussion of humanistic knowledge—at Berkeley, when the College of Arts was split, in 1893, into a College of Social Sciences and a College of Natural Sciences. Between 1893 and 1915 the College of Social Sciences contained departments of Jurisprudence, History and Political Science, Engineering Design (Architecture), and Economics. The division, since 1915 a part of the College of Letters and Science, has expanded over the years; by 1967 it included ten departments (Anthropology, Demography, Economics, Geography, History, Journalism, Philosophy, Political Science, Psychology, and Sociology) and three schools (Criminology, Public Affairs, and Social Welfare).—The development at Harvard was different. In 1890 there were many small divisions; among these was a Division of History and Political Science with two departments (History and Roman Law; and Political Economy) and a Division of American Archaeology and Ethnology. By 1940, seven departments may be considered parts of the area of social sciences (Philosophy, Psychology, Sociology, Anthropology, History, Government, and Economics). The inclusion of Philosophy may be inaccurate, since it first had stood alone as a separate division; later, however, (in 1919) it comprised Philosophy and Psychology, and Social Ethics.—Princeton has held the social sciences to a small scale. In 1919 it had a Division of History, Politics, Economics and Social Institutions, consisting of only three departments. The same three departments (History, Politics, Economics and Social Institutions) made up the social sciences in 1949, though there was now also a School of Public Affairs. Later, in 1960 and 1970, respectively, Sociology and Anthropology became independent departments. Philosophy was counted among the humanities, Psychology among the natural sciences.

Some institutions have solved the problem of questionable allocations of "mixed" disciplines to particular groups or divisions by making double or multiple assignments. The University of Chicago used this device from the beginning of its academic reorganization in 1930. Five departments were listed exclusively as members of the Division of the Social Sciences (Anthropology, Economics, Education, Political Science, and Sociology), and two with double allegiance (Geography, "also in the Physical Sciences"; and History, "also in the Humanities"). In addition, two departments in the Division of the Biological Sciences (Home Economics and Psychology) were listed as "represented in the Social Sciences." If one wonders why Home Economics is considered a biological science, one may have to realize that cooking, especially in its dietary aspects, has a strong tie to physiology.—The most sensible arrangement seems to be the one now in effect at Swarthmore College, where six of the nine departments in the Division of Social Sciences have double or triple allegiance. Two departments (History and Linguistics) are also in the Division of Humanities; one (Engineering) is also in the Division of Natural Sciences and Engineering; and three (Mathematics, Philosophy, and Psychology) are in all three divisions. Only three departments (Economics, Political Science, and Sociology and Anthropology) have exclusive allegiance to the Division of Social Sciences.

The Sense of It All

Enough has been said to justify the conclusion that it would not be helpful to use the organization charts of academic institutions, the breadth requirements for undergraduates, or the voting regulations for faculty members as guides to the classification of higher learning. Nor would it be helpful to use the arbitrary criteria chosen by committees of professors to sort the disciplines into prefabricated boxes of subject groups. None of the conventional or unconventional taxonomies, no matter how interesting they are from historical or philosophical points of view, can provide useful arrangements of scientific, scholarly, or intellectual knowledge.

Classification schemes where the actual filing or cataloguing raises puzzling questions in 10 or 15 per cent of all entries have to be tolerated; but, when the ratio of doubtful cases reaches one third, or even more, of the total, the effort ought to be abandoned. Governments, of course, will not give up; undaunted by philosophical contradictions, they can legislate any distinctions and differentiations they like to make. As a result, specialized knowledge which the trained expert cannot consistently "order" into fixed classes can be sorted by a skillful administrator into the "appropriate" category, especially if the decision is related to the allocation or denial of funds for teaching and research.

In subsequent volumes of the present work where, especially in the analyses of education and research, statistical disaggregations of funds for the creation and dissemination of knowledge of various types will be required, I shall prefer a finer breakdown than into the broad classes discussed in the present chapter. To inquire into course enrollments or research activities in psychology or in history may be of interest, but aggregated data for broader, inconsistently defined classes of knowledge, say, natural sciences, biological sciences, social sciences, and humanities, would tell us little.

Are "the arts" branches of knowledge? This question has no definite meaning as long as one is not clear on what is meant by "the arts"—and this has changed in the course of history and, moreover, it changes even today with the context in which the word is used.

Liberal, Professional, Mechanical, and Fine Arts

Unquestionably, the "liberal arts" in the curriculum of the medieval university were branches of learning: the trivium—grammar, rhetoric, and dialectic (logic)—as well as the quadrivium—music, arithmetic, geometry, and astronomy. The liberal arts were juxtaposed to the "professional arts," which were taught in other faculties of the university, chiefly, medicine and law. There were, of course, also the faculties of theology, but this branch of learning escaped being called an "art." The "mechanical arts" referred sometimes to technology, surely an important branch of knowledge, sometimes, however, to techniques in practicing various crafts. The reference to practice or action was not intended to deny that any kind of doing presupposes a knowledge of "how to." (Jeremy Bentham told us—as I shall show in the next volume, in Part One, Chapter 5—that science was "knowledge" whereas art was "practice," but he also stressed the fact that every branch of learning was both art and science and that each needed the other.) The "fine arts" are rather different things; they surely involve not only "how-to" knowledge on the part of the performer, but they also convey to the beholder impressions which I include in the wide concept of knowledge. Incidentally, our language distinguishes between performers of mechanical arts and fine arts by designating them, respectively, as artisans and artists.

To look to academic institutions for an authoritative meaning of the arts is hopeless, because word usages differ widely. If some innocents believe that "arts and sciences" are meant to express a dichotomy, they will be quickly disabused of this error if they recall the organization of the University of California (Berkeley) from 1868 to 1893, where the College of Arts was composed of the College of Social Sciences and the College of Natural Sciences. Other institutions used the expression "liberal arts" in conformance with the ancient model, which included arithmetic, geometry, and astronomy and was enriched by substantial doses of natural sciences. And, to complete the round, several colleges and universities have a division of art to serve mainly the visual and performing arts.

Performance versus Precepts for Performance

Some writers wanted to distinguish between art and science by having the former consist of "instrumental" propositions, the latter, of positive propositions, but they did not deny the designation "knowledge" to either.[52] Does this make the cookbook a work of art? Or is it the practice of cooking that constitutes art? Those who speak of cooking as an art do not mean to say that it is an art to read a cookbook and carry out its instructions, or to cook without instruction the simple dishes commonly eaten by most of us. They refer, instead, only to the work of those rare cooks who prepare very special meals, using unusual imagination and a fine sense of taste, form, and color. The "art" in this activity lies precisely in the deviation from common practice and from common precepts.

This meaning of art as a performance superior to that of most practitioners is, however, contrary to the meaning of art as a body of precepts for practice; the latter happens to be one of the dictionary definitions and has been widely used as an antonym of science. Art in this sense is, like science, systematic knowledge but arranged in a different way, suitable for more immediate practical application. As John Stuart Mill has proposed, science is a body of knowledge classified according to causes, art a body of knowledge classified according to effects, the causes of which are often the subject of several different sciences.[53]

Clearly, not all knowledge is science and not all practice is art. Perhaps one may say that highly qualified knowledge (rather than common, everyday knowledge) is science, whereas highly qualified practice (rather than common, everyday practice) is art. But, since virtually all practice, and certainly all qualified practice, presupposes knowledge, it is not unreasonable, as some writers have proposed, to use art and applied science as synonymous terms.

Those who have defined art as practical knowledge have usually

[52] This and the next four paragraphs repeat an earlier discussion of the same topic in my essay "Positive and Normative Economics" in Robert L. Heilbroner, *Economic Means and Social Ends* (Englewood Cliffs, N.J.: Prentice Hall, 1969), pp. 106-107; reprinted in Machlup, *Methodology of Economics and Other Social Sciences*, pp. 432-433.

[53] In a similar vein, Mill said about science and art that "the one deals in facts, the other in precepts. Science is a collection of *truths*; art, a body of *rules*, or directions for conduct," John Stuart Mill, in *Essays*, p. 124. As to the chronological order in which art and science develop, Mill said "In every department of human affairs, Practice long precedes Science." *Principles of Political Economy with Some of Their Applications to Social Philosophy* (London: John W. Parker, 1848), p. 1.

failed to differentiate various degrees of practicality and various degrees of practice. There are important differences between, say, a handbook of technology, technological advice in a concrete situation, actual instructions given for immediate action, and the final, perhaps manual, execution of the instructions. Yet all four phases of practical knowledge or practical application of knowledge have indiscriminately been called art.[54]

An important idea in designating certain kinds of practical activity as art is, I submit, the recognition that these activities presuppose a combination of human qualities that cannot be obtained solely from books or lectures. These activities are "art" in that they call for judgment, intuition, inventiveness, and imagination; they call for skill in making the correct diagnoses and prognoses required for successful prescriptions and good performance. Here lies a real distinction from science or scientific knowledge, and even from technology and general practical precepts.

Creation and Communication

The most important distinction for the purposes of this study is between art as *application*, or use, of knowledge and art as *communication*, or conveyance of knowledge. In the former aspect, knowledge is an input, in the latter, it is an output. That the artist *uses* knowledge in his performance—as a writer, composer, painter, sculptor, actor, musician, singer, dancer—is not of great importance from the point of view of an inquiry into the production of knowledge. That the artist *creates* knowledge in the minds of his readers, viewers, listeners, and spectators is what matters in the context of this book. It presupposes a very wide concept of knowledge, as in fact I use when I define knowledge production as any human (or human-induced) activity effectively designed to create, alter, or confirm in a human mind a meaningful apperception, awareness, cognizance, or consciousness of anything whatsoever.

Knowledge without Words

My wide concept of knowledge permits me to recognize the existence and importance of knowledge without words. Nonverbal knowledge may be of many different kinds: we see shapes, colors,

---

[54] The German word for art is *Kunst*, but the German language offers the compound nouns *Kunstlehre* (for art as a body of general precepts, technology), *Kunstregel* (for art as a precept or rule for practical application), and *Kunstfertigkeit* (for art as technical skill).

and pictures; we hear noises, melodies, harmonies, and rhythms; we touch surfaces, rough and smooth; we smell odors; we taste flavors; and all these impressions we can reproduce or reconstruct in our minds. The deliberate production of sense impressions of these sorts and of consequent cognitive or affective processes in human minds is a part of the total production of knowledge.

Verbal and Nonverbal Arts

The literary arts communicate knowledge expressed in words, but the feelings and affections they produce in the reader or listener are integral parts of the effects in the recipients' minds. The knowledge conveyed through a work of literary art is both cognitive and affective. It is a characteristic of all works of art that the beholder's experience is only partly cognitive, inducing a process of conceptualization and verbalizable reasoning; it is chiefly emotional, inducing nonverbal reactions. Art addresses the soul more than the mind, if I may indulge in using this romantic metaphor.[55] The playwright and the novelist often speak chiefly to the intelligence of their public, but the poet is more likely to arouse in his audience a mixture of reactions in which feelings may outweigh thoughts.[56]

[55] On a less metaphorical and more physiological level, one may perhaps replace the reference to the mind and the soul with a reference to the left and right hemispheres of the human brain—provided one accepts the contention, advanced on the basis of experimental research, that the one half is responsible for verbal skills, the other for nonverbal artistic skills.

[56] I may present two poets, Wordsworth and Shelley, as witnesses supporting my statement. ". . . poetry is the breath and finer spirit of all knowledge; it is the impassioned expression which is in the countenance of all science." William Wordsworth, *Lyrical Ballads*, vol. 1, 3rd ed. (London: T. N. Longman and O. Rees, 1802), p. xxxvii.—"Poetry . . . is at once the center and circumference of knowledge; it is that which comprehends all science, and that to which all science must be referred." Percy Bysshe Shelley, *A Defence of Poetry* (published posthumously, first in Mrs. Shelley's edition of Shelley's *Essays, Letters from Abroad, Translations and Fragments* [1840]; the passage here is quoted from a reprint of the 1845 edition of *Essays* and is entitled *A Defence of Poetry* [Indianapolis: Bobbs Merrill, 1904], p. 76).—The philosopher John Dewey attempted to reduce these poetic declarations on poetry to the statement that "in both production and enjoyed perception of works of arts, knowledge is transformed; it becomes something more than knowledge because it is merged with nonintellectual elements to form an experience worth while as an experience." John Dewey, *Art as Experience* (New York: Minton, Balch, 1932), p. 290.—Another witness testifying in support of my statement about knowledge may be Hermann Broch with his pronouncement that "scientific and artistic cognition are branches of a single trunk—which is, simply, cognition [Erkenntnis]." Hermann Broch, "Einheit wissenschaftlicher und dichterischer Erkenntnis [Unity of Scientific and Poetic Cognition]," first published in 1933, reprinted in Hermann Broch, *Erkennen und Handeln*, Essays, vol. 2 (Zürich; Rhein-Verlag, 1955), pp. 83-89.—For earlier views on

Visual Arts

The visual arts—drawing, painting, modeling, sculpturing, etc.—
produce primarily pictures and shapes, not words. This does not
mean that these art objects do not address the mind and do not induce thought; but not all thinking is words and sentences, it may
just as well be images of things viewed or only suggested by the
drawings, paintings, plastics, and sculptures.

The effects on the viewer are probably different in the case of
realistic and in the case of abstract art. A realistic painting lends itself
more easily to verbal reasoning in that the objects represented in the
picture may produce associations with the viewer's earlier experiences of the same or similar objects and with the designations which
his language has provided for them. An abstract painting, however,
with its lines, shapes, colors, and shades may impress the viewer
chiefly as beautiful, comical, strange—or puzzling if he is used to
seeking definite meanings in what he sees. The thought processes
induced by the painting may be in images or in words, but the
feelings it arouses in him may depend on his previous acquaintance
with abstract art.

In looking at a sculpture, imagining how it might feel to touch the
object—how smooth and pleasant to the palm—may be part of he
viewer's reaction. He may verbalize his impressions in his own
thoughts and, of course, in expressing them to others, but his immediate response is in images, shapes, and surfaces, appealing to his
senses rather than his intelligence. Knowledge comprises the nonverbal feelings and the nonverbal thoughts, along with the verbalized thoughts in the recipient's mind.[57]

Performing Arts

Much of what has been said about the visual arts applies also to instrumental music, just as some of the observations about poetry
apply to vocal music. Vocal music communicates verbal knowledge,
but its appeal may be chiefly affective, not cognitive, particularly so
if the singer's diction is such that his words cannot be comprehended.

---

poetry and other art forms as branches of human knowledge, see Part One, Volume II
of the present work, especially the sections on Francis Bacon and the French ency-
clopaedists.

[57] "Knowledge which is verbally expressed is superior to that which is satisfied
with having something before its eyes; but the latter, too, is a kind of knowledge. Let
the reader try to describe in words what he is seeing at any moment, and he will be
surprised at how little he can 'say' about what he so clearly sees in front of him." José
Ortega y Gasset, *On Love: Aspects of a Single Theme* (New York: New American Library, 1957), p. 111.

Instrumental music impresses just through the sounds produced, through the succession of notes that makes a melody, the simultaneity or instantaneity of sounds that make for harmony, the variations of time intervals that make for rhythm, and so forth. The listener's responses may be entirely noncognitive, except for the recognition of musical shapes (melodies, etc.) previously heard and remembered, vaguely or accurately. On the other hand, the listener with musical training may have cognitive responses as he discerns the difference between major and minor keys (if the music is not atonal), identifies the beats and measures (say, two-four, three-four, four-four, six-four), recognizes themes and variations, notices the exposition and development of principal and subordinate themes, their returns in the same or in different keys or different tempi, the beginning of the coda, and so forth.

The impressions produced by repeated hearings of the same piece (say, a concerto or a symphony) may be quite different. Some music "grows on you" the more often you hear it, whereas other music, though pleasing at first or second hearing, may prove shallow and increasingly tedious if heard repeatedly. As different listeners exchange their views of particular compositions or particular performances, one may wonder about the differences in their reactions. These may be due to differences in their background, training, experience, or familiarity with the work, but some may be due to differences in the ways they listen to the music. Some listen with analytical and critical attention to technical details, but some of us just "let the sounds of music creep in our ears." Either way, the listener receives knowledge, largely of the nonverbal kind. He learns to know the piece—the concerto, the symphony, the string quartet, the sonata, etc.—and knows it better after several hearings.[58]

Two other performing arts, pantomime and dance, convey nonverbal knowledge to the audience. Pantomime and some kinds of dance with expressive gestures may be regarded as quasi-verbal in that they communicate knowledge to the spectator by means of a sign language, with facial and bodily movements replacing the spo-

[58] In this context I may quote from an address by an eminent physicist on certain aspects of human experience, in particular, the "expression" of music: "A Beethoven sonata is a natural phenomenon which can be analyzed physically by studying the vibrations in the air, as well as chemically, physiologically and psychologically by studying the processes at work in the brain of the listener. However, even if these processes are completely understood in scientific terms, this kind of analysis does not touch what we consider relevant and essential in a Beethoven sonata—the immediate and direct expression of the music." Victor F. Weisskopf, "The Frontiers and Limits of Science," *Bulletin, The American Academy of Arts and Sciences*, vol. 27 (March 1975), p. 23.

ken word. Classical ballet, with its explicitly designed plots, is supposed to tell a story. It is sometimes a very elaborate story, as in
Giselle, The Sleeping Beauty, Swan Lake, or *Romeo and Juliet.*
These danced dramatic plays, with music but without words, create
verbalized thought along with nonverbal thought and deeply felt affections. Abstract ballet, on the other hand, is not designed to
suggest a plot or story but only to appeal to the viewer through the
beauty—and technical difficulty—of bodily movements in harmoni-
ous conjunction with the music. Yet, neither the choreographer nor
the performers will object if an imaginative spectator reads a story
into the movements and gestures of the dancers and into the sounds
of the music. If some in the audience indulge in such imagery and
quasi-verbal interpretation of a nonverbal artistic performance, one
may affirm that nonverbal art may, without the artists' intentions,
create verbalized knowledge in the spectator's mind. No survey
exists to tell us what percentage of the audience would actually receive verbalizable knowledge from viewing strictly nonverbal, absolutely plotless, abstract dance. But even if the percentage be small,
the impressions received by the audience may still be placed in the
category of knowledge: nonverbal knowledge in the form of images
and sounds.[59]

Mundane Experiences

The production of knowledge without words is of course not confined to artistic creations. The most mundane experiences, in everyone's everyday life may create in one's mind impressions—awareness, consciousness—which ought not be denied the designation of
knowledge. Just as we know what we have been told or what we
have read, we also know a person we have met, a bird or a tree we
have seen, an animal's cry or a thunderbolt we have heard, a rose's or
a skunk's scent we have smelled, a thistle or nettle we have touched,
a lemon or pepper we have tasted. Thus, all sense perceptions may
be known by experience, whether they are visual, auditory, olfac-
tory, tactile, or gustatory. We know images and shapes, sounds,
scents, touches, and tastes even if we do not know the names language has assigned to them.

  Though our nonverbal memories may be better or worse than
those of other people, most of us know and recognize our friends by
their faces, by the shapes of their heads and, even from great dis-

[59] The program of the Colloquium on Semiotics (Berlin, October 1975) included
sessions on "linguistic, paralinguistic, and nonlinguistic systems of signs" and on
"complementarity in multi-media communication." Papers in the latter session were
on "complementarity of language, image, and music" in film and in advertising.

tances, by their gait and way of moving. We know and recognize them by their voices and, some of them, by the fragrance of their perfumes or the natural odor of their bodies. And a very few—our spouses, mates, and lovers—we know by the touch of their skin. However, knowledge by nonverbal sense experiences is not confined to persons, animals, or tangible objects in general. We perceive and conceptualize in nonverbal form events and happenings we witness. We know what "goes on" when we witness a tree falling, cars colliding, or the sun setting, even if we may not know the theories that explain such events. Explanations are predominantly in the form of verbal propositions. But the actual occurrences can be observed and remembered, and reoccurrences can be recognized as such and placed into abstract classes of events even by those who have never learned the meaning of class and of abstraction.[60]

Most philosophers confine their discourses on knowledge to verbal propositions; pragmatists, to true knowledge as a guide for action; linguistic analysts, to a variety of statements which the knower supposedly has a right to be sure of knowing are true. In this book I use the word knowledge in a much wider sense, because a narrow (or "strong") sense of knowing would restrict its meaning unnecessarily. If Tom, Dick, and Harry say that they know somebody or something, we admit that it is reasonable, and indeed philosophically necessary, to ask what kind of knowledge they claim; but it is not reasonable to insist on so restrictive a definition of knowledge that 90 per cent of all that Tom, Dick, and Harry claim to know is "really" not knowledge. I am making this declaration in defense of my wide concept of knowledge, and I shall have to repeat it on several occasions, because, for the purposes of my study of economic activities designed to produce (disseminate) knowledge, the "strong" sense of knowing is largely irrelevant.[61]

[60] That animals, likewise, may have the capacity of nonverbal cognition is stated by Donald R. Griffin, *The Question of Animal Awareness* (New York: Rockefeller University Press, 1976). Griffin holds, and makes fully plausible, that animals have "mental experiences" and are conscious of having them; that they have "awareness" of the "whole set of interrelated mental images of the flow of events . . . close at hand in time and space, like a toothache, or enormously remote" (p. 5). Griffin does not use the term "knowledge," but my own concept of knowledge comprises his terms "mental experience," "awareness" and "consciousness." However, I am concerned solely with human knowledge and need not extend my discussion to "cognitive ethology."

[61] The notions of nonverbal knowledge and nonverbal "communication" have been gaining recognition among psychologists. A team of researchers has looked "into how people vary in the accuracy of their judgments of other people's feelings as conveyed through a variety of nonverbal channels, such as facial expression, tone and rhythm of voice, body gestures and posture." And some of these studies "suggest that when people have a choice between attending to verbal messages and nonverbal messages,

With this pronouncement I may return to the question of knowledge without words, of both the mundane and artistic type.

Knowing a Tune and Knowing a Feeling

What can it mean if Jane tells me: "I know this tune"? Let us list some of the possible meanings.

1. "I know this tune—I have heard it before." (We cannot verify this statement. Even if Jane proves to me that she was present at an earlier performance of the piece in which the tune appears, this is no evidence for her knowing it.)

2. "I know this tune—I remember and recognize it." (Although we cannot prove that she actually remembered the tune at the time she made the statement, we might test her capacity to recognize it again in a "line-up" of ten or twenty tunes that are played for her with the instruction that she identify it. A recognition test, however, is excessively rigorous. To remember a tune does not imply the capacity of identifying it if the line-up contains several tunes one has heard before.)

3. "I know this tune—I can sing it or pick it out on the keyboard of a piano. (This is a testable proposition.)

4. "I know this tune—it is from a string quartet, but I have heard it in an orchestral version in a concert conducted by Toscanini." (Parts of this statement can be verified, though Jane may not be able to produce evidence of her having heard the concert conducted by Toscanini.)

5. "I know this tune—it is the introductory theme of the third movement in Beethoven's String Quartet opus 132." (This statement is readily testable from the score.)

6. "I know this tune—it is an adagio in the Lydian mode." (Again a statement which a good musician can verify.)

In the parenthetical comments to each of these statements I appear to have accepted the insistence of logical empiricists on using a truth test for what, by their standards, may be admitted to the status of knowledge. I made these comments, however, only to help distinguish the various claims to knowledge, for I would not fail, dismiss, or disallow *any* of them and, indeed, would accept as knowledge all of the mental processes described even if they were not expressed by the knower. If Jane had not said a word, if she had merely thought

---

they frequently weigh the nonverbal information more heavily. This is done outside of conscious awareness—people seem to have a gut sense that there is truth in nonverbal channels." These quotations are from a report on the research of Dr. Judith Hall in "Feminine Intuition: Is There a Scientific Basis for It?" *Johns Hopkins Journal* (Winter 1977), p. 3.

these things silently, I would be satisfied calling these types of mental cognition her "knowledge." And, in my book, the playing of the tune in question is unquestionably production of knowledge, partly of the reinforcing type.

Analogous reflections regarding nonverbal knowledge of mundane experiences would come to the same conclusions. All retained experience and all retrievable, reconstructable experience of a nonverbal character qualifies as knowledge in the sense relevant to this inquiry.

Knowledge of feelings and mental states deserves special mention. The meaning of statements of the type "I know toothache" has been analyzed in many treatises on epistemology, as have claims by individuals to know pain, fear, anger, anguish, happiness, and other emotional and mental states. Many writers on the philosophy of knowledge deny the status of knowledge to "first-person reports" on "direct knowledge."[62] One of their misgivings lies in the different meanings of three closely related statements: (1) I have a toothache, (2) I know that I have toothache, and (3) I know toothache, that is, I know how it feels to have toothache. Analysts fuss about the difference between the first two statements; in particular, they ask the person who tells about his present pain "how do you know it? what evidence do you have for it?" In general, they distrust all direct knowledge if it cannot be "objectively" verified by others. The third statement, too, is vulnerable on this ground. There are (fortunately, I would say) other epistemologists who admit that our memories contain plenty of nonverifiable, nontestable, and nonfalsifiable knowledge, for which we have no better name than knowledge and that it is an arbitrary restriction to limit the use of this word to facts that meet standards of evidence dictated by a set of fastidious norms.[63]

For the purposes of our inquiry we shall not need the tests which epistemologists prescribe for knowledge in the strong sense; we shall not need to establish whether anybody "really" knows, and knows that he knows, and whether we really know that he knows

[62] "For rather than constituting a sort of knowledge which the man who asserts them is either best or uniquely qualified to claim—since they refer to states of himself . . .—the recent view is that there is no speaking of knowledge here at all." Arthur C. Danto, *Analytical Philosophy of Knowledge* (Cambridge: at the University Press, 1968), p. 32.

[63] The fastidious philosophers of knowledge assume "that there is something, for which we need to have a name, for which 'know' is the name that our language in fact provides. But we [they] want to discover exactly what that something is. This we [they] can do (it is alleged or assumed) by considering how we use the word 'know' when we speak carefully." A[kept secret]. M. MacIver, "Knowledge," *Proceedings of the Aristotelian Society*, supplement, vol. 32 (1958), p. 5.

that he knows. Our "loose" concept of knowing will do for verbal communication (through spoken, written, or printed words), quasi-verbal communication (through gestures, silent sign language), and entirely nonverbal communication.

Knowledge as a Mere Euphemism

My leniency in admitting to the status of knowledge all sorts of mental processes which most philosophers of knowledge disqualify as not meeting their standards may cause many raised eyebrows among critical readers. They may object to my accepting at its face value almost anything that anybody claims to know, even if, more appropriately expressed, he merely believes, guesses, or feels it, or was exposed to it. My indulgence, however, has its limits. Where the word "knowledge" is used as a mere euphemism for a physical act customarily designated by very different words, such acts will not be placed under the heading of knowledge or knowledge production. I refer to the biblical use of "knowing" in Genesis 4:1.

Carnal knowledge is only a euphemism for sexual intercourse. It is, of course, associated with mental processes and with sensations, and indeed these sensations may be the most immediate and most eagerly expected and intended effects (in contrast with the female partner's "conception"); but this does not make sexual activities knowledge-producing activities. Eating, drinking, smoking, the use of drugs, and many other things are also associated with sensations felt pleasurable by many individuals, yet these sensations will not be included in the category of knowledge produced by said activities. Knowledge *about* these activities and their effects is again a very different thing; books or articles on food, drink, smoking, and sex qualify fully as media disseminating knowledge.

CHAPTER 4

ALTERNATIVE CLASSIFICATIONS
OF KNOWLEDGE

SO MANY TYPES of knowledge have been discussed and so many distinctions made in the previous chapter that it may appear excessively pedantic to present another collection of distinctions and classifications. Yet, philosophers and administrators of knowledge have proposed sets of distinctions which must not be overlooked in a discourse of this sort. A review of customarily distinguished aspects of knowledge is in order before we can come up with classifications most appropriate for the purposes of this book.

VARIOUS ASPECTS AND DISTINCTIONS

Without going into details and without engaging in an "in-depth" analysis of the differences, I shall place the following distinctions on the agenda: basic versus applied knowledge; theoretical versus historical knowledge; general-abstract versus particular-concrete knowledge; analytical versus empirical knowledge; knowledge of enduring interest versus knowledge of transitory or ephemeral interest; knowledge for many versus knowledge for only a few; and instrumental versus intellectual versus spiritual knowledge.

Basic and Applied Knowledge

The dichotomy, used by administrators of funds for the support of research and by compilers of statistical reports, of "basic" and "applied" knowledge is not easy to carry through when it comes to sorting out the things researched, found, and disseminated. But it does make sense and serves some good purposes. There are, in the first place, certain functional relations between basic knowledge and applied knowledge: the former may permit us to derive practical knowledge from it, which explains the name "applied" knowledge; but sometimes it is the other way around—that is, the discovery of some pieces of practical knowledge may suggest the need for new basic knowledge and may provide clues for finding it. Second, there is the perennial question of the right division of emphasis in our teaching: the liberal arts versus the vocational curriculum, the former stressing basic and general knowledge, the latter stressing the applied and practical. The most distinguished scientists, scholars, and educators try to sell the former, whereas the majority of parents and students buy the latter. Third, there is the question of the right allocation of funds between basic and applied research: the former oriented towards general knowledge of wide and indirect or of unknown applicability, the latter oriented towards specific knowledge of practical use in particular activities. The scientists cry for more liberal money allocations to basic research, while the dispensers of funds devote ten times as much for applied research and development. All these issues will be examined later in this book.

It should be noted that knowledge regarded as "basic" because of its wide and indirect applicability—"indirect" by way of knowledge deduced from it—is not confined to the natural sciences. There is much practical knowledge based on the theoretical social sciences—just think of tax legislation, monetary policy, labor relations—and on the humanities—think of the practical use of foreign languages or of the teachings of history applied in international relations. Moreover, a great deal of practical knowledge is not based on anything that can be attributed to science or scholarship of any sort: for example, where I can shop at lowest prices, which is the fastest route from my home to my office, how I can tie my shoelaces if they are too short, at what time the last train for Princeton leaves Pennsylvania Station, New York. That is to say, not all practical knowledge needs a particular "base." On the other hand, one may be impressed by the large amounts of resources society allocates to the production of practical knowledge in the form of technology in the narrow sense of the word, and for these efforts surely a stock of knowledge of the natural sciences is basic.

Theoretical and Historical; General-Abstract and Particular-Concrete; Analytical and Empirical

Some philosophers of science used to distinguish between "theoretical" ("scientific") and "historical" knowledge. The former would be concerned with generalizations (regularities, tendencies, rules, laws) regarded as relevant to the explanation or prediction of recurring phenomena. The latter would be concerned with individual facts and unique events, regarded as significant for the understanding of past developments of importance to states or nations.

This division again focuses largely on school learning and leaves out most of the knowledge, general and particular, that is not taught in schools, and even a good part of what is taught. A lot of knowledge, some of which is taught at school and most of which is not, is neither theoretical nor historical. Not that the distinction is inappropriate; it simply fails to cover enough ground.

More helpful in this respect is the distinction between "general-systematic" and "particular-concrete" knowledge. By not confining "general-systematic" (or "general-abstract") to "theoretical," or "particular-concrete" knowledge to "historical" knowledge, the proposed classification embraces a much larger universe. Used chiefly for logical and epistemological analyses, it has been regarded by many as insufficiently discriminating. One of the proposed amendments distinguishes three kinds of knowledge: (1) of logically necessary universals, (2) of empirically probable universals, and (3) of particulars (chiefly events in the past, including the immediate past). Others want to stress chiefly the difference between analytical and synthetic propositions but have some difficulty in deciding the logical nature of theories using abstract constructs designed to be useful in the interpretation of the empirical world. Distinctions of this sort, though indispensable in an introduction to methodology, are not serviceable in studies of the social and economic significance of different types of knowledge.

In order to build bridges between classifications serving logical analysis and classifications designed for other purposes, it is sometimes helpful to make cross-references. They may be utterly "irrelevant" to almost anything and yet aid in orientation: students of one discipline may feel more at home in another if they can see how the categories of the alien field relate to the categories of their own.

Knowledge of Enduring and of Transitory Interest

One of the distinctions which may serve as a helpful bridge-builder between different disciplines is that between knowledge of enduring interest and knowledge of only transitory or ephemeral interest. Schools supposedly teach only what is considered to be of enduring interest; but undoubtedly the mass of things known but only of ephemeral interest bulks large in the total of knowledge.

Knowledge of the battle of Waterloo may be of enduring interest, whereas knowledge of a fight in a tavern on Main Street may be of transient interest, though there are probably more Americans who know of a recent tavern brawl than who know of the battle of Waterloo. The death of Marat may be more lastingly important than the death of a retired salesman who left his fortune to his widow and his brain to Johns Hopkins, but this does not mean that the one piece of information is "knowledge" and the other is not.

These examples refer to "particular-concrete" facts, to "historical" events. But knowledge of merely transitory interest is by no means always knowledge of particular events. Many generalizations, likewise, are not of enduring, but only of transitory and spatially limited, interest. Take, for instance, the proposition, true in 1962, that "in dialing telephone numbers the first three letters of the exchange are dialed in London, but only the first two letters in New York." A few years later this piece of knowledge was out of date and uninteresting. The knowledge of the present train schedule from New York to Washington will remain of interest to several thousand people until next October or April, when it is changed.

Some of the mass of knowledge, general-systematic or particular-concrete, which is of only transitory relevance has nevertheless great economic value. Certain services of specialists in particular kinds of transitory knowledge have a market value, not because it takes especially scarce qualifications to acquire this knowledge, but because the "division of knowledge" is a great time-saver and thus a highly productive arrangement in the economy.[1] For example, the freight forwarder knows which lines operate between particular places, when their vehicles depart and arrive, what the rates are, etc. The importer knows where to find certain materials, what they cost, to whom to apply for an import license, how to declare the goods in order to get the lowest import duty, how to procure the foreign exchange, etc. Most of this knowledge is picked up by the individual practitioner in the course of his business operations. Some transitory knowledge, however, is acquired through organized research. For example, many millions of dollars are spent every year in market research by business firms exploring the outlets for their products, the preferences of the consumers, the acceptability of alternative quality improvements, the sensitivity to price changes, etc.

This kind of knowledge, of great social and economic importance, finds no place in any of the classes of knowledge distinguished by some philosophers. This remark is not intended as a criticism; few of these thinkers have been concerned with knowledge of transitory value. But we cannot help being concerned with it since society devotes large amounts of resources to the production of such knowledge.

The distinction between enduring and ephemeral knowledge is not entirely a question of the length of time during which it remains relevant; there is also the question of how long all kinds of knowledge not incorporated in a durable and easily accessible physical re-

---

[1] Friedrich A. Hayek, "The Use of Knowledge in Society," *American Economic Review*, vol. 35 (1945), pp. 519-530. Reprinted in Hayek, *Individualism and Economic Order* (Chicago: University of Chicago Press, 1948), pp. 79-91.

cord will be retained in the recipients' memories. Thus, both obsolescence and forgetfulness may make knowledge perishable. The
second of these limits to the durability of knowledge relates less frequently to the nonexistence of physical records than to the people's
unwillingness to go back to existing records and refresh their memory. Much of the knowledge acquired in school and in compulsory
or voluntary study from teachers, magazines, and books is forgotten
sooner or later. The memories of most people are not capable of re-
taining all that they have received; this holds for practical knowledge no less than for academic (intellectual) knowledge. In effect,
the durability of knowledge is almost the same as the duration of
people's interest in it.

Knowledge for Many and Knowledge for Only a Few

Knowledge may also be classified by the number of persons who find
it interesting or relevant. Some messages may concern only a single
recipient; other bits of knowledge may concern a small group of persons; some kinds of knowledge may be of interest to large groups,
and some to masses of people. Such differences in the number of
persons interested may exist regarding all kinds of knowledge:
transitory and enduring, particular and general, practical and academic, historical and theoretical, and so forth. It is not difficult to
give examples of every kind of knowledge of interest either to only a
few or to very many persons.

The time schedule of an airline conveys transitory knowledge, as
it may stay in effect for only three or four months; and it is practical,
though only for a limited group, namely, for the ticket officers, the
travel agents, and the traveling public, including potential travelers.
The multiplication table is enduring knowledge, intellectual as well
as practical, and relevant for virtually all but the most primitive
people. The knowledge of the infinitesimal calculus, on the other
hand, though equally enduring, is limited to a very small group of
well-schooled persons. The history of ancient Rome is potentially
enduring knowledge, but it interests only a relatively small part of
the population in developed countries; if knowledge is what people
know—what they have in their heads, not just in their books—then
this knowledge may be transitory even for those who were forced to
acquire it at school. The knowledge conveyed by a bird book may be
more or less enduring, though chiefly for naturalists and amateur
bird watchers, usually residing in suburbs and rural districts, rarely
in big cities. On the other hand, knowledge of Mozart's *Jupiter* Symphony, a highly enduring work of art, may be limited to a very small
number of people, chiefly city dwellers and suburbanites with re-

fined taste. In contrast, the knowledge found in cookbooks, more or less enduring and highly practical, may be of very wide interest.

Both the durability of knowledge and the number of the knowledgeable persons were referred to in these examples. As a matter of fact, the two questions—knowledge for how many and for how long—are positively correlated if the groups of people to whom knowledge of a particular subject is interesting or relevant are not limited to our contemporaries but include future generations. Thus, although knowledge of matrix algebra, nuclear physics, molecular biology, Shakespeare's plays, and Beethoven's quartets is limited to a small elite of persons now living, the elites of future centuries will still be interested in this esoteric knowledge. Indeed, with a wider time horizon, one may find that the number of persons who regard this enduring knowledge as relevant to themselves is as large as the number of persons interested in knowledge as ephemeral as today's price of beef or yesterday's scores in college football.

In any case, a classification of knowledge according to the number of persons likely to be interested seems to be as significant as any of the classifications by other criteria.

Instrumental, Intellectual, and Spiritual Knowledge

To the extent that ephemeral knowledge helps people *do* certain things, it would fit into the scheme proposed by Max Scheler: it would be what he called "Herrschaftswissen." Scheler distinguished three classes of knowledge, *Herrschaftswissen, Bildungswissen,* and *Erlösungswissen*[2]—that is, knowledge for the sake of action or control, knowledge for the sake of nonmaterial culture, and knowledge for the sake of salvation; let me call them instrumental knowledge, intellectual knowledge, and spiritual knowledge.

One might be inclined to characterize intellectual knowledge as knowledge for its own sake, but Scheler rejected this explicitly. "There is no such thing as knowledge just for the sake of knowing," he insisted; intellectual knowledge has a purpose too, namely, "the free self-fulfillment of all mental capacities of the individual and the continual growth of his mind."[3]

There is no place in this scheme for knowledge of merely transitory value that is neither instrumental to action nor regarded as intellectual. The scheme is, nevertheless, vastly superior to such simple divisions as that between "basic" and "applied" knowledge. If

[2] Max Scheler, *Die Wissensformen und die Gesellschaft* (Leipzig: Der Neue-Geist Verlag, 1926), p. 250.
[3] Ibid., p. 251.

anybody wishes to regard *all* intellectual knowledge as "basic," I would not quarrel with him, though I believe it can be basic only in the sense in which Darwin regarded poetry and music as required exercises because "the loss of these tastes . . . may possibly be injurious to the intellect and more probably to the moral character. . . ." I doubt that Darwin would have included most of our films and television plays or our books and magazines in this category of valuable taste-builders, or that Scheler's scheme would accommodate them in any of his categories since so few of them convey instrumental, intellectual, or spiritual knowledge. To be sure, some films, TV plays, books, or magazines do qualify for one of these three groups. But we need a class of knowledge for what is neither instrumental nor intellectual nor spiritual. It would be too arbitrary to say that a cookbook conveys instrumental knowledge, a Shakespeare play intellectual knowledge, the Bible spiritual knowledge, and most other books no knowledge at all. They do convey a type of knowledge, however low-brow, and we need a name for it.[4] I shall presently propose one, together with a more comprehensive classification.

THE CHOSEN CLASSES

With regard to all schemes of classification of knowledge, I believe that an objective interpretation according to *what* is known will be less satisfactory than a subjective interpretation according to the meaning which the knower attaches to the known, that is, *who* knows and *why* and *what for*. For example, to stay for the moment with Scheler's classification, what is spiritual knowledge for the religious man may be intellectual knowledge for the man of learning and instrumental knowledge for the cleric and the therapist. What is instrumental knowledge for the professional man is intellectual knowledge for the man outside the field. Thus, economics is instrumental knowledge for an economic consultant, but purely intellectual knowledge for a physicist; contrariwise, physics is instrumental

[4] A classification proposed by Anthony Downs, *An Economic Theory of Democracy* (New York: Harper and Row, 1957), p. 215, would put it under "entertainment knowledge," which would include both intellectual and low-brow entertainment. Downs, who is chiefly interested in political information, distinguishes two main classes, (1) information "procured solely for the edification it provides" and (2) information used for decision-making. The former he calls "entertainment information," the latter he subdivides into "production information," "consumption information," and "political information." Whether he would class religious knowledge as entertainment, production, consumption, or politics is not clear; he probably has not thought about it.

for the physicist and the engineer, but purely intellectual for me, an economist.

Incidentally, I would prefer to use the words "training" for learning what is needed for one's job and "education" for learning what is not needed for it. Thus, no amount of knowledge of economics could make me an educated man; I am educated only to the extent that I know Latin, music, literature, physics, geography, etc. In this book, however, I shall not, or shall only occasionally, use the word "education" in this restricted sense.

Five Classes of Knowledge

Using then the subjective meaning of the known to the knower as the criterion, I propose to distinguish five types of knowledge:

(1) Practical knowledge: useful in the knower's work, his decisions, and actions; can be subdivided, according to his activities, into

  a) Professional knowledge
  b) Business knowledge
  c) Workman's knowledge
  d) Political knowledge
  e) Household knowledge
  f) Other practical knowledge

(2) Intellectual knowledge: satisfying his intellectual curiosity, regarded as part of liberal education, humanistic and scientific learning, general culture; acquired, as a rule, in active concentration with an appreciation of the existence of open problems and cultural values.

(3) Small-talk and pastime knowledge: satisfying the nonintellectual curiosity or his desire for light entertainment and emotional stimulation, including local gossip, news of crimes and accidents, light novels, stories, jokes, games, etc.; acquired, as a rule, in passive relaxation from "serious" pursuits; apt to dull his sensitiveness.

(4) Spiritual knowledge: related to his religious knowledge of God and of the ways to the salvation of the soul.

(5) Unwanted knowledge: outside his interests, usually accidentally acquired, aimlessly retained.

Subjective Sorting and Operational Criteria

The adequacy of a classification cannot be judged before one knows what is done with it. And, with its subjective point of view, the proposed classification may look as if it could not be used for anything. I submit, however, that many, perhaps most, "meaningful" classifications in the social sciences begin with subjective-sense interpretations, for only then are they truly adequate for explanatory purposes.[5] Many of the subjectively meaningful concepts, however, have objectively discernible (operational) counterparts. As to the types of knowledge, we shall of course not ask each knower for his personal evaluation of every piece or bit of information that he has obtained, but there are ways for the social scientist to judge the typical status of various classes of knowledge in the value systems of their typical recipients.

How do the various classifications that have earlier been mentioned or discussed in this chapter fit in with the proposed quinquesection? The dichotomy scientific and humanistic knowledge or the trichotomy scientific, humanistic, and artistic knowledge can peacefully coexist with the five-class scheme: these types of knowledge (distinguished in a traditional though not very logical fashion) are either intellectual or practical. Nonverbal knowledge may have intellectual, practical, or pastime character. Basic knowledge will with few exceptions be intellectual, whereas applied knowledge may be practical as well as intellectual. Of the pairs—generalized versus historical, general-abstract versus particular-concrete, theoretical versus empirical, analytical versus synthetic, etc.—each member can be intellectual or practical knowledge, or even pastime knowledge in some instances, depending on the use which the knower makes of it. This holds also for the dichotomy enduring versus ephemeral, or rather for the spectrum from the one to the other, though ephemeral knowledge will mostly be either practical or pastime knowledge. More will have to be said about the five classes proposed here, but I should like to deal first with a few important problems which I may subsume under the heading "quality of knowledge."

[5] I am referring to Max Weber's postulates of Sinnadäquanz and Kausaladäquanz. See Fritz Machlup, *Methodology of Economics and Other Social Sciences* (New York: Academic Press, 1978), pp. 221, 237, and 246-247.

PART TWO

QUALITIES OF KNOWLEDGE

THE PROBLEMS reserved for discussion in Part Two are usually regarded as the exclusive domain of professors of philosophy. They include highly controversial issues of language philosophy, epistemology, ethics, aesthetics, and other philosophic specialties. I can foresee some snide remarks such as "fools rush in where angels fear to tread"—though I shrink from the possible implication of philosophers as angels. I can also foresee some protests against my treating truth as a quality of knowledge, but I can point to a precedent: Bertrand Russell, neither fool nor angel, has said that "truth is the *quality* of belief in facts."[1] Truth is one of several qualities of knowledge to be dealt with in the three chapters of Part Two.

Chapter 5   Truth, Beauty, and Goodness
Chapter 6   Other Standards of Quality
Chapter 7   Notions of Negative Knowledge

[1] Italics are mine. The qualification "in facts" after the word "belief" is in turn qualified by the statement that "when we entertain a correct belief, that which we believe may be called a fact." Bertrand Russell, "On the Nature of Truth," in *Proceedings of the Aristotelian Society*, n.s., vol. 7 (London: Williams and Norgate, 1907), p. 45. Similarly, Whitehead wrote that "truth is a generic quality with a variety of degrees and modes." Alfred North Whitehead, *Adventures in Ideas* (New York: Macmillan, 1933), p. 309.

CHAPTER 5

TRUTH, BEAUTY, AND GOODNESS

DIFFERENT SCHOOLS of philosophy differ in essential ways in defining knowledge and relating it to cognate terms. The major problems concern the truth value and probability value of assertions or knowledge claims and the logical relations among knowledge, belief, conjecture, hunch, promise, expectation, conviction, evidence, verification, confirmation, verisimilitude, falsification, refutation, and other members of the family of notions that may come to mind when we hear someone—or rather a man of science or learning—say "I know."

KNOWLEDGE VERSUS BELIEF

A large issue for philosophers, especially of the linguistic-analytic school, is whether knowledge is a particular kind of belief, whether belief is a particular kind of knowledge, or whether knowledge and belief are different things. Some philosophers taking the third of these positions declare that, when we reflect, "we cannot mistake belief for knowledge or vice versa."[1] To others, however, knowledge is "warranted belief," "certified belief," or "justified true belief," where not only the truth of the predicated thing (event, situation, etc.) is certified (supported by generally accepted evidence) but also the knower (or believer) is sure of that truth, that is, feels sure that he is justified in feeling sure about the truth of what he predicates.[2] Contrariwise, there are philosophers for whom belief is knowledge of which the believer (or knower) is not quite sure; it is uncertain knowledge or merely conjectured knowledge.[3]

[1] Harold Arthur Pritchard, *Knowledge and Perception* (Oxford: Clarendon Press, 1950), p. 88.

[2] Several authors could be cited as holders of this view or of variants of it; two quotations should suffice: "Knowledge is belief which not only is true but also is justified in its believing attitude." Clarence Irving Lewis, *An Analysis of Knowledge and Valuation* (La Salle, Ill.: Open Court Publishing, 1946), p. 9.—". . . the necessary and sufficient conditions for knowing that something is the case are first that what one is said to know be true, secondly that one be sure of it, and thirdly that one should have the right to be sure." Alfred J. Ayer, *The Problem of Knowledge* (Harmondsworth: Penguin Books, 1956), p. 35.

[3] At least one of the language philosophers made the helpful suggestion to distin-

The three semantic positions are mutually exclusive: in the first case, knowledge is one kind or species of belief; in the second, belief is one kind or species of knowledge; and in the third, knowledge and belief are different genera. The arguments behind these positions, merging philosophy of knowledge (epistemology) with philosophy of language, sound highly sophisticated but can be rather simply interpreted as a fusion of the two meanings of the term knowledge: the *known* and the *knowing*. In my blunt simplemindedness I have referred to the double meaning as an equivocation. (See the first page of the previous chapter.) "Knowledge as that which is known" and "knowledge as the state of knowing" are two different things, and for most purposes it is of little help to rivet them together in a single definition and to make matters even more complex by fussing (a) about the knower's "right to be sure" and (b) about the "certified truth" of that which he knows. The truth of what people know (or think they know or believe) is a different story, which is told rather differently depending on the school of philosophy in which the storyteller has enrolled.

KNOWLEDGE AND TRUTH

The range of views on the relationship between knowledge and truth is wide, but within the range the nuances which particular philosophers wish to emphasize are sometimes difficult to distinguish. I shall try to point to some of the nuances but prefer to do so in the form of questions rather than affirmations. Some of the possible answers may be gleaned from quotations or paraphrases supplied in footnotes. I see no need to commit myself to any particular philosophical platform. Perhaps the questions are more important than the answers, though the philosophers who have taken a firm stand on these issues would probably not agree with this suspicion of mine. They may resent my neutrality—especially if they notice that I am not really neutral but merely noncommittal.

---

guish knowing "in the strong sense" from knowing "in the weak sense"; the latter does "not absolutely exclude the possibility that something could prove it to be false," that is, it allows "for the possibility of a *refutation* ." Norman Malcolm, *Knowledge and Certainty* (Englewood Cliffs, N.J.: Prentice-Hall, 1963), pp. 58-72, esp. p. 61. Malcolm's essay is reproduced under the title "Knowledge and Belief" in Michael D. Roth and Leon Galis, eds., *Knowing: Essays in the Analysis of Knowledge* (New York: Random House, 1970), pp. 17-32. This collection contains a good selection of pertinent literature from the point of view of language philosophy.

Facts and Propositions

Do we "know" propositions (statements, assertions, sentences) or do we "know" facts? Do the "known" propositions have to be about facts and do the facts have to be physical (observable, certifiable)?[4]

Should we accept as knowledge only propositions of unquestionable truth?[5] Should we recognize that knowledge may be imperfect?[6] Is not all knowledge uncertain and only partial?[7]

Verifiability, Confirmability, Falsifiability

Is there a "truth" that is independent of the knowledge of it, so that "a fact remains unaffected by our awareness or lack of awareness of it"?[8] Is "truth . . . a physical property of physical things, called sym-

---

[4] Some neopositivists (logical empiricists) have insisted that only physical facts be "admitted." In his earlier writings Carnap embraced (or at least suggested) a strong physicalist position, for example in the following statement: "If, because of its character as a universal language, we adopt the language of physics as the . . . language of science, then all science turns into physics." Rudolf Carnap, "Psychologie in physikalischer Sprache," Erkenntnis, vol. 3 (1932), p. 108. Later Carnap accepted "observable facts" without insisting that they be physical. Thus he regarded a sentence as confirmable if its confirmation . . . is reducible . . . to that of a class of observable predicates." Rudolf Carnap, "Testability and Meaning," in Philosophy of Science, vol. 3 (October 1936), p. 456. Other philosophers close to the Vienna Circle distinguished "logical facts" from "object facts." Hans Reichenbach, Experience and Prediction: An Analysis of the Foundations and the Structure of Knowledge (Chicago: University of Chicago Press, 1938), p. 11. Reichenbach did not restrict the meaning of "object facts" to physical facts. Philosophers of different persuasions, likewise, used the term "object" in a wider sense. Whitehead, for example, spoke of "sense objects" and "thought objects," and even the sense objects were not confined to those perceived by any of the five senses but included "emotion objects." Alfred North Whitehead, The Aims of Education (New York: Macmillan, 1929), pp. 180-201.

[5] See above, Chapter 2, for the position of the astronomer Sir John Herschel.

[6] Joseph Agassi, "Imperfect Knowledge," Philosophy and Phenomenological Research, vol. 32 (June 1972), pp. 465-477.

[7] "All human knowledge is uncertain, inexact, and partial." Bertrand Russell, Human Knowledge: Its Scope and Limits (New York: Simon and Schuster, 1948), p. 507. This is especially stressed with regard to "scientific truth." Einstein found it "difficult even to attach a precise meaning to the term 'scientific truth'. So different is the meaning of the word 'truth' according to whether we are dealing with a fact of experience, a mathematical proposition, or a scientific theory." Albert Einstein, "On Scientific Truth," Essays in Science (New York: Philosophical Library, 1934), p. 11.—According to Popper "We do not know: we can only guess . . . every scientific statement remains tentative forever." Karl R. Popper, The Logic of Scientific Discovery (New York: Basic Books, 1959), pp. 278 and 280.

[8] This question is answered in the negative by Felix Kaufmann, Methodology of the Social Sciences (London and New York: Oxford University Press, 1944), p. 60. Kaufmann shows that the question is inconsistent with scientific procedure and that the

bols" and does it consist in the correspondence between these symbols "and other things, the objects"?[9]

Should we insist that only verifiable propositions have meaning, and only meaningful propositions deserve the designation "knowledge"?[10] Does either the truth or the meaning of propositions depend on their usefulness for decisions or actions?[11] Do we test our knowledge by applying it for practical purposes or by trying to refute it?[12] Should efforts to "verify" what we believe we know be replaced by (less demanding) attempts to "confirm" or by attempts to disconfirm or falsify?[13] Should the concept of truth be replaced by the conception of "degrees of verisimilitude"?[14]

---

word "true" has to be replaced by "verified" or even by "verifiable in principle" (pp. 61-63).

[9] This question is discussed by Hans Reichenbach, Experience and Prediction, p. 32. Reichenbach proceeds to an analysis of the statement that "truth is not a function of meaning but of the physical signs; conversely, meaning is a function of truth." Reichenbach distinguishes a "truth theory" of meaning, where physical truth and logical truth have to be kept apart, and a "probability theory" of meaning, which always refers to "physical meaning" only (pp. 37-57). However, he rejects the absolute "verifiability theory" of meaning (p. 53). In a helpful ranking, in descending order of respectability, he lists "physical truth meaning, probability meaning, and logical meaning," and even "super-empirical meaning" (pp. 62-63). He does not join the majority of logical positivists in denying meaning to propositions with only "super-empirical meaning"; indeed, he concedes that statements for which "the truth-value . . . is known, but by super-empirical methods," and even statements for which "we have no means at all for knowing their truth-value" (p. 64) may have empirical meaning.

[10] "The meaning of a proposition is the method of its verification," declared Ludwig Wittgenstein, Tractatus logico-philosophicus (London: K. Paul, Trench, Trubner, 1922). Although this sentence is not verbally contained in this work, "it expresses [Wittgenstein's] ideas very adequately and has been used, with this intention, within the 'Vienna Circle.' " Reichenbach, Experience and Prediction, p. 49. His declaration makes all nonverifiable propositions into "meaningless pseudo-propositions." Carnap in his early writings subscribed to this position and wrote that "a string of words" has meaning only if "it is derived from 'protocol sentences' " (that is, observation reports) and if "the way to verification . . . is known." Rudolf Carnap, "Überwindung der Metaphysik durch logische Analyse der Sprache [Overthrow of Metaphysics through Logical Analysis of Language]," Erkenntnis, vol. 2 (1931), p. 224.

[11] Various kinds of pragmatism and instrumentalism are associated with the names of Charles S. Peirce, William James, John Dewey, and others.

[12] Whereas pragmatists point to testing through attempted application, Sir Karl Popper emphasizes testing by attempts to refute. Karl R. Popper, Conjectures and Refutations: The Growth of Scientific Knowledge (New York: Basic Books, 1962), p. 112.

[13] Popper presents powerful arguments against verificationism, and also confirmationism, and in favor of falsificationism. Ibid., esp. pp. 280-281.

[14] Popper regards the (regulative) idea of truth as essential for the understanding of human knowledge since "we simply cannot do without something like the idea of a better or worse approximation to truth." Ibid., pp. 232, 233. (Personal communication from Sir Karl, 24 March 1000)

Relevance for the Purposes of this Study

Scores of questions of this sort have been asked, and the proposed answers have been thoroughly analyzed and heatedly debated. My own positions on most of these philosophical issues need not be spelled out; it will suffice to explain why they are not really relevant for the purposes of this book on the production and distribution of knowledge.

For much of the knowledge (in the weak and wide sense) produced (acquired, disseminated) in our society, the requirements of verifiability or falsifiability would be quite unmanageable. This can be readily seen with regard to spiritual knowledge. If knowledge is warranted belief, what kinds of warranty are accepted, or "ought" to be required, in order to decide whether belief in God and salvation can reasonably be accepted as "knowledge" of God and salvation? For the purposes of our study of the production (dissemination) of knowledge, there is no need to enter into epistemological discussions of this sort. Sermons and Sunday-school classes have to be included in our study no matter what one holds concerning the truth value of the contents taught. There are ways of making it all true knowledge regardless of the strength of belief in it or warranty for it. For example, whether or not I believe what the minister told me from the pulpit, I know that he said it, and thus I have full knowledge, verified by witnesses and documents, of what he and others have said about God and salvation. There may be less sophistical ways of accomplishing our purpose; in any case, the concept of knowledge used here must not be limited by positivistic restrictions.

A requirement that knowledge be "true," tested, verified would not be much less embarrassing with regard to other classes of knowledge, so-called scientific knowledge not excluded. It is one of the postulates of a scientific attitude that one is willing on good evidence to reject or correct at any time what today is considered verified or "not yet falsified" knowledge. The possibility that our present knowledge, say of statistical mechanics or cytology, might in the future be shown to be largely erroneous does not mean that what we now believe to be true in these fields cannot qualify as "knowledge." Conflicting hypotheses are often equally good explanations of the same set of events, and only one of them, at best, may eventually turn out to be correct. Yet all the competing hypotheses are part of our knowledge. The cosmogonists and the earth scientists have no tested knowledge of the origin of the universe or the earth, but they have knowledge of what has been written about it and of the comparative merits of the competing hypotheses. Similarly, the fact that most of what Copernicus or Newton taught has later proved to be in need of correction, and thus was not "true knowledge," should not mislead anybody to deny that he possessed knowledge. "Knowledge" need not be knowledge of certified events and tested theories; it may be knowledge of statements and pronouncements, conjectures and hypotheses, no matter what their status of verification may be. The history of past errors in science is a highly important part of our knowledge today.[15]

The Wrong Fifty Per Cent

The idea that most of our knowledge, even so-called scientific knowledge (in the wider sense permitted in the last two hundred years), is *uncertain* knowledge, was charmingly expressed by Sir William Osler of the Medical School at The Johns Hopkins University, around 1900, when he warned his students of that uncertainty: "Fifty per cent of everything I've told you is wrong. The trouble is, I don't know which 50 per cent."[16] I shall later return to "wrong scientific knowledge" when I speak of the notion "negative knowledge."

Pastime and Artistic Knowledge

The problem of truth is least bothersome in the case of what I have called "small-talk and pastime knowledge." The knowledge of a rape and murder which the newspapers disseminate in all gory details should, of course, be "possibly" true if it is to be effective, but the eager readers—and there must be many or the papers would not give so much space to such stories—do not care very much whether it is really true. They would read with almost equal interest a fiction story about the same rape and murder if it were equally brief and equally selective with regard to the details described. The main element is probably the possibility of identification with the criminal, the victim, the detective, or someone close to any one of them: "It

[15] Compare these statements with Popper's remarks on the subject: "Even Newton's theory was in the end refuted; and indeed, we hope that we shall in this way succeed in refuting, and improving upon, every new theory. And if it is refuted in the end, why not in the beginning? One might well say that it is merely a historical accident if a theory is refuted after six months rather than after six years, or six hundred years. Refutations have often been regarded as establishing the failure of a scientist, or at least of his theory. It should be stressed that this is an inductivist error. Every refutation should be regarded as a great success; not merely a success of the scientist who refuted the theory, but also of the scientist who created the refuted theory and who thus in the first instance suggested, if only indirectly, the refuting experiment." Ibid., pp. 242-243.

[16] Quoted from *Johns Hopkins Magazine*, July 1977, p. 31.

could have been me!" Since every true story has elements of fiction, and all pure fiction has elements of truth, they both should be regarded as objects of knowledge—not necessarily as knowledge of events that have actually taken place but, nevertheless, knowledge of reports of events.

All this refers, with small or no modifications, to many kinds of intellectual knowledge. Knowledge of the *Iliad* or of the *Nibelungen Saga* is knowledge of works of art—poetry, fiction—which, in the opinion of almost all who possess it, enriches them. It is partly for this reason that we call it intellectual rather than pastime knowledge. Other great literary works may contain more "historical truth," but this does not necessarily add to the amount of knowledge the knower of these works possesses. The reader of *King Richard the Second* does not acquire more knowledge than the reader of *King Lear* just because the former play is closer to history than the latter.

To know a play, a novel, or a poem qualifies as knowledge, no matter whether this work of literary art represents pure fiction or is partly based on bits of historical truth or perhaps contains references to general-abstract knowledge or even unrefuted scientific truth. There is no need, however, to rely completely on the subterfuge of having knowledge of, or being acquainted with, the particular literary work of art, for there is usually much more involved in the total mental experience it affords. A different kind of knowledge is *implied* in a work of art, a message it conveys to the understanding reader—a knowledge which can be said to be true in a sense not approved under the standards of "scientific method"; it is what Hermann Broch called "heart-truth" and placed above "body-truth."[17] Thus, besides the knowledge of the work, there is the knowledge of the heart-truth it conveys. In a similar vein, Whitehead taught us that "truth is various in its extent, its modes, and its relevance." Speaking of truth in art, he said this: "Appearance summons up new resources of feeling from the depths of Reality. It is a Truth of feeling, and not a Truth of verbalization."[18]

Practical Knowledge Had Better Be True

Perhaps one might say that the questions of confirmed truth, accuracy, verifiability, and falsifiability matter only for practical knowl-

[17] Hermann Broch, *Der Versucher* [The Tempter] (Zürich: Rhein-Verlag, 1953). The statement that "heart-truth is greater than body-truth" is made by the main character of the novel, Mother Gisson, whose name is an anagram of *Gnosis* in the sense of positive knowledge.

[18] Alfred North Whitehead, *Adventures of Ideas* (New York: Macmillan, 1933), p. 343.

edge, not for the other types of knowledge. Inaccuracy may have
serious consequences in the application of practical knowledge. For
example, misinformation about the time schedule of the railroad
may cause me to miss my train; misinformation on the ingredients of
a pharmaceutical product may cause my untimely death. There is a
reason why "pragmatism," or rather one of the thirteen philosophical systems that go under that name, is understood as a theory of
truth: lack of truth has no consequences in the case of nonpragmatic
knowledge; when it has, the knowledge in question is pragmatic. If
intellectual knowledge or pastime knowledge is told by somebody to
impress others, but proves false and causes the teller to lose face, it is
because he has actually used his knowledge in a practical way. Intellectual knowledge stops being intellectual when it is exhibited by
the show-off.

KNOWLEDGE AND BEAUTY

As we proceed to a discussion of knowledge and beauty, we should,
before all, try to separate different aspects of the relation between the
two notions. Knowledge in the sense of an individual's state of
knowing or his (her) act of acquiring knowledge may give him (her)
a pleasant feeling that some call (in rather metaphoric language)
beautiful. "It is beautiful" to know and to learn. This sense of satisfaction or exhilaration does not concern us in a discussion of the
quality of knowledge, which surely refers to that which is known (or
learned), that is, to the object or contents of knowledge. Even in the
sense, however, at least two aspects have to be kept apart: (1) the
known thing, thought, or image may itself be judged to be beautiful;
(2) the way in which it is presented, the form in which the knowledge is expressed or conveyed, may strike its recipient as beautiful.

The Object and the Form

The difference between these two aspects can be most readily perceived in the cases of literary or visual works of art that may be beautiful presentations of beautiful, plain, or ugly objects. Thus, the plot
of a beautiful novel, drama, or poem may be gruesome, gory, or disgusting, whereas the form in which it is expressed may be beautiful
by accepted standards. The images and shapes shown in paintings
or sculptures may be unattractive, ugly, or terrifying though the beholder may be impressed by the exceptional beauty of the work of
art. Botticelli's Venus (The Birth of Venus) is a beautiful painting of
a beautiful woman, but Caravaggio's Medusa (The Head of Medusa)
is a beautiful painting of a hideous woman. The monsters in the fantastic pictures by Hieronymus Bosch are frightening or ridiculous,

but usually quite ugly; yet the paintings are rightfully acclaimed for
their beauty. The contrary relationship occurs too: many beautiful
women have been shown in mediocre, bad, or awfully tasteless
paintings. The connoisseur regards them as cheap art, or kitsch.

Performing Arts

In the performing arts we may be confronted with a third dimension
of the beautiful. In a stage play, for example, this attribute may
apply, first, to a character in the play, second, to the way the playwright has succeeded in shaping this character in his drama or comedy, and, third, to the way in which the actor succeeds in making the
character alive for us to see and to hear. Think of Cleopatra, the beautiful queen of Egypt, of Cleopatra in Shakespeare's *Antony and
Cleopatra* or of Cleopatra in Shaw's *Caesar and Cleopatra*, and of
Cleopatra as played by Peggy Ashcroft, Maggie Smith, Vivian Leigh,
Ingrid Bergman, Elizabeth Taylor, Elizabeth Ashley, some of the ac-
tresses best remembered in that role. Our knowledge of history's
Cleopatra, of the author's Cleopatra, and of the actress's Cleopatra
may give us the feeling of beholding a beautiful object of thought or
sight in all three manifestations. Any reader whose interests include
history, literature, and the theater will be able to think of examples
where the attribute "beautiful" cannot reasonably be awarded to all
three objects of his knowledge. I can easily imagine that Shakespeare's beautiful characterization of King Richard the Third, ugly
in physical shape and odious in his personal qualities, receives on
some stage a performance that is, or is not, beautiful.

In music, another performing art, only two awards for beauty can
be given: for the composition and for the performance. It is possible,
of course, to judge different aspects of each. In a symphony, for
example, we may find the tunefulness, the melodic lines, beautiful,
but the orchestration not beautiful at all. In the performance of a
sonata, we may find the display of the instrumentalist's technical
skill beautiful, but the conception of the entire work deficient. In
another type of the performing arts, the ballet, we may find beauty or
lack of beauty in the music, in the orchestra's performance, in the
choreography, in the scenery, in the costumes, in the dancing, and
in the acting; this is not surprising in an art form that calls for the
collaboration of so many producers of artistic knowledge.

Beautiful Theories, Beautiful Exposition

The problem of knowledge and beauty is not, as one may think at
first blush, related only to artistic work; it is pertinent to most other
types of knowledge as well, especially knowledge expressed in
words, including scientific knowledge. Again, we must distinguish

substance (contents) and form. A scientific proposition (conjecture, hypothesis, theory) may be regarded as beautiful in its grandeur, its inherent elegance, its harmony with other scientific propositions—observation reports, generalizations, models, hypotheses, theories. On the other hand, its formulation may be awkward, clumsy, pedestrian, without grace or it may be elegant, sparkling, graceful, charming. It was in the former sense that Popper spoke of the beauty of a theory, even a refuted one.[19] Many examples of the second sense of beauty in knowledge—beautiful exposition—can be found in all sciences, formal (logico-mathematical) as well as empirical, natural as well as social and humanistic.[20] Even the driest bits and pieces of scientific knowledge may, by a master of stylistic taste, be presented in a way that elicits the reader's acclaim: "beautiful!" By the style of his exposition, a scientist becomes an artist.

KNOWLEDGE AND GOODNESS

Having treated truth and beauty as qualities of knowledge, one is tempted to do likewise with the third member of the triad: goodness. The True and the Beautiful are commonly seen in company of the Good, and this suggests that we probe whether knowledge can have the quality of goodness. We do not, of course, mean good in the sense of "good for somebody" or "good for something"—which would refer to utility or usefulness—but good in an ethical sense, say, virtuous or in accord with moral precepts, the opposite of wicked or immoral. Can we reasonably attribute this quality of goodness to any kind of knowledge?

Ethics

Neither knowledge of the Good nor knowledge about goodness justifies attributing goodness to such knowledge. A volume of ethical precepts or the knowledge it conveys may be useful, interesting, beautiful, but I cannot see any sense in calling that knowledge good in the ethical sense. Whether such knowledge of ethical precepts can be true or false depends on whether we regard it as empirical rather than normative. If it is interpreted as empirical knowledge—for example, assertions that particular valuations are in fact entertained by many people—truth or falsity can be attributed to it. On the other

---

[19] "Even if a new theory . . . should meet an early death, it should not be forgotten; rather its beauty should be remembered and history should record our gratitude to it." Popper, *Conjectures and Refutations*, p. 243.

[20] On the notion of "humanistic sciences," see above, Chapter 3 in this volume and Chapter 6 in Volume II, especially where I discuss Carnap's thoughts on "unified science."

hand, interpreted as a code of conduct, a set of norms promulgated by churchmen, peers, or other moralists, ethical (value) judgments would be excluded by neopositivist and analytic philosophers from the universe of verifiable knowledge—and, by orthodox exponents of these schools, excluded altogether from the universe of knowledge.[21] But even if the category of normative statements is accepted as knowledge, and even if normative judgments are translated into empirical judgments, this does not carry with it a justification for attributing goodness to the statements and judgments in question. In other words, neither ethical knowledge nor knowledge of ethics (the science of ethics) can be judged to be good or wicked. (Parenthetically it may be added that a possessor or asserter of ethical knowledge—or of knowledge of any sort—may of course be found good or wicked, but, though the "knower" can be good or bad, the "known" cannot.[22]

Normative and Empirical Statements

I have spoken about the possibility of translating normative statements into empirical ones. For some philosophers there is no need for such a translation; they hold that "valuation is a form of empirical knowledge."[23] For others, however, transformation of a normative or evaluative statement into an empirical one, or of a sentence in the imperative mood into one in the indicative mood or, better still, in a conditional form, may be reassuring. Thus, "stealing is bad" or "thou shalt not steal!" can be translated into "if you steal, you will be despised by many." Likewise, "helping the poor is good" or "help the poor!" can be translated into "if you help the poor, you will feel good."

Moral Education

My denial of the attributes good or bad to particular pieces of knowledge, including ethical knowledge, was perhaps too rash. We con-

---

[21] For Carnap, "a value statement is nothing else than a command in a misleading grammatical form. It may have effects upon the actions of men, and these effects may either be in accordance with our wishes or not; but it is neither true nor false. It does not assert anything and can neither be proved nor disproved." Rudolf Carnap, *Philosophy and Logical Syntax* (London: K. Paul, Trench, Trubner, 1935), p. 24.

[22] This statement is not the same as—but may remind us of—the famous line in *Hamlet*: "There is nothing either good or bad, but thinking makes it so" William Shakespeare, *Hamlet*, Act 2, line 259.

[23] Lewis, *An Analysis of Knowledge and Valuation*, p. vii. Regarding aesthetic judgments, Lewis holds that "the value found in the experience is evidence of value in the object," though "it is always subject to possible correction by later experience" (p. 457). Of course this principle of permanent control (revisability) holds for all empirical propositions.

stantly read and hear about accusations that our educational system fails to instill in the minds of our youth an adequate appreciation of moral values, sufficient knowledge of what is right or wrong, good or bad. If moral education is called deficient, does this not mean that more knowledge of what is morally right would be "good"? Would this not, after all, justify our judging knowledge of moral values as morally good? Such knowledge of widely accepted moral values can be disseminated in a variety of ways, for example, in the teaching of religion, philosophy, history, social studies, literature, and other humanistic areas of knowledge. There are many beautiful stories, in literature and in history, which can impress the student not only through their relevance to his own life experiences and interests but also through their ethical connotations, and which can have effective and lasting influence on his actions and reactions. If education succeeded in giving most of the people a firm knowledge of right and wrong, it would surely be "a good thing." It would be good for the majority of the people; without hesitation one would consider it useful, beneficial to society. Still, I must leave it to the professors of ethics to decide whether their science[24] is "good" in a moral sense.

A Special Class of Knowledge?

With all this talk about ethical knowledge, one must wonder whether ethical knowledge should not have been given a place on the list I proposed as appropriate for the purposes of this book. Should it be regarded as a class of knowledge separate from the five that were enumerated? I do not think so. To the extent that ethical knowledge serves as a guide to action, it qualifies as *practical* knowledge. To the extent that it is knowledge of values actually recognized by others, but does not form a basis on which the knower judges his or their actions, it qualifies as *intellectual* knowledge. A treatise on ethics would be regarded by most of those who read it as conveying intellectual knowledge, though it may have a lasting influence on the value systems of some readers and thus contribute to the production of practical knowledge. Thus, as ethical knowledge is either intellectual or practical, it falls into either of two of the five classes included in the proposed scheme, and there is no place for a separate box labeled "ethical knowledge."

[24] "Nor is there good reason for refusing the adjective *scientific* to such works as Aristotle's *Politics* or Spinoza's *Ethics* and applying it to statistical 'investigations' or 'researches' that do not advance the understanding of anything." Morris R. Cohen, *Reason and Nature: An Essay on the Meaning of Scientific Method* (Glencoe, Ill.: Free Press, 1931), p. 89. (I have quoted this statement on an earlier occasion.)

CHAPTER 6

OTHER STANDARDS OF QUALITY

TRUTH, BEAUTY, AND GOODNESS, the triad of qualities more or less applicable to knowledge (in the sense of what is or may be known or conjectured), command the stage of philosophical discourse; but in less sophisticated, everyday parlance, a few additional qualities receive casual attention. These refer chiefly to knowledge disseminated by print media and electronic media of communication. I propose to examine a few pairs of opposites—serious versus lightweight knowledge, workmanlike versus shoddy knowledge, wanted versus unwanted knowledge—and a few special qualities, such as noncomprehended knowledge, forbidden knowledge, dangerous knowledge, and supposedly unwholesome knowledge.

HIGH-GRADE AND LOW-GRADE KNOWLEDGE

Two pairs of opposites can be distinguished under this heading: serious versus lightweight knowledge, and superior, workmanlike versus inferior, shoddy knowledge. The difference between these pairs of opposites is that the first refers to the level of intellective effort required, the second to the level of workmanship and care devoted to the product.

Serious versus Lightweight Knowledge

The distinction between serious knowledge and lightweight knowledge impressed me as so important that I incorporated it into the five-class scheme I adopted for inquiries needed in various parts of this book. The distinction between intellectual knowledge and pastime knowledge is meant to correspond to that between serious and lightweight knowledge.

Readers of books and sellers of books commonly contrast "light" reading with difficult or "heavy" reading; catalogues of phonograph records are divided into popular and classical music; opera houses in large cities refuse to include light operettas and musicals in their repertoires; museums and art galleries want to exhibit only "genuine" art to the exclusion of fake and cheap art; and so forth. These examples should clear me of possible charges that I am trying to impose my personal taste or an elitist standard of excellence upon a public that does not really care. To be sure, there are many audiences indifferent to the fare offered by the media (publishers, editors, theatrical producers, broadcasters, etc.) as knowledge designed to satisfy people's curiosity, their ambitions to learn, and their desires to be entertained. I submit, however, that the wide currency of the expressions used in my examples proves that these distinctions are actually made both by transmitters and by recipients of knowledge.

The line between intellectual and pastime knowledge is not hard and fast. The differences I have proposed as the characteristic ones lie in the attitude of the knower, in the accessibility of the knowledge, and in the effects of the knowledge on the knower. Most decisive for the distinction are perhaps the active questioning and intelligent concentration required in absorbing intellectual knowledge, in contrast to the passive reception of pastime knowledge. In addition, intellectual knowledge usually keeps its "cultural value" for longer periods, perhaps forever, whereas small-talk and pastime knowledge is only of ephemeral value.

To give an example of the difference, I may point to a comparison between chamber music and rock 'n' roll music. It is a serious strain to listen to and appreciate a difficult chamber-music composition, at least the first few times; even on repeated hearings, the typical listener will try to discover nuances in rhythm, in harmony, in counterpoint, which he has not taken in previously, or differences in interpretation by the performers. In contrast, few rock 'n' roll listeners will concentrate on the aesthetic form and patterns of the composition; the enjoyment they get from listening will not be an intellectual one, and probably not one subject to aesthetic analysis.

The choice of these extremes in musical knowledge has made it easier for us to differentiate between them. Had we chosen an "easy" symphony or a melodious opera and compared it with a popular march or a "cheap" operetta, we might have found it hard or impossible to make the difference stick and to draw a clear line between intellectual and nonintellectual knowledge. Here the reference to the "typical" listeners may not help us any longer in classifying the objects of knowledge and, to do it conscientiously, one would have to resort to an analysis of the "particular" listeners and their attitudes to the works presented. For a statistical study designed to show broad orders of magnitude, such resort to individual analysis is quite unnecessary; arbitrary distinctions according to "general opinions" on the aesthetic nature of the artistic offerings would not make much difference as far as aggregate quantitative estimates are concerned.

For wide ranges of the spectrum between the extremes, the assignment to one or the other class will cause few qualms. No one will question the judgment that Goethe's *Faust*, Kant's *Critique of Pure Reason*, Gibbon's *Decline and Fall of the Roman Empire*, Darwin's *On the Origin of Species*, and Einstein's *General Theory of Relativity* are all rather heavy stuff, surely not light reading. There will be similar agreement on putting Erich Segal's *Love Story*, Jacqueline Susann's *Valley of the Dolls*, Grace Metalious' *Peyton Place*, Zane Grey's *The Knights of the Range*, and Peter Benchley's *Jaws* into the category of light reading. The knowledge conveyed by the first group of books is well characterized as intellectual, whereas the books in the second category convey pastime knowledge. The same distinction holds for "general-interest" journals. Magazines like *The American Scholar* and *Commentary* supply intellectual knowledge, whereas magazines like *The Ladies' Home Journal* and *True Confessions* supply pastime knowledge.

Similar contrasts can be shown with regard to knowledge without words. Bach's *Goldberg Variations* and Berg's *Violin Concerto* are rather difficult music to appreciate, even by well-trained audiences. On the other hand, John Williams' popular music to the film "Star Wars" and Sinding's piano piece "Rustling of the Spring" are light music, pleasing to the untrained ear and listened to without effort. In the visual arts, Michelangelo's *Creation* and Rembrandt's *Nightwatch* demand concentration and exertion on the part of the viewer to be fully appreciated, whereas Maxfield Parrish's *September Morn* (a young nude coyly covering her female parts) can be taken in (and enjoyed by many) at the briefest glance. The characterization as intellectual knowledge and pastime knowledge, respectively, will hardly incite protests from those who know the works in question.

If we attempt to make estimates of the relative amounts society expends to produce the different types of knowledge—and we shall try to do so, for example, when we study the expenditures on books and newspapers, radio and television—we shall rely on "expert opinion" in classifying the contents of the presentations in question. This may look like a deviation from the methodological postulate of subjective interpretation, of "accepting" the knower's own evaluations of the knowledge. That postulate, however, does not mean reliance on empirical survey research; it involves no more than the construction of "ideal types" of knowers. The investigator makes his distinctions with what I like to call the aid of "imagined introspection." He asks himself how he would feel acquiring certain pieces of knowledge if he were the typical person acquiring it. To be sure, the investigator's imagination can hardly be free from the influence of his personal interests and tastes, though he will do his best to study and evaluate "representative" opinions and thus avoid serious biases due to his own background and experience.

Such problems of possibly biased evaluation and classification may arise several times in this study. Thus, when we come to the analysis of the mass media of communication we shall ask ourselves how their offerings are divided among the five types of knowledge which we distinguished, and to what extent the impression gained from "casual observation"—that by far the greatest part is pastime knowledge—is borne out by an examination of the contents. What in official statistics is called "entertainment"—the movies, theaters, operas, concerts, variety shows, etc.—will likewise be divided into intellectual and pastime knowledge, and my decisions may possibly be judged, by my critics, as high-brow or even snobbish. Similar differences in value judgment may show up in connection with education, since schools and other institutions of education produce knowledge of all five types—not merely practical and intellectual knowledge, as some idealists might prefer.

Workmanlike versus Shoddy Knowledge

All knowledge industries, especially educational institutions and mass media of communication, produce sometimes low-quality output. Every one of us who has attended school, or has children attending school, knows full well that many teachers are ineffective, badly prepared, or without the natural gifts required for good teaching, and that many textbooks are badly organized, poorly written, partly obsolete, and in some respects plainly wrong. Every one of us who reads a daily paper is aware of considerable amounts of misinformation disseminated in news items, feature articles, and editorials. All of us who listen to radio or watch television know that much of what is offered by these media is in poor taste, deficient in many respects, or downright shoddy. And, as readers of books and book reviews, we cannot fail to be cognizant of the fact that many of the products of the publishing industry are mediocre or even bad, no matter whether they purport to convey intellectual knowledge, practical knowledge, or merely pastime knowledge. How much of the total output of our knowledge industries falls below standards of acceptability, let alone standards of excellence?

Important as this question is, I see no way to answer it. Neither the masses who receive the deficient knowledge nor the experts who are appointed to evaluate its quality agree either on the standards by which it should be judged or on the degree to which individual products deviate from any specified standard. The same book that is highly praised by one reviewer is savagely attacked by another. A film is rated as a masterpiece by one critic and as trash by another. A stage play is recommended in one paper as the best of the year while other papers warn their readers against wasting their time seeing such tedious rubbish. Who is to be believed? And do we not know that some of the greatest music played by our symphony orchestras or in our opera houses was roundly rejected at its first performance, by the audiences as well as by the learned critics?

The conclusion is cogent: we have no infallible judges of the merits of works of art, scholarship, and even "scientific" research. We cannot accept the judgments of arbiters, be they appointed censors or self-appointed "cognoscenti." I shall not undertake to evaluate the superior or inferior quality of any knowledge disseminated by institutions or media and to assign cardinal indices, numerical ratings or letter grades. I may in some instances vent my idiosyncrasies, display my prejudices, show my respect for some intellectual achievements and my disrespect for others. But I shall not be so bold as to say what portion of our educational offerings is worthless and what percentage of the output of the print media or electronic media ought to be regarded as a dead loss.[1]

UNWANTED KNOWLEDGE

When I included "unwanted knowledge" in my scheme of classification, I was not thinking of the required subjects taken by unwilling pupils at schools and colleges. What these pupils dislike is not the knowledge but rather the effort of acquiring it. Thus, when I de-

---

[1] Strangely enough, some of my critics have complained about my disregard of the quality of the information conveyed, for example, by advertisements, especially the commercials on radio and TV. "Does the information contained in them really outweigh the misinformation?" asks Joseph A. Kershaw in a review of my 1962 book in Public Opinion Quarterly, vol. 27, no. 3 (Fall 1963), p. 508, and he chides me for simply adding the money costs of the advertisements regardless of their "positive or negative" contribution to the listeners' judgments in spending their incomes. At the same time he scolds me for distinguishing the intellectual and pastime character of the knowledge conveyed by phonograph records, although in these statistics I had some guidance from the industry's classification of "popular," "classical," "jazz" and "other" releases. I remain unconvinced; I shall not judge the truth value of advertisements and other literary communications or the aesthetic value of artistic communications, but I shall make an effort to categorize knowledge according to type and subject matter where it is possible.

scribed what I think is unwanted knowledge, I spoke of knowledge "usually accidentally acquired and aimlessly retained," though outside the interests of the knower.

Wanted by Some, Unwanted by Others

The existence of such unwanted knowledge will hardly be contested by anybody who has his radio or television program rudely interrupted by long-winded commercials, or who has to wade through pages of advertising in his newspaper or magazine in order to find the end of the story that began on an earlier page. Some of the jingles which advertise the wonderful qualities of this or that product on the radio or TV may stick to the musical memory of some unhappy listeners like wads of chewing gum to the shoe soles of unhappy pedestrians and resist all efforts to remove them. The inclusion of this unwanted knowledge in an economic study of the production of knowledge is justified by the very large expenditures incurred in the process. Of course, this knowledge is not unwanted by everybody; there are always a few of the recipients who want it as practical information aiding their decisions about what to purchase and where. It is unwanted knowledge for the majority of listeners because they either have already absorbed it or do not care. Incidentally, that those for whom it is "wanted" knowledge are small minorities is not an argument against its dissemination. Help to a few may well justify a minor inconvenience to many.

The trouble with this class of knowledge lies in the difficulty of estimating the proportions of the recipients who want and those who do not want to receive the messages in question. Assume, for example, that several thousands of people are at a large airport, some waiting to board a departing plane, others waiting for an incoming plane bringing the relative or friend they plan to meet. The loudspeaker announces in short intervals the airlines, flight numbers, and origins or destinations of landing or departing planes. Only between 100 and 300 persons are interested in any one announcement, whereas thousands of others are uninterested, disturbed, and perhaps annoyed listeners to many messages which are not for them, although they are impatient to hear the one about "their" plane. The ratio of wanted to unwanted announcements received may be 1 to 100, which means that each message is unwanted by 99 per cent of those exposed to it. Yet, for the 1 per cent, the information is crucial, and there seems to be no technique available by which this small minority can be reached and the unwilling recipients spared. Since the recipients of the unwanted knowledge know the importance of the information to the small minority, they tolerate the stream of for them irrelevant and annoying messages. Perhaps, though, they resent that the loudspeakers in the departure hall blare out the arrivals of incoming planes, and that the loudspeakers on the arrival side have to disseminate to people meeting their expected parties all of that unwanted knowledge about departing planes. Technology could provide for more discernment in the transmission of knowledge to presumably interested recipients.

Nuisance Commercials as the Price of Desired Gifts

There may be advertisements in newspapers and magazines, or on radio and television that are unwanted by virtually *all* readers, listeners, and viewers, respectively, but which are inserted by advertisers in the hope that they may hit at least a few potential buyers and thus attract some new customers and reinforce the loyalty of old ones. It is conceivable that the particular knowledge is unwanted by all recipients but, after all, it is its supplier who wants it disseminated and who pays for it. We cannot be sure the advertiser's hopes are justified, but we have reason to presume that he has duly considered the uncertain benefits and the certain costs of his decision to advertise. On this presumption, one may conclude that advertisements are, by and large, regarded worth their cost by those who pay for them. The nuisance to the unwilling recipients of this knowledge is a "third-party effect," or, in economic jargon, an "external diseconomy"; but it is possible that this injury or cost imposed on them is offset by a benefit in the form of a lower price, or even zero price, of the medium or of other, desired pieces of knowledge transmitted by the medium. For example, the newspaper or magazine may be sold at a much lower price than would be possible in the absence of revenue from advertising; likewise, highly desired musical or theatrical presentations on radio or television could not be offered without charge to listeners or viewers were it not for the payments the advertisers make to the broadcasting stations.

The described examples of unwanted knowledge are communications addressed, so to speak, "to whom it may concern," but they are so widely distributed that they reach many who are quite uninterested. Fortunately, our memories are quite selective and most messages which we see or hear but do not care to take notice of drop out of our memories almost instantaneously. If not retained but for seconds or minutes, they are in the nature of noise, audial or visual, undesirable but not producing "unwanted knowledge retained against our will." If the noise is loud, we resent it, but it produces no knowledge. Only if the message is "aimlessly retained" for a time does it represent unwanted knowledge.

Noncomprehended Knowledge

The distinction, which I made in the preceding discussion, between unwanted knowledge and mere noise suggests similar questions regarding noncomprehended and only partly comprehended messages. Had a noncomprehended message better be regarded as knowledge or only as noise?

A message fully comprehended but not retained in the memory for any length of time was designated as mere noise; if retained, though unwillingly, it was called unwanted knowledge. What about a message not comprehended but nevertheless retained in the memory for a significant length of time? If it is sheer gibberish, or in a foreign language which the recipient does not understand, or in the form of a code which he cannot decipher, but if he nevertheless retains it, deliberately or aimlessly, should this noncomprehended sequence of sounds or visual signs be regarded as noise or as knowledge? I have concluded that it merits the designation "knowledge." Indeed, great importance may be attached to knowledge encoded by a transmitter in a form unintelligible to an intermediary who passes it on to a third party who can decode it.[2]

An imaginative reader will quickly think of spy stories in which the spy wants to send a secret message to some agent through an intermediary who is not supposed to know the decoded information and must commit it to his memory in the form not comprehensible to him. The sequence of sounds he has to learn, retain, and finally to reproduce for the appointed ears is surely knowledge to all parties including the noncomprehending middleman.

The messenger carrying in his head a nondecoded message is not the only example of a possessor of noncomprehended or only partly comprehended knowledge. The soprano singing German *lieder* by Schubert and Schumann in a recital in a concert hall or salon may be another case of a person having memorized sounds which she fails to comprehend fully but undertakes, more or less successfully, to reproduce for a more, or even less, understanding audience. I remember a singer who learned to perform a song in Japanese without knowing the meaning of the words. And surely many of us are aware of the fact that thousands of people of all ages, as members of religious congregrations, know prayers and hymns in Latin or Hebrew which they have learned, have committed to memory, and faithfully reproduce on specified occasions, without comprehending precisely

---

[2] Specialists in information science make fine distinctions between data, signals, information, and knowledge. These distinctions probably have their place in the analyses in which they are used. They are not relevant for my purposes.

(or even vaguely) what they know. Yet it surely is part of their stock of knowledge.

I see no good reason for creating a special class for noncomprehended or partly comprehended knowledge. It may fall into any of the five classes enumerated in my scheme. It may be practical, intellectual, pastime, spiritual, or unwanted knowledge. The fact that it is not fully, if at all, comprehended by the knower may not be ascertainable by an outside observer. Hence, a statistical investigation attempting to assess the part of noncomprehended knowledge in the total stock or distribution of knowledge does not seem to be feasible.

RESTRICTED OR FORBIDDEN KNOWLEDGE

In the introductory chapter of this book, I casually referred to the widespread tendency of publicists to speak of knowledge as a good thing of which never too much can be had; at the same time it has been argued that there are some kinds of knowledge the dissemination of which "ought" to be restricted or forbidden by authorities, governmental, religious, or parental. In other words, some knowledge has been deemed to be bad—either for those who acquire it or for others, who may suffer some ill effects of acts by those who have acquired it. The motivation to restrict the acquisition or dissemination of "dangerous" knowledge is, accordingly, either of the sort "don't read this book and don't look at these pictures, because it's bad for you (for your mental or physical health)" or of the sort "these publications and pictures should not be read or viewed, because they will lead those exposed to them to actions injurious to others."

The Victims of Dangerous Knowledge

Who are these "others," who are to be protected from the effects of possible acts by recipients of dangerous knowledge? One may think of a variety of possible victims: innocent people suffering from acts of violence incited by exposure to such knowledge; men in power (in government, church, or public institutions) who may suffer from acts of disobedience or violence induced by the dissemination of antisocial (or antiestablishment) knowledge; groups in society who may suffer from prejudice, intolerance, or acts of repression fostered by biased, derogative, or hate-inspiring expositions of knowledge, warranted or not; people whose property, health, or life may be jeopardized by armed forces in war or revolution and by terrorist bands who have learned to exploit new technological knowledge for making and using more destructive, more deadly weapons; unknown numbers of people in the future who might be attacked by escaped microbes or other organisms produced in experiments of gene-splicing (DNA recombinants), organisms against which the life sciences may be unable to develop effective mechanisms of protection; unknown portions of the members of future generations who might be incurably deformed as a result of gene mutations induced by still only vaguely known ecological developments (atmospheric or other) in the course of searching for, or applying, novel technologies.

All these actual or hypothetical dangers ascribed to the creation and dissemination of various kinds of knowledge have been widely discussed, and most of them taken very seriously, in scientific, academic, political, juridical, and journalistic quarters. They have given rise to proposals or adoption of measures designed to suppress or restrict pornographic, subversive, and heretical communications, and to regulate research and teaching in astronomy, anatomy, nuclear physics, biophysics, genetics, demography, and various other social sciences. I cannot afford the space for discussions of all sorts of forbidden, restricted, or discouraged knowledge, but I shall single out for special attention two broad categories: allegedly unwholesome knowledge, which may wreak its presumed injuries on society gradually, and inflammatory or explosive knowledge, which may have its presumed destructive effects in a sudden burst or outbreak.

Unwholesome Knowledge

The two major candidates for restriction (or suppression if this were possible) as unwholesome knowledge are subversive communications and obscene communications—more concretely, dissident and pornographic literature, graphics, and films.

The authorities have been zealous in their attempts to stop the distribution of such presumably dangerous knowledge, dangerous chiefly because it might undermine the authority of the authorities concerned. Their attempts have been only partly successful. The most draconic punishment of producers and distributors of subversive literature has not completely silenced the dissidents nor stopped the political underground press in countries under authoritarian regimes. Likewise, even the harshest measures by church authorities, state legislatures, and local police have not stopped the under-the-counter sale of pornographic books and magazines.

This is not the place to discuss the constitutional, legal, political, and philosophical issues concerning freedom of speech and freedom of the press. The point to stress is that in most countries, even where guarantees are written into their constitutions, the governments do not honestly believe in these freedoms. It is easy to understand why a ruler, desiring to stay in power, is determined to silence those who speak out against him in the hope of subverting his regime. It is not quite so easy to understand why governments are so hostile to the production and distribution of pornography. Where secular and religious authorities collaborate, attempts of the former to suppress pornography can be understood as a scheme of mutual assistance: the state helps enforce the teachings of the church and expects the church in return to support the power of the state. But why should the state continue to enforce the churches' ban on recreative sex where the state has become largely independent of the church? The explanation is possibly in terms of a cultural lag: popular beliefs cultivated during thousands of years do not disappear when the direct control exercised by the expounders and persistent reinforcers of these beliefs declines or disappears. Large and highly vocal groups continue to demand that the state protect its citizens, especially the younger ones, from sinful knowledge which encourages them to seek sexual gratification for pleasure instead of procreation.

To be sure, there are also other motives behind the opposition to erotic realism and pornography. There is, for example, a widespread belief that masturbation is unhealthy[3] and, hence, that any reading matter or pictorial presentation that stimulates sexual self-gratification conveys unwholesome knowledge. The theory that indulgence in solitary sex is unhealthy has been contradicted and refuted by psychologists and physiologists but still dominates the thinking of the masses. Hence, there is a strong popular demand that the health of the people be protected from exposure to titilating, sexually arousing pictures and reading matter.[4]

---

[3] The Oxford Dictionary gives "self-abuse" as the meaning of masturbation.

[4] I suspect that the two major groups who want to ban pornography, the one because it incites "sinful" conduct, the other because it incites "unhealthy" conduct, overlap so extensively that they are in effect only one group. That is to say, among irreligious people—persons who care little about religion, sin and salvation—probably few can be found who want to censor or prohibit pornography. This statement should not be taken as an argument against religion or religiously inspired opposition to the distribution of "filth," "smut," and "hard porn." It is intended, instead, to encourage research on the sources of the popular pressures for the prohibition of pornographic materials. The techniques of survey research could adequately provide the answers. We ought to know whether the attribution of unwholesomeness to this sort of knowledge is conditioned by religious, physiological, psychological, or criminological beliefs. After we find out, the various hypotheses can be examined with greater clarity and honesty than is possible when the arguments are confounded.

Obscene Knowledge and Pornography

This may be the place to clarify the semantic relation between obscenity and pornography.[5] Both words have come to be used to denote the reactions of readers, viewers, or listeners: obscene is what offends them, pornographic is what arouses them sexually. These are highly unsatisfactory word usages because they refer to entirely personal responses. What is offensive to some may be acceptable or even pleasing to others; what is sexually arousing to some may leave others cool. It depends on family background, religious attitudes, education, experience, intelligence, age, and other factors, including mood and other momentary conditions, whether a given description of sex acts, sex fantasies, or sex organs leads to a person's sexual arousal. To rely on the personal sensibilities of juries and judges, police officers and magistrates is to let judicial decisions be determined by subjective states of mind rather than objective facts. If definitions are to be "nonloaded" they have to remove the emotional connotations of the words "obscenity" and "pornography"; these words have to be defined, not in terms of effects on, or reactions of, people, but in terms of what they are: descriptions of matters related to certain human functions normally performed in privacy.[6]

Whether pornography has a psychological effect on a particular reader or viewer in his capacity as an appointed or self-appointed arbiter or censor is one thing; it is quite another thing whether pornography has objectively observable effects on masses of readers or

[5] The etymology is clear. Obscene is derived from the Latin preposition ob (or obs) and caenum, which means dirt; pornography from the Greek words pornè, which means harlot, and graphos, which means drawn or written. Thus, obscene means dirty, but is used chiefly to mean indecent, grossly offensive. Pornography means literally "description of the life, manner, etc. of prostitutes and their patrons." (The quoted words are from the Oxford English Dictionary.)

[6] An official commission, reporting in 1970, tried to solve this terminological problem in a different way: "Some people equate 'obscenity' with 'pornography' and apply both terms to any type of explicit sexual materials. Other persons intend differences of various degrees in their use of these terms. In the commission's report, the terms 'obscene' or 'obscenity' are used solely to refer to the legal concept of prohibited sexual materials. The term 'pornography' is not used at all in a descriptive context because it appears to have no legal significance and because it most often denotes effect. The report uses the phrases 'explicit sexual materials,' 'sexually oriented materials,' 'erotic,' or some variant thereof to refer to the subject matter of the commission's investigations; the word 'materials' in this context is meant to refer to the entire range of depictions or descriptions in both textual and pictorial form—primarily books, magazines, photographs, films, sound recordings, statuary, and sex 'devices'." Report of the Commission on Obscenity and Pornography, September 30, 1970 (New York: Bantam Books, 1970), p. 5, note 4.

viewers as members of society, for example, inciting them to engage in patently antisocial actions, such as rape or child molestation.[7] Only the second question should matter in deciding whether the legislature ought to prohibit or penalize the dissemination of pornographic knowledge. The question whether a causal relationship exists between exposure to pornography and engagement in sexual assault cannot be answered by merely anecdotal "evidence" and expert impressions (prejudice). The answers must be sought in empirical research, and they have thus far been negative.[8]

The widespread belief regarding supposedly injurious effects of pornography on private or social conduct has been characterized as a "patriarchical hysteria" and illuminated by the following observation: "We know of no case where any juror or judge has admitted that he found material erotically stimulating or a stimulus to irregular conduct; on the contrary, the expression of concern is always that someone else or some other class of people will be corrupted."[9] This observation is quite astute in recognizing that the would-be censor, proscriber, and avenger of pornography regards himself as guardian of society against the weaknesses of other people, who, less virtuous or fortitudinous than he, would, by reading or viewing erotic and sex-oriented materials, develop into dangerous criminals. The quoted comment, however, is poorly formulated in that it speaks of a stimulus to "irregular conduct." What is irregular to some may be regular or even wholesome to others. To be relevant to public policy, the fears and warnings should be of rape, child molestation, torture, killings—not of deviant sex practices among consenting adults.

---

[7] Needless to say, "abnormal sex acts" between consenting adults are neither injurious to society nor encroaching on the freedom of any of its members. That many persons judge such conduct to be a sinful or disgusting abomination does not make it antisocial.

[8] "In sum, empirical research . . . has found no evidence to date that exposure to explicit sexual material plays a significant role in the causation of delinquent or criminal behavior among youth or adults. The Commission cannot conclude that exposure to erotic materials is a factor in the causation of sex crime or sex delinquency." Report, p. 32. A dissenter from the majority report preferred to rely on authority. Among others, he quoted St. Paul and J. Edgar Hoover, the director of the Federal Bureau of Investigation. See Report, pp. 616 and 637, respectively. The majority of the commission had guarded itself against such dissenting views: "It is no longer necessary to rely on expert opinion alone. Several empirical studies are now available to inform discussion regarding the relationship between erotic material and antisocial behavior among minors." Report, p. 258. The same conclusion was reached regarding adults.

[9] Quoted from Peter Michelson, "An Apology for Pornography," in Douglas A. Hughes, ed., Perspectives on Pornography (New York: St. Martin's Press, 1970), p. 63.

Erotic Knowledge and Intellectual Freedom

In arguing the case for freedom of speech, of the press, and of the reading, listening, and viewing public, we probably should make some distinctions among different media of communication: books, magazines, sculptures, pictures, motion-picture films, burlesque shows, so-called live shows (live sex shows), and television. The case for freedom is strongest when the allegedly unwholesome knowledge is transmitted through the printed word, especially in books. No one whose sense of propriety is offended by erotic literature or explicit description of sex has to read the "obscene" books. If adolescents acquire such books, perhaps we ought to welcome the chance that they may develop an appreciation of books and join the small "elite" of book readers.

The case is not so strong for pornographic articles in magazines, and much weaker for entire magazines devoted to explicit sex, especially because of their multimedia approach—the marriage of words and pictures, so much more appealing to those who like to avoid the effort of reading but are prepared to do a little of it when lured by salacious or erotogenic pictures. Still, the case for freedom is stronger than that for governmental restriction, especially because the restrictions cannot be enforced except in a brutal police state. In the case of motion pictures, one may argue for an exclusion of children and youngsters, a restriction that can be enforced without undue cost in resources and freedom. No strong case can be made for antipornographic restrictions in theatrical performances—the stage, burlesque shows, and live shows. Youngsters can be kept out without much difficulty, and prudish adults can stay away.

The case against pornography is strongest in television broadcasting, because in this medium it is practically impossible to keep it from children and immature youngsters. Moreover, if there is not a multiplicity of TV channels available, unwilling adults without sufficient strength of character may be exposed to what they do not *choose* to view but *have* to view because they cannot bring themselves to turn off their TV.

The public's demand for pornographic materials has been enormous, and supply, whether permitted or prohibited under the laws of the countries at various periods, has sought to meet the demand. This has been true in all civilized societies from antiquity to the present. The *Register Librorum Eroticorum*, compiled by Rolf S. Reade (Alfred Rose) and published in London, 1936, lists more than 5,000 English, French, German, and Italian titles, not including "the vast amount of ephemeral erotica in the shape of pamphlets, drawings, photographs, films, postcards, and the like, which have formed the stock-in-trade of the commercial pornographer since Victorian times."[10] The size of the pornographic business at the present time will be discussed in Volume V. The belief that repressive actions by government (Federal, State, or local) can be effective is utterly naive; such actions lead to waste of public funds, neglect of really important public services, and infringements of the freedom of the press that is essential to a free society. The well-meaning fighters for chaste and clean morals had better learn to recognize that "erotic realism and pornography . . . fulfill certain functions and answer basic needs in the human psyche."[11]

Prior to a recent decision of the Supreme Court of the United States, the dissemination of explicit sexual materials had been regarded as protected by the Free Speech Guarantee of the Constitution except when they were found to (1) appeal to the prurient interest, (2) exceed the standards of candor in the representation of sexual matters, and (3) be "utterly without redeeming social value." In a decision in 1973, a work was defined as criminally obscene if, taken as a whole, it was found to (1) appeal to the prurient interest, (2) portray sexual conduct in a patently offensive manner and (3) be lacking in any serious literary, artistic, political, or scientific value. "Patently offensive" were representations of ultimate sexual acts, masturbation, excretion, and lewd exhibition of genitalia. The other criteria were to be assessed in terms of "community standards"—though it was not said whether community referred to a geographic subdivision of the United States or the country as a whole. These criteria allow judicial assessments to be determined by the degrees of prudishness and bigotry of the particular juries.

It is well known that unquestionably scientific treatises, such as the Kinsey Report or the studies by Masters and Johnson, have been bestsellers, not because of the scientific character of the findings, but because of the sexual stimulation which most of their readers expected from these works. The enormous popularity of such literary masterpieces as John Cleland's Fanny Hill, D. H. Lawrence's Lady Chatterley's Lover, and Henry Miller's Tropic of Cancer—all of which had been banned in English-speaking countries until the 1960s—is not due to the graphic pictures of social conditions at various times or places which they provide, or to the excellence of their

[10] H. Montgomery Hyde, A History of Pornography (London: Heinemann, 1964), pp. 14-15. The number of titles has probably been multiplied many times between 1936 and 1975.

[11] Hughes, Perspectives, p. 15.

style, but rather to their erotic contents.[12] As far as the local community standards are concerned, the correlation between these and religious attitudes is probably so close that one must wonder how supporters of the separation between church and state can accept the primacy of local sensibilities over freedom of the press.

Reflection on the criteria by which legitimate pornography is separated from illegitimate pornography raises several hard questions. Regarding the deference to community standards despite evident regional differences in the degree of liberation from Victorian fig-leaf mentalities, one must ask why the same knowledge of particular subject matters deemed to be harmless in New York should be condemned as unwholesome and dangerous in Tennessee? (Are inhabitants of Memphis more easily incited to rape?) Regarding the attestation of scientific value of a work that includes explicit descriptions of sexual matters, one must ask why such descriptions are less unwholesome to the reader if they are offered with an appropriate admixture of scientific jargon and statistical tables than if they are served unblended? (Is the same total of erotic content less harmful if taken with scientific soda water than if taken straight?) Regarding the attestation of artistic value of a sexually explicit drawing, one must ask whether the implicit incitement to acts dangerous to innocent victims is really reduced by the picture's artistic design. (Can many of the rapists and child molesters distinguish between great art and vulgar illustration?)

If pornographic knowledge were to constitute a "clear and present danger" to society, its suppression could be justified; but there has been no conclusive evidence to that effect.[13] To rule on the legitimacy or illegitimacy of sex-oriented literary or pictorial presentations on the basis of arbitrary standards of tastes, morality, sensibility, enlightenment, and similar subjective criteria is incompatible with the principles of a free society. Those who dislike pornography can avoid the offensive books, pictures, and magazines. Those who like it should not be barred from reading and viewing what gratifies their tastes and desires. Incidentally, we may remember that the types of knowledge distinguished in the classification scheme pro-

---

[12] A literary masterpiece, James Joyce's *Ulysses*, was also among the forbidden works in England as well as the United States because of the "obscenity" of certain passages and of its "coarse" language. It was only in 1933 that the American courts legalized its imports, publication, and sale. I did not include the work with the three mentioned in the text, because its appeal to the reader was not due to the explicitness of the language, though the notoriety of its "illegality" may have contributed to the sales volume.

[13] This is the essence of the dissenting opinion of Judge Frank in the 1956 case of Philip Roth, the author of *Portnoy's Complaint*.

posed for this book are basically characterized by the knower's own attitude toward the knowledge he acquires or possesses. If the principle of subjective evaluation of the stock and flow of knowledge is applied also to the appraisals of its quality, the judgment that particular kinds of knowledge are unwholesome to him is reserved to the knower; it is none of the business of the authorities.

Inflammatory or Explosive Knowledge

Whereas subversive and pornographic knowledge are feared by the authorities and by public opinion chiefly as unwholesome, as poison slowly debilitating the body politic and society at large, other areas of knowledge are feared for their possibly inflammatory or explosive effects. Indeed, only if acquisition and dissemination of any kind of knowledge can be shown to constitute a clear and present danger will a believer in the freedoms of speech, research, and teaching concede that restrictions are at all legitimate.

The first of three examples offered here of interferences with academic research and teaching is highly questionable on precisely this ground. Some members of the academic community, chiefly students but also some professors, have tried, through intimidation by a variety of means, to discourage genetic research on suspected race differences in mental ability. The discouragement of such research is defended because its findings, however tentative, could reinforce racial prejudice and might be used in support of prejudicial racial policies.[14] But why should such prejudices be feared since "error of

[14] The following quotation from an editorial on "Social Determinism and Behavioral Genetics," by Bernard D. Davis, Science, vol. 189 (26 September 1975), p. 1049, may help us understand the background of the controversy:

Unfortunately, the idea of genetic diversity has encountered a good deal of resistance. Some egalitarians fear that its recognition will discourage efforts to eliminate social causes of educational failure, misery, and crime. Accordingly, they equate any attention to genetic factors in human behavior with the primitive biological determinism of early eugenicists and race supremacists. But they are setting up a false dichotomy, and their exclusive attention to environmental factors leads them to an equally false social determinism.

Ironically, this opposition parallels that of theologians a century ago: both saw the foundations of public morality threatened by an implication of evolution. But neither religious nor political fervor can command the laws of nature. One might accordingly expect scientists, knowing this very well, to encourage the public to accept genetic diversity—both as an invaluable cultural resource and as an indispensable consideration in any approach to social equality. . . .

To be sure, in behavioral genetics premature conclusions are all too tempting, and they can be socially dangerous. Moreover, even sound knowledge in this field, as in any other, can be used badly. Accordingly, some would set up lines of defense against acquisition of the knowledge, rather than against its misuse. This suggestion has wide appeal, for the public is already suspicious of genetics. It

opinion may be tolerated where reason is left free to combat it" (Thomas Jefferson)? Is there really a clear and present danger of a violent outburst, a violent confrontation apart from one organized by the very same people who oppose the controversial opinion? The actual danger is not of a violent response by those who may be persuaded by the findings presented by the unpopular researchers, but of violence threatened by groups unwilling to tolerate statements of disliked opinions—statements they may not even have read but which they prefer to have suppressed rather than combatted by reasoned argument.

The second example of proposed restrictions on scientific inquiry relates to "recombinant DNA" research. (DNA stands for dioxyribonucleic acid.) A set of safety guidelines for the conduct of federally financed experiments "involving recombinant DNA molecules" has been formulated, but a coordinated effort is being made to obtain federal legislation imposing guidelines on all such research, or even to stop it altogether. The fear is that the techniques may be usable for genetic engineering, deliberate modification of the genes of complex organisms, including man. Another fear is that new microorganisms may be developed in the course of experimentation and might "escape" and attack the human body, which is not constituted to defend itself against them.[15] Such fears are exploited by sensation-seeking journalists and popularity-seeking politicians. Biological researchers are still hopeful that they will be able to prevent the enactment of unduly restrictive regulations.[16]

---

recognizes that earlier, pseudoscientific extrapolations from genetics to society were used to rationalize racism, with tragic consequences; and it has developed much anxiety over the allegedly imminent prospect of genetic manipulation in man. . . .

[15] An appeal for a temporary moratorium on experimental DNA research was signed by a group of scientists that included James D. Watson, who had shared a Nobel Prize for his work on the structure of DNA. He later conceded that "The vision of the hysterics has so peopled biological laboratories with monsters and super-bugs that I often feel the discussion has descended to the realm of a surrealistic nightmare." Quoted from *The New York Times*, Sunday, July 31, 1977.

[16] Several lessons of history should warn against exaggerated optimism of progressive scientists. To secure a sober judgment of the strength of prohibitionism in teaching and research we need not go back to the trials of Galileo; it suffices to recall that during the lifetime of most of us the teaching of biological evolution was forbidden by law in some States of this country, and that we can always count on some excessively cautious scientists to lend their support to the prohibitionists. Even Isaac Newton decided against publishing some of his findings because he thought that some knowledge was not to be communicated "without immense damage to the world." See Betty Joe Teeter Dobbs, *The Foundations of Newton's Alchemy or The Hunting of the Greene Lyon* (Cambridge: at the University Press, 1975), p. 195. The fact that Charles

The third example of proposed restrictions on research, development, and dissemination of knowledge is probably the best known, best documented, and perhaps also the most reasonable. It stems from the fear that mankind has been developing the technology to destroy itself, and that only the strictest control over that technology can prevent the final catastrophe. When research and development concerning the hydrogen bomb was ordered, some of the most distinguished physicists—Robert Oppenheimer most notoriously—argued against that undertaking. When the United States had the monopoly of knowledge of this most destructive of all weapons, it did its utmost to prevent or delay the spread of that technology to other countries. Yet it did not take very long before four other countries had developed their nuclear technology and the capacity to produce hydrogen bombs. As long as only the largest and most powerful countries possessed the bombs, one could hope that the principle of mutual deterrence would save the world by keeping each of the bomb-owning countries from ever considering a "first strike." However, as the number of countries with the capacity to make their own bombs increases, reliance on the principle of mutual deterrence becomes questionable. But the worst of all dangers lies in the possibility that terrorist groups might come into possession of atomic bombs. They could hold up the world for ransom and, in order to appear credible and be sufficiently feared, they might put their bombs to use.

Proliferation of the knowledge to make nuclear devices for nonpeaceful purposes is regarded as the greatest threat to humanity. Here, then, is a case where knowledge is of immense danger to nations and to civilization.

Darwin delayed by twenty years the publication of his most important theories on natural selection is indicative of the inhibitions of a scientist whose findings may subvert the teachings of the authorities.

CHAPTER 7

NOTIONS OF NEGATIVE KNOWLEDGE

IS THERE SOMETHING that should be called *negative* knowledge? If so, what is it?

Accepted Knowledge Negated by New Knowledge

Some who have suggested the term "negative knowledge" want it to mean erroneous knowledge, or knowledge which has proved false or will prove false when properly tested.[1] Others have used the term in a different sense, namely, to refer to knowledge that negates propositions previously or potentially held, by themselves or by others. These are just two of a much larger family of notions that may somehow deserve designation as negative knowledge. I shall first introduce, and then discuss, several members of this family: erroneous knowledge, contradicted knowledge, contradicting knowledge, obsolete knowledge, alternative knowledge, rejected knowledge, inadequately supported knowledge, questionable knowledge, uncertain knowledge, vague knowledge, illusive knowledge, confusing knowledge, and knowledge fertile of negative predictions.

Frank Knight, the well-known philosopher-economist, once quoted approvingly a humorist's dictum to the effect that "It ain't ignorance that does the most damage, it's knowing so derned much that ain't so."[2] If I know, or believe I know, something that in actual fact is not so, my knowledge is erroneous, or "negative." But on whose authority or on what evidence can I say that "in actual fact it is not so"? Either *you* know better and consider *my* knowledge false or I myself will find out later that I was in error. In the first case we are faced with two inconsistent knowledge claims; in the second, with a prediction that I "shall find out" or, alternatively, a postdiction that my previous knowledge-belief was in error. If we think that the term "negative knowledge" helps characterize these situations or sequences, we have to choose which of the two contradictory pieces of knowledge better deserves to be called negative: the previous one, which at one time I considered a (positive) part of my stock

---

[1] I am indebted to Kenneth Boulding for an interesting correspondence on this point.

[2] Frank H. Knight, "The Role of Principles in Economics and Politics," *American Economic Review*, vol. 41 (March 1951), p. 5.

of knowledge, or the new knowledge claim, which contradicts or negates the previous one. If the negation eliminates a part of my stock of knowledge, perhaps it should be called negative. Is not my stock of knowledge reduced now that I have to discard a part of it? Does not the new knowledge, which negates the previous one, compel me to make a subtraction from the minuend (the quantity to be diminished), and, therefore, does it not constitute the subtrahend, the negative magnitude?

Disproved and Suspended Knowledge

This, admittedly, is sheer quibbling. It does, however, lead to the question whether accepted knowledge becomes nonknowledge when it is successfully contradicted or whether it merely becomes another kind of knowledge. If something that has long been regarded as true knowledge is eventually shown to be false, it is not erased either from the memories of those who have believed it to be true or from the written or printed records in our collections and on our library shelves.

If the disproved fact, event, or theory belonged, for example, to the systematic body of knowledge called physics, it will be moved into another file, kept in the department of history of physics, another systematic body of knowledge. Seen from this angle, contradicted knowledge is not negative knowledge but only knowledge moved into another file. It may go into a file for historical knowledge or obsolete knowledge, or, perhaps, if many are not convinced by the disproof, it may go into a file for "pending matters." It has happened that some of the relegated pieces of knowledge have been moved back into an active file, not only from the pending file but also from the obsolete file.

Knowledge Losing Relevance

Not all obsolete knowledge consists of erroneous, contradicted, disproved knowledge; an even larger part may simply have lost its relevance or timeliness. Most of such now irrelevant knowledge was, at one time, true knowledge, neither erroneous nor irrelevant; but it related to circumstances that no longer exist. Much of it was practical knowledge, useful in guiding decisions and actions of a certain period. To give examples, knowledge of market conditions in, say, 1952, was of value to some businessman of the time, knowledge of technology important to an entrepreneur and producer, knowledge of highway conditions to a freight carrier, and so forth. Today, all this once timely knowledge is obsolete; it is irrelevant to businessmen, producers, and freight carriers of our day. However, there may be records of such obsolete knowledge in various documents, and it may be also in the memories of a few living persons. If someone wishes to call it negative knowledge, he is free to do so, but such nomenclature hardly contributes to our understanding of the types of knowledge.

Alternative Knowledge: Acceptance Pending

The reference to the logical opposites, contradicting knowledge and contradicted knowledge—which induced me to the quibble about which of the two had a better claim to the designation "negative"— presumed a rather simple situation: the successful negation of an erroneous proposition. In many instances, however, we are faced with alternative hypotheses with no strong clues as to their relative truth or probability values.

To know that something is either this or that or both constitutes knowledge, to be sure, but it is not sure knowledge—and it is not negative knowledge either. The hope, typical in such instances, is that one day, sooner or later, we shall find out; but for the time being, things are not settled and we must be satisfied that the knowledge of two or more possibilities is preferable by far to no knowledge at all.

Demoted Sciences

There is a great deal of rejected knowledge, possibly rejected forever, and no respectable scientist would dare to hold out any hope for its restoration or vindication. Among once widely accepted sciences, or systematic bodies of knowledge, which are now repudiated and in utter disrepute, are astrology, demonology, necromancy, and studies of supernatural phenomena.

Astrology, defined in the Oxford Dictionary as the "practical application of astronomy to the prediction of events, natural and moral," was classified as Natural Astrology, concerned with the foretelling of natural phenomena, and Judicial Astrology, concerned with judging the occult influences of the stars upon human affairs (Astromancy). Is this "negative" knowledge? Webster's calls it a "pseudo science." It is no longer taught in universities; and most of us smile at quaint acquaintances of ours who believe it highly significant that I was born under the sign of Sagittarius and that one ladyfriend is a Virgo and another a Libra. I have sometimes been scolded for my ignorance in these matters, which means that this is a body of knowledge taken seriously by many of our contemporaries and even (or, rather, consequently) by newspapers and magazines catering to the masses.

Knowledge of the influences of the stars upon human affairs is unscientific (which may not say much since the same adjective is used

to downgrade systematic knowledge of unquestioned truth or probability) and almost certainly erroneous. None the less, systematic
knowledge of astrological beliefs, for example, a history of astrology,
or anthropological and sociological studies of astromancy, cannot
reasonably be denied the status of scientific research projects (in the
international sense of science). They may be good science or bad science; for example, the historian may have relied on poor translations
of foreign documents, or the anthropologist may have misinter-
preted his evidence or overlooked the availability of relevant data.
Still, the research and the findings, and the knowledge derived from
the analysis, are scientific and positive, no matter how irredeemably
erroneous are the beliefs which the investigator set out to study.

Controversial Knowledge Claims

These considerations suggest comments on some fields of knowledge or ignorance regarded as science, pseudo science, semiscience,
or nonscience, depending on which of the protagonists or an-
tagonists you consult. Think, for example, of extrasensory perception (ESP) or parapsychology. The convenient operational definition
of science as any systematic body of knowledge studied (researched,
taught) at several reputable universities would give research on ESP
the status of science—centers for ESP research exist at several top-
rated universities—were it not for the heated arguments of a highly
respected and very vociferous opposition. Much of the evidence for
the defense has been exposed as untenable, in some instances even
as downright fake. But not all evidence has been toppled and, although the "prosecution" considers it weak and doubtful, the defense has not conceded defeat and continues to hold its ground. To
call research on ESP and parapsychology erroneous knowledge, or
negative knowledge, would be to take sides in an ongoing scientific
controversy, largely on the basis of sympathy and respect for particular members of the academic establishment.

   If some quixotic champions of "scientific method" should protest
and pronounce that the burden of proof is on those who make positive knowledge claims, not on those who contest them, one may rule
them out of order. The notion that only empirically verified propositions are accepted in a science has been found wanting (see above,
Chapter 5). Indeed, an overwhelming portion of the propositions accepted in nearly every empirical science is unverified and even unverifiable: they certainly cannot be verified on the basis of observation or observation statements.[3]

---

[3] According to Sir Karl Popper, theories are "never empirically verifiable." Karl R.
Popper, *The Logic of Scientific Discovery* (London: Hutchinson; New York: Basic
Books, 1959), p. 40. Even the neopositivist Rudolf Carnap retracted his early tenets

This recognition disposes of another candidate for the class of negative knowledge: inadequately supported knowledge. None but analytical knowledge—logical inferences from formal definitions, conventions, and postulates—is really supported by unquestionable evidence. There are degrees of confidence with which one accepts knowledge that has "proved its mettle,"[4] and degrees of significance of sentences judged by rules of correspondence between theoretical postulates regarding "unobservable entities" and sentences with "terms designating observables."[5]

Questionable Knowledge

One may see a difference between inadequately supported knowledge and questionable knowledge; the difference is at best one of degree, not a difference of kind. All empirical knowledge is questionable. The "principle of permanent control"—the recognition that all empirical knowledge is uncertain and the willingness to consider its potential modification or rejection—has been regarded as the sign of a truly scientific attitude.[6]

Vague Knowledge

Knowledge may be vague. To know something only vaguely is not the same as to recognize the essential uncertainty of any part, or all, of empirical knowledge. Uncertain knowledge, incomplete knowledge, and vague knowledge are rather different things, although in some instances and to some extent vagueness may be due to the uncertainty and incompleteness of knowledge. More often, however, vagueness is due to inadequate comprehension by the knower or to inadequate exposition on the part of those who communicated their knowledge to him. I have discussed these possibilities in the preceding chapter. Vague knowledge may be more or less useless for purposes of making decisions and taking actions, but it is nevertheless not without value where the knower's major concern is intellectual satisfaction, entertainment, or salvation. This too has been pointed out earlier: clear and accurate knowledge may be essential to a per-

---

regarding verification and confirmation: "It was clear that the laws of physics could not possibly be completely verified. . . ." and "we must abandon the earlier view that the concepts of science are explicitly definable on the basis of observation concepts." *The Philosophy of Rudolf Carnap*, edited by Paul A. Schilpp (La Salle, Illinois: Open Court, 1963), pp. 57 and 59.

[4] Popper, *The Logic of Scientific Discovery*, p. 33.

[5] Carnap, *The Philosophy of Rudolf Carnap*, p. 8.

[6] Felix Kaufmann, *Methodology of the Social Sciences* (New York: Oxford University Press, 1944), p. 53.

son who relies on it for practical action, but most knowledge is not of this type, notwithstanding the contrary opinions of pragmatists, be they active practitioners or thinking philosophers.

Superstitions

Some of my friends are particularly negative when it comes to superstition. For them, superstitions are false beliefs, errors, negative knowledge. I grant them that superstition is defined as erroneous and useless knowledge, but just which of a person's beliefs are superstitions is a matter of judgment. We know that many people, indeed, millions of people, act on the basis of knowledge which they believe to be valid and true but which we believe to be invalid or false. They may despise us for our disbelief, whereas we may condescendingly smile at, or seriously disapprove of, their naiveté, credulity, blind conviction. Let us recall that "one man's superstition is another's religion," that "one religion is as true as another," and that "superstition may be defined as constructive religion which has grown incongruous with intelligence."[7]

In these circumstances, the distinction between superstitions and religious beliefs becomes a matter of arbitrary judgment. I have accepted knowledge of God and salvation as spiritual knowledge and am willing to admit certain kinds of superstitions under that heading. Profane or mundane superstitions, not concerned with sacred beliefs, but earnestly believed with great conviction, constitute practical knowledge if the believers' decisions and actions are based on them. Some industries flourish thanks to superstitions. Large quantities of amulets and charms are purchased by people who believe in their power to avert accidents, disease, or other dangers.

Beliefs in the curative powers of certain drugs and patent medicines, despite warnings and condemnations by highest medical authorities, are knowledge acted upon by thousands of people. The prescription of supposedly effective, though probably poisonous, cancer cures, such as laetrile, is undoubtedly based on "knowledge of controversial probability value." If legislatures often side with the believers in knowledge claims which have been scientifically rejected, they may be motivated by (a) a sentiment for personal freedom ("everybody has a right to his foolishness"), (b) a feeling that the supposedly wrong ideas may after all be true, and (c) an inkling

---

[7] The first of these three quotations is of (to me) unknown origin; the second is from Robert Burton, *Anatomy of Melancholy*, Part 3, section 4; the third, from John Tyndall, "Science and Man" in *Fragments of Science*, quoted from John Bartlett, *Familiar Quotations*, edited by Christoper Morley (Boston: Little, Brown, 1950), p. 543.

that the majority of the voters may reelect legislators who let the people act on their beliefs or on particular beliefs.

I realize that the subject of superstition merits more discussion from several angles. From the point of view of my work, however, there is little or no reason to pass judgment on the knowers' or believers' warrants for their beliefs or knowledge. For my purposes, knowledge is what people think they know. Whether or not I agree with them is irrelevant for my study.

Illusive Knowledge

The next item on my agenda relates to illusive or deceptive knowledge, and I select optical illusions as my example. The subject of visual illusions is very old: the ancient Greeks wondered why the moon looks bigger near the horizon than it does high in the sky—even in our day different explanations coexist.

A favorite example is that of two parallel lines of equal length that are made to look different after different "arrows" are drawn at their ends.[8] The tentatively accepted theory posits an acquired mental ability, named "size constancy," which enables the brain to reinterpret the relative sizes of images on the retina of the eye. The brain can apply alternative interpretations about what sort of object the eye perceives. The unconscious rule of size constancy enlarges or reduces the perceived image. The mind's interpretations of the eye's perceptions may lead to corrections as well as to illusions. Can we always decide with assuredness whether the knowledge acquired from our "experience" is correct or illusive? Evidently not. Illusive knowledge is surely not negative in any meaningful sense.

Confusing Knowledge

Perhaps I have failed, in connection with some of the types of knowledge discussed, to differentiate sufficiently between current flows of knowledge—messages, information—and stocks of knowledge, knowledge recorded or remembered. If a subclass of "confus-

---

[8] This is the Müller-Lyer illusion, called after Franz Müller-Lyer, who showed it in 1889:

Line A looks shorter, probably because it is interpreted to be closer to the viewer than line B. Recent research on visual illusions has been done by Richard L. Gregory, Bionics Research Laboratory, University of Edinburgh. (Cited from a feature article by Boyce Rensberger, "What Optical Illusions Do to the Brain," New York Times, January 23, 1979, p. C3.—See also the interesting article by Edmond L. Wright on "Illusion and Truth," Philosophy and Phenomenological Research, vol. 39 (March 1979), pp. 402-432.

ing knowledge" is recognized as one of the class which some may regard as negative, one should probably intimate that it is more likely a new piece of information than an old part of the knowledge stock that may be confusing.

There are so many possible causes of confusion that any attempt at enumeration would be futile. Inconsistencies, contradictions, ambiguities, gaps, mutilations, technical noise, linguistic deficiencies, equivocations, and other sources of semantic noise are all possible causes of confusion. Some confusions may be attributable to the information source, the encoding and transmitting processes, others to the receiving and decoding processes and to deficiencies in the background knowledge of the message recipient. The problems alluded to in these expressions are treated in the theory of communication, on which more will be said in a later volume of this work.

Excluded Possibilities and Negative Predictions

I am coming to the last item on my agenda for the discussion of knowledge types qualified by the adjective "negative."

Karl Popper had shown that the conclusions to which theoretical knowledge can lead are eventually in the nature of prohibitions or exclusions that "forbid" the occurrence of certain kinds of events. A positive prediction tells that *only one* of several possibilities will be observed.

Following Popper's reasoning, Friedrich Hayek, in a methodologically important article, stated that some sciences can provide the basis for specific positive predictions, excluding all but one of a large number of possibilities, whereas other sciences may at best select a few alternatives as the most likely outcomes, and thus exclude the rest.[9] In some disciplines, however, even this may be outside the investigator's capacity to predict; he may have to confine himself to select one event, or a few, that *cannot* occur under the conditions specified. Such negative predictions, specifying what cannot occur or is most unlikely to occur, but allowing a very large number of possible outcomes to be realized, can be very important. To know that what others expect to result from certain actions will in fact not happen is the economist's most significant achievement, and to disseminate this negative knowledge may be his greatest contribution to society.

Frank Knight expressed the same view: "I do wish to stress the importance of negative conclusions, particularly in relation to ac-

[9] Friedrich A. Hayek, "Degrees of Explanation," *British Journal for the Philosophy of Science*, vol. 6 (1955), pp. 209-225.

tion, the advisability of not doing things that will make matters worse, and the fact that principles of economics do have in a high degree this unromantic sort of value."[10]

Conclusion

Having reviewed the various meanings and connotations attached to the expression "negative knowledge," I conclude that some of the types of knowledge to which it may refer can be given a negative, others a positive, evaluation; but in view of the semantic diversity, it is wiser to avoid using the term.

[10] Knight, "The Role of Principles," p. 5.

PART THREE

KNOWLEDGE AS A PRODUCT

IN THIS PART we are going to move closer to economic aspects of human knowledge. We have left behind us the issues that concern the theorists of knowledge, the language philosophers, and the professors of moral, political, and legal philosophy; we are now ready to look at knowledge as a product, as a result of economic activity. This examination is not a fullfledged essay either on the economics of knowledge or on the economics of information; but it is prerequisite to it.

Chapter 8   Choosers and Users of Knowledge

Chapter 9   Stocks and Flows of Knowledge

Chapter 10   The Economic Cost of Knowledge

Chapter 11   Transmission and Reception

Chapter 12   Consumption, Investment, Intermediate Product

Chapter 13   Uses, Value, and Benefits of Knowledge

Chapter 14   Knowledge Industries and Knowledge Occupations

CHOOSERS AND USERS OF KNOWLEDGE

WHO DECIDES what kinds of knowledge, and how much of each kind, are to be produced in the country? In the usual microeconomic model for market economies, the theorist has imaginary, idealized producers make the decisions about what and how much to produce, and these decisions are based on the potential salability of the product, that is, on their expectation that their product will meet the preferences of consumers (or intermediate producers). The producers' initiatives or, alternatively, their reactions to market signals are interpreted as being controlled by the consumers' free choices. Does such a model of decision-making apply to supply and demand in the "market" for knowledge?

Consumers' Choice, Entrepreneurial Initiative,
Political Decision

The customary model used by economic theorists in the analysis of an "industry" represents schematically a market in which would-be buyers and would-be sellers of the product trade with one another; as a result, prices for the products emerge, which give producers "signals" that guide them in their decisions as to what and how much to produce in order to profit from satisfying the effective demand of the consumers. This primitive, though in many cases useful, model does not easily, and surely not generally, fit the case of knowledge as a product. To be sure, one can conceive of the transmitters of knowledge as "supply," and of the recipients as "demand" in a market for knowledge; and this conception may be most suitable where the recipients pay for the service and where these payments cover the costs incurred by the transmitters. Where, however, the recipients pay either nothing or only a small part of the costs, and the transmitters cover their costs out of other revenues (say, taxes), the model of a free market for knowledge will be less helpful, or downright misleading.

Some part of all knowledge disseminated in this country can reasonably be said to be determined by the consumer's free choice and guided by "consumer's sovereignty." That is to say, there is some scope for profit-oriented decisions of entrepreneurs to produce knowledge (offer information) for sale to nonsubsidized buyers who follow their own preferences (sometimes informed, sometimes mis-informed, perhaps misled by advertising). Examples may be chiefly in the production and sale of books, certain kinds of information services, and instruments and appliances used in the reception of in-formation. A survey of all the branches of knowledge production may show, however, that knowledge produced for profit and sold to consumers in a free market is but a small part of the total.

For the greater part, the production of knowledge is not guided by the market mechanism. Much of the knowledge produced is not purchased by the consumer at a price but is offered to him free of charge. The largest item is the expenditure for schools, colleges, and universities, paid for chiefly by government, with smaller portions defrayed by philanthropists and parents; the contents of the teaching are determined in a complicated process by political bodies, lay boards, and professional educators. Another large item is the cost of research and development; in the United States, many of the projects are selected by the government, which often has paid more than half their total cost. Radio and television are mostly paid for by "com-mercial sponsors" in the United States, and by government in most other countries; the programs are chosen on the basis of considera-tions of (1) what the masses of listeners and viewers seem to like best and (2) what is thought to be good for them, the mixture of consider-ations varying between 2:1 and 1:2, depending on whether advertis-ing agents or government officers do the choosing. To what extent the recipients of knowledge—the "consumers"—actually influence the product—the knowledge transmitted by the suppliers in any of the mentioned branches of the "knowledge industry"—is difficult to decide. In any case, there is ample justification for investigators to question the opinions of the suppliers, or of those who give the specifications, concerning what the people want and what they "ought" to want or "would" want if they were better prepared to make their choices.

In many instances, business decisions are involved at both ends, demand as well as supply. When we hear the expression "con-sumer's choice" we first think of individuals and households con-sidering the purchase of goods and services for consumption, that is, for immediate satisfaction. Much information, however, is sought by business firms, which need it for the efficient management of their operations, that is, for productive purposes. They need to know the best sources of supply of equipment and materials, of funds and human resources; they need to know the best outlets for their prod-ucts, the requirements, preferences, and loyalties of their customers; and they need to know the best methods of organization and production. To reduce it to the simplest categories, they are seekers of knowledge of markets and of technology. Regarding the latter, not only are they eager to be apprised of the most up-to-date technology in their fields, but they also look out for novel techniques the use of which may give them a headstart over their competitors. This kind of knowledge will be produced, in the first place, by activities designated as research and development.

The role of the government in the knowledge sector of the economy is not easily described. If the government pays for the larger part of the expenditures for research and development, does it do so as a supplier of knowledge, as a buyer of knowledge, as a user of knowledge, or simply as a promoter of knowledge (that is, as a sort of sugar daddy of the producers and users of knowledge)? Since in most instances the government merely provides the finance for, but does not itself perform, the research and development work, whereas in some instances the performance of these activities is also done by governmental agencies, it is important to make a distinction and reserve the designation of *producer* of knowledge for the second set of circumstances. Where the R and D activities are undertaken to design or improve spacecrafts, ballistic missiles, military weaponry, and other defense items for use by the government, the question arises whether the government should be regarded as the *user* of the technological knowledge obtained. On the other hand, the hardware ordered by the government is manufactured by private American corporations; the manufacturer, not his customer, receives and uses the knowledge conveyed in the form of blueprints and detailed specifications. Hence, although the government pays for both the research and development which generate the technology and the manufactured hardware in which that knowledge is eventually embodied, the government is neither supplier nor user of the knowledge in question. Yet, the government is the chooser of the type of knowledge as it contracts first for the R and D and then for the manufacture of the engineered items.

The government supports also another range of research and development, where the initiative rests with the researchers. Groups of scientists affiliated with universities or other research organizations submit proposals to governmental departments or agencies which, if they approve of the projects, make grants in aid of the research proposed. The proponents formulate their projects in accordance with their own interests but also with a view to the acceptability to an appointed review panel, whose general preferences are usually known to the academic profession. Thus, the reviewing panel, which may be considered as an arm of the government (if not a part of the brain

of the government), has a twofold influence on the selection of research topics: through its past actions of approval or rejection, it influences the proponents in what they submit in their applications for
research grants; and then it evaluates the submitted projects and
recommends their acceptance or rejection. Thus, although the initiative in the selection of the new knowledge to be generated is private,
and the actual performance of the research is also in the private sector, government and the political considerations that ultimately
guide its actions are major factors in the choices made.

This discussion of knowledge generated by research and development work suggests another distinction, for which the classification scheme presented in Chapter 4 has not provided a special
place. We have to distinguish *new* knowledge from *existing* knowledge, but we must not forget that what is new today will no longer be
new tomorrow, and that what is new for some need not be new for
all.

Subjectively New and Socially New Knowledge

The last remark regarding the subjectivity of novelty calls for some
additional observations. The distinction between the production of
subjectively new knowledge—a process resulting in one or more
persons knowing what he or they had not known before—and the
production of *socially* new knowledge—a process resulting in a person (or persons) knowing what neither he (or they) nor anybody else
had known before—is important because society devotes increasing
amounts of resources to the latter (although the total spent on socially new knowledge is much less than the amount spent on communication and dissemination of existing knowledge). Most of the
efforts and funds allocated to the production of socially new knowledge—chiefly in the form of scientific and industrial research and
development—are designed to obtain generalizations about predict-
able effects resulting from specified acts under certain conditions.
Many of these generalizations are of enduring value. Some new
technological knowledge, pertaining to particular industrial products, may be of value only for a relatively short time. The same is
true with regard to some socially new knowledge of social phenomena or relations. For example, the findings of market research may be
relevant for a few weeks or months only; similarly, the results of investment analysis or financial research. It may, nevertheless, be well
worth while for people—households and business firms—to spend
large amounts of money on such activities or for the information obtained.

The reporting of news is a special case in the production of knowledge because it is doubtful whether even the first reporter—who has discovered that the particular event has taken place—is really the first who has obtained knowledge of it, if the event is one in which one or more human beings have taken part. For, evidently, the participants have had knowledge of their actions, sufferings, or other experiences before the first reporter discovered what happened. But the problem involved here is trivial and easily disposed of by resolving that the first who makes a report in communicable form be deemed to be the one who produces the socially new knowledge of the reported event. This first reporter will usually be a detective, a policeman, a "spokesman," an "authoritative source," a "usually reliable source," a newspaper reporter; it may be any sort of observer or analyst. In any case, the overwhelming part of the total cost of news-reporting lies in the phase of dissemination, not in the production of socially new knowledge. Thus, the work performed by the mass media of communication (newspapers, magazines, books, radio, television), as also the work performed by schools and other institutions of education, is essentially reproduction of knowledge, its production in new minds—that is to say, its transmission by "haves" to "have nots."

Knowledge as an Intermediate or a Final Product

One more distinction must be made, one that is essentially based on economic principles. Knowledge can be classified either as a final product or as a necessary requirement in the production of other goods and services. The class "knowledge as a final product" is subdivided into two subclasses, consumption and investment. For example, education and scientific research produce knowledge which one may wish to regard as investment, whereas the publication of comic papers and the performance of burlesque shows produce knowledge which one may prefer to regard as consumption. On the other hand, market research and financial analysis produce knowledge which will commonly be regarded as an intermediate product. Intermediate products share with most investment goods the significant fact that they are used in the production of other goods, but they differ significantly with regard to the time in which they are used: If they are used only in the future or if their use is spread over a time that extends into a distant future, they are treated as investment; if they are used immediately or in the near future and, thus, will not remain valuable beyond, say, a year or two, they are treated as intermediate products and, hence, as current cost of production of some final products.

This trichotomy, knowledge produced for consumption, knowledge produced for investment, and knowledge as an intermediate product used in the production of current output (and, therefore, a current cost of producing other things) will occupy us throughout this work. The discussion at this point has been merely preliminary; it will be elaborated later on.

CHAPTER 9

STOCKS AND FLOWS OF KNOWLEDGE

IN ECONOMICS a fundamental distinction is commonly made between stocks and flows, usually with reference to goods, to capital funds, to money. The distinction applies also to knowledge. At any moment of time, there is a stock of knowledge; during any period of time, there is a flow of knowledge.

As far as the stock is concerned, we should distinguish between knowledge on record and knowledge in the mind. *Recorded knowledge* may be written, printed, drawn, painted, or engraved on paper or other material, or encoded on disks, tapes, or other implements, for people to read, listen to, or decode in order to get it into their heads. Such recorded knowledge may be available to all interested persons or restricted to a selected few. *Knowledge in the mind* is in the memory of an individual person, in the memories of small groups of persons, or in the memories of many members of society.

As to the flows of knowledge, we should distinguish between *communication from transmitter to recipient* and a *continuing stream from a source to beneficiaries*, the former being a flow through space, the latter a flow at a rate per unit of time. The flows through space may be of three kinds: transmissions from persons to records, from records to persons, and from person to person without record. The flows per unit of time are expected to continue for a definite or indefinite period, though not necessarily in an unchanging quantity or at a constant rate.

The relation between stock and flow is similar but not the same with regard to the two flow concepts: regarding the flow through space, or communication, our attention will be chiefly on the possible increase in the recipients' stocks of knowledge (where the recipients may be nonhuman records or human minds), whereas, regarding the stream of knowledge at some rate per period, our attention will be on the valuable source (or stock) that yields the services in question (benefits) and on the investments made when beneficiaries use some or all of such services for building up valuable stocks of knowledge for future use or enjoyment.[1]

---

[1] An abridged version of this chapter was published in *Kyklos*, vol. 32, nos. 1-2 (1979), pp. 400-411, in honor of Gottfried Bombach. I later received helpful comments from Israel Kirzner, who directed my thoughts to the distinction between a flow of

Our main task in this chapter is to ask whether there are any ways to measure or estimate the magnitudes of the stocks and flows of knowledge.

The Stock of Recorded Knowledge

Various proposals have been made with regard to "measurements" of society's stock of recorded knowledge, mostly in the form of books and journals stored on the shelves of libraries. The essence of these measures is that they are in terms of physical units, such as volumes or titles. Counts of volumes and counts of titles lead to very different results, not only because one title may involve several volumes (especially in the case of reference works, journals, and other serials), but also because of the holding of duplicates, to some extent in any one library but mainly in the total of the existing collections (in the country or in the world). None of the title counts can cope with another problem of duplication: the coverage of the same bits of knowledge in different publications. Some scientometricians—if I may borrow Derek Price's term for measurers of scientific knowledge—have confined themselves to counting journal articles, especially in the natural sciences and technology. They argue that growth of knowledge in society is more meaningfully estimated by the number of articles than by the number of books, particularly on the assumption that scientific journals publish articles refereed for novelty and advancement of knowledge.

Whether estimates of the accumulated journal literature would be more indicative of the stock of recorded knowledge if the number of articles were counted, rather than the number of words, pages, issues, or volumes, is debatable. Is the very short article in which an experimental physicist or biologist reports on his findings an equivalent of a long article (of almost monographic length) in which a historian of science surveys the research achievements of decades or a theorist argues for a major change in a basic "paradigm" of his scientific discipline? This question may prove to be irrelevant if, over the years, the ratio of short to long articles has not changed very much. A similar question arises with regard to the number of issues per year. Perhaps the simplest kind of estimate would be in terms of volumes, assuming that the issues of a journal for any one year have been bound in one volume. Can we estimate the number of annual volumes of scientific and scholarly journals that would have accumulated on the shelves of a "universal library" that had not missed or lost a single publication?

knowledge as communication from transmitter to recipient and a continuing stream from source to beneficiary.

A Collection of Scientific Journals

The first two scientific journals, so we are told, were published in 1665: *The Philosophical Transactions* of the Royal Society of London, and the *Journal des Sçavans* [*Savants* in modern French], founded by Denis de Sallo in Paris. The growth in the number of journals published has been remarkably constant from about 1760 to the present, if we can accept the estimates of Derek Price.[2] If the growth rate is known and has really been constant, and if the number of journals published at present is known, a simple calculation can tell us the number of annual volumes of journals accumulated in a hypothetical universal library. The "ifs" in the preceding sentence unfortunately are counterfactual; for example, estimates of the number of "scientific periodicals" currently published varied, a few years ago between 25,000 and 100,000, a rather substantial variance.[3] Other estimates of the number of "scientific periodicals" came to 25,000 in existence between the years 1900 and 1921, and 60,000 between the years 1900 and 1960, which, however, includes those that had become defunct some time during that period.[4] Price proposed that we use a figure of 50,000 for the number of scientific, technical, and scholarly journals currently published in 1975.[5] The number of journals ever published would be much higher, because their mortality rate has been considerable. But, although many periodicals have been discontinued, new ones have been started, and the birth rate has exceeded the death rate. According to Price's estimates, the birth rate is roughly twice the death rate; if this relation has been stable over the decades and centuries, the number of journals alive must be about one-half the number of journals ever founded. Taking account only of the surviving scientific journals, Price, at one place, estimated that the number of journals published

[2] Derek J. de Solla Price, *Science since Babylon*, 2d enl. ed., 1975 (New Haven: Yale University Press [1st ed. 1961]), pp. 164-165.

[3] "Information Processing," *Encyclopaedia Britannica*, Macropaedia (1974), vol. 9, p. 568. Some of the variance is probably due to the ambiguity of the term "scientific," and some to the vagueness of the term "periodical." Scientific may mean a restriction to natural and technological sciences; periodical may include all sorts of serial publications, including conference reports, statistical and bibliographic services, newsletters and magazines, as well as regular journals.

[4] These numbers come from four consecutive editions of the *World List of Scientific Periodicals*. The journals published between 1900 and 1933 numbered approximately 35,000; those published between 1900 and 1950 numbered 50,000. The fourth edition (London: Butterworths, 1963) eliminated some 10,000 entries, because they were only of "social and commercial interest," but added some 20,000 new periodicals that were published between 1950 and 1960. The number of 60,000 for the period from 1900 to 1960 is therefore limited to the physical and biological sciences and technology.

[5] Price, in a letter to me, May 19, 1977.

would double every fifteen years. This would imply a compound rate of growth of 5 per cent a year. With the volume of journals increasing by 1/20 every year, the total number of volumes published since the beginning (that is, since the publication of the first journal) must be 20 times the number published now in one year.[6] If this number is 50,000, the total accumulation of volumes is 1,000,000.

Although the arithmetic of our question is simple, the census of the present population of scientific journals is rather complex. Price once had estimated the present population of surviving scientific journals to be 100,000; indeed he had claimed "an extraordinary regularity" in the growth of journals.[7] This estimate was far too high. The total number of "serials" listed in the ISSN Index (International Standard Serial Number) in 1975 was only about 70,000, and this included all sorts of serial publications—annual reports, bulletins, circulars, directories, regular and occasional newsletters, preliminary and final reports, conference programs, proceedings—besides journals. It included, moreover, all sorts of subjects—clothing-trade fashions, clubs, colleges and alumni, food and food industries, gardening, giftware and toys, hobbies, hotels, interior design, jewelry, leather and fur industries, patents, pets, real estate, shoes and boots, sports and games, theater, tobacco, travel and tourism, and women's interests—besides science and technology. To be relevant to scholarly (scientific, technological) journals, the overwhelming part of the number of serial publications has to be eliminated.

Such reductions, from serials to journals, and from all subjects to science and technology, result in numbers estimated as between 400 and 4,000, depending on the criteria adopted for recognition as "primary-research journals."[8] If 4,000 is taken as a plausible number

[6] I am indebted to Derek Price for the mathematical argument underlying the statement in the text. He kindly responded to my request for advice on how to estimate the number of journal volumes accumulated over the years. In his letter, however, he used an annual growth rate of 7 per cent, or 1/14, so that the number published currently would have to be multiplied by 14 to obtain the total number of volumes accumulated over the years: 50,000 journals published now would mean 700,000 volumes on the shelves. In later correspondence Price commented on the wide variations in estimates of the number of scientific journals currently published.

[7] ". . . it is immediately obvious that the enormous increase in the population of scientific periodicals has proceeded from unity to the order of a hundred thousand with an extraordinary regularity seldom seen in any man-made or natural statistic. It is apparent, to a high order of accuracy, that the number has increased by a factor of ten during every half-century, starting from a state in 1750 when there were about ten scientific journals in the world." *Science since Babylon*, 1st ed., p. 96, 2d ed., p. 165.—Note that on these assumptions the number 100,000 should have been reached by 1950.

[8] For a survey of estimates, see Fritz Machlup, Kenneth Leeson et al., *Information*

of the present population of scientific and technological journals, and if 5 per cent is still taken as a plausible rate of annual growth of that population, the universal library would have to possess a collection of 80,000 volumes of primary-research journals. This would be the stock of recorded knowledge in the natural sciences, mathematics, and technology. The question must be raised, however, whether a growth rate estimated for the kind of periodicals included in a present population of 50,000 periodicals would still be applicable for a more select population of only 4,000 primary-research journals. There is no reason why the ratio of such journals in the universe of periodicals should have been constant and, hence, why the rates of growth should have been the same. I conclude that all these speculations about the holdings of our "universal library" ought not to be taken very seriously.

The Role of Books

We have to recall, moreover, that the foregoing discussion was based on the assumption (or belief) of the scientometricians that all primary-research findings in the "hard sciences" were reported in journals and that books therefore did not matter as a measure of scientific knowledge. Such an assumption, whether valid or not for the natural sciences and mathematics, is surely untenable regarding the accumulation of recorded knowledge in the social sciences and the humanities. In these areas books matter. Indicators for the numerical proportions of journals and books in the universe of scholarly publication (or in the total holdings or acquisitions by libraries) may be found in some statistical ratios which I have developed elsewhere.[9] For example, the share of the natural sciences in total subscriptions to periodicals by 119 American libraries in 1976 was 22.1 per cent, which is more than the 21.1 per cent of social sciences and much more than the 15.7 per cent share of the humanities. The combined share of social sciences and humanities in total subscriptions was 36.8 per cent, against their 57.2 per cent share in the acquisition of books. To look at other combinations, the natural sciences, engineering and technology, and the health sciences together commanded a share of 40 per cent in subscriptions to periodicals, but their combined share in the acquisition of books was only 19.5 per cent. In a different sample, of academic libraries with the largest budgets, the book collections in the humanities alone accounted for over 37 per cent of the total holdings of books.

through the Printed Word: The Dissemination of Scholarly, Scientific, and Intellectual Knowledge (New York: Praeger Publishers, 1978), vol. 2, Journals, pp. 12-18.
    [9] Ibid., vol. 3, Libraries, pp. 103-105 and 136-141.

An estimate of all books and journals ever published was made by Daniel Gore in a paper he presented in 1975 at a conference on academic libraries which was dedicated to the theme: "Touching Bottom in the Bottomless Pit." He estimated that there have been "50 million books published since Gutenberg; 400,000 new ones each year, plus some 300,000 new serials volumes." He cited these (perhaps somewhat exaggerated) figures in order to show that the principle or ideal of the great Library of Alexandria—to possess everything that had ever been published—would be both impossible and undesirable. "Every square foot" of Egypt's surface would be "occupied by the Alexandrian Library."[10] This statement is absurd, unless it is assumed that the library were to be only one story high and were to be planned for all accretions in the next century. A high-rise building block the size of the World Trade Center in New York could accommodate 90 million volumes shelved for easy access or 135 million volumes stored in compact shelving.[11] Gore had a plan for our libraries. He held that no university library should aspire to have a collection larger than a reasonable fraction of what its patrons may want to read, and that the libraries should dispose every year of as many old volumes as they acquire new ones. Between three and six national libraries would be the repositories or "storage libraries" to hold one or two copies of each of the many volumes withdrawn (discarded) by the academic libraries. Gore estimated that each of the storage libraries would initially hold 860,000 volumes and would add 133,000 volumes per year.

This proposal, bidding farewell to the Alexandrian ideal for academic libraries, implies of course that there would be six quasi-Alexandrian libraries in the United States. That these storage libraries would not hold anything near the 50 million books published since Gutenberg is due to the fact that none of our libraries has a complete collection, and their discards therefore cannot give the national storage libraries any complete collections. The combined holdings of all academic libraries in the United States are at present

[10] Daniel Gore, "Farewell to Alexandria: The Theory of the No-Growth, High-Performance Library," in Daniel Gore, ed., *Farewell to Alexandria: Solutions to Space, Growth, and Performance Problems of Libraries* (Westport, Connecticut: Greenwood Press, 1976), pp. 170, 171.

[11] According to the "cubook formula," developed by Robert W. Henderson of the New York Public Library, 100 volumes can be shelved per single stack sections 3 feet wide and $7\frac{1}{2}$ feet high, which requires 10 square feet of floor space. With compact shelving, 150 volumes can be stored on 10 square feet of floor space. See Keyes D. Metcalf, *Planning Academic and Research Library Buildings* (New York: McGraw-Hill, 1965). The World Trade Center, consisting of twin towers and three low buildings, provides 9 million square feet of office space.

(1975) about 440 million volumes, but the largest portion of these consists of multiple copies of the same books. The ratio of titles to copies is estimated to be 1 to 50,[12] which would mean that our combined library collections contain less than 9 million titles.

The Stock of Knowledge in Human Minds

One may contend that the stock of knowledge in society is more meaningfully related to what people have in their heads than what is recorded in their books and journals. It is conceivable that not a single person in the country knows even the smallest fraction of what is printed in the volumes in the library stacks. People may be illiterate and thus incapable of getting to know what *could* be known from the printed records; but, even in the most literate society, some of the knowledge potentially obtainable from the stored tomes in the libraries is probably unknown to any living person.

To make it quite clear that the size of the accumulated stock of recorded knowledge is not the essential measure for some purposes, one merely has to imagine several different societies of equal population and with exactly the same stock of recorded knowledge on the shelves of their national libraries. In one of these societies, people are completely illiterate; in another, 10 per cent of the adult population is literate, and one half of the literates has read and absorbed some tiny fraction of what is stored in the journals and books of the library; and in a third society, 95 per cent of the adult population is literate, between 10 and 15 per cent of the people are so well educated that they have in their heads more than minimal fractions of what the printed pages can transmit, and another 5 per cent are capable of absorbing much larger quantities of the stored knowledge, and actually do so by various groups specializing in various fields of knowledge. Can anyone doubt that these three societies, despite the equal size of their stocks of recorded knowledge, are totally different in their knowledgeability? From various points of view, "living knowledge," or what living people know, may be the relevant stock of knowledge in society.

The stock of knowledge accumulated in the head of an individual person is something different from the stock of knowledge shared by two or more persons, let alone by a majority of the members of a community. "Phenomenological theory of knowledge," if I may propose this term, significantly began its analysis with experiences in the daily life of an individual that have gradually built up the private stock of subjective knowledge in his mind, a stock that influ-

---

[12] Gore, *Farewell to Alexandria*, p. 178.

ences his plans and actions vis-à-vis his fellowmen.[13] The theory proceeded to the problem of intersubjectivity, communication, and interaction between two individuals with a good deal of shared experiences and, hence, private stocks of subjective knowledge relevant to their common interests and their potential as well as actual dealings with each other.[14] The theory then extended the analysis to more anonymous types of actors who share a general social environment, though not necessarily the immediate surrounding, and have learned to orient their individual actions in accordance with their private stocks of subjective, but intersubjectively valid and partly objectivated knowledge of other minds and other people in the social world in which they live. The theory concluded with the fully objectivated knowledge of a society, a social stock of knowledge which in some sense is the result of a socialization of knowledge and contains at the same time more and less than the sum of the private stocks of subjective knowledge. If I may quote from the best source, "the social stock of knowledge contains not only 'more' than the subjective, but also 'more' than the sum of them [the private stocks of subjective knowledge]"—but also " 'less' than any particular subjective stock of knowledge," which "contains elements which refer back to the biographical 'uniqueness' of subjective experiences, and elements which evade an objectivation in language."[15]

This most ingenious phenomenological theory of the stock of knowledge in society is not equipped to deal with the problem that we have raised: the problem of assessing the size of the stock and its growth. As we have decided to focus on the stock of knowledge in the minds of the people, the problems of measuring its size or its growth become forbidding. Of course, there have been attempts to assess the extent of school learning. Several school systems annually rate the cognitive achievements of pupils and students at all levels; and a national assessment of our schools has tried to ascertain how well students at various ages have succeeded in learning some of the basic subjects or skills taught at school. In the United States, College Entrance Examinations have been testing the achievements of high-school graduates, and Graduate Record Examinations have tested

[13] See Alfred Schutz and Thomas Luckmann, The Structures of the Life-World, translated by Richard M. Zaner and A. Tristram Engelhardt, Jr. (Evanston, Ill.: Northwestern University Press, 1973), especially chapter 3 on "Knowledge of the Life-World" and chapter 4 on "Knowledge and Society."

[14] The term "mutual knowledge" has been suggested. Anthony Giddens, New Rules of Sociological Method: A Positive Critique of Interpretative Sociologies (London: Hutchinson, 1976), p. 16.—For a good statement on Schutz's notion of "multiple realities," see Giddens, p. 30.

[15] Alfred Schutz and Thomas Luckmann, Structures of the Life-World, p. 264.

the verbal and numerical aptitudes of college graduates and their mastery of particular subjects. In all these cases, it is not the complete stock of knowledge in the heads of the examined students that is measured, but only the degree to which they have mastered particular batches of knowledge in well-circumscribed areas.

If we are interested not only in how well certain things are known to a certain group of persons in school but also in the scope of their knowledge, we are confronted with again another problem. There arises the question how the social stock of knowledge is related to the private stock of knowledge in the mind of each individual in society. Should we claim "additivity" of the individuals' stocks of knowledge? Should we for each bit or bite of knowledge find out the number, or the percentage, of the people who know it?

In any case the conception of "growth" becomes highly complex if we want to apply it to the stock of knowledge in society. This stock is increased if more people come to know, to absorb and retain, a given quantum of knowable things—but also if a given number of persons come to know more. The same thing may be known to more people or more things to the same people. But what weights should be assigned to different accretions of knowledge? If knowledge of the multiplication table is successfully transmitted to an additional five million people, does this represent more or less growth in the stock of knowledge in society than if knowledge of gene-splicing and recombinant DNA is transferred to an additional five hundred people? We may want both, but choices are often necessary, and indeed are being made, between more new knowledge in the heads of a few and old knowledge in more heads.

Such choices are made even if the stock of knowledge in society cannot be measured and its growth cannot be quantified. The weights that are assigned to various kinds of growth, or rather the priorities that are assigned to alternative directions and advancements of knowledge in society, are probably not very consistent. The decisions are either compromises between different preferences of different political factions or majority votes of the legislatures or other collective bodies in charge of such decisions. We have seen that the appropriations of public funds for space explorations— generating knowledge accessible to very few—have successfully competed with appropriations for remedial education of retarded, neglected, or unwilling learners, but the latter, in turn, have outranked the funding of enriched or accelerated education of especially gifted youths. Political decision-making does not, and cannot, wait for solutions of unsolved problems of measuring the probable consequences of these decisions. Thus we must content ourselves with raising questions and pondering the difficulties of finding good answers.

The Flow of Knowledge

One should think that the problems of quantifying the flow of knowledge are just as difficult as those connected with the stock of knowledge in society. Indeed, in some economic applications—to wit, in the case of some nonperishable good—flows are measured by changes in stocks. This is not so, and cannot be so, in the case of flows of knowledge. Flows of knowledge, in the sense of communication from transmitter to recipient, are different in a very special and important sense from flows of material goods. A flow of goods from one person to another reduces the stocks of the former and increases the stocks of the latter. By contrast, a flow of knowledge may increase the recipient's stock of knowledge without reducing the stock of the transmitter. This implies that every flow of knowledge may bring about an increase in the combined stock of knowledge.

I have said "may," because it is not necessarily so. Although the flow never reduces the stocks of knowledge possessed by the transmitters, it does not always increase the recipients' stocks. First, a recipient may not fully comprehend. Second, he may be unable to retain what was supposedly disseminated.[16] Third, knowledge may be perishable, ephemeral: that is, it may quickly lose relevance for (and perhaps be forgotten by) the recipient. The third reason will not often apply to scientific and scholarly knowledge, but it often applies to information of a mundane type, especially pastime knowledge, and also practical knowledge needed for actions today, not tomorrow or any time later. Many information services, highly valued and paid for, are not designed to increase the stock of knowledge for any length of time, or, if they do increase it, the increment may be subject to rapid obsolescence.

Although the preceding statements were made with reference to flows from person to person, they could be reformulated for transfers of knowledge from persons to records and from records to persons. The only difficulty would be that some of the formulations might imply additivity of knowledge in man-made records and knowledge in human minds, which would compound the problems of quantification and estimation. This can be avoided by assuming that all newly recorded knowledge is actually read (listened to, decoded)

[16] There is the problem of subconscious retention: a message received but not consciously retained may on later occasions, as a result of an appropriate stimulus, be retrieved or reconstructed. Should such potential recovery of knowledge lost for the time being be included in the accumulated stock?

and absorbed by at least one mind. Those scientometricians who are resolved to measure the flow of knowledge in terms of physical units have chosen the alternative of concentrating on recorded knowledge.

Not in all areas of knowledge transmission will it be possible to count physical units, but such counts are feasible in publishing, library operation, broadcasting, motion pictures, performing arts, telephone service, to mention some examples. The physical units are not comparable, however, either among the different branches of knowledge production or even within any one branch. We need only note the difference in volumes, titles, and copies of books; in the numbers of journals, issues, subscriptions, articles, pages, and words printed; in library materials acquired and circulated; in hours of broadcasting, the number of receiving sets, and the size of the audience; in the numbers of motion-picture films produced or presented, the footage of film shown, the cinemas, the audience; in the numbers of teachers employed at various levels of education, the students enrolled, degrees granted, hours spent in classrooms; and so on. Every single one of these units, and especially their rates of growth, may be meaningful for some purposes, but none lends itself to a measurement or estimate of the magnitude of the annual flow of knowledge.

There is, however, one common denominator: dollars spent, or dollars collected, for any of the activities during a given period; and the dollar figures can be compared with such large aggregates as the national income or the gross national product. Costs or revenues expressed in dollars permit the one measure or estimate that applies to *all* types of knowledge disseminated within a period.[17] This magnitude can even be broken down, though only on the basis of imaginative and arbitrary judgments, by different types of knowledge and, within intellectual knowledge, by field or subject matter. (This is one of the tasks to be attempted in this study.) The production and distribution of knowledge in the United States is, in essence, the annual flow of knowledge disseminated at a cost (defrayed or borne by some members of our society).

This statement applies to both concepts of flow which I distinguished at the beginning of this chapter: flows of knowledge over space in the sense of communication between transmitters and receivers, and flows of knowledge at a rate per unit of time, yielded by

[17] Boulding reminds us of "the measuring rod of money" employed in the *Economics of Welfare* by Pigou. See Kenneth E. Boulding, "The Economics of Knowledge and the Knowledge of Economics," *American Economic Review*, Papers and Proceedings, vol. 56 (May 1966), p. 2.

lasting or gradually exhausting sources. One might ask why the distinction was made if it makes no difference for problems of measurement or estimation. The answer is that differences of theoretical (causal or functional) relationships are sufficient reasons for making distinctions, no matter whether measurement is possible, questionable, or impossible.

The theoretical relationships for which the concept of flows of knowledge attributable to long-lasting sources is essential are twofold: there are, on the one hand, the sources, or resources, which we call capital, yielding streams of services period after period; and there are, on the other hand, these streams of services of which some portions are used, not for immediate benefits, but for producing new long-lasting resources, new capital, expected to yield additional flows of services (benefits) in a more distant future. The theoretical model of capital yielding income, and of income being invested to accumulate more capital, is needed for the understanding of many economic problems. In the theory of knowledge production this model is of great help. Incidentally, although numerical estimates may be problematic, we shall, in our statistical investigations, take great pains to find out how much of the cost of current knowledge production has been incurred for investment purposes.

Much of the capital that yields flows of knowledge is in the nature of human capital, and much of the investment portion of knowledge production is formation of human capital. My plan for this work provides for an entire part in Volume II devoted to Knowledge as Human Capital. I cannot at this point elucidate in a few paragraphs ideas which I intend to treat later in several chapters. I may, however, give one or two examples to illustrate what is involved. Think of education and research. The services of educators and researchers can be had only thanks to previous knowledge production having formed human capital. Human resources had to be improved in order to equip them with the knowledge and skills required for the tasks of teaching and research. Thus, the production of knowledge through education and research relies on the flows of knowledge from the human capital accumulated in the past. At the same time, the process of education largely serves the production of human capital for the sake of benefits in a remote future. The model of stocks of knowledge yielding flows of knowledge, and some of these flows being used to accumulate stocks is, I hope, sufficiently clear.

Perhaps I may now suggest that the concept of a flow of knowledge through space is not something completely separate; it may be involved in the notion of a flow of knowledge-producing services attributable to existing knowledge resources. That the process of communication of knowledge from transmitters to receivers represents a stock-flow-stock relationship is clear. This process takes place in connection with the flows of knowledge yielded by human capital when its services are rendered by communication over space. For example, the teacher disseminating knowledge to his students, and the researcher committing his findings to printed or written records, are engaged in communication, in transmitting flows of knowledge "through space." We should behold, however, that there can be knowledge production without communication, though only in exceptional instances, as long as we confine our interest to activities that have economic significance. One such instance would be the researcher who keeps his findings secret, not divulging the new knowledge to anybody. Another instance is the growth of knowledge in the human mind through processes of maturation. Such maturation occurs, for example, when persons attain a deeper understanding of material previously learned, or develop new ideas through flashes of insights or chance discoveries.[18] Although such internal flows of knowledge, taking place entirely within single minds, may be of utmost importance to the individuals themselves or, through their subsequent "practical" use, to society at large, they will not count heavily in the national-product accounts, where knowledge flows are measured by money value, money costs, or imputed costs.

Generation, Dissemination, and Use of Information

In the literature on information services, especially regarding "scientific and technical information," we often find that generation, dissemination, and use of information are distinguished. (Equivalent nouns are creation, diffusion, and utilization, respectively.) *Generation* evidently refers to "socially new knowledge," previously not known to anyone and now known only to the one person or small groups of persons who have come upon it. *Dissemination* refers to the intended transfer of knowledge—by means of speech or some such record as a written or printed page, from the minds of

---

[18] I acknowledge my indebtedness to Israel Kirzner. Other aspects of knowledge production without communication will be discussed in the next chapter.—I have failed to deal with several other points Kirzner made in discussion and correspondence. For example, he notes the importance of expectations regarding the rate at which a potential stock of knowledge may yield future internal flows of knowledge—benefits to its possessor. These expectations have significant implications for the forms in which investment in stocks of knowledge is undertaken. Individuals and business firms may have a choice between investing in a stock of knowledge now to derive internal flows of knowledge-services from it in the future and, alternatively, planning to buy these services from outside sources later when they need them.

those who generated it, or who learned it from them or from intermediaries—to other minds, which have not hitherto possessed it.[19] *Use*, if it is to mean something other than the receiving end of the transfer (like the reading of a journal article), must refer to activities guided or influenced by the knowledge received.[20] For example, a researcher "uses" it as an input in his own research, perhaps as a stepping stone in his advancement towards further insights, where the knowledge he received, perhaps somewhat modified, may be a part; or it may have served him merely as a clue in his thinking about quite different theories, or as a hint for the design of some experiments helpful in his own investigations. A developer "uses" the received knowledge for further work on some raw invention, or on certain modifications or refinements of technological ideas still to be made reducible to practical application. Finally, the innovator "uses" the received knowledge by applying it practically in actual construction or production.[21]

The distinctions—generation, dissemination, use—are appropriate for certain purposes, but not for any estimates of the flow of knowledge (or information) in society. It is not possible, even in the vaguest sense, to quantify the use made of any bit or piece of information. Whether some newly received knowledge of a scientific idea has inspired a researcher to change the direction of his thinking or his laboratory work cannot possibly be ascertained, except perhaps from a detailed diary kept by him. Whether a novel technological idea was adopted or adapted by a developer or innovator in his development work or in his methods of production, respectively, is

[19] I speak of "intended" transfer of knowledge because not all dissemination is effective. For example, the researcher's or consultant's findings may not reach the manager or executive who is too busy to read the reports; the teacher's words are not heard by students who sleep or let their minds wander.

[20] "Activities" may include inaction, that is, decisions not to take actions that had been considered. Indeed, information influencing the recipient to abstain from acting in certain ways may be a very important use of the knowledge received.

[21] Even the decision of a recipient of a report to reject recommendations for action may be regarded as use of the received knowledge. There is also the phenomenon of delayed use and of "waves of utilization." See Robert F. Rich, "Uses of Social Science Information by Federal Bureaucrats: Knowledge for Action versus Knowledge for Understanding," in Carol Weiss, ed., *Using Social Research in Public Policy Making* (Lexington, Mass.: D. C. Heath, 1977), pp. 203-204.—In the case of teaching and learning, most of the uses of the produced knowledge are delayed, often distributed over the recipient's entire life. Where the dissemination of knowledge is not designed to produce learning or to induce action but merely to entertain or to please, one may quibble whether the act of receiving (hearing, viewing, reading) should be separated from the pleasurable effect on the recipient and only this effect be regarded as "use" of the knowledge produced.

difficult to prove, as can be seen from the countless controversies and litigations about patent infringements where the plaintiff argues, and the defendant denies, that the patented invention has been used. Not even in the sense of having read a paper or article on the new piece of knowledge can its "use" be certified, unless on the reader's admission or on a witness's testimony. In terms of the conceptual framework in which the discourse on information or the flow of knowledge is carried on, becoming informed, that is, receiving the disseminated knowledge, is surely included, but its "use" is outside that frame unless it involves the generation of additional knowledge or the retransmission of the received knowledge to additional recipients.[22]

Generation of socially new knowledge is another nonoperational concept as long as generation is not complemented by dissemination. If a single person has generated some knowledge which no one else has and if that single person keeps it to himself, others may either be unaware of the existence of his secret or may not believe him if he tells them that he has it. Only if he shares his knowledge with others can one recognize that new knowledge has been created. Generation of knowledge without dissemination is socially worthless as well as unascertainable. Although "tacit knowledge" cannot be counted in any sort of inventory, its creation may still be a part of the production of knowledge if the activities that generate it have a measurable cost.

Of the supposed three functions of society's information sector, we should now realize, dissemination, not generation and not use, is the essence of this study. This realization validates my earlier terminological resolution to merge production and distribution of knowledge into one broad concept of knowledge production, which includes all kinds of activities that are designed to create (directly or indirectly) meaningful impressions or thought processes in a human mind—one's own or anyone else's. These activities constitute the flow of knowledge in society.[23]

[22] This is not to deny the importance of the use (or "utilization") of knowledge. Indeed, as I have tried to show in Chapter 2, an attempt to distinguish different types of knowledge is largely based on differences in the uses or purposes which the knowledge is supposed to serve. Still, the use of knowledge is only in special instances a part of the production of knowledge. See below, Chapters 12 and 13.

[23] I want to recall that the term "information" should not be used for a stock of knowledge, but only for a flow of knowledge. This follows, as I have pointed out, from the meaning of the verbs that are correlative to the nouns. To know is a state of mind, and hence refers to a stock of knowledge at any moment of time; to inform or getting informed is a process, and hence refers to a flow of knowledge during a period. To speak of "information dissemination" or "information transfer" is redundant, since

Accumulation, Replacement, Current Input,
Consumption, and Waste

A set of concepts, introduced earlier and elaborated later in other contexts, deserves a brief side-glance in connection with the dichotomy of stocks and flows of knowledge. A flow of knowledge—from person to person, by word of mouth or via some sort of record—may be regarded as accumulation, replacement, current input, consumption, or waste—but sometimes as a combination of two or more of these alternatives.

A flow of knowledge will give rise to *accumulation* if it results in a net addition to the stock of knowledge in society. It will be *replacement* to the extent that it, though a gross addition to the stock, offsets (compensates for) parts of the stock that have been forgotten, become obsolete, or been wiped out by the death of the persons in whose minds it had been stored. It will be *current input* if it serves the current production of other goods and services but is not expected to aid such production in the future. (See the last subsection in Chapter 8 for a brief reference to knowledge as an intermediate product used in current production.) The flow will be *consumption* if it serves the current enjoyment of the recipients. It will be *waste* if it does none of the four things.

It is easy to see that combinations of the five possibilities are quite normal. If a given flow of knowledge is designed as entertainment or some other form of immediate satisfaction, but succeeds only partly—for example, because it is mixed with excessive amounts of unwanted knowledge, noncomprehended knowledge, or unpleasant noise, so that it is boring instead of amusing, or if it is produced at excessive cost—the outcome will be judged to be a combination of waste and consumption. If a given flow of knowledge constitutes a gross addition to the stock of knowledge in society, usually some share of that addition will be considered a replacement of knowledge lost by the various kinds of attrition (death, loss of memory, obsolescence).[24] The same flow of knowledge may be partly current input and partly accumulation for future use in production. To give an example of a triple combination, a given flow of knowledge may

---

information is always disseminated or intended to be transferred. Even if some user of the word "information" means the contents rather than the process of dissemination, it should be clear that information relates, by definition, to knowledge disseminated.

[24] It was Boulding who, in a review of my book *The Production and Distribution of Knowledge*, raised the question of replacement of knowledge lost by death, loss of memory, and obsolescence. Kenneth E. Boulding, "The Knowledge Industry," *Challenge*, May 1963, p. 37. Perhaps we should add retirement of trained people from active service as an additional factor of attrition calling for replacement.

be regarded as yielding current consumption (immediate enjoyment by the recipients), accumulation of a stock of knowledge expected to yield future benefits, and also some waste.

Virtually every flow of knowledge may have an admixture of waste, some of the efforts of producing knowledge proving either abortive or superfluous. Incidentally, if efforts at disseminating knowledge are abortive, the failure may be the fault of the transmitters, lacking understanding, discernment, or skill, or the fault of would-be recipients, being ill prepared, uninterested, or otherwise nonreceptive. On the other hand, the admixture of waste may often be so small compared with the benefits derived from the contributions which the flow of knowledge makes to consumption and production that the effort devoted to the dissemination may still be fully worth while. Where the benefits exceed the costs by a sufficiently wide margin, one may be inclined to overlook the waste involved in the fact that the benefits *could* be higher or the cost *could* be lower. (The question of benefits will be discussed in Chapter 13 below.)

In some particular areas of knowledge dissemination, it is possible to undertake estimates of waste by analyses of the cost effectiveness of resources employed or by comparisons of the benefits and costs of alternative techniques. However, where questions of the actual or potential stocks of knowledge enter the argument, we had better acknowledge that attempts at quantification are not promising; the essential concepts are not statistically operational, and, hence, neither accumulation nor replacement are subject to estimation, let alone measurement. To say this, however, is not to question the significance of the conceptual framework for the analysis of fundamental relationships that remain important as long as we are satisfied with understanding the social world without insisting on measuring the nonmeasurable.

CHAPTER 10

THE ECONOMIC COST OF KNOWLEDGE

WE HAVE tentatively concluded that stocks of knowledge are neither measurable nor comparable, whereas flows of knowledge can be quantified and appraised by the "measuring rod of money" applied either to what is being paid for the knowledge by those who buy it (for themselves or for others) or to what is being given up for it to be made available. This statement, however, is far too general and inaccurate to be accepted without qualification, for it will be seen in a moment that large components in the flow of knowledge require neither payment nor sacrifices.[1]

The Private and Social Cost of Acquiring Knowledge

It is well known that in many activities private cost may be different from social cost. The divergences are most impressive in those fields of knowledge production where the producers—original creators or transmitters—defray only a small part, or none, of the cost, and the recipients of disseminated knowledge may obtain it at a low price or entirely free of charge. In many of these instances, however, the cost to society may be substantial; that is to say, sizable parts of the cost of production are defrayed by members of the community other than the creators, transmitters, or recipients, for example, by the taxpayers. Thus, we are not surprised to find that the private cost of some flows of knowledge is little or zero, whereas the social cost is substantial.

Besides these flows of knowledge which are costless only to the private parties directly involved but not to society, there are large flows of knowledge acquired at zero or near-zero cost, social as well as private. The existence of costless knowledge calls for an explication of its nature as well as of the implications it has for the study of knowledge production.

Knowledge at No Cost

A constant stream of knowledge is received without any effort and without any sacrifice on the part of the recipients or anybody else

---

[1] This chapter was prepublished, with only minimal alterations but under the same title, in Emil Küng, ed., *Wandlungen in Wirtschaft und Gesellschaft*, Festschrift für Walter Adolf Jöhr (Tübingen: J.C.B. Mohr—Paul Siebeck, 1980), pp. 381-388.

simply as a result of people being alive, awake, and conscious of what goes on around them and inside them. The stream of experiences of individuals in their everyday lives—either as casual observers or as actors engaged in more or less ordinary activities as workers, consumers, family members, citizens, businessmen, and in all the hundreds of other roles they play during any day—will normally induce reflection, interpretations, discoveries, and generalizations, all of which are accretions to their knowledge. They include, or are the same as, what Bertrand Russell meant by "individual knowledge" (see above, Chapter 2), what William James meant by "knowledge-of," or "knowledge by acquaintance" (again, Chapter 2), and what Alfred Schutz meant by "private, subjective knowledge" (above, Chapter 9)—to mention only a few of the philosophers who have recognized this primary source of knowledge obtained without cost to anybody. To mention also a philosophically inclined economist, I may quote George Shackle's remark that "so far as men are concerned, being consists in continual and endless fresh knowing."[2]

Not all people are equally perceptive, observant, and reflecting; some are alert, others obtuse, some wide awake, others half asleep. These differences in receptiveness make for wide differences in the richness, variety, and cognitive fertility of the individuals' personal experiences and the knowledge they distill from them. Still, with all these differences, every person alive (and not in a coma) has at his disposal an almost continuous flow of free knowledge.

One may wish to distinguish those of an individual's personal experiences that stem from his passive observation of his "life-world"[3]—verbal or nonverbal impressions that force themselves upon his consciousness—from what two or more individuals can learn from one another through intercommunication, that is, through talking, exchanging views, telling about their own experiences and comparing them with the reported experiences of the others. These are also streams of life-worldly knowledge, continuously acquired with a minimum of effort or sacrifice. These communications are from people around us, talking (without cost to themselves) chiefly to satisfy their propensity to talk. Many of our daily or occasional companions—members of the household, neighbors, friends, co-workers, strangers on the bus or in a queue, and all

[2] George L. S. Shackle, Epistemics and Economics (Cambridge: at the University Press, 1972), p. 156.

[3] The individual's "life-world" is the world in which he lives and acts, in contrast to the social "model-world" which the social scientist constructs as a mental tool employed to interpret and analyze observations of social phenomena.

the rest—are great chatterers, conveying endless streams of knowledge to our defenseless ears and minds. Some of these flows of communicated knowledge may be interesting, entertaining, useful, stimulating; some may be irrelevant to our actual interests, not fully comprehended, or plainly unwanted. In any case, however, it is knowledge, and costless (though not always painless).

Precisely because this individual, highly personal, subjective, or intersubjective knowledge is acquired without appreciable effort or sacrifice, it will usually be regarded as a free good. Where no choices are involved, no alternative opportunities given up, we do not count our activities—looking and listening, in the present case—as economically relevant. Our personal cost accounting omits items that cost us nothing and have no alternative use. If these items cause no cost or inconvenience to any other members of society, they do not figure in social cost accounting either. The measuring rod of money is not applied to the flow of freely transmitted and freely acquired knowledge, no matter how important that knowledge may be in our everyday lives and how essential it may be as raw material for subsequent systematic analysis, the creation of knowledge of a higher order, scientific knowledge.

The noneconomist may object to this omission of useful knowledge from our national accounts. Let him be reassured, there is method in this suspected madness of the social accountants. Many of the goodies the nation enjoys cannot be entered in the tabulations of national product and income, at least not with the accounting techniques now considered acceptable; likewise, many of the bad things suffered by the people cannot be deducted, as negative contributions to the nation's welfare, from the national income produced. Technical difficulties force the statisticians who prepare the national accounts to omit substantial and important parts of the flows of knowledge transmitted and received. Knowledge as a product in the economic sense is thus only a part of the knowledge produced in a wider sense, more plausible to many. In a general analysis of the production of knowledge, all flows of information, costly or free, have to be examined for the role they play in the lives of the people; but, in an analysis that undertakes to estimate the share of knowledge production in the gross national product, no account can be taken of items that cannot be evaluated either at market prices or at factor cost.

The Scarcity Value of Alertness

The conclusion that the production of costless knowledge is not included in the account of the gross national product seems to contradict my earlier observation regarding the different capacities of people to see, to spot, to discover knowledge of great practical usefulness. If only a few people are alert, perceptive, and imaginative enough to see novel and timely opportunities, will not this knowledge of newly detected promising ventures, including business ventures, be scarce and, hence, a valuable product of the detectors' activities?

Economic theory has recognized this problem but has decided to deal with it in the analysis of the profits of enterprise. The scarcity of sharp-eyed entrepreneurs will lead to scarcity values of their novel products, reflected in relatively high market prices. The value of the knowledge—the discovery of promising opportunities to innovate—will in this case not be separated from the value of the products for which their knowledge is essential. Only in instances in which costly search, expensive exploration, or extensive research and development precede, or are otherwise distinct from, the new industrial or commercial undertakings, does it appear practical to separate, in corporate and national accounting, the production of knowledge and the production of the goods and services in which that knowledge is embodied.[4]

The Intentions of the Recipient of Knowledge

The issues and arguments presented in the last two or three pages suggest that certain distinctions be made with regard to the intentions of the recipients of knowledge.

The two cases with which we have become familiar in the preceding pages are those, first, of unintentional, purely accidental, passive reception, and, second, of vibrant reception supported by a conscious and alert receptiveness, a special readiness and willingness to receive knowledge. The third case is that of an eagerness to find out, to embark on a search even at considerable cost in terms of effort and foregone alternatives. Let us examine these possibilities.

Taking the three cases in reverse order, we will note that the one of intentional search by a knowledge seeker who is prepared to incur costs has been analyzed most frequently in the context of decision theory and of the objectives of a business firm looking for opportunities for promising innovation in products, product qualities, production techniques, and marketing. Analysts have pointed to significant

---

[4] In writing this and the next two subsections I was stimulated by, and have learned from, reading the draft of a paper by Israel M. Kirzner, "Knowing about Knowledge: A Subjective View of the Role of Information," included in his book, *Perception, Opportunity, and Profit: Studies in the Theory of Entrepreneurship* (Chicago: University of Chicago Press, 1979).

differences in the clarity of the vision and interests of those ordering or undertaking the search: how vague or how certain are they about just what they want to know? They can hardly know precisely what they want to know, but they may be more definite or less regarding the target of their curiosity, more confident or less that their curiosity can be satisfied, that answers to their questions can be found. Thus, their search may be for what they believe to be *known to some* other person or persons, somewhere; or their search may be for what, though unknown to them, they *feel sure* can be found out; or their search may be for what they have *some hope* can be found. According to these and similar circumstances, the degrees of uncertainty and the willingness to incur large costs for the search in question will differ. Whether the search will be done "in house," that is, by the staff of the interested organization or firm, or farmed out to others, say, to consultants or specialized research organizations, does not change the nature of the project: it is intentional search for answers to specific or to vaguely circumscribed questions.

Absence of intentional search but presence of a special receptiveness to new knowledge mark the second case. Some alert and quick-minded persons, by keeping their eyes and ears open for new facts and theories, discoveries and opportunities, perceive what normal people, of lesser alertness and perceptiveness, would fail to notice. Hence, new knowledge is available at little or no cost to those who are on the lookout, full of curiosity, and bright enough not to miss their chances.

Finally, there is the third case, reception of new knowledge by those who neither embark on intentional and costly searches nor possess the qualities of extraordinary alertness and perceptiveness, but who just stumble upon the hitherto undiscovered. Accidental discovery is an undoubtable source of new knowledge.

With these observations, we have surveyed some of the ways in which socially new knowledge may be generated in the minds of painstaking searchers, alert watchers, and lucky finders. Although most economic analysts, when they engage in discussions of this sort, have entrepreneurial innovators in mind, the distinctions are valid for gainers of knowledge of all sorts. Yet, though the distinctions look so very neat—the diligent searcher, the wide-eyed rover, and the accidental finder—they fail to take account of the role of accidental finds in the work of the diligent searcher. Many unintended and unexpected discoveries and inventions have been made in the course of search, research, and development work designed for very different objectives. The word "serendipity" has been coined to denote chance discoveries that are made while looking for very different things.[5]

The possibility and probability of chance discoveries and unintended inventions by eager searchers for solutions to quite different problems makes the terms "accidental" or "lucky" finders of new knowledge ambiguous. Many *diligent* searchers are at the same time *accidental* finders of valuable facts and theories, techniques and procedures, products and ideas. We need a term to distinguish those who are engaged in diligent search activities designed for well-defined targets but find something they have not been looking for from those who look for nothing but stumble upon something they cannot help noticing. I submit that the diligent searcher's discovery is not due to a lucky accident but is a byproduct of his diligence and circumspection, hence, not really accidental but just unexpected; it is *incidental* to his other search activities. I can thus reserve the expression "accidental" for discoveries of the nonlooking finder.[6]

The Initiative to Produce Knowledge

If, having just emerged from a (not very entertaining) disquisition on the *intentions* of the seekers and finders of knowledge, we turn to a discussion of *initiatives* in knowledge-producing activities and *inducements* to undertaking them, many a reader, especially the noneconomists, may balk at this succession of "quibbles." Instead of reassuring them, I must warn them that they will later be invited to a discourse on *incentives*, especially institutional devices or governmental measures designed to increase the inducements to produce knowledge. At this point I propose to look into the question whether the initiative to engage in the production of knowledge comes more often from the demand side or from the supply side of the "market."

Reference to a market implies the presence of two groups, one offering knowledge for sale, the other desiring to acquire it and willing

[5] Horace Walpole coined the word (in 1754) to denote the faculty of making lucky and unexpected finds by accident. He formed the word from the title of a fairy tale, *The Princes of Serendip* (an ancient name for Ceylon, or Sri Lanka), because the princes, as Walpole wrote, "were always making discoveries, by accidents and sagacity, of things they were not in quest of."

[6] One of the economic problems connected with incidental discoveries and inventions made in the course of costly research and development work concerns the allocation of R and D expenditures. Should a portion of these expenditures be allocated to the incidental finds? If so, what portion? Or is incidentally acquired knowledge a costless windfall, with all expenditures charged to the findings they had been intended to produce? What if the intended purposes of the expenditures have not materialized at all?

to pay for it. A larger supply may be forthcoming either because demand has increased (or is expected to increase), which would be a demand-induced increase in knowledge production, or because producers (transmitters) of knowledge have stepped up their activities on their own initiative or have become more productive and have more to offer, which, if the demand is responsive and receptive, would be a supply-induced increase in knowledge production. This model of a market where sellers and buyers transact business has no explicit place for those who themselves produce what they want. Economists usually adjust their market model by adding the "self-providers" (who provide for their own needs) to both sides. Supply and demand are increased by the same quantities, as all in-house production to meet in-house demand (or "the producers' demand for their own product") is added laterally to supply curves and demand curves of the customary graphs.

As has been said before, the market model does not fit well for several areas of knowledge production, but it may be helpful in some. In the case of consulting firms, independent research-and-development organizations, and other information services, descriptions in terms of supply and demand may be very much to the point. Searches undertaken by such firms or institutions, public or private, may be entirely demand-induced in the sense of customers taking the initiative in ordering some particular information, which is then generated and delivered on demand. There is also demand-induced production of knowledge if the suppliers of information services can confidently expect a recurring demand for knowledge of particular data and, in anticipation of customers' orders, accumulate a stock (data bank) from which the orders can then be filled as they come in.

On the other hand, the initiative may be entirely on the side of the suppliers. They may undertake to generate and accumulate knowledge for which no effective demand exists at the time; few, if any, may know that the particular knowledge will become obtainable; and few, if any, may know that they will want that knowledge. The suppliers may eventually create not only the knowledge but also the demand for it. Clearly, this is supply-induced production of knowledge.

In many instances the question of the locus of the initiative is moot. There may be a latent demand for certain types of knowledge, a demand that becomes effective when suppliers offer to satisfy it at a reasonable price, and there may be a latent supply that becomes effective when the existence of the demand is sufficiently manifest. The case of books, journals, and magazines suggests itself as an example of divided initiative. Should we say that the production of mystery stories or sex magazines is supply-induced or demand-induced? Surely, in such cases, supply creates its demand, and demand induces the supply, and it does not make much sense to ask whether sellers or buyers are more eager. To be sure, choices and decisions are made by several groups of people. In the case of books, the authors, editors, publishers, booksellers, and librarians, on the one side, and the buyers and borrowers, on the other side, are involved in this production of knowledge; and, although their roles are different, their relative importance cannot be meaningfully appraised.

TRANSMISSION AND RECEPTION

HAVING LEFT no doubt about the essential duality of knowledge as that which is known and as the state of knowing it, I need not hesitate to repeat that knowledge production can mean producing additional new ideas—extending the universe of the known—but also producing a state of knowing in additional minds—extending the population of knowers. For reasons that have become clear (or at least less obscure) in the discourse on stocks and flows of knowledge, an examination of processes or methods of producing knowledge will be more fruitful if it places primary emphasis on activities designed to effect or affect states of knowing.

To repeat also the definition appropriate for my purposes, I understand by production of knowledge any human (or human-induced) activity effectively designed to create, alter, or confirm in a human mind—one's own or anyone else's—a meaningful apperception, awareness, cognizance, or consciousness of whatever it may be. This is, I must admit, a rather broad definition; but it is not, I submit, unduly so. I find comfort in others' having chosen similarly broad concepts—for example, Warren Weaver's using the word "communication . . . to include all of the procedures by which one mind can affect another."[1]

Techniques and Intents of Knowledge Production

Where the result of the knowledge-producing activity is upon the actor's own mind, that activity will typically be watching, listening, reading, experimenting, inferring, intuiting, discovering, inventing, or (often also in connection with received messages) interpreting, computing, processing, translating, analyzing, judging, evaluating—to give an illustrative, not an exhaustive, list.

Where the result is upon someone else's mind, the activity by which it is produced will typically be talking, writing, typing, printing, motioning, gesturing, pointing, signaling, but also drawing, painting, sculpturing, singing, playing, or performing in any other visible or audible way.

[1] Warren Weaver, "The Mathematics of Information," in *Automatic Control* (New York: Simon and Schuster, for *The Scientific American*, 1955), p. 97.

All these examples have stressed the use of two of our five senses, seeing and hearing; knowledge production through touch is less frequent (except for the blind and in certain psychotherapeutic efforts); and smelling and tasting are confined to a few very specialized activities and occupations.

The same techniques of producing impressions upon another mind may be used for a large variety of purposes. When the communicator talks, he may do so, for example, in order to teach, to insult, to persuade, to impress his audience, or for many other purposes. To compile a list of possible intents of communication—of producing knowledge in another mind—would be like copying many pages of Roget's *Thesaurus*. Merely to give an impression of the variety of the intents, let us list a score of verbs signifying "talking for a purpose": conversing, chatting, reporting, confessing, complaining, denouncing, scolding, threatening, warning, requesting, begging, advising, persuading, directing, commanding, convincing, permitting, teaching, entertaining, showing off, edifying, reassuring, consoling, confirming, affirming, denying, misleading, teasing, insulting, harassing, embarrassing. This is only a sample. Among the economically most important of the intents of communicating are reporting, advising, directing (managing), teaching, and entertaining. These constitute the activities of a large number of persons who derive their incomes from the services they render in this fashion: for example, the reporters of news, research findings, etc., the consultants, advisers, and staff officers in business and government, the directors, managers, and administrators of all sorts of organizations, especially in business, the teachers at all levels, the entertainers and performers of arts, high-, middle-, and low-brow. Again, these are only illustrations, a small sample from a long list. Incidentally, a much longer list of knowledge-producing occupations will be used in Volume VIII.

Types of Individual Knowledge Transmitters: Eight Levels

Modern communication theory has given a description of the process between and within two persons or units in a system, one, the transmitter, the other, the receiver of the message. The transmitter selects the message from his information store, transmits it, usually after encoding it into a "signal," through a "communication channel" to the receiver, who, after decoding the signal, puts the message into his information store. (The use of the personal pronoun in this statement makes it pertinent to human transmitters and receivers, though the application is more frequently to machines. No sex discrimination is intended by using the masculine. Every "he" is meant to be "he or she.")

If we want to analyze the activities of an *individual* person engaged in the production of knowledge, the sequence of acts usually has to be turned around: he will receive first and transmit afterwards. The "receiving" is of course not confined to messages addressed to him, nor to messages identifiable as the "input" to which the outgoing messages can be attributed. For there may be plenty of "storage" and therefore an inventory of knowledge in the individual's mind. In contrast to most other inventories, his knowledge inventory will as a rule not be reduced when he transmits knowledge to others. On the contrary, the more often he sends out a certain message, the more firmly will its contents be retained in his own mind. Only in the simplest forms of forwarding a message will no storage on the part of the forwarder be involved. For example, the honest mail carrier retains nothing, and the oral-message bearer, the typist, and the printer, and even some processors of knowledge who can do the processing "mechanically," in a routine fashion, will retain little or nothing unless they try hard to commit part of the message to memory.

Before we attempt to make distinctions between the various types of knowledge conveyors, we may note that the transmission or delivery of a message may be "prescheduled" or "upon demand" or "spontaneous." The written message, in the form of a postcard or letter, which the mail carrier receives for delivery will (or should) reach the addressee at a prescheduled time, unless it was marked "general delivery" or "poste restante," in which case it will be delivered at the post office upon demand. The teacher delivers his lectures according to a fixed schedule, the consultant or medical doctor gives his advice upon demand, the creative artist, scientist, or inventor communicates his message spontaneously.

According to the degree to which the messages delivered by a person differ from the messages he has previously received, we may distinguish several types of communicators, or knowledge producers, as we have chosen to call them. A *transporter* of knowledge will deliver exactly what he has received, without changing it in the least; for example, the messenger carrying a written communication. A *transformer* of knowledge changes the form of the message received but is not supposed to change its contents; for example, the stenographer receiving a message in sound, changing what he hears to penciled shorthand notes and then to a typed letter, which he dispatches. A *routine processor* of knowledge changes both form and contents of what he has received, but only by routine procedures which subject different pieces of knowledge received to certain operations, such as combinations, computations, or other kinds of rearrangements, leading to definite results, independent of the processor's tastes, moods, or intuition, dependent solely on conventions concerning such processing rules; for example, the bookkeeper receiving separate debit and credit advices, which he combines in definite ways to enter on particular accounts, to prepare statements of accounts, or to show net balances.

A *discretionary processor* of knowledge is similar to a routine processor except that he may or must use his judgment or intuition to decide which routine procedure to follow; for example, a senior accountant may decide which method of inventory valuation best suits the requirements of the firm at the particular time. A *managerial processor* of knowledge receives reports from his staff, from consultants, clients, government offices, and others, and may pass extracts or summaries on to his superiors. In addition he receives instructions from his superiors in the hierarchy. The second kind of messages may be general or specific instructions. The managerial processor will, to the degree he deems necessary, change the form and substance of the message and issue specific instructions to his own subordinates.

An *interpreter* of knowledge changes form and contents of the messages received but has to use imagination to create in the new form effects equivalent to those he feels were intended by the original message; for example, the translator of a subtle speech or sensitive poetry in a foreign language. An *analyzer* of knowledge uses so much of his own judgment and intuition in addition to accepted procedures that the message he communicates bears little or no resemblance to the messages received. An *original creator* of knowledge, although drawing on a rich store of information received in messages of all sorts, adds so much of his own inventive genius and creative imagination that only relatively weak and indirect connections can be found between what he has received from others and what he communicates.

That all these activities are designated here as knowledge production may be resented by some who wish to reserve such a high-sounding phrase for the upper strata, perhaps the analyzers and original creators. I find it more convenient to use the phrase for the entire spectrum of activities, from the transporter of knowledge up to the original creator. Surely, in many instances one may ask whether a particular communication is, for example, the work of an analyzer or rather of a discretionary processor. Such questions, however, are of little relevance since we are less interested in characterizing particular acts of communication than in characterizing the kind of activities and, more often, the mixture of activities typically performed by persons in certain occupations. Few occupations fall entirely into one class of activity or fit entirely one type of knowledge producer. Examining a "job description," one usually finds that the occupation in question comprises activities of several types, so that for different parts of his duties the performer of the job is, say, a routine processor, a discretionary processor, an interpreter, and an analyzer of knowledge as well.

In Volume VIII of this work, in the discussion of the occupational structure of the United States, an attempt will be made to produce estimates of the composition of the labor force by type (or level) of mental activity required in carrying out the typical occupational duties; as these estimates will be based on statistical data for 1940, 1950, 1960, 1970, and perhaps 1980, they will suggest what kinds of changes have taken place over the years. Since the judgments regarding the nature of occupational duties are quite speculative, the validity of the findings may be questioned. But I see no point in questioning, or quarreling about, the assumption that all kinds of communication are designed to produce knowledge in another mind.

Knowledge Receiving as Knowledge Production

In the discussion in the preceding section, the emphasis was on knowledge transmitting as knowledge production. All acts of knowledge transmission were treated as productive. This was perhaps premature, and we may have to take back part of what was said. Some acts of communicating knowledge may be designed chiefly for the pleasure of the transmitter—for example, when he satisfies his desire to chat or to show off. In these instances the production of knowledge in the other mind may be only a byproduct of his activity, and not necessarily one that is at all valued by the recipient. Although this is production of knowledge in a technical sense, one must question whether it should be regarded as production from an economic point of view.

In the case of receiving knowledge, the presumption will even more often be against regarding the required activities as economic production of knowledge in the recipient's mind. Most frequently these activities are listening, watching, and reading. In a technical sense they are undoubtedly part of the process of knowledge production. Indeed, the writers, editors, publishers, demonstrators, and teachers succeed in their functions of communicating and disseminating knowledge to the extent only that there are readers, listeners, watchers, and learners of adequate intelligence, diligence, and interest to receive and absorb the message. Still, this does not imply that the receivers' activities should be accepted as "production" from an economic point of view.

An analogy may be helpful at this juncture. In the production of nourishment, the sequence of activities near the end of the line includes wrapping, taking to the kitchen, unwrapping, cooking, cutting, slicing, salting, lifting to the mouth, chewing, swallowing. Although most of these activities are technically necessary parts of the production process, we draw the line at an earlier point and rule that "economic production" ends when the foodstuff passes into the possession of him who takes it home to prepare a meal for himself or members of his household. Of course, we may be going too far in accepting the "lesson" of this analogy. Taking in food is always viewed as consumption. As has been said before, taking in knowledge may be, but need not be, consumption.

When the acquisition of knowledge (or the exposition of one's receiving organs to the signals which are convertible into knowledge) serves the purpose of giving immediate or early satisfaction to the recipient, his activity to this end will not be regarded as knowledge production from an economic point of view. Although his listening, watching, or reading is necessary to produce the impact on his mind which the productive activity of the talker, performer, or writer is designed to produce, his part in this process is consumption, not production, if the chief aim is the immediate pleasure it gives.

When the acquisition of knowledge is designed to increase the productive capacity of the recipient, when his listening, watching, or reading is intended as *learning*, and therefore intended to serve future ends, his activities should be regarded as production from the economic point of view. In these circumstances the receiving and absorbing of messages constitute, economically as well as technically, production of knowledge in the actor's own mind.

There is a third possibility: the recipient of information may use it for other things he is doing; it may serve him as a directive in physical work, in productive or consumptive activities of all sorts. He may watch for signals directing him in the best timing of his movements; he may listen to a foreman telling him what to do, or he may read the instructions for a medicine he takes or for a gadget he installs. In almost everything we do as physical workers, as consumers, as passengers, as drivers, as pedestrians, or in any capacity whatever, we are aided directly or indirectly by information received. The activity of the knowledge recipient in such instances will not be viewed as production of knowledge from an economic point of view. Instead, it will be regarded as an integral part of the productive or consumptive activity in which it is supposed to be of assistance.

In summary, the activities of the knowledge recipient are technically always, but economically only in certain situations, part of the production of knowledge. They should be recognized as production of knowledge in the economic sense if they are designed to increase the productive capacity of the recipient for future use. They should not be so recognized if they are part of activities in which the recipient is engaged for other purposes; they may even be part of the cost of doing these things. Nor should they be recognized as economic production of knowledge if they are motivated by a desire for immediate or early satisfaction.

One must guard against a misunderstanding on this point regarding "knowledge for consumer's satisfaction." Technically such knowledge is produced by activities on the part of both the transmitter and the receiver. We have ruled that the receiver's activities in this process should not be recognized as production of knowledge, but only as consumption. This does not change the status of the transmitter's activities. He does produce knowledge in the receiver's mind, even if it is pastime knowledge. The entertainer is therefore a knowledge producer, and his products, the pleasurable impressions on the minds of the receivers, are final output. Production for purposes of consumption by others remains production from every point of view.

CHAPTER 12

Consumption, Investment, Intermediate Product

DISTINCTIONS provisionally made in a previous chapter with a promise of later elaboration have been casually used in the preceding pages; it is time to reexamine them with greater care. I refer to the distinctions among different ends of producing knowledge, to wit, immediate consumption, investment, and intermediate services in the production of other goods—goods which in turn may be destined for consumption, investment, or inputs for producing still other goods.

Production: The Use of Valuable Input for
Valuable Output

In economic theory, "production" implies that "valuable input" is allocated to the bringing forth of "valuable output." The input is valued in terms of foregone opportunities—that is, by the magnitude of the sacrifice of alternative outputs that could be produced in lieu of the output actually obtained. The output is valued in terms of someone's willingness to pay for it. Thus, we do not speak of production if all inputs are "free," that is, if no other output is being "missed" in consequence of the inputs—human energy plus things of any sort—being allocated to the particular activity. Nor do we speak of production if the output is wanted by nobody, neither by those who put it out, nor by those who cause it to be put out, nor by those who are in any way affected by its being put out.

Let us apply these criteria to the transmission of information, say, of a report that the New York Yankees beat the Baltimore Orioles 8-5 in a baseball game. This activity will be regarded as production (in the sense of the conceptual scheme chosen for theoretical consistency) if those who telephone or otherwise transmit the report could have done something else with their time (something they or someone else would appreciate) and if some of those who receive the report would "give something" to hear it (either because their curiosity is thereby satisfied or because they are in any other way "enriched" or "gratified" by receiving or having received the information). The communication of this piece of knowledge would *not* be called production in an economic sense if its transmitters did it for the fun of it without sacrifice of otherwise employable time and effort and if its receivers were totally uninterested and no third party were interested in the transmitters' giving, and the receivers' getting, the information.

The need for statistically operational concepts forces the exclusion of those knowledge-producing activities which, although they require sacrifices on the part of the communicators and give satisfaction to the recipients, fail to give any clue to the statistician of the amounts of cost and satisfaction involved. A man in love may spend several hours a day describing in letters to his beloved his feelings, thoughts, and activities, and he may neglect his work doing so. The recipient of his affection and of his letters may derive the greatest happiness from these reports and would give anything for this knowledge were it not received gratis. The costs and the satisfactions connected with this romantic knowledge escape the statistician's eye and remain unrecorded. Where there are no records of money payments or other transactions, the statistician will usually, perhaps with a regretful shrug, pass on to other matters; purely hypothetical, private opportunity costs and psychic incomes are, as a rule, of no concern to him.

The best-known example of this—from another area—is the classification of cooking in the national-income accounts. Labor employed in the production of meals in restaurants and taverns is entered under national income originating in service industries; labor engaged in the production of meals in private households appears as part of the national income only if it is performed by a hired cook, maid, or housekeeper—domestic service—but is entirely omitted from the statistics if it is performed by the housewife or another unpaid member of the household. That the production of a meal in the household is an effort (disutility) and yields a benefit (utility) is not denied, but it is nevertheless disregarded in the statistics of national product and income. Similar or analogous considerations are valid for the analysis of the production of knowledge.

The production of knowledge will appear in the customary national-product accounts only where it requires the paid services of people or the paid use of installations and materials, so that the costs can be estimated, or where the information services rendered are paid for by somebody—by those served or by a third party, such as the government—so that these payments can be interpreted as an expression of the value of the services rendered.

Investment in Knowledge and Investment for Knowledge

When knowledge is produced in order that, or in the expectation that, the productivity of resources—human, natural, or man-made—will, as a result, increase in the foreseeable future, the production of knowledge can be regarded as an investment. The types of knowledge which chiefly qualify for this designation are those flowing from scientific and technological research and development and from improved or extended schooling, training, and education.

The decision in each particular instance of whether the production of knowledge should be regarded as investment, as consumption, or as intermediate output in the production of other things is rather arbitrary, a matter of judgment. We shall see in subsequent chapters that no reliable objective criteria are available for making this judgment. To anticipate one of the points to be made in interpreting our national-income accounts, we cannot accept all business expenditures for research and development as necessary cost of *current* production, even if our tax laws allow business firms to treat them as such. These expenditures are undertaken in order to improve or secure the competitive position of the firms in the *future*, either through cost reductions or through product improvements. Thus, from an economic point of view they are investment expenditures even if they are "expensed" rather than "capitalized." Where research and development expenditures are financed by the government, our national-income statisticians treat them as "final output," without, however, committing themselves as to whether they are investment or consumption. If one regards the part of these expenditures that is futile or wasted as necessary and inseparable from the apparently successful expenditures, then the entire outlay for research and development should be counted as investment.

The effects of improved and extended schooling will be discussed in both Volumes II and III. The only point to anticipate here is that it would be certainly wrong to regard the entire cost of schooling as *net* investment, and probably wrong to regard it all as *gross* investment. The decision as to what part of the cost of schooling should be characterized as consumption would, I am afraid, be rather controversial, and one may prefer to avoid making such a decision.

Investment in knowledge should not be confused with investment in durable goods needed in the production of knowledge, no matter whether that knowledge may be investment, consumption, or an intermediate product in the production of current output of other things. If, for example, a firm builds another research laboratory, it invests in a durable asset which, for years to come, will be used in the production of technological knowledge designed to increase its productivity; hence, it makes an investment *for* the production of knowledge, a production which in turn will be also an investment *in* knowledge. If, on the other hand, a TV station builds another studio or transmitting plant, it invests in a durable asset which over the years will be used for the most part in the production of pastime knowledge, that is, for consumption purposes. If, to give an example of the third possibility, a manufacturing company buys an electronic computer for use in its payroll, billing, and accounting departments, it invests in a durable asset which over the years will be used in the production of business knowledge for use in its operations as producer of manufactured goods.

Knowledge as Intermediate Product

In a statistical analysis, *investment* expenditures for knowledge and *consumer* expenditures for knowledge are relatively easy to ascertain only if the National Income Division of the Commerce Department has regarded the knowledge in question as "final output" and therefore recorded the expenditures in question in gross national product and national-income accounts. Considerable reinterpretations and modifications may have to be made even in these cases. Serious complications, however, arise in connection with estimates of knowledge produced as an intermediate service in the production of other output.

The statistical problem of obtaining cost estimates of knowledge used in the production of other output can only be overcome without great trouble where firms are specialized in the production of knowledge for business use and are grouped into special service industries whose total sales are reported. For example, where information services and consultation services are sold by incorporated businesses to incorporated businesses engaged in the production of things, statistical problems arise only to the extent that some sales are made to nonbusiness buyers, to consumers. Thus, the services of investment analysts and securities brokers are sold partly to business firms and partly to consumers.[1] On the other hand, the services of certified public accountants, marketing-research organizations, and consulting engineers are sold almost entirely to business firms.

[1] That consumer expenditures for such services are counted as "consumption," although they do not yield direct satisfaction but instead serve to increase the returns from personal savings, is one of the flaws of the accepted techniques of social accounting. It is analogous to the consumer expenditures for transportation to the place of employment, which are officially counted as "consumption" although they are a cost of earning income.

Whether the firms buying these services use them for producing consumer goods or capital goods (durable producer goods) does not matter for our purposes; in either case the production of knowledge serves in the current production of other things, and the cost of the production of knowledge will be part of the cost of these other things, not a separate item in the national product, gross or net. The services of consulting engineers will perhaps be used more often in connection with new construction than with the current production of manufactured goods, and it might be interesting to see what portions of the investment in new plant are payments for knowledge produced in its planning and design. The services of architects are altogether of this sort; whether for industrial or residential construction, they furnish knowledge to be embodied in durable assets, and the cost of this knowledge becomes part of the investment in fixed plant or dwellings.

Where knowledge for business use as an intermediate product in the production of other things is produced, not in separate knowledge-producing industries, but rather within the firms that use it, the problems of statistical compilation become very difficult. If separate departments served these functions, and separate cost accounts were published for these departments, the problem could be solved. Assume, for example, that the information services maintained by large firms were organized as separate departments with separate accounts, or that such accounts were available for all public-relations desks or departments; the costs of providing this sort of public information could then be compiled. But in fact we do not have these data.

Even if the cost data for all special information-producing departments of business firms were available, they would comprise only a small part of the relevant total. For, under modern techniques of manufacturing, a great amount of knowledge is produced and used in one and the same department or even in one and the same operation. In many cases it would be impossible to distinguish the mental, knowledge-producing from the manual, knowledge-using phase of the operation. The operator tending certain machines or apparatuses may have to watch measuring instruments and react by quick manipulations to the information they convey; he may have to turn valves, press pedals, push buttons in accordance with information-giving signals produced by others in the group, by instruments he has to read, or even by information he himself produces by mental operations on the basis of information read from the instruments. The knowledge produced in these instances is an indistinguishable part of the physical operations performed. It would be impossible to quantify this kind of knowledge production. Wherever mental and physical labor are combined in the activities of a person, it will be sounder procedure for our purposes not to attempt an analytical separation of the output. (It can and will be separated in the analysis of labor input, when the occupations approach will be used in Volume VIII.)

Knowledge-Producing Personnel in Business Firms

In every business a considerable percentage of the work force consists of persons specializing in the production of knowledge. This can be said not only of the research, development, planning, and designing personnel but of the entire body of executive, administrative, supervisory, technical, and clerical personnel, from the chairman and president of the firm to the switchboard operator and stock clerk. All the people whose work consists of conferring, negotiating, planning, directing, reading, note-taking, writing, drawing, blueprinting, calculating, dictating, telephoning, card-punching, typing, multigraphing, recording, checking, and many others are engaged in the production of knowledge in the sense in which we understand these words. If complete sets of numerical data on this division of labor within firms were available, we could examine differences in the relevant ratios among various industries, regions, and countries, as well as changes that have taken place over time. It is a fact that the increase in factor productivity in American industry over the years has been associated with an increase in the ratio of knowledge-producing labor to physical labor. And it is very likely that the association has been a causal one. We have often been shown the secular increase in the amount of capital per worker and the enormous rise of the use of machine-generated energy (horsepower) per worker. It would surely be interesting to see statistical evidence of the increase in the quantity of knowledge-producing labor per manual worker.

Evidence of this sort will be produced in later volumes of this work. It will not, we may repeat, relate to the problem of the division between the use of intelligence and the use of physical skill or strength by a manual worker. This cannot be done. But where there is a division of labor, where some members of the work force specialize in the production of information (reports, advice, directions, orders), statistics can show the numbers and ratios involved. A discussion of some of the theoretical problems involved will be found in the last chapter of this volume.

Instruments for the Production of Knowledge

Although we shall have only fragmentary data on human knowledge producers within business firms, we may be able to obtain data on engineering products that serve as knowledge producers. Every firm has a battery of machines, apparatuses, instruments, and gadgets for this purpose.

There are first of all the various devices for the communication of messages, such as bells and light signals, telephones and intercoms, typewriters and multigraphing equipment, and telegraph and teletype systems. There are, furthermore, many devices for the automatic initiation of information, such as thermometers, manometers, speedometers, voltmeters, ammeters, and scores of other measuring instruments. Simple scales, tapes, gauges, calipers, compasses, counters are among nonautomatic measuring devices which aid human knowledge producers in the acquisition of information on such things as weight, length, thickness, all sorts of numbers. Finally there are the devices for the processing of information, such as adding machines, cash registers, calculating machines, up to the complicated computing machines of recent vintage.

For an estimate of the annual cost of knowledge-producing equipment, we should have to know its value, depreciation rates, and maintenance. In lieu of these unavailable data we might do with the annual sales of measuring instruments and office equipment, which can be had from census data. For the most part these sales are to business firms and it is probably not too serious an error if the total (apart from government purchases of electronic computers) is included in business investment.

Some knowledge-producing instruments are sold to consumers. We all buy watches and clocks, which tell us the time of the day; thermometers and barometers, which tell us about the weather; bathroom scales, which tell us whether we have gained too much weight; cameras, which give us pictures preserving the images of our young friends or babies; phonographs, records, and tapes, which reinforce our knowledge of musical compositions; and radios and television sets, which provide us with an abundance of pastime knowledge and with some unwanted knowledge to boot. Consumer expenditures for knowledge-producing instruments figure prominently in the national income, and there is a clear upward trend in this outlay and its share in the consumer's budget.

Who Pays for It and How?

Whether a particular output is regarded as consumption, investment, or nonfinal product is decided, in national-income accounting, not by an analysis of the use made of it, but rather on the basis of who pays for it and how it is treated in private accounting. As a rule, products paid for by consumer expenditures, government expenditures, and those business expenditures which are entered as capital assets in the books of a firm are regarded as final output, whereas business expenditures which are treated as costs of sales are deemed to be for intermediate products.

These rules would not do for our purposes, as I have mentioned before in connection with expenditures for research and development. Since business firms in their tax accounting may treat these expenditures as current expenses, the production of new technology would be regarded as intermediate, as cost of current output of manufactured goods. Yet, in the context of our study, it should be regarded as investment. The fact that government expenditures for research and development are regarded as paying for final output points up the conceptual contradiction and the need for correcting it.

Another instance of contradictory treatment in national-income accounting is radio and television broadcasting. There are in principle three ways of paying for this service: the consumer, the government, or business may pay the bill. If business pays for it and treats it as advertising cost, the national-income accountant calls the service an intermediate output in the production of the goods advertised by the sponsors. If government pays for the service, or if the consumer pays for it, then the national-income accountant calls it final output. Just as the national income is statistically reduced when bachelors marry their cooks, the national income is statistically increased when radio and TV are nationalized. Such a contradiction requires correction in our study: broadcasting will here be regarded as final output, chiefly as consumption, no matter who pays for it and how.

Chatting and Other Knowledge Production by Amateurs

A friendly reader with little sympathy for my wide concept of knowledge, and still less understanding of my conceptual decisions about the knowledge-producing activities that do or do not qualify for inclusion in the calculation of the relevant parts of the national-product account, has presented me with an interesting argument. Since a large part of all knowledge is conveyed from person to person by word of mouth—plain talking—and since people in most societies, the most primitive no less than the most advanced, spend much of their waking hours talking to one another, should not all this talking and chatting be included in what I have called production of knowledge?

The question, seemingly plausible, will hardly bother any reader who has grasped the distinctions I have proposed. To be sure, the majority of people in all walks of life and in all sorts of gainful employment, including completely manual labor, engage in a lot of talking and listening to the talk of fellow workers, bystanders, acquaintances, friends, and relatives. To be sure, all this chatting can create or reinforce knowledge in people's minds, and some of it gives pleasure to the talkers and perhaps also to the listeners. On these two counts—that the chatting produces knowledge and that it is pleasurable—does it not qualify for admission into the product accounts that I am setting up for the totality of knowledge production?

The answer is negative. Indeed, this answer has been explicitly given at various points and has been implicit in several other statements. An implicit statement was contained in the immediately preceding subsection "Who Pays for It and How"? If nobody pays for that knowledge, neither the recipient nor anybody else, its production will not be entered in the product account. Explicit statements were made in the first subsection of this chapter, "Production: The Use of Valuable Input for Valuable Output." There I wrote that production, in economics, implies that "valuable input" is allocated to the bringing forth of "valuable output," that input is valued in terms of foregone opportunities, of alternatives sacrificed by engaging in the activities in question, and that the output is valued in terms of someone's willingness to pay for it.

The fact that some knowledge production is not included in our "product accounts" should not be unduly disturbing. Those who are interested in national accounting and statistical distributions are likely to be more disturbed by too many inclusions than by any exclusions. They would prefer the closest conformance with the principles adopted for official statistics of national income and product. Those who are annoyed by my decision to exclude knowledge production when all inputs are free (neither paid for nor causing opportunity costs) are probably not overly concerned with accounting procedures and statistical distributions. They should accept that most economists have their own preconceptions regarding the treatment of incomes and outputs.

There is, however, one aspect of this discussion that deserves more comment. For it is not only the casual chatting that I exclude from the national accounts of knowledge production, but also many other amateur performances, activities the performers do for fun, for their own pleasure and/or that of their audience. Amateurs—speakers, actors, dancers, painters, sculptors, or musicians—receive no pay for their activities; even if their audiences enjoy the knowledge (verbal, visual, musical) which they receive, they enjoy it "for free." To the extent that no one incurs any cost in connection with these activities, they remain outside the statistical compilations of knowledge production.

CHAPTER 13

USES, VALUE, AND BENEFITS
OF KNOWLEDGE

THIS CHAPTER owes its existence to a sense of frustration about some very hardy misconceptions on the part of information scientists, management consultants, educators, librarians, engineers, R and D specialists, inventors, and many other producers of knowledge.[1] Any producer is interested in what use is being made of his product; he rejoices at the thought of producing something useful—useful especially to society or all mankind. He is convinced that anything that is useful must be of value, and he is pleased to hear that his efforts bestow benefits upon society.

It is not surprising, therefore, that many writers on knowledge and information have proposed research designed to measure the value of knowledge and the social benefits derived from it. A few enterprising ones have actually embarked on such research and have come up with "findings" quite flattering to those who have had a part in producing knowledge or rendering information services. Unfortunately, most of these proposals, let alone the findings, are rather ill conceived, unsound, or even fantastic. In this large study of the production of knowledge and of the "value" of the annual flow of information services, I must not shirk the responsibility of clarifying the issues involved.

USES OF KNOWLEDGE

In earlier chapters I have made a few casual observations on uses of knowledge or of information, but I must not be squeamish about repetitiveness in a work which no one will ever read in one sitting. Indeed, it may be helpful to some readers if my widely dispersed obiter dicta are brought together at one place, where they can be reexamined and reevaluated.

---

[1] This chapter was prepublished, with only minimal alterations but under the same title, in Knowledge: Creation, Diffusion, Utilization, vol. 1, no. 1 (September, 1979), pp. 62-81.

Information Service and Knowledge Acquired

One obstacle to obtaining a clearer vision of the issues in question is the inability of many participants in the discussion to distinguish between the process of information and the contents of the message, that is, the knowledge transmitted. (I discussed the difference between informing and knowing first in Chapter 1 and again in Chapter 2, and this is not the last time I shall come back to it.) If someone speaks of the "value of information" when information is understood as the *act* of informing, this is as if the value of a delivery service depended on the value of what is being delivered; as if the mail carrier conveyed a greater benefit upon society when the letter he delivered contained a secret formula, not just Christmas greetings from a friend. But I have jumped an important step in speaking of value before speaking of use. To "use" information—a process, mind you—is to listen, to look at, to read; in short, it is the reception and, if possible, the understanding of the message, full or partial, by the recipient. The use of the knowledge conveyed is something else. The act of delivering is one thing, the object delivered is another.

This difference is quite obvious in the case of tangible objects. If a parcel service delivers a knife, no one will doubt that the use of the delivery service and the use of the knife are totally different and separate. Such separation is not always possible in the case of services that are performed directly on an object or person. Certain "delivery services" are inseparable from what they deliver. For example, a barber (or hair stylist if he charges higher prices) delivers haircuts with the effect that the recipients emerge with shorter hair on their heads. The recipients have no chance of "not using" the services that have been rendered to them. In contradistinction, the recipient of a letter can decide to throw it unread into the wastebasket. Has he "used" the information service in question? Does use of information—the process of transmission and reception, say, of a letter—mean (a) receiving it and thus getting a chance to read it; (b) receiving it and actually reading it; (c) receiving, reading, and understanding it; (d) receiving, reading, understanding, and appreciating it; (e) receiving, reading, understanding, and appreciating it, plus making it the basis of a decision; or (f) receiving, reading, understanding, and appreciating it, plus letting it help you in making a decision and taking an action (or refusing to act) in line with the decision reached with the help of the knowledge obtained? I submit that the convention of information scientists to mean by information the process of informing, and not the content, should be a cogent reason for restricting the meaning of "use of information" to the first two alternatives, (a) or (b). The other alternatives refer no longer to information as a process, but rather to its contents, the knowledge conveyed.

Pastime Knowledge and Practical Knowledge

Assume we are told a joke; we hear it, understand it, appreciate it, indeed we roar with laughter. Where in this sequence does the "use" of the information stop? Should the appreciation and laughter be included in the "use" or should these be seen as separate effects of the use? If you include the enjoyment and its physiological manifestation among the elements that make up "use of the information," would you not have to say that a joke that does not make you laugh has not been "used"? It seems more reasonable to keep use and effect of use separate. And if you decide to amuse your friends by telling them the joke you have found so hilarious, you are initiating numerous separate processes of information (or, more correctly, communication). You are then using the knowledge acquired from your informant to render the same service to others by passing it on to them.

Ascending from frivolous or pastime knowledge to more serious matters, say, to the practical knowledge a consultant or market researcher intends to impart to his client or superior in business management, we confront similar occasions for hairsplitting. Assume that this "management-information service" takes the form of preparation and submission of a lengthy report. Can we say that it is being used when it is merely received and filed away without being read, let alone studied? What operational definition of "use" should we adopt? Should we perhaps administer oral or written examinations to the business managers in order to ascertain that they have read and understood the report? Should we just ask them and believe their answers? Should we play historian and test whether the recommended actions have actually been taken? The latter test would be quite inconclusive, for it is possible and not unusual that the client or superior after studying the report decides against taking the recommended action. The opposite, incidentally, is also possible (and I know of instances in which it happened): the manager in charge may have taken the recommended action without ever having read or even seen (or heard of) the report in question.

Apart from these obstacles, an operational definition of use is practically impossible also because of the time lags involved. Action may follow a recommendation after years of delay and without recollection of the recommendation, at least without conscious recollection. In all these cases, however, whether the reasoning, the recommendations, the ideas contained in the report were used immediately or with great delay or not at all, the "use" refers not to the *information*, not to the process of transmitting messages, but to the *contents*, the knowledge conveyed by it.

Process versus Contents of Information

Most people are not fussy in the use of words. Since sloppy speech drives out meticulous speech, we find that in the same breath speakers use information as a process interchangeably with information as the contents of a message, and no one is the worse for it. One may object, however, to inconsistency in the speech of specialists, experts who want to set us an example in the discriminating choice of terms. Information scientists have solemnly declared that they refer to a *process* when they say "information," and do not refer to the *contents* of the message conveyed by the process. Alas, these declarations are contradicted by hundreds of statements about the "use of information," where it is quite clear that it is the use of the message or of the knowledge resulting from its interpretation that is actually meant.

This was surely the case in some of the examples above, say, in the telling of a joke and the report to business management. If one wants to be consistent in keeping separate the process of informing and the message or knowledge conveyed by that process, one would be well advised to avoid altogether speaking of "uses" of information, except if one wishes to refer to choices among alternative modes of information. One may select a particular mode of information in preference to others; thus one may consider using the telephone or writing and posting a letter, or using a typewriter or a tape recorder. But as far as the use by the recipient is concerned, his part in the process of information is confined to listening or reading; everything that goes beyond reception, decoding, and interpreting is no longer a part of information as a process. I come back to the analogy of a transport-and-delivery service in relation to the object transported and delivered. Use of a mode of transportation and use of the transported object are different things. Likewise, use of a mode of information should not be confused with use of the message or knowledge conveyed.

Some More Examples of Use

I hope I have succeeded in making my point. Those who, in linguistic permissiveness, do not mind using the word "information" for the contents of the message as well as the process by which it is transmitted have every right to speak of (immediate or delayed) "uses of information." Linguistic purists, however, who have defined information as a process, as activities designed to transmit and receive messages, cannot reasonably speak of "uses of information" when they mean to refer to the decisions made and actions taken by the recipients of the knowledge obtained.

If I propose to give a few more examples illustrating the reasonable meanings of "use" of knowledge transmitted by information, it is chiefly in order to avoid the impression that information is always oriented towards decisions and actions. This impression has been fostered by information scientists whose primary concerns are studies of the design of information systems for clients such as the military establishment or business management. The objectives of systems design are foremost in their minds, so much so that decision-making and action-taking become parts of the definitions which they propose. They overlook the fact that most information systems in operation have objectives other than to facilitate action.

The most expensive of the information systems operated by our nation is public education. Its major purposes are to improve basic skills, to develop reasoning power, to induce and satisfy intellectual curiosity, to foster accepted moral standards, and to impart knowledge of all types. Of all this, only a minute fraction serves to "facilitate action." At best, one may say that any actions induced by the learning acquired at school are distributed over the whole lifetime of the students and graduates and are only very indirectly related to the processes of information employed in the school system or to the contents of the educational communications.

Another large portion of the nation's production of knowledge is what goes on under the heading of research and development. In the part of this work in which we shall discuss R and D, we shall find that the legislature, in authorizing and appropriating funds, adheres to a rather myopic pragmatism. The legislators want "practical results" as soon as possible and thus favor applied research and development. Basic research, designed to generate findings not immediately applicable, is treated quite niggardly, although the science advisers try hard to show that basic research and the fundamental knowledge it is designed to generate are essential for the long-run advancement of "useful knowledge." But, obviously, basic research is not mission-oriented, and the information system for the dissemination of the new insights of that research does not facilitate action—unless the term "action" is used in such a wide sense as to include further research, basic or applied, in the future.

Some subjects of basic research may never lead to anything that may be called useful knowledge in a materialistic sense. There is such a thing as knowledge for the sake of knowledge—let us recall the *Bildungswissen* in Max Scheler's classification (see above, Chapter 4). By its very definition it excludes any possible use other than being the mark of an educated person. No action of any sort is facilitated by an information system designed for the dissemination of such purely intellectual knowledge.

Pastime knowledge is another category of knowledge transmitted without any thought of action based on it. Much of what is disseminated by the mass media of communication, both the print media and the electronic media, is of that sort. Its only purpose is to entertain or to satisfy a kind of curiosity that cannot qualify as intellectual, it is acquired in "passive relaxation," without intellectual exertion (see above, Chapter 4). The objectives of communicating this type of knowledge are to please, to entertain, to stimulate, to satisfy; if these functions are regarded as "uses of knowledge," so be it. But "action-oriented"—that is, oriented towards action on the part of the recipient—they are not.

The Value of Knowledge

The preceding discourse on Uses of Knowledge can be seen as a logical preparation for a discourse on the Value of Knowledge. Readers acquainted with theories of value, especially in economics, will remember that "use value" has long been a favored expression, particularly as an antonym for "exchange value." This pair of expressions has played an important role in solving the "paradox of value," or "antinomy of value," which confronted early economists anxious to explain that the most useful things, such as air or water, commanded a low or zero price, whereas rather useless things, such as precious stones or pearls, fetched highest prices. Hence the apparent antinomy of low use value and high exchange value, and vice versa.

The solution to the paradox lay in the consideration of the relative quantities in which the various goods or services are available. Air is indispensable for our survival, but one single cubic inch of air, with all the air around us, makes no difference to our well-being. Relative scarcity, or marginal utility,[2] has proved to be the determining factor in explaining the value of a small unit of the object, no matter how much or how little the total availability may mean to any individual or to society as a whole. The value of a small unit of whatever it may

---

[2] "Marginal," because utility, usefulness, or valuation refer only to the *last* unit, not to the total supply.

be cannot be high as long as there is plenty of it available, so that little depends on having that one unit at one's disposal.[3]

Value of Information

We are all by now fed up with the ever-recurring argument about information versus knowledge. To those who have accepted the definition of information as a process, as a set of activities regardless of what it is that people are informing (or getting informed) about, it is clear that the value of these activities depends only on the scarcity values or opportunity values of the productive factors—labor, materials, equipment—employed in producing the service of transmitting and receiving messages or pieces of knowledge.

To the less discriminating or more permissive word users who allow information to stand also for the contents of the messages conveyed, it should not be difficult to understand an argument in terms of messages or pieces of knowledge, avoiding the expression "information" when the reference is to content rather than process.

Value of Knowledge to Individual Would-Be Knowers

The value to an individual of any quantity of any tangible or intangible good is measured by what he would give in exchange for it—what he would pay for it—if he did not have it. This is quite simple—indeed too simple, in that it assumes that the individual is aware of what that commodity, or that additional quantity of it, would do for him. For most things this assumption is acceptable: people usually have a pretty good idea of how much an extra cup of coffee or ounce of meat per day would contribute to their happiness. But can they know this also about an extra piece of knowledge which they neither possess nor ever have possessed and which they cannot know how important it might be for them to have, because if they knew it they would possess it? We cannot know what a piece of knowledge may be worth to us before we know what it is. Is this a logical trap from which we cannot extricate ourselves? It is not a serious one and does not cause much trouble, at least not with regard to most types of knowledge. After all, knowledge is not a homogeneous good and the problem of its valuation is quite different for different kinds of knowledge.

Let us begin with a bit of pastime knowledge in the category of gossip about some acquaintance of ours. Assume that Tom and Dick

---

[3] This brief comment may have served readers who have little background in economics as a helpful introduction to a discussion of the "value" of knowledge. To economists I must apologize for a superfluous and simplistic "filler" in my exposition.

whisper to each other something they know about Harry; I am curious, but they do not divulge their little secret. I would be willing to pay them for "letting me in" on their secret. Not that I would anticipate any action I might take on the basis of the probably trivial piece of gossip; but I am curious and want to know what I now do not know. (It is even conceivable that I actually do know it and merely believe that it would be news to me.) It may be worth a few dollars to me to have my curiosity satisfied—the amount of my payment depending on how much I care about Harry and, of course, on the size of my income. In this case the knowledge in question is valued precisely because of the state of my ignorance. Having acquired the knowledge at a price, I may conclude that it was not worth it, but this happens often for other purchases too; values are based on expectations ex ante, not on regrets ex post.

Incidentally, is the value of this piece of knowledge to me dependent on the use I plan to make of it? I surely do not contemplate any action, but to make use of knowledge need not mean to act on it. If the disclosure of the secret satisfies my curiosity, this is all the use that I get out of this particular piece of knowledge. There is nothing special about this use of a thing acquired; I value and buy a piece of candy to satisfy my appetite, and I value and buy a glass of orange juice to satisfy my thirst. In all these cases the use of the acquired object—the juice, the piece of candy, and the piece of knowledge— lies in their meeting my desire, and their value to me is determined by the satisfaction that I as their consumer anticipate.

Practical and Intellectual Knowledge

Let us proceed to an example of practical knowledge. We have concluded in an earlier chapter that the acquisition of such knowledge may be in the nature of consumption, current production cost, or investment, but it will be sought as a basis for action. (This is what makes it practical—and, incidentally, what makes it fit better into the models of information scientists.) Practical knowledge can be acquired for consumption if it serves household purposes of an ephemeral character (like a weather forecast); it is investment if it is of enduring usefulness (like a cookbook). Expenditures for practical knowledge serving business management are current cost of production if it is incurred only for the current year's output (like a shortterm analysis of the market for raw materials); it is business investment if it is expected to be of lasting usefulness (like an advance in technology, perhaps a patented invention or some secret technical know-how). In all these cases, the values of the knowledge to be acquired are based on anticipations; ex post surprises (pleasant or disappointing) do not count, except as experiences from which one can learn and improve one's judgment regarding future valuations of practical knowledge.

A methodical reader will want me to go on to examples of intellectual knowledge. By definition such knowledge is valued, not for purposes of action, but only for the satisfaction of intellectual curiosity, for the enjoyment of intellectual appetites for the "appreciation of the existence of open problems and cultural values" (see above, Chapter 4), and it can be acquired only "in active concentration" by people willing to exert themselves for the sake of becoming more knowledgeable and better educated for no practical purposes whatever. The value of such knowledge to individual would-be knowers is difficult to ascertain because much of it is subsidized by society (or rather by acts of legislatures and executive decisions made by people spending other people's money). The need for subsidies is explained by the fact that the taste for intellectual knowledge is an acquired taste, and that it can be acquired only if large doses of intellectual knowledge are forced upon or thrust upon rather unwilling individual investors. (Since the early administrations of such knowledge are rarely enjoyed by those exposed to it, the recipients cannot be regarded as consumers but only as reluctant investors in intellectual benefits which authorities, donors, and teachers hope will accrue eventually, in a remote future.)

Only after the taste for intellectual knowledge is well developed—as a result of parental example and exhortation, of peer-group pressures, and with the considerable help from the snob appeal of elitism—can one expect a self-sustaining desire and effective demand for additional quantities of intellectual knowledge. Thus, the economic value of this type of knowledge to individual customers depends on their earlier-accumulated stocks of knowledge and their moral allegiance to the cultural values of a beau monde, an elitist upper crust of society. The incremental thirst for intellectual knowledge will manifest itself in an effective demand for books (scholarly, general, fiction, poetry), journals (reporting on research and surveying scholarly literature), magazines (intellectual, literary, opinion), theater tickets (drama, opera, ballet), concert tickets and subscriptions (symphony, chamber music), lectures, seminars, courses (continuing and recurrent higher education), and so on.

The value of schooling at all levels is still more difficult to ascertain, even if we carefully distinguish the value to the individual and the value to society. Although this distinction is essential, the difference between the "private" and the "social" value of education can be better explained when both are discussed together.

The Private and Social Value of Education

This topic will be treated in considerable detail in at least two other parts of this work: in Volume II in chapters on knowledge as human capital, and in Volume III in chapters on benefits of education, on comparative differences in schooling and earnings, and on the productivity of education. With the prospect of these elaborate discussions, I may, and should at this juncture, confine myself to presenting the major issues in utmost brevity, without trying to examine them in depth.

The distinction between private value of education—value from the students' and parents' point of view—and its social value—value from the point of view of "society as a whole"—was dictated by the realization (fact? belief? hypothesis?) that the benefits from schooling that accrue to the entire community or society exceed the benefits that accrue directly to those of its members who actually receive the schooling, that is, the students. Such a statement presupposes that one can *identify* all effects of schooling (positive, negative, on the students and on others, over the long run) and can measure, or at least *estimate*, their magnitude or importance. Several of these effects, however, resist quantification in any terms and valuation in terms of money or of any common denominator that would allow summing up and comparing with alternative uses of available resources.

Some examples of nonpecuniary effects on society at large, effects emphasized by writers on the social value of formal education, are inculcation of high moral standards, cultivation of desirable social attitudes, facilitation of political maturity, development of critical abilities, and refinement of styles of living.[4] Can these and similar achievements of our educational system be proved, quantified, appraised? Some of these attributions are controversial; but even if they were undisputed, would we find an approach to an objective, or perhaps a widely accepted subjective, valuation? With such doubts, it is understandable that most economists have preferred to abstain from putting dollar values on the nonpecuniary "spillover effects" on society at large. (The professional jargon calls them "external benefits," because they are not included in the internal calculations and considerations of the direct users of educational services.)

Even the internal benefits—the effects on the students at school and afterwards for the rest of their lives—include some that are not

[4] A reader of my manuscript raised the question whether the increased investment in formal education during the 1960s had these or perhaps the opposite effects. As I say in the next lines of the text, I have not found a way to answer such questions. I believe that those who have the answers rely largely on their prejudices.

pecuniary and not subject to quantification. One may make lists of what these effects might be; one may add judgments about their importance; but again, one cannot easily come up with valuations in terms of money, except if one indulges in highly subjective speculations. Economists have therefore confined themselves to valuations that can be based on money figures found in official statistical records, namely, in the statistics of incomes earned by graduates with different numbers of years of school attendance.

Higher Earnings for Longer Schooling

If persons with sixteen years of schooling (plus given years of work experience) earn more than those with only fifteen years, or only twelve years, of schooling, the difference in earnings can conceivably be attributed to the difference in the years at school. Conceivably—but not really, because other factors may be involved.

Many factors may determine actual differences in earnings, and some of these factors are interrelated and also connected with the length of time the students devote to school attendance. For example, higher native intelligence, greater diligence, stronger motivation and ambition, more drive and energy, better parental guidance, larger family income, a family background more conducive to a desire to learn, better connections in the search for jobs.

It is difficult to disentangle the effects of these factors, which at the same time predestine the young people to stay at school for more years, to study harder and more effectively, to get better jobs, and to be more productive in these jobs. A simple attribution of higher earnings to longer schooling would surely be wrong, and the use of multiple-regression analysis to parcel out the earnings differentials among the contributing factors would presuppose that they can be quantified and that the quantities are known. This is not the case, and the use of some statistical "proxies" is highly questionable. For example, although one could conceivably measure diligence by the hours spent on studying, it would not be practically possible to obtain accurate data. One has not yet found acceptable statistical proxies for ambition, energy, and drive, perhaps the most important factors of all.

Some enterprising analysts have taken the position that "we shall do what we can to eliminate those of the contributing factors on which we can get a numerical handle; but then we shall accept the residual as the effect of longer schooling, which we are convinced plays a large role." This is not an unreasonable position, but it leaves many conceptual and statistical problems to deal with. I shall defer their discussion for later, but I must not defer pointing to some ques-

tions regarding the underlying theory. Does the attribution of incremental lifetime earnings to incremental years of schooling furnish
an unambiguous value of the earnings-producing capacity of schooling and of its productivity-increasing capacity? These are two
different things, since a graduation certificate or diploma will often
procure higher rates of pay even if the school attendance has not increased the graduate's productivity. Moreover, what exactly is
meant by the "value" of education: the capitalized value of one
year's increment in earnings? or the increment in lifetime earnings?
And does the *increment* in earnings attributed to an *increment* in
schooling give us the value of the *total* stock of education embodied
in the *total* labor force? Some of these questions have been explored
and answered rather convincingly, but one cannot assert with confidence that we have found an unambiguous method of measuring the
money value of education either for the students or for society.

These brief remarks on a big and difficult subject have not yet included any reference to the quality of education and to its contents.
It can hardly be assumed that, say, three years of poor teaching of
"civics" at high school can be the equivalent of three years of good
teaching of mathematics. Or that it makes no difference to the
graduates' productivity—in the sense of their capacity to add to the
nation's product—whether they have studied law, anthropology, or
engineering. To be sure, we have no alternative but to take the
employees' earnings as a reflection of the value of their work to their
employers and, on the basis of certain theories of competitive-
market mechanisms, also as a reflection of the value of their work to
the whole economy. Yet, several qualifications regarding the
applicability of these theories to conditions of the real world—
which probably deviate from those postulated for the theoretical
model—will warrant some reservations regarding possible divergences between private and social values. Research on differential
incomes earned by graduates of different departments at colleges
and universities is not yet sufficiently advanced to justify more than
speculative statements on the comparative productivity of different
curricula.

An Alternative Notion of the Value of Schooling

The foregoing discussion may have served as a brief (and superficial)
introduction to the most widely employed and most carefully developed technique of arriving at a private value of education. The main
idea in examining the values of anything is to find the underlying
reason for the demand for it. If a "demand curve" can be ascertained
or at least imagined, and intersected with a (hypothetical) "cost

curve," the quantity purchased can be "shown" (in a graph) and "explained." (I use all these quotation marks in order to indicate that none of the terms so marked is unambiguous.) The marginal valuation—marginal utility, marginal productivity—is supposed to explain what quantity the would-be buyers will demand at a particular price or cost to them. If the marginal valuation for various quantities of schooling (formal education) is determined by the incremental lifetime earnings attributed to incremental units (courses, years) of schooling—with the stream of earnings duly discounted at the relevant rate at which expected future accruals are capitalized to present values—we can explain the quantity purchased by private individuals (by parents for their young children, later by the adolescent or adult students themselves) at the "private cost" they have to incur.

The private cost depends in a large measure on the size of the public subsidy. For primary school, the state pays most or all of the cost in most countries. For upper-secondary schools (senior high schools), colleges, and graduate schools, varying portions of the capital cost and operating cost of the educational institutions are often paid from public funds and endowment incomes rather than by the students. On the other hand, foregone earnings will be a large cost to these students since they are of working age and have to sacrifice large sums of potential earnings, as they refrain from seeking gainful employment and devote their time to studying, or at least to attending classes.

To make sense of the concept of a genuinely private demand for formal education, one would have to "assume away" not only all subsidies but also all forms of coercion. Compulsory school attendance, through statutory enactments, government regulations, or social pressures (including peer-group pressures) affect the position of the demand curve: the number of units of schooling (course credits or years) taken by persons of school age are then not determined by their own valuations of schooling but by the legislators and other authorities.[5] There have been suggestions of drawing demand curves for formal education and deriving the "value" to the students from the amounts they actually pay for the quantity acquired plus the amounts they would have been prepared to pay if they did not get it for less. These are ideas which economists have often discussed under the heading of unpaid value, or "consumer surplus." Since

---

[5] The private value of education, or school attendance, to perhaps myopic (but still rational) pupils (or their parents) may be influenced or even determined by the height of penalties they risk for violating the laws or ordinances that make school attendance compulsory.

the same ideas have been advanced for several other kinds of information services and knowledge goods, it might be helpful to some readers if we offered further examples.

The Private and Social Value of Scientific Journals

In a statement on the "Value of Journals to Society," in a report of a task group of a committee formed by the National Academy of Science and the National Academy of Engineering, we are told that "one can make rough quantitative estimates of certain portions of the value of [scientific and technological] journals to society, estimates that show that this value exceeds a certain lower bound already many times larger than the total cost of producing the journals."[6]

The argument begins with the perfectly acceptable definition of the "social value of journal" as the sum of its "value to current subscribers, that is, to the users they represent" and its "value to others, including future generations." The value to current subscribers is stated to be the sum of "current direct value" and "current indirect value," the former being the value to the direct "user" (reader, I suppose) of the journal, the latter the value to those who "receive information via contacts with others who have used journals." The task group believes that the "two terms [direct and indirect value] are comparable with each other," which I translate to mean that the indirect value is not much less than the direct value—whatever that may be. The report then proceeds to apply to the task of estimating the "direct value" the time-dishonored method of taking the integral of all (unknown) marginal utilities which the users would obtain from their copies of the journal (or the integral of all likewise unknown maximum prices they would be prepared to pay for them).

This method has been accepted by some economists for *small* changes in prices charged or quantities taken but has been roundly rejected for determining *total* values obtained by buyers or takers of any goods or services. The literature on the integrability of unpaid utility or "consumer surplus" is quite complex, and only those who are untroubled by any familiarity with it would dare to apply these notions to actual estimates of total value.[7] Yet, the report boldly as-

[6] Committee on Scientific and Technical Communication, *Report of the Task Group on the Economics of Primary Publication* (Washington, D.C.: National Academy of Science, 1970), p. 9.—It is interesting to note that the task group did not include any professional economists.

[7] For the benefit of noneconomists, references to selected items in the literature on the concept of consumers' surplus shall be given: Alfred Marshall, *Principles of Economics*, 8th ed. (London: Macmillan, 1920 [1st ed. 1890]), Book 3, chapter 6, sections 1-4, pp. 124-133; Arthur Cecil Pigou, *The Economics of Welfare*, 4th ed. (London:

serts that the "sums of the value estimates of all the subscribers who actually get the journal"—a "good general physics journal"—can "hardly be much less than" five times its production cost, and "the total social value of such a journal is likely to be over ten times its production cost".[8] If these and similar conclusions had been submitted to a panel of renowned economists, they would have advised the authors of the report to abstain from publishing them.[9]

Perhaps it would be fair at this place to offer some hints that may enable the noneconomist to judge some of the arguments against the use of the theory of consumer surplus to estimate the "total value" of goods. Think of the total value of air, now available at a zero price; should we ask each person to tell us how much he would pay, if necessary, for the first cubic inch of air, for the second, third, and so forth, up to the total quantity he consumes? Since air is indispensable for survival, the total value, in the sense of the integral of the maximum price offered for each successive unit, would surely exceed the entire national income; no one could afford to pay any price at all for anything else. Moving now to less important goods, such as various foodstuffs, pieces of clothing, or books, we should immediately understand that the maximum prices people could offer to pay for successive units of any one good would depend on the prices at which they can obtain other goods. This means that the total value of any good would be high, low, or zero depending on the prices of other goods. The total value of *all* goods, if it were not taken to be based on the prices *actually* paid but on prices *potentially* extorted from the buyers, would obviously be a nonsense concept. The total value of the quantity of any one good actually bought cannot be estimated as the integral of prices potentially extorted with prices of all other goods and services assumed to be given and unchanged, because, if this same method were used for these other goods and services, we would obtain an enormous multiple of total production and consumption. What sense does it make to say that the national

Macmillan, 1950), pp. 56-57; John R. Hicks, *Value and Capital* (Oxford: Clarendon Press, 1939), pp. 38-41; Hicks, "The Four Consumer's Surpluses," *Review of Economic Studies*, vol. 11, no. 1 (1943), pp. 31-41; Hicks, *A Revision of Demand Theory* (Oxford: Clarendon Press, 1956), pp. 95-106 and 169-179; Fritz Machlup, "Professor Hicks' Revision of Demand Theory," *American Economic Review*, vol. 47 (March 1957), pp. 119-128.

[8] *Report*, p. 8.

[9] Most of the argumentation is based on an appendix for which Dr. Conyers Herring took responsibility. It was in turn based on much highly creditable research but went too far in accepting questionable conceptions. Herring probably relied too much on the reasoning employed in the doctoral dissertation by Sanford V. Berg, "Structure, Behavior, and Performance in the Scientific Journal Market" (Yale University, 1970).

product has a "total value" a thousand times higher than the value based on market prices? Moreover, comparisons among total values of *each* separate good estimated by this method would be irrelevant to any kind of economic valuation or policy.[10] To come back to the case of journals: that a few persons might offer thousands of dollars for a subscription if they could not get it otherwise has absolutely nothing to do with the total value of these journals and cannot tell us anything about the social desirability of subsidies or other supports favoring journals over medical care, whiskey, tobacco, or diapers.

Benefits from Knowledge

If you suspect that in a section on benefits after one on value you will get "more of the same" under another name, you are quite right. Many writers have used value—gross and net, private and social—just as an equivalent of, and completely interchangeably with, benefit—again, gross and net, private and social. Some have differentiated them a little by stating that the value (of knowledge as of anything else) is derived from, or determined by, the benefits expected from it. But, if there is a one-to-one relationship between the two, the proposition that value is not the same thing as benefit but a logical consequence of it is not saying very much from a pragmatic point of view.

Some writers have a better excuse for focusing on benefits rather than on value: they want to get away from doctrinal controversies, for example, whether the value of a good or service is determined by its cost or by its utility. To make it quite clear that they want to compare benefits with costs, and estimate or calculate the difference, the avoidance of the term "value" may be justified.

[10] The reader may wish to see what some other economists have thought of the applicability of the theory of consumers' surplus. Paul Samuelson concluded that consumers' surplus is a worse than useless concept—worse because it confuses. *Foundations of Economic Analysis* (Cambridge: Harvard University Press, 1947), pp. 194-195. Ian M. D. Little regarded it as no more than a "theoretical toy." *A Critique of Welfare Economics*, 2d ed. (Oxford: Clarendon Press, 1957), p. 180. A qualified defense of the conception was offered by Robert D. Willig, "Consumer's Surplus Without Apology," *American Economic Review*, vol. 66 (September 1976), pp. 589-597. Willig gave a rigorous proof for the validity of estimates of consumers' surplus provided it refers to only *one single consumer* and uses not the usual (Marshallian) demand curve but the (Hicksian) compensated demand curve—compensated for the changes in income parameters, which vary with each change in price. Thus, ". . . *at the level of the individual consumer*, cost-benefit welfare analysis can be performed rigorously and unapologetically by means of consumer's surplus" (p. 596).

Benefit-and-Cost Analysis

Economic analysis of benefits expected to be derived and costs expected to be incurred becomes important whenever market prices for certain goods or services either do not exist or are regarded as irrelevant or misleading as guides in decisions aiming at an efficient allocation of resources. Many decisions about public investment, public regulation, public subsidization, and other public intervention can be made sensibly only if expected benefits can be compared with expected costs, that is, if they are based on a benefit-and-cost analysis.[11]

The case for government action arises ordinarily in connection with "collective" goods and services. These have one or both of two properties: (1) they are *public* goods and/or (2) their production or consumption has *external* effects. Public goods are those which nonpaying people cannot be kept from using; if these goods (or services) exist at all, it is not possible, or not practicable, or too expensive, to exclude nonpayers from using them. (Examples: streets, street signs, street cleaning, better air thanks to a large park, police protection.) Externalities are benefits (or injuries) from producing or consuming that accrue to others than the producers or consumers and are therefore not reflected in the prices charged or paid. "Market prices are not, in those cases, adequate measures of social value."[12]

Benefit-and-cost analysis is then used for projects or government-action programs where market prices are strongly suspected of disregarding some important parts of social benefits or social costs. In the case of public goods the benefits of the nonpaying users (beneficiaries) are not reflected in the prices received and revenues collected by the producers. In the case of external economies accruing to other producers, these economies, though possibly passed on (under the pressure of competition) to consumers, are not reflected in the prices and revenues received by the producer.

The existence of such instances, where benefits to others than the producers and direct consumers are not paid for to those who are re-

---

[11] Sensitive readers may wonder about the variants in which this combination of words is used; they find cost-benefit analysis more often than benefit-cost analysis, and they see the pair of nouns in their role as adjectival modifiers of "analysis" linked by hyphens more often than by the conjunction "and." Why? Because many economists are tone-deaf and have forgotten that they say "profit-and-loss account," "income-and-expense statement," and "pleasure-and-pain calculus"; a better feeling for rhythm or more orderly thinking would dictate the order (first the plus, then the minus) as well as the use of the conjunction.

[12] Robert Dorfman, "Introduction," in Robert Dorfman, ed., *Measuring Benefits of Government Investments* (Washington: Brookings Institution, 1965), p. 5.

sponsible for generating them, is taken as a justification of governmental subsidies, regulation, or even investment or production by the government. It has been widely assumed and asserted that such instances are especially frequent in various kinds of knowledge production and information services. This makes benefit-and-cost analysis particularly relevant for the undertaking on which we have embarked in this treatise.

Typically, such an analysis begins with "listing the various social and economic groups likely to be affected by the particular . . . program under investigation." Next comes "a listing of the various impacts" and also longer-run influences on the various groups. Then comes the attempt to place values on each influence upon each group.[13] Alas, many significant influences cannot be quantified, and still less valuated, in terms of money. Where valuations are not possible, one may substitute for them wide ranges of money equivalents, say, "more than one million dollars but less than one billion dollars in the admittedly prejudiced opinion of the analyst."

Five Types of Benefit-and-Cost Comparisons

Since there is a full spectrum of meanings, ranging from an implicit sentiment about the worthwhileness of certain favorite projects to an explicit calculation based on statistical data, we must do what is usually done when a spectrum is analyzed or examined: we must separate it arbitrarily into distinct bands. I propose, then, quite arbitrarily, five different types of what may be meant by benefit-and-cost comparisons.[14]

Type 1 is the implicit sentiment, sans analysis, in favor of the particular project, the worthwhileness of the project or program being taken entirely for granted. Everyone with a favorite project will, when asked, assert that "of course" the benefits from it are greater than the costs. (If you put the question to the legislators in Congress who vote for certain river projects and against increased aid to education, they will certainly say that these river projects come out much better in a benefit-and-cost comparison than further aid to education—even if they have neither theoretical arguments nor empirical data to support such contentions.)

Type 2 may be seen in explicit propositions about the value of the program, in which you impose your own value judgments upon the

[13] Ibid., p. 9.

[14] This subsection is taken almost verbatim from comments I made on a paper by Burton A. Weisbrod as reported in Dorfman's volume of proceedings of the Brookings Conference. See Fritz Machlup, "Comments," in Dorfman, Measuring Benefits, pp. 150-151.

people of the commonwealth. You "know" what is best for society, though you do not care to say why, or to defer or refer to the opinions of others.

Type 3 is more than an imposition of your individual value judgments; it is an assumption that you and others know what society wants, what kinds of benefits it may derive from the program, and how big these benefits are. There is still no analysis, but the assumption appears to be moving closer to matters that deserve to be taken seriously.

Type 4 is based on theoretical analysis, where you at least state what kind of empirical information you would need to make a calculation or an estimate of the benefits and costs: data on prices and incomes, and on all sorts of actual and potential outputs, individual valuations, willingness to pay, demand and supply elasticities, future increases in the labor force, future changes in technology, and so on. If you knew all these, then you would be able to tell us just how the relevant benefits and costs could be calculated.

Type 5 is the actual calculation of benefits and costs in which all or much of the required information is available and utilized. Since there are always some relevant items for the estimation of benefits or costs that are not measurable, due allowance for these items must somehow be made. Some opportunity costs, for example, may not be available in any usable statistical form, and you will have to rely on rather speculative chains of reasoning leading to some estimates, however vague. After you make a good case for the numerical values chosen, you will put them into your calculation.[15]

Eager Ophelimetricians

Most economists have long since abandoned as hopeless and irrelevant the aim of measuring the total utility or the total benefits obtained from the existence, availability, or consumption of a class of good or service. Some overzealous advocates of measurement, however, impressed by the claim that "science is measurement" (and its corollary, "no measurement, no science"), continue their ef-

[15] In light of the above, I shall classify a research project in which I was engaged some twenty-five years ago, involving benefit-and-cost analysis, as Type 4. I had no actual data and merely attempted to state just what data I would have to have for an evaluation of benefits and costs. In any case, I wrote some 200 pages of a draft on the benefits and costs of the patent system. The draft is still sitting in my bookcase, and I shall probably never use it. At the time I certainly lacked the courage to publish, feeling sure that everybody would say: "What of it? You don't have the data. Why make all that fuss?"

forts at measuring the total benefits which society derives from having a particular class of good or service available.

We can find these eager ophelimetricians[16] among the analysts of virtually all specialties of information services, such as publication of scientific journals, design for retrieval systems of documents, programs for the reproduction and distribution of reports, and so forth. They seek methods for the "quantification of benefits," even for "objective measures of value," and for "dollar calibration"—by which they mean "the evaluation, in dollar terms, of the pluralistic self-interest judgments" and which they call "the crucial step in establishing a connection between the benefits of a service and the world of dollars." They even advance a "theory of social value," which presupposes that "the dollar-calibration data . . . obtained from market response" are supplemented by "some assumptions about the behavior of the demand curve beyond the range that is empirically accessible."[17]

Some of the zeal of the would-be measurers of the total benefits that are conferred upon society by the provision of scientific information as "a public good" was reinforced and supported by a doctoral dissertation in economics in which the author attempted to "measure" the demand for journals in physics and chemistry.[18] The gist of the thesis was reported later in the *Journal of the American Society for Information Science*.[19] The exposition was misleading in many respects, especially in failing to distinguish estimates of *marginal changes* in benefits attributable to *small changes* in prices and quantities from estimates or "measurements" of *total* benefits. The author made assumptions about shapes (linearity) and about parallel and nonparallel shifts of demand curves, which he drew from one axis to the other, that is, from the price at which the quantity purchased would be reduced to zero to the quantity that would be purchased at a zero price. He thus hypostatized a teaching device, a

[16] *Ophelimon* is the Greek word for helpful, and *metron* means measure. "Ophelimity" was used by Vilfredo Pareto for what Austrian and English economists had meant by utility. Vilfredo Pareto, *Cours d'économie politique* (Lausanne: F. Rouge, 1896-97). Pareto, who had first believed in cardinal utility, later (after 1900) ridiculed the idea of its measurability.

[17] Victor J. Danilov, Conyers Herring, and Donald J. Hillman, *Report of the Panel on Economics of the Science Information Council* (Washington: National Technical Information Service, January 1973), pp. 23, 25, 28, 32.

[18] Sanford V. Berg, "Structure, Behavior, and Performance," p. 26.

[19] Sanford V. Berg, "An Economic Analysis of the Demand for Scientific Journals," *Journal of the American Society for Information Science*, vol. 23 (January-February 1972), pp. 23-29.

heuristic idealized geometric and algebraic model, into an operational set of empirical data, which in fact are unknown and unknowable. And what is even worse, he failed to point out that all these fictitious empirical data are irrelevant for the purpose of sound decision-making for public policy.

Why they are irrelevant for decisions on public policy bears repeating. The looks of a demand curve in its upper ranges, far above the level of the cost of producing the good or service in question, may be a nice subject for teaching and philosophizing, but for policy decisions designed to increase social welfare it makes no difference whether this purely hypothetical curve is linear, concave, convex, flat, steep, elastic, inelastic. That people get a huge benefit from breathing air, for which they pay nothing, is neither a reason for making them pay for this free gift of nature nor a reason for subsidizing the production of more air. That some people or firms get a very large benefit from reading a journal in physical chemistry, and might be prepared to pay $10,000 for a subscription if they had to, does not make it sound public policy either to extort this price from them or to subsidize the journal, reduce its price, or add more pages to it. There may be economic reasons for subsidies, price discrimination, or more pages, but the shape of the demand curve in its upper ranges, and the large benefits to buyers who do not have to pay these imaginary prices, have nothing to do with the case. Let us bear in mind that the demand curve for any one good or service is drawn on the assumption that the prices of all other goods and services are given and unchanged, and hence the benefits which buyers of a particular good obtain by paying less than what they might pay for it in a pinch—their so-called consumer surplus—would be entirely different if other prices were changed. Even if the unpaid benefits were measurable—which they are not—they would depend on millions of other prices. We must ask our ophelimetricians to get this idea out of their heads.

Who Pays? Who Benefits?

Having said a great deal about benefits to society, I feel an obligation to recall that this "collective" is not taken equally seriously by all. Society is all the people who live in a particular territory (perhaps minus the ones who are about to leave or to die, and plus those who are going to be born or to immigrate). It is widely agreed that all members of society should—from a moral point of view—weigh equally in our considerations. Should this be taken as a good reason for disregarding the question who are the most likely recipients of any additional benefits to be derived from a particular government action and who will have to pay its cost?

For many kinds of public regulation or subsidization, majority opinion holds that the benefits are larger than the cost, thus yielding a net gain to society. Should we be indifferent to the most likely distribution of benefits and costs? If we are convinced that the benefits would accrue almost entirely to a small group of people whereas the cost would have to be borne by other groups, large or small, should we endorse such a measure with the same enthusiasm as we would if the benefits were widely diffused? Or should we examine the worthiness of the special-interest group favored by the program?

If the beneficiaries, for example, are handicapped persons—think, for example, of subsidized production of books in Braille or of phonograph records of novels for the blind—we might not mind if other people had to contribute to the modest cost of the program. But would we feel the same way if the beneficiaries of some public measure were a privileged group, without special merits, much richer and better endowed than those who have to pay the bill? There are many cases where it is hard to solve the question of "equity"; indeed, problematic cases may be more frequent than easy ones. For example, if an extension of the duration of copyright protection forces readers of books of enduring popularity to pay higher prices, so that the heirs of the author, say some grandnieces or distant cousins, can collect royalties long after the author's death, should this count as a clear net advantage to "society"? The benefit to society would rest on the (questionable) hypothesis that more and better books are written when authors can anticipate that royalty payments will in a distant future go to their still unknown heirs.

It is customary in economic analysis to separate questions of allocative efficiency—how to use resources most productively—from questions of distributive equity—how to redistribute incomes most equitably. Yet, a reminder may not be uncalled for that many decisions of public policy are designed to aid special groups at the expense of other people; indeed, the political chance of the adoption of public programs is greater if the benefits are more "visible" and are vociferously claimed by special-interest groups, whereas the costs are so widely diffused that the majority of the people may think they do not have to pay any part of it.

Lest there be a misunderstanding, it should be said that an analysis of the most probable directions of change in resource allocation and income distribution induced by a public measure—subsidy, regulation, investment, etc.—does not presuppose any measurements of total benefits. It is therefore no contradiction if I first denied the possibility of measuring the total gross or net benefits due to an entire program introduced by the government, and then discussed marginal effects of relatively small changes of some parameters of a program. Even these marginal effects can rarely be measured or estimated with any degree of accuracy; but the directions of induced changes can often be indicated, with a reasonably good chance of being right, with regard to both resource allocation and income distribution.

KNOWLEDGE INDUSTRIES AND
KNOWLEDGE OCCUPATIONS

A FEW TIMES in discussing the various types of knowledge and the methods of knowledge production, I have used the phrase "knowledge industry." Although we shall soon find that this phrase is not really appropriate, even as an analogy, I shall go on using it, especially when I embark on a discussion of the conceptual and operational difficulties of an analysis of knowledge-producing "industry." No conceptual difficulties are encountered in an analysis of "knowledge occupations." Definitions of these terms will be formulated after it becomes a little clearer what is involved.

KNOWLEDGE INDUSTRIES

A statistical analysis of any industry and of its role and performance in the economy involves data of many kinds. Ideally they should include measures of physical output, total sales broken down by major products, purchases of intermediate products, total employment, value added and income originating in the industry, changes in the composition of output, changes in selling prices, changes in productivity, and a few more things. Unfortunately, little of this can be had for some of the most important knowledge industries.

What We Don't Know about Some Knowledge Industries

There are several insurmountable obstacles in a statistical analysis of some knowledge industries. In the first place, there is no physical output (except for what I call information machines). Indeed, for most parts of the production of knowledge no possible measure of output can be conceived that would be logically separate from a measure of inputs; and those relatively rare kinds of knowledge for which independent indices of output can be concocted cannot in any meaningful way be compared, let alone aggregated, with other kinds of knowledge.

In addition, most of the services of some knowledge industries are not sold in the market but are instead distributed below cost or without charge, the cost being paid for in part or in full by government (as in the case of public schools), by philanthropists (as in the case of some private schools), and by commercial advertisers (as in the case of newspapers, magazines, radio, and television). Hence we lack the valuations which for most other industries the consumer puts on the product by paying a price for it. There are no "total sales" and no selling prices.

Because of the nonmeasurability of the product, the consequent lack of productivity data, and the absence of market prices, one cannot even state with assurance that an increase in the expenditures for knowledge, relative to gross national product, will result in more knowledge being provided to society. This is a problem to which we may have to return more than once or twice, for it has special importance in the evaluation of data on education and on research and development. Even in the few exceptional instances where we do have consumption expenditures in the form of purchases of products at market prices, the heterogeneity of the product makes a quantification of output most difficult. Book publishing may serve as an example: "increased sales" may mean that more books ("titles") were published or that more copies (of perhaps fewer titles) were sold, or that more hard-cover rather than paperback editions were sold, or that perhaps more books requiring expensive typesetting or printing were sold, all this quite apart from differences in the types of books and their potential contributions to knowledge.

For the most part, employment data or factor-cost data are the only available sources of financial information about the production of knowledge in these industries. A fundamental question arises here: if inputs are essentially the only thing that can be measured, would it be more appropriate to select for the statistical compilation the inputs according to the type of contribution they make to the production process in which they are engaged or according to the type of product which they help produce? In other words, speaking of labor input alone, should an "occupation" approach be used, or an "industry" ("product") approach?

The Type of Product or the Type of Labor

Examples can make clear what is asked here. A chemical engineer employed in the food industry, a designer in the shoe industry, an accountant or a lawyer in the chemical industry, all are engaged in the production of knowledge according to their *occupation*, but not according to the *industry* in which they work. On the other hand, a janitor in a school building, a charwoman in a research laboratory, a mechanic in a television studio, all are engaged in the production of knowledge according to the *industry* in which they work, but not according to their *occupation*. If the phrase "knowledge industry" were to be given an unambiguous meaning, would it be a collection of firms producing knowledge or rather a collection of occupations producing knowledge in whatever industries they are employed? Would it thus include all people employed, and factor cost paid, in education, research and development, book publishing, magazines and newspapers, telephone and telegraph, radio and television? Or would it include all people employed, and compensation paid to them, anywhere in knowledge-producing occupations, for example, as accountants, actors, architects, artists, auditors, authors? The results may be quite different, at least as far as the relative magnitudes—knowledge production relative to total production—are concerned. It may be that the results are not very different when one looks at growth rates over time, for it is quite likely that knowledge production has been increasing on both counts, by occupations and by industries.

INDUSTRIES AND OCCUPATIONS

Having found that there are (at least) two approaches to a sizing up of the role of knowledge production in the economy—an industry approach to the total value of the output of all firms, agencies, departments, etc., that generate or disseminate knowledge, and an occupation approach to the amount or value of the input of knowledge-producing labor—we must no longer defer formulating definitions of knowledge industries and knowledge occupations.

Knowledge Industry

The usual definition of an industry as a group of producers, ordinarily firms or enterprises producing a certain kind or set of products, does not easily fit our purposes. I regard education as a knowledge industry although very few firms in the usual sense are in this business. Schools may be public or private establishments, church-related or other not-for-profit corporations or associations, and only a small fraction are commercial enterprises. Moreover, education in the wider sense of the word takes place also outside schools: in the home, in the army, or as "training on the job" in many firms that produce physical products. I regard research and development work as a knowledge industry although only a fraction of its output is produced for sale by firms undertaking R and D as their sole or primary business. Much research and development is done in government agencies and universities, but the largest part is done in departments of industries, such as the chemical, electronic, aeronautical, and other industries producing physical products. This complicates attempts at defining "knowledge industry."

I define a knowledge industry as a group of establishments—firms, institutions, organizations, and departments, or teams within them, but also, in some instances, individuals and households—that produce knowledge, information services or information goods, either for their own use or for use by others. The knowledge they generate and/or transmit may be of any type, sort, or quality (provided only that its value or cost can be estimated within limits, however broad). Information goods are tangible products serving chiefly to generate, transmit, or receive knowledge, things such as writing paper, newspapers, journals, books, records, tapes, utensils, and "information machines," that is, instruments, appliances, apparatuses, and machines that serve chiefly to generate, transmit, or receive knowledge.

The inclusion of information goods in the definition of knowledge industry raises the question of double-counting. If, for example, the computer industry is regarded as a knowledge industry, and computers are used in R and D and in many information services, can one reasonably count both the output of the computer industry and the output of the computer-using knowledge industries when the share of knowledge production in the gross national product is calculated? An answer to this question is suggested by the generally accepted principles of national-income accounting. Durable capital goods are treated as final products and the annual user cost of these capital goods (chiefly depreciation) is treated as a cost of producing the output of the industries that use them. (Depreciation is deducted when net national product is derived from GNP.) Thus, there is no objection to having both the output of the computer industry and the output of the computer-using knowledge industry regarded as parts of knowledge production. This answer is not applicable to all knowledge goods. For example, paper used for printing newspapers or books is not a final product and will enter the account of knowledge production only once, as a cost of the newspaper or book. Likewise, books acquired by libraries, though they are durable goods, will not be entered twice—once as output of the publishing industry and again as cost of library services—when the aggregates are calculated.

Knowledge Occupation

I define a knowledge occupation as one that involves activities, gainful or costly, that are designed chiefly to aid in the generation, transmission, or reception of knowledge of any type, sort, or quality, including giving, directly or through instruments, visual, aural, or otherwise sensible signals, and ranging from carrying messages to creating new knowledge.

If the role of knowledge-producing activities in the economy is to be sized up by the occupation approach, one has the choice of doing this either in terms of manpower—the number of men and women employed in knowledge occupations—or in terms of the value of cost of their labor. The first technique requires estimates of physical inputs of labor (man-years or man-hours), the second, estimates of compensation paid, incomes received, or alternative incomes foregone. Both these procedures focus on inputs. The contrast between input and output can perhaps help us best to comprehend the difference between the industry approach and the occupation approach. Knowledge *industries* are defined by their *output*, produced by any and all types of input; knowledge *occupations* are defined by the kind of work performed as *input* for whatever product in any industry whatsoever.

Thus, knowledge industries employ workers in many kinds of occupations, knowledge occupations as well as others, (that is, occupations involving chiefly manual labor). The output of these industries is regarded as part of knowledge production no matter how much or how little input from knowledge workers it "embodies." (I apologize for the metaphor so widely used in economic discussion: embodying is not a suitable word when the output is intangible.) And, of course, other inputs besides labor contribute to the output. On the other hand, as I have said, the labor of workers in knowlege occupations is input for all sorts of products in many industries other than knowledge industries.

Degrees of Arbitrariness

An important difference between knowledge industries and knowledge occupations lies in the degree of arbitrariness in meeting the criteria of the definitions. There is some arbitrariness in the breakdown of the labor force by occupation. (Take the categories of foremen or engineers; both of them may include workers who do chiefly manual work and others who chiefly produce knowledge. For the degree of arbitrariness, much depends on how detailed is the breakdown of the labor force, how realistic are the descriptions of the work typical for the occupations distinguished, and how accurate are the assignments of workers to each category. Yet, none of this introduces anything near the degree of arbitrariness that is inherent in the definition of "knowledge industry."

Let us recall that the proposed definition allows promoting a department of a firm, or even a team within a department, to a member of a knowledge industry even if the firm itself is not. R and D, for example, is given the title of a knowledge industry even though most of the R and D work is done within industries producing chemicals and drugs, airplanes, ballistic missiles, nuclear devices, military equipment, and what not. Our definition gives us a license to lift the R and D teams out of the firms where they are employed and to reassign them to the R and D industry, where they are joined with research professors and their assistants working in universities, perhaps only part time, on research projects, and with some governmental agencies doing demographic, medical, environmental, or energy research. Similarly, it would give us a license to lift the accounting and bookkeeping departments out of all business firms and to join them with the auditors and certified public accountants in an accountancy industry, if we chose to do so. (I choose not to do so, but only because I do not have the statistical data that would enable me to estimate the cost of "accounting information.") These examples should suffice to explain the arbitrariness involved in the industry approach to an estimation of the aggregate magnitude called knowledge production.

Some investigators might consider this degree of arbitrariness a sufficient reason for resignation and for abandoning the project of a statistical inquiry into the knowledge sector of the economy, its size and its growth. I am not discouraged. I shall proceed with both boldness and caution, in that I shall make hundreds of arbitrary decisions, but shall always state my reasons as well as all appropriate reservations and warnings. Anyone who disagrees with my decisions regarding questionable inclusions or exclusions will be able to adjust the ultimate findings in accordance with his judgments.

A Heuristic Fiction: "Complete" Division of Labor

Could one possibly conceive of an imaginary economy in which specialization is carried so far that each occupation is organized in special firms selling its particular services and nothing else? If so, could the imaginary statistics of such an imaginary economy be so organized that the occupation approach and the industry approach become one and the same?

In such a completely "disintegrated" economy, no firm could have an engineer, a typist, an accountant, a cashier, a salesman, a messenger boy; it would have to buy these services from engineering firms, typing bureaus, accounting offices, collection and disbursement firms, sales agencies, message carriers (just as the small firms in our world have no lawyers on their staffs but retain outside legal service). However far this scheme can be pushed, a limit will be reached with management. Decision-making is one activity which the firm must perform internally, or it stops being a firm. There may be professional "management consultants" and there may be "management contracts" between a parent company and its subsidiary, but every independent firm must have its own management and, hence, the occupation "manager" can never be so organized that it becomes available only to specialized "management firms," forming a "management industry."

The economies of the real world are far removed from the scheme just considered: most firms employ members of various occupations, and larger firms, no matter what they produce, employ members of various knowledge-producing occupations. In other words, there is "internally-produced knowledge" which is "used" within the firm. Where it is produced by persons statistically listed as members of some "white-collar" occupation, the occupation approach to our statistical problem may give us clues which the industry approach cannot possibly provide.

Production for Interindustry Trade and Intraindustry Use

A few comments on the division of labor between knowledge producers and producers of physical goods and services may be helpful in this connection. This (as any other) division of labor may take different forms: entire *industries* specializing in particular types of output; some *firms*, within more broadly defined industries, specializing in particular outputs or including a specialized service among the several it supplies; *departments* within firms specializing in certain activities that serve other departments in the same firm; *groups or teams* of workers specializing in certain performances required within the same department; *individual workers* specializing in particular tasks needed within a team of collaborating workers.

Where input or output data are broken down only by broadly defined industries, only the first of these five forms of division of labor can be statistically captured. Thus, the industry approach will yield immediate results for our study only where knowledge transmission is the entire output of the industry, as for example in "newspapers and magazines" or even in "printing and publishing." If industry classes are broad and the firms included produce various goods and services, some of which qualify for our survey whereas others do not, the industry approach will help us only to the extent that we are able to make educated guesses about the share of the total sales of the industry that the output in which we are interested may constitute. For example, if "electrical appliances" include radio and television receivers (for which we want data) along with vacuum cleaners and dishwashers (which are outside our present interests), we need a separation which the industry breakdown may not provide. In the particular case of radio and TV receivers, we are able, fortunately, to obtain relevant information; but in other cases we may have to resort to guesses based on the flimsiest evidence.

Where the division of labor gives rise to interindustry trade, so that knowledge instruments or knowledge services produced by one industry are purchased by another industry, we face problems of double-counting in some instances and of lack of information in others. National-product accounts will omit such production entirely because it does not represent "final output." Where the division of labor is of any of the last three forms—namely, within a firm—and knowledge is produced for intraindustry use, the industry approach will yield no data at all. In these cases, the occupation approach alone can shed light on our problem.

On the other hand, the occupation approach will leave us in the dark with regard to several essential matters. Thus, some of the most important ways of producing knowledge require as input intermediate products largely made with types of labor from non-knowledge-producing occupations. For example, books, newspapers, and magazines are printed on paper produced by labor not in the knowledge-producing category; the same is true for the equipment for telephone, telegraph, radio, television, all of which are eminently involved in the production of knowledge. There could be large increases in the production and use of all these means of communicating knowledge without any accompanying increase in the relative number of workers from knowledge-producing occupations. We conclude that both industry analyses and occupation analyses are needed in order to find out about the past development and present role of knowledge production.

The Major Knowledge Industries and Branches

Both approaches will be followed in this study, though the major emphasis will be on the industry approach. This allows for more interesting subdivisions. Detailed analyses of the major product classes in the knowledge category will open up vistas that might be missed were we to follow the occupation approach only.

I classify knowledge production into six major product classes: education, research and development, artistic creation and communication, media of communication, information services, and information machines.[1] Each of these is further subdivided, so that I shall describe, analyze, and evaluate the output of some sixty or seventy industry branches. Although most of these correspond to industry branches defined by the standard classification used in official statistics of the United States, several do not. Differences between the official breakdown and the one employed in my study will be explained and justified.

Probably the most important product class to be studied is education. It would be wrong to be satisfied with a review of published data on the explicit cost, or monetary expenditures, incurred for the provision of formal education. Several implicit cost items have to be estimated and added to what is reported in the conventional national-income-and-product accounts. For example, the costs of education in the home, instruction in the armed services, and training on the job have to be ferreted out from various sources; and the earnings foregone by students of working age who sacrifice wage incomes for the sake of extended schooling have to be estimated. The intricacies of benefit-and-cost analysis may look forbidding, but this is no acceptable excuse for dodging an attempt to deal as best we can with the problems of cost effectiveness and productivity of the educational activities of the nation. The different, sometimes contradictory, findings regarding private and social returns to successive or alternative investments in education—improvement of working capacity, development of human resources—have to be examined for conceptual, methodological, and empirical validity and soundness. (Several chapters on human capital in Volume II, and all of Volume III, will be devoted to the study of education in general, and to that in the United States in particular.)

Research and development is generally regarded as the primary activity designed for the generation of socially new knowledge. I take a good deal of conceptual license in transforming, in narrative as well as statistical analysis, R and D activities into a separately named industry. Many of these activities are performed within firms and industries that are entirely outside any branch of any knowledge industry. The reason for the wide acceptance of the elevation of R and D activities—dispersed over academic institutions, governmental agencies, and private firms—to the status of knowledge industry par excellence is probably found in the importance which the academic establishment, the industrial-military complex, the popular mass media, and the government, in virtual unanimity, have at-

---

[1] In my book *The Production and Distribution of Knowledge in the United States* (Princeton: Princeton University Press, 1962), I had merged artistic creation and communication with media of communication.

tached to new knowledge in science and technology. If R and D is supposed to serve the production of socially new knowledge, it shares this objective with many kinds of artistic creation and communication. (It will, therefore, be understandable if I propose to let scientific, technological, and artistic knowledge creation share Volume IV of this work.)

Dissemination of knowledge through the media of communication is a different area of inquiry. The print media of communication—books, journals, magazines, newspapers, etc.—and the electronic mass media—radio and television broadcasting, and also phonographic recording—will raise hard problems of statistical disentanglement and moral judgment. Both types of mass media give rise to legal questions, for example, protection of copyrights. Several industries are related to the mass media of communication, for example, advertising and public relations, and conventions and conferences. Finally, there are the media of addressed communication—telephone, telegraph, and postal services—all calling for narrative as well as statistical treatment. (Volume V is intended for this.)

Information services have proliferated during the last two decades. Apart from libraries, probably the oldest providers of information services, many specialized information services have sprung up. They are operated for profit or not for profit, on a cost-covering basis or subsidized from public or private sources. Science information and technological information enjoy much public interest and have become most-favored subjects of research and supportive government policy. Management, including business management, has been treated as an information system and a communication process. Many information services are joint products of industries primarily engaged in producing other services; in such instances it may be difficult to separate the costs of the information services, or the information component, from the costs of the other outputs. Many of the researcher's decisions regarding the estimation of the appropriate figures cannot help being arbitrary.

The last of the six product classes, information machines, comprises the wide range of apparatuses, appliances, and machines designed to assist in information processes. Historically these reach from the sundial and the stylus to the electronic watch and the laser-controlled disease scanner; in a modern cross-sectional view, the products of this industry include printing presses and typewriters, copiers and intercoms, thermometers and thermostats, phonographs and microphones, eyeglasses and hearing aids, and thousands of measuring instruments, recording appliances, and control apparatuses. The information machine that has had the fastest growth in the last few decades is the computer. The statistical work in the description of the information-machine industry is complicated by several problems: some of the information machines, especially the less durable ones, are, if used by business, regarded as intermediate products the cost of which is included in the current production cost of whatever the user produces; information machines with longer service lives are counted as final goods, parts of the purchasers' investment; if purchased by individuals and households, they are treated as final goods, parts of consumption. Then there is the problem of double-counting. Where information appliances are acquired by knowledge industries—say, schools, research organizations, printing establishments—and the purchases are counted among the current cost of the information produced, we must exclude the sales price of the appliances either from the output of the industry that produces them or reduce the current cost of the industry that uses them. That is to say, we must not count the same item twice. On the other hand, where these appliances are acquired by firms or organizations producing goods and services other than information, the sales price of the appliances must be counted as an outlay for knowledge production. The fear of counting an item twice should not lead us to omit it altogether.

Only after all these inquiries into the various knowledge industries are completed shall we be prepared for a comprehensive statement on the size and growth of knowledge production in the United States. (This will be in Volume VII, according to present plans.) The analysis of knowledge *occupations* and of changes in the occupational structure in the United States will have to wait until the *industry* approach has reached its end.

FIRMS, INDUSTRIES, AND THE WHOLE ECONOMY

If the occupational structure of the whole economy changes so that the ratio of knowledge-producing occupations to the entire labor force increases, this may or may not be associated with a similar change in the occupational structure of individual firms. It would be possible for the composition of the work force of most existing firms to remain virtually unchanged while new firms employing chiefly members of knowledge-producing occupations appear on the scene.

The Occupational Structure of Single Firms

There are strong indications that the change has in fact been taking both forms: many new firms with substantially greater ratios of knowledge-producing labor have been emerging *and* many old firms have been employing increasing shares of white-collar labor. The hypothesis suggests itself that technological progress has forced firms to make such changes in their employment patterns and that firms in the forefront of technological innovation have moved faster in this direction than firms following merely adaptive policies. One may advance an even stronger hypothesis, holding that firms that are more innovation minded than those representative of their industry will employ substantially higher ratios of white-collar labor because they need research and development laboratories, planning divisions, and market-research departments.

A hypothesis of this sort was advanced in a brief and suggestive pamphlet by Harbison and Hill and subjected to empirical tests.[2] Several firms in the same industries were studied and their employment patterns and innovative policies were compared. The sample was too small to permit conclusive results, but whatever findings were obtained seemed to be consistent with the hypothesis.

There are at least two grounds, however, on which the hypothesis may be challenged. First, technological change need not always—and least so in the individual firm or particular industry—take the form of a displacement of physical labor. Although this may be the way in which technological advance proceeds in the economy as a whole, innovation in some industries and some firms may be of a different nature. It may very well happen, for example, that a novel technique of data processing is introduced which decimates the clerical work force of the firm. Second, a firm leading all the other firms in the industry in the adoption of new technologies need not perform the necessary research and development work within its organization. It may instead retain firms of consulting engineers to do the research and development for it. There is no need for it to maintain a staff of its own for the inventive and developmental activities required for its innovative program if it can buy all these services from the outside.

These arguments do not invalidate the hypothesis, but they can explain why empirical tests may yield negative results in a large number of cases. One may hit upon several instances in which the rate of innovation in the firm has been faster than in the rest of the industry, and the proportion of white-collar labor in the work force has nevertheless declined instead of increased. It would not be likely that the results of empirical tests come out this way if the sample of firms investigated is large and the time period over which they are

---

[2] Frederick H. Harbison and Samuel E. Hill, *Manpower and Innovation in American Industry* (Princeton: Princeton University, Industrial Relations Section, 1959).

observed is long. But one must not expect all tests to confirm the hypothesis; it could survive negative results, which presumably contradict it.

On principle, however, this is not a sufficiently significant hypothesis to seek its verification. If it is possible for innovation to proceed without this "expected" change in the employment pattern of the firms concerned, we should not stake much effort on empirical tests proving that the patterns do change. We should put our money on the hypothesis that the employment pattern changes in the economy as a whole as technology advances. This is what really matters. This is the problem to which we shall return in the last volume of this work.

A Different Model of the "Information Economy"

After all that I have said about the arbitrary decisions to be made in arranging the data, estimating the subaggregates, and arriving at an aggregate of knowledge production, no one will be surprised to learn that the first follow-up to my 1962 investigation, Marc Porat's The Information Economy,[3] was cast in a mold different in some respects from the one that I had constructed. Marc Porat's study was based on 1967 data; his overall findings are well in tune with the aggregates I had presented on the basis of the 1958 data.[4] The conceptual framework used by Porat, however, is sufficiently different from mine to invite my reaction.

Briefly, Porat distinguishes two "information sectors," a primary and a secondary one. "The 'primary information sector' includes those firms which supply the bundle of information goods and services exchanged in a market context. . . . The 'secondary information sector' includes all the information services produced for internal consumption by government and noninformation firms."[5] This distinction is largely dictated by Porat's "major goal . . . to build a set of accounts . . . that are completely consistent with the National Income

---

[3] Marc Uri Porat, The Information Economy: Definition and Measurement, vol. 1, and The Information Economy: Sources and Methods for Measuring the Primary Information Sector, vol. 2 (Washington: U.S. Department of Commerce, Office of Telecommunications, 1977).

[4] "The total information activity, including both market and nonmarket transactions, accounted for 46% of GNP in 1967" (Ibid., vol. 1, p. 8). "Total knowledge production in 1958 was almost 29 per cent of adjusted GNP. . . ." (Machlup, Production and Distribution of Knowledge, p. 362). The increase from 29 per cent in 1958 to 46 per cent in 1967 seems well in line with the relative growth rates which I calculated for the production of knowledge and of other goods and services (Machlup, Production and Distribution of Knowledge, p. 374).

[5] Porat, The Information Economy, vol. 1, p. 4.

& Product Accounts."[6] Porat does not always adhere to this rule or to his definitions. For example, he admits the expenditures for public education into the primary information sector although few educational services are sold in the market; he defends this as a "direct analog" to services sold to satisfy final demand. (But he would not admit any implicit costs—because this would deviate from the established national-accounting practices.) For at least one industry, Porat found his presumably authoritative data source inadequate.[7]

Porat himself provides a useful "Comparison to the Machlup Study." He summarizes it as follows:

> First, Machlup's accounting scheme innovated rather liberally on the National Income Accounts concepts and practices, whereas this [Porat's] study does not. Second, his [Machlup's] work includes an admixture of both 'primary' and 'secondary' type activities, whereas this study keeps them distinct. Third, a variant of final demand is used by Machlup as a measure of the knowledge industry size, whereas this study uses primarily the value added approach but reports both sets of figures.[8]

Strict conformance with the "National Income Accounts concepts and practices" was, and is, no "major goal" of mine. If we want to know, for example, the total expenditures for research and development in the United States, we cannot use the data reported in the national-income accounts (NIA) and have to depart from NIA practices, which treat R and D differently, according to who pays for it. R and D remains knowledge production (or information service) no matter whether it is financed by government, private industry, or private nonprofit organizations, and regardless of whether the R and D output is sold by one firm to another or produced and used within the same firm. We must not omit large expenditures for R and D just because of existing tax provisions and accounting practices. Likewise, if we want to know the cost of producing, transmitting, and receiving television programs, we cannot make inclusions or exclusions on the basis of who pays for it all. Governments may pay out of general tax revenues; consumers may pay fees for possessing receiving equipment or for receiving selected programs; individuals,

---

[6] Ibid., p. 5.

[7] For "communications, except radio and TV broadcasting," Porat stated that "unfortunately, the NIA procedure is somewhat oblique in providing meaningful industry detail, so we shall resort to other data sources to explain the industry's activities." Porat, The Information Economy, vol. 2, p. 4.

[8] Ibid., vol. 1, p. 44.

foundations, or corporations may make voluntary contributions; private business firms may sponsor programs in public-relations efforts; or they may pay for commercials (advertising). Regardless of these and other differences, broadcasting remains the same kind of activity, producing intellectual, practical, or pastime knowledge. We should, of course, subdivide the total cost of any knowledge-producing activity according to sources of funds, so that the figures can be reconciled with those shown in national-income-and-product accounts.

Perhaps I have trotted out these examples too often and should apologize for being so repetitive. Another, entirely hypothetical, example would perhaps clinch the argument. Suppose a statute compelled business firms to pay for the education of the children of their employees. Should these expenditures be shown as current production costs of automobiles, textiles, soap, or other products, or should they be included in the cost of education? Or, to make the point still more striking, suppose the law provided that the full cost of operating all schools must be paid directly by the business firms located in the district. Should this eliminate education as a knowledge industry? I submit that for some purposes the concepts and practices of national-product accounting have to be departed from: there are questions that require different arrangements of the data.

That my arrangement of industries involves an "admixture of primary and secondary" information sectors is, of course, true; this "admixture" is, I submit, called for in the interest of consistency. Porat uses the very felicitous expression "quasi-firm" for a department producing information services for internal use by the firm of which it is a part, and the expression "informational quasi-industry" for the horizontal aggregation of "quasi-firms" producing the same type of information for use by "noninformation industries."[9] Examples of such "informational quasi-industries" would be electronic-data-processing services, advertising, letter-typing services, accounting and bookkeeping services; many others are listed by Porat.[10] I have alluded to this problem in earlier chapters and also earlier in this chapter, for example, in the subsection "Production for Interindustry Trade and Intraindustry Use" (reproduced without alteration from my 1962 book). For most of the quasi industries, I was unable to obtain statistical data for the compilation of knowledge production in 1958, but I mentioned that those knowledge-

[9] Ibid., pp. 148-149.
[10] See "Table 9.1: Partial List of Information Quasi-Firms Within Non-Information Enterprises," ibid., p. 150.

producing activities could be captured by the occupations approach. I felt, and still feel, that the industry approach and the occupations approach should be kept strictly apart. The information services produced by Porat's "quasi-firms" and "informational quasi-industries" should be included in the industry approach to the estimation of total information activities only if the data are not the same as those derived from labor-force statistics. Porat, contrary to my methodological resolution, does include in his secondary information sector data on employee compensation of information workers, labor income of proprietors performing informational tasks, and capital consumption allowances taken on information machines, in "noninformation industries." In other words, he mixes information *inputs* in industries outside the information sector with *outputs* of industries in the information sector.

On the third divergence of Porat's measurement technique from that proposed and employed by me, I cannot help finding my procedure preferable. Porat recommends the value-added approach, whereas I use what he called "a variant of final demand." Expressed in my own words, I use total sales or total cost of output, whichever is higher, for the money value of the product, that is, the knowledge generated or disseminated. To use only value added by the producers of the knowledge goods and knowledge services would understate the cost of the product. To use a simple analogy: if we want to know the share of steel production in gross national product, we want not just the value added by steel producers but also all the things they had to purchase from other firms in order to produce the steel. Likewise, if we want to know the total of book production, we must not confine ourselves to the value added by the publishers; we need their sales receipts for the books produced or, if books were produced for free distribution, we would need the full cost of production, including the paper, the printers' bills, and all other intermediate products and services purchased. And if the publishers were working in rent-free offices, provided by governments, foundations, or universities, we would have to add the rental values of these offices as implicit cost of the product. Value-added statistics may provide important data for the measurement of the output of some knowledge industries, but it is not the appropriate basis for the purposes of our inquiry.[11]

[11] Estimates of final-demand output and estimates of value added by all producers come, of course, to the same aggregate figure if, but only if, value added by supplying industries is included in a full regress down to the first intermediate output supplied as input to the subsequent processor.

Strategies and Tactics in Quantitative Analysis

The preceding comparison of alternative approaches may be baffling or puzzling to noneconomists; on the other hand, it may serve to establish or clarify some of the principles to be observed in the estimation of the product of knowledge industries. I ought to mention, however, that these principles can only determine the general strategies, not the detailed tactical decisions that become necessary in the process of any quantitative analysis. Anybody who has been engaged in such a task has learned that general principles do not provide blueprints for action. Innumerable decisions will have to be made, and many of them will be ad hoc, without much guidance from the principles adopted for the broad strategy of the inquiry.

LIST OF PAGES WITH LINES OF TEXT RETAINED
FROM THE 1962 VOLUME

Chapter Number and Running Head		Number of Lines	Page in This Volume	Page in 1962 Volume
The Story of This Work		10 lines	xvii	iii
		2 lines	xviii	10
		43 lines	xix	10-11
		43 lines	xx	11-12
		4 lines	xxi	12
	TOTAL	102 lines		
1 Introduction		30 lines	3	3
		43 lines	4	3-4
		37 lines	5	4-5
		43 lines	6	5-6
		37 lines	7	6-7
		16 lines	8	8
		29 lines	9	8-9
		43 lines	10	9-10
		7 lines	11	10
		3 lines	16	vi
		8 lines	17	vi
	TOTAL	296 lines		
2 The Known and the Knowing		31 lines	27	13
		36 lines	28	14
		15 lines	56	14-15
		5 lines	57	15
		7 lines	58	15
	TOTAL	94 lines		
3 Classes of Knowledge		21 lines	59	15-16
		7 lines	60	16
	TOTAL	28 lines		

Chapter Number and Running Head		Number of Lines	Page in This Volume	Page in 1962 Volume
4 Alternative Classifications		8 lines	101	16
		40 lines	102	17-18
		41 lines	103	18-19
		40 lines	104	19-20
		18 lines	106	20
		30 lines	107	20-21
		39 lines	108	21-22
		8 lines	109	22
	TOTAL	224 lines		
5 Truth, Beauty, and Goodness		26 lines	117	23
		19 lines	118	23-24
		17 lines	119	24
		14 lines	120	24
		9 lines	124	24-25
	TOTAL	85 lines		
6 Other Standards of Quality		33 lines	126	25-26
		13 lines	127	25-26
		21 lines	128	26-27
		4 lines	129	27
		22 lines	130	27
	TOTAL	93 lines		
8 Choosers and Users of Knowledge		25 lines	156	28
		23 lines	158	28-29
		31 lines	159	29-30
	TOTAL	79 lines		

Chapter Number and Running Head	Number of Lines	Page in This Volume	Page in 1962 Volume
11 Transmission and Reception	21 lines	186	30
	40 lines	187	31
	43 lines	188	32
	26 lines	189	32-33
	20 lines	190	33-34
	41 lines	191	34-35
	25 lines	192	35
TOTAL	216 lines		
12 Consumption, Investment, Intermediate Product	21 lines	193	36
	43 lines	194	36-37
	41 lines	195	37-38
	35 lines	196	38-39
	43 lines	197	39-40
	39 lines	198	40-41
	42 lines	199	41-43
	26 lines	200	43
TOTAL	290 lines		
14 Knowledge Industries and Knowledge Occupations	25 lines	225	44
	41 lines	226	44-45
	16 lines	227	45-46
	11 lines	230	46
	40 lines	231	46-47
	38 lines	232	47-48
	10 lines	235	49
	40 lines	236	49-50
	12 lines	237	50
TOTAL	233 lines		

GRAND TOTAL   1,740 lines

INDEX

a priori knowledge, 65
ability, critical, 211; improving in, 46;
    kept in reserve, 43; physical, 42; race
    and, 141; to demonstrate, 35, 44, 47,
    51; to explain, 47, 51; to take tests,
    35-36, 53; to recognize, 49; to sing, 51
abortive information, 57
abstract, art, 94; ballet, 96; constructs,
    103; knowledge, 63
abstracting and indexing services, xxix
Académie des Sciences Morales et Po-
    litiques, 65n
academies of sciences, 14, 23, 68
Accademia Nazionale dei Lincei, 68
accountancy industry, 230
accountants, xxv, 227
accounting, corporate, 181; departments
    in business firms, 230; machines, 196;
    national, 181
accuracy, of knowledge, 35, 55-56, 119-
    120, 148; of measurement, 224
Acknowledgments, xiv
acquaintance, knowledge by, 29, 43, 47,
    50, 119, 179; nodding, 41
action, based on knowledge, 90, 148,
    174, 206, 207; information inducing,
    206-207; guided by knowledge, 17, 31,
    33, 97, 106, 124, 145, 148, 149, 150,
    151-152, 174, 191, 203, 204, 206-207,
    209; sequence of, 44
actor, 16n, 92, 121, 201, 227
additivity of knowledge, 169, 170
administrators, 10, 101, 187, 198
advertising, 23; as current input in pro-
    ducing goods, 200; by newspapers
    and periodicals, 130, 131, 226; by
    radio and television, 129n, 130, 200,
    226, 239; competition for, 15; income
    from, 131; in mass media, 129-131,
    234; knowledge conveyed by, 129-131;
    misleading, 128, 129n, 155, 156; paid
    for business, 131, 156, 200, 239; pro-
    fessionals, xxv; truth in, 129n; un-
    wanted knowledge through, 129-131
advising, 36, 187
aesthetic, form, 126; knowledge, 83, 126

aesthetics, 21, 83, 111
affective versus cognitive knowledge,
    xxiv, 50, 87, 90, 93, 94
Agassi, Joseph, 63-64n, 115n
agriculture, 24
Aiken, Henry David, xxiv, 76n, 78n
airline, 105
airport, 130
alertness, 42, 179, 180-181, 182-183
Alexander the Great, 31
Alexandrian Library, 166
algebra, 74, 106
Allen, Don Cameron, 84n
allocation, of resources, 5, 218, 223; of
    research funds, 102
amateurs, 201
American Council of Learned Societies,
    73, 74
American Scholar, 127
Ampère, André Marie, 85
Amsterdam, 39
analytic versus synthetic propositions,
    32, 103
analytical, inquiries, 33; knowledge, 109,
    148; propositions, 32, 64, 103
analyzers of knowledge, 16, 159, 189
analyzing, 186
anatomy, 134
anger, 99
animal cultures, 70
anonymous ideal types, 168
anthropologists, xiv, xxv, 30, 147
anthropology, 37, 65n, 80, 85, 87, 88, 89,
    147, 213
antihumanism, 79
antiscientism, 76-81
antisocial action, 137
Antony and Cleopatra, 121
aplopathoscopic, 87
apodictic certainty, 64
apologies and charges, 20-24
applied, knowledge, 31, 46, 69, 101-102,
    106, 109; research, 101-102, 206; sci-
    ence, 80; versus basic knowledge,
    106-109
archaeologists, 67

archaeology, 88
architects, 197, 227
architecture, department of, 88; of Notre
    Dame, 36
Aristotle, 62-63, 66n, 124n
arithmetic, 90
aroma of wine, 41
art, abstract versus realistic, 94; as
    applied science, 91; as performance,
    44; as practice, 44, 90, 91-92; critic, 45;
    dollar value of, 23; gallery, 15n, 125;
    genuine versus fake, 125; historian, 45;
    knowing a work of, 34, 42; low-brow,
    127, 187; meanings of, 90-92; of doing,
    44, 45, 90; of knowing, 45; precepts as,
    91, 92; total expenditures for, 19, 23,
    24; works of, 34, 42, 125-129
artifacts, 70, 87
artificial intelligence, 14
artisan, 90
artist, 15n, 16n, 70, 92, 188, 227
artistic, communication, xvi; creation,
    xvi, 15, 16n; knowledge, xvi, 15, 54,
    74, 90-96, 109, 118-121, 129n, 234;
    skills, 54; taste, 91
arts, and the humanities, 70, 73, 74; ex-
    penditures for the, 23; fine, 15, 16n, 24,
    90, 92, 94, 120-121; liberal, 76, 90, 102;
    literary, 119; mechanical, 90; perform-
    ing, 15n, 94-96, 121; professional, 90;
    theater, 15n, 16n; visual, 94, 120-121,
    127
Arts and Sciences, 88, 90
Ashcroft, Peggy, 121
Ashley, Elizabeth, 121
astrology, 146, 147
astromancy, 146, 147
astronomers, 63, 64
astronomy, 90, 134, 146
atonal music, 95
attention, in performance, 32, 42, 45; to
    details, 95
Austria, 41
authoritarianism, 134; Teutonic, 27
authors, 185, 223, 227; unborn heirs of,
    223
automobile, 32-33, 59; collision, 97
Avogadro's number, 31
awareness, an element of knowing, 92,
    96; animal awareness, 74n; focal, 45;
    knowing as, 47, 48; truth dependent
    on, 115

awe, 36
axioms, 62, 64
Ayer, Alfred J., 37n, 113n

Babbitt, Irving, 79n
Bach, Johann Sebastian, 127
Bacon, Francis, 63, 85n, 94n
Bailey, Herbert, xiv, xviii
ballet, 16n, 96, 121, 210
Baltimore Orioles, 193
barometers, 199
Bartlett, John, Familiar Quotations, 149n
Bartok, Bela, 40
Barzun, Jacques, 75n, 78
baseball, 59, 193
basic, knowledge, 31, 46, 101-102, 106,
    109; versus applied knowledge, 31, 46,
    101-102, 109; inquiry, 11; research, 24,
    101-102, 206; skills, 22, 33, 60, 61, 168,
    206
Battle of Waterloo, 103
BEA, see Bureau of Economic Analysis
beauty, and knowledge, 120-122; in
    dance, 96, 121; of a stage performance,
    121; of a theory, 122; of exposition, 122
Beethoven, Ludwig van, 39, 48, 95n, 98,
    106
behavioral genetics, 141n
belief, certified, 113; confident or firm,
    31, 43; justified true, 38, 43, 113;
    strength of, 117; versus knowledge,
    33n, 38, 43, 100, 113-114, 117; war-
    ranted, 113, 117
Benchley, Peter, 127
benefit-and-cost analysis, xv, 24, 131,
    217n, 218-219, 233
benefits, and costs, xv, 217n, 220n; ex-
    ceeding costs, 131, 177, 211, 223; fu-
    ture and immediate, 6, 31, 33, 69, 91,
    159, 161, 172, 173n, 174, 176, 177,
    191-192, 210; more visible than costs,
    223; non-pecuniary, 10, 24, 194, 211,
    212, 218-219; of education, 211-212,
    219, 233; of knowing better, 53; private
    versus social, 5, 10, 24, 210-215, 218-
    219; unpaid, 214, 215-217, 222
Berg, Alban, 127
Berg, Sanford V., 216n, 221n
Bergman, Ingrid, 121
Bible, the, 100
bicycle, 61, 61n
bigotry, 139

Bildungswissen, 106, 207
biological sciences, 82, 85, 88-89, 163n
biology, 63, 71, 81, 85, 106, 142, 162
biophysics, 134
bird watchers, 105
Birth of Venus, 120
birth rate of journals, 163
Black, Max, 67n
blueprinting, 198
body-truth, 119
bomb, 12, 143
Bombach, Gottfried, 161n
book designer, 16n
bookkeepers, 189, 230
books, acquired by libraries, 166-167,
    228; and knowledge production, xvi,
    6, 19, 60, 234; art cannot be learned
    from, 92; as information goods, 228;
    consumer's choice of, 156; counts of,
    162-167; dangerous, 133, 138, 140;
    good and bad, 128; hardcover versus
    paperback, 226; in Braille, 223; in the
    humanities, 80-81, 165; in the social
    sciences, 165; journal articles versus,
    162; lightweight versus serious, 127;
    mutiple copies of, 162, 167; paper for,
    232, 240; physical inputs in produc-
    ing, 232; pornographic, 134, 138,
    139-140; praised or damned, 129;
    printers' bills for, 240; proportion of
    journals to, 165; reproducing knowl-
    edge, 159; scholarly, 210; subsidized
    production of, 223; supply and de-
    mand for, 156, 184-185, 210; the role
    of, 165-167; value added versus total
    cost of publishing, 240; versus labora-
    tories, 80; volumes, titles and copies,
    162, 171, 226
booksellers, 184-185
Bosch, Hieronymus, 121
Botticelli, Alessandro, 120
Boulding, Kenneth E., xiv, xxi, 8n, 144n,
    171n, 176n
Bowman, Mary Jean, xxi
Brahms, Johannes, 52
Braithwaite, Richard, 79n
British Association for the Advancement
    of Science, 65n
broadcasting, paid for by business, 33,
    131, 156, 200, 238, 239; paid for by
    consumers, 200, 238, 239; paid for by
    government, 156, 200, 238, 239

Broch, Hermann, 93n, 119
Broudy, Harry S., 34n
Buddenbrooks, 39, 53-54
Bullock, Lord Alan, 75n, 77-78, 83
Burck, Gilbert, xxvi-xxvii
Bureau of Economic Analysis (BEA),
    xxviii, 196
burlesque show, 138
Burton, Robert, 149n
business, information, 156-157, 196-197;
    knowledge, 55, 104, 108, 156-157, 196,
    197, 209; management, 6, 55, 156, 204,
    206, 234
business expenditures, for advertising,
    131, 156, 200, 239; for information ma-
    chines, 156, 195-196, 199, 200, 235; for
    information services, 156, 158, 181,
    184, 196, 197, 209, 234, 238; for jour-
    nals and other print media, 184, 215-
    217, 222; for knowledge in general, 33,
    196; for radio and TV broadcasting, 33,
    131, 156, 200, 238, 239; for research
    and development, 157, 158, 181, 195,
    196, 197, 200, 209, 238; for schooling,
    239; for training on the job, 227, 233

cabarets, 34
Caesar and Cleopatra, 121
Caesar, Caius Julius, 71n
calculating, 32n, 198
calculating machines, 199
calculus, 41, 43, 44, 105
California, 40
Cambridge University, 72
camera man, 16n
cameras, 199
Campbell, Norman R., 66n
capacity, built up by training, 45; intel-
    lectual, 45; mental, 106; productive,
    191; reasoning, 206; to discover, 181;
    to identify, 98; to perform, 31
capital, per worker, 198; stock of knowl-
    edge as, 8, 172; yielding flows of ben-
    efits, 172
Caravaggio, Michelangelo M. da, 120
card-punching, 198
cardinal measuring, 53
Carl, Martin L., 71n
carnal knowledge, 100
Carnap, Rudolf, 66n, 79n, 115n, 116n,
    119n, 122n, 123n, 147n, 148n
cash registers, 199

censors, 129, 135n, 136, 137
certainty, 62-64; apodictic, 64
certified public accountants, 196, 227, 230
Ceylon, 183n
chain reactions, intellectual, xv
chamber music, 50, 61n, 95, 98, 126, 210
Chambers, Ephraim, 63
charges and apologies, 20-24
charms, 149
charwoman, 226
chatting, 60, 179-180, 190, 200-201
checking, 198
check marks, 51
chemistry, 31, 78, 87, 221, 222
Cherpack, Clifton, 84n
chess-playing, 41, 42, 44, 50
chewing gum, 130
Chishiki Sangyō, xxv
"Chopsticks," 52
choreographer, 16n, 96, 121
chrematology, 85
Christmas greetings, 203
church, authorities, 134-135; separation
    of state and, 140; state enforcing teach-
    ings of, 135
churches, in Paris, 34
Churchman, Charles West, 8n
Cicero, Marcus Tullius, 71n
cinemas, films for, 16n; in Paris, 34;
    number of, 171
city, knowing a, 32, 33, 34
Clarke, Martin L., 71n
classical, humanities, 76; studies, 71;
    music, 125, 126
classics, 71, 76
classification, and evaluation of knowl-
    edge quality, 128; of academic sub-
    jects, 23; of elements of knowing, 47;
    of higher learning, 89; of knowledge,
    59-100, 101-109; of major knowledge
    industries, 232-235; substituting for a
    definition, 59
Cleland, John, 139
Cleopatra, Queen of Egypt, 121
cleric, 107
cognate versus constituent fields, 14
cognitive, achievement tests, 53; knowl-
    edge, xxiv, 15, 51, 55; plus affective,
    93; processes, 50; versus affective,
    xxiv, 50, 87, 90, 93, 94
cognoscenti, 129

Cohen, Morris R., 66n, 124n
collective goods and services, 218-219
college entrance examinations, 168
Collingwood, Robin G., 66n
color, 92, 94
Columbia University, 87
combustion, 41
comic books and funnies, 159
Commentary, 127
Commission on Obscenity and Por-
    nography, 136n, 137n
Commission on the Humanities, 82
communicating, 8
communication, addressed, 16, 234; and
    creation, 15; artistic, xvi, 15; as part of
    knowledge production, between
    transmitter and receiver, 171, 173,
    184-192; channel, 187; media of, xvi,
    15, 207; media, in 1962 volume, xix-
    xx; multimedia, 96n; obscene, 136-
    141; of messages, 199; processes of,
    204; subversive, 134; system, 14;
    theory, 3, 8-9, 14, 22, 151, 186, 187;
    verbal, nonverbal, and quasi-verbal,
    100
competition, and monopoly, xvii, 3; de-
    grees of, 22; for advertising, 15; for
    good students, 76; pure theory of, xv
composer, 16n, 45, 92
composition, musical, 54, 199; of knowl-
    edge production, 19; of labor force, 190
Compton, John, 79n
computer, xiii, xvii, xx, xxviiin, 196, 199,
    228, 235
computer science, 14, 22
computing, 186
Comte, Auguste, 85
conception, mental, 100; physiological,
    100
concert, 40, 98, 128, 132, 210
concrete, piece of information, 58; situa-
    tion, 92; versus abstract knowledge,
    102-103
conductor, 16n, 50
conferring, 198
confidence in knowledge, 55-56
confirmability, 115-116, 148n
confusing knowledge, 150-151
conjecture, 63, 118, 122
connaissance, 67n-68n
connaître and savoir, xiii, 29
connoisseur, 41, 45, 120-121

consciousness, 28, 31, 48, 57, 92, 96, 97n, 179
construct, 83, 103
construction, of broadcasting stations, 196; planning and design, 197
consultants, 184, 187, 188, 189, 196, 202, 204, 231
consumer expenditures, for information machines, 156, 199, 235; for information services, 33, 158, 196, 197; for journals and other print media, 138, 156, 184, 230; for knowledge in general, 33, 138, 159, 196, 210; for radio and TV, 200, 238, 239; for schooling, 156, 214
consumer sovereignty, 155
consumers, choice, 155-158; surplus, 214, 215-217, 217n, 222
contents, of information, 8-9, 56-57; versus form, 120-122
control, devices, 234; mechanism, xx, 199; principle of permanent, 148
conventions and conferences, 15n, 234
convincing, 36
cookbook, 91, 106, 107, 209
cooking as a biological science, 89; as an art, 91; as production or consumption, 191; in national-income accounts, 194
Copernicus [Kopernik, Mikolaj], 115
copying machines, 234
copyright, 15, 16, 223, 234
Cornell University, xvii
correspondence, between symbols and objects, 116; rules of, 148
cosmogonists, 117
cost-benefit analysis, see benefit-and-cost analysis
cost effectiveness, 177, 233
counterculture, 81
Cournot, Antoine Augustin, 85
Creation, 127
creation and communication, of artistic knowledge, 15, 16n, 92; of knowledge, xvi, 7, 15, 16n
creative, arts, 70; imagination, 189; thinking, 57
crime, 108, 141n
criminology, 88, 135n
critic, 45, 67, 128, 129
Critique of Pure Reason, 127
Croce, Benedetto, 66n
cubook formula, 166n

cultural, activities, 24; aspirations, 33; lag, 135; resources, 141n; sciences, 68n, 70-84, 87; values, 21, 23-24, 78, 83, 126, 210
culture, animal, 70; human, 70, 78; nonmaterial, 106
curiosity, idle, 207, 209; intellectual, 11, 13, 108, 206, 210; knowledge satisfying, 31, 33, 108, 126, 182, 193, 206, 207, 209, 210
cyberneticists, 14
cytology, 117

d'Alembert, Jean LeRond, 64n
dancer, 92, 95, 96, 201
dancing, 16n, 52, 61, 95
Danilov, Victor J., 221n
Danto, Arthur C., 99n
Darwin, Charles, 107, 127, 142n-143n
data, bank, 184; ideally required, 225; obtaining, 39; raw versus interpreted, 8; relevant, 147; statistical, 19; versus information, 132n
Davis, Bernard D., 141n
Debussy, Claude, 40
decision-making, 31, 55, 107n, 148, 155, 156, 169, 174n, 204, 206, 218, 222
decision theory, 181
Decline and Fall of the Roman Empire, 187
decoding, 132, 151, 170, 187, 205
definitions, and axioms, 62; formal, 148; loaded, 136; of art, 91, 92; of Bildungswissen, 207; of cultural sciences, 70; of humanities, 70, 74, 82, 84; of industry, xxivn; of information, 205-206; of intellectual knowledge, 108, 210; of knowing how, 44; of knowledge, 113; of knowledge industry, 228; of knowledge occupation, 228-229; of knowledge production, 92, 175, 186; of obscenity and pornography, 136; of production, 193-201; of science, 63-69; of social value of journals, 215; of unemployment, 39; of use of knowledge, 204-205; persuasive, 59-60; place of, 27; versus classification, 59
delivery service, 203, 205
demand, curve, 213-215, 221; for books, 156, 184, 185, 210; for concerts and theater performances, 210; for information services, 22, 184; for journals, 184,

demand (*cont.*)
  210, 215-217, 221, 222; for knowledge,
  155, 183-185; for pornographic materials, 138, 139; for schooling, 210,
  213-214; latent or generated, 184
demographers, 4
demography, 81, 88, 134
demonology, 146
demonstrating one's knowledge, 35, 44,
  51, 53
demonstration, syllogistic, 63
departmentalization, in universities, 23,
  87-89; of business firms, 230
departments of erudition, 14
depreciation, 199, 228
Descartes, René, 63
descriptive, inquiries, 33; knowledge, 32
designer, costume, 15n; shoe, 226
designing, 8
detailed knowledge, 55
detectives, 159
Dewey, John, 93n, 116n
dialectic, 80, 90
dictating, 198
Diderot, Denis, 64
differential equations, 41, 44
diphtheria, 31
directing, 198
directives, 33
disciplines, as fields of study, 34, 60;
  humanistic, 70
disclosure, 7, 28
discovering, 8, 28, 57, 186
discovery, accidental, 173n, 182, 183; incidental versus accidental, 183; induced by experience, 179
discretionary processor of knowledge,
  189
disseminating, 8
dissemination, not the contents but the
  process of, 176n; of knowledge, 7, 22,
  23, 97, 133, 173-176; to entertain or to
  please, 174n
distinguishing, 47, 49
Diumulen, I. I., xxvn
divine studies, humanist reaction to, 75
division of labor, between mental and
  physical workers, 6; imaginary
  "complete," 230; within and between
  firms and industries, 198, 231, 232; in
  performing arts, 15-16n
division of knowledge, 104

DNA (dioxyribonucleic acid), 81, 134,
  142, 169
Dobbs, Betty Joe Teeter, 142n
doing versus knowing, 45, 51
dollar calibration, 221
dollar tags, 23-24
Dorfman, Robert, 218n
double-counting, 228, 232, 235; versus
  not counting at all, 235
Downs, Anthony, 8n, 107n
drawing, 94, 186, 198; a map, 32, 41, 42,
  44
drill, 45
driving an automobile, 32-33, 34
Drucker, Peter, xxviii
drugs, 12, 100, 149
dumb knowledge, 29
Duncan, William, 63
durability, 105, 106
durable goods, used in knowledge production, 195-196

Earhart Foundation, xiv, 20
earnings, by graduates, 212; differential
  schooling and, 211, 214; foregone, xxi,
  xxii, 214, 233; lifetime, 213-214; non-
  recorded cost of recorded, 196n
earth scientists, 81, 117
ecological developments, 134
econometrics, 35
economics, as a theoretical science, 85;
  as instrumental or intellectual knowledge, 107; chiefly negative
  conclusions in, 151-152; in the National Academy of Science, 65n; in the
  third culture, 81; knowing, 35-36, 50;
  of education, 5; of knowledge and information, 15, 21, 52; of knowledge
  production, 11; of research and development, 5; special fields of, 35; university departments of, 88, 89; welfare,
  10, 35, 217n
economists, xiv, xxv, 9, 18, 33, 55, 62,
  67n, 81, 108, 184, 208n, 211, 212, 214,
  215, 216, 218n
education, and knowledge stocks, 172; as
  investment or consumption, 159, 195;
  as a knowledge industry, 227, 233; assume business paying for, 239; basic
  research and higher, xvi, xix; broader,
  81; contents of, 213; continuing and
  recurrent, 210; cost of, 19; demand for,

210, 213-214; department of, 88; economics of, 5; efficiency of, 10; elementary, 61; embodied in labor force, 213; explicit and implicit costs of, 233; for retarded or unwilling learners, 169; government expenditures for, 33, 156, 214, 219, 226, 238; higher, xvi, 60; humanistic, 84; in the army, 227, 233; in the home, 227, 233; in the 1962 volume, xix; input-output ratios in, 10; investment in, 24, 195, 210; liberal, 108; money value of, 23, 213; moral, 123-124, 206, 211; national-income accounts omitting implicit costs of, 238; of laymen, 73; outside school, 227; overspecialized, 80; private and social value of, 210-215; private expenditures for, 156, 214; purposes of, 206; quality of, 28, 213; remedial, 169; subsidized, 214; total expenditures for, xix, 5, 19, 23; treated in volume III, 15; valuation of data on, 226; value of, 23, 210-214; value judgments on, 128; valuation of data on, 226; versus training, 108; vocational, 102

educational, failure, 141n; system, xvi, 22, 211; testing, 53, 76; theorists, 22

educationalists, xiv, xxv, 11, 22

educators, 102, 202

egalitarian, 20, 141n

Egypt, 31

Eiffel Tower, 34

Einstein, Albert, 115n, 127

Eisenhower, Milton S., 84n

elective system in colleges, 76

electrical engineering, 22

Eliot, Thomas Stearns, 58

elite, 138

elitist, 126, 210

emotion objects, 115n

emotions, 70, 83, 84, 93, 136

empirical, research, 127, 137; sciences, 62-65, 66, 67, 69, 122; world, 103

empiricism, 63

encoding, 132, 151, 187

encyclopaedia, xiii, 28, 60

Encyclopaedia Britannica, 71, 163n

endogenous variable, 5

enduring knowledge, xvi, 57-58, 103-105, 106, 109, 158, 159, 209

Engelhardt, A. Tristram Jr., 168n

engineering, 14, 60, 88, 89, 213

engineers, xiv, 3, 108, 196, 202, 226, 229

Ennis, Robert H., 34n

entertainers, 187, 192

entertainment, desire for, 126; either intellectual or pastime knowledge, 128; knowledge for, 33, 107n, 108, 126, 128, 148, 174n, 176, 180, 207

entomologists, 80

entropy, 40

environmental programs, 24

envy, 36

ephemeral, 57-58, 103-105, 106, 126, 138, 158, 170, 209

epistemology, 21, 27, 37, 99, 103, 111, 114, 117

equivocation, 27, 114, 151

Erlösungswissen, 106

erotic, contents, 140; knowledge, 135-141; realism, 135

ethical, knowledge, 85, 122-124; judgments, 123; precepts, 122-124

ethics, 21, 63, 111, 122-124

ethnology, 65n, 85, 88

ethology, 97n

evaluating, 186

everyday knowledge, 59-62, 96-97, 167-168

evidence, 37n, 43, 55, 65n, 98-99, 113, 117, 137, 147, 148

examinations, 36

exogenous variable, 5

expansion, of 1962 volume, xiii, 13-23

expansionism, 20-24

expectations, ex ante versus regret ex post, 209-210; heuristic, 37n; valuations based on, 209

experiences, comparing, 179; human, 83; inner, 79; learning from, 210; mental, 119; mundane, 99, 167-168; musical, 95; of animals, 97n; personal, 28, 30, 36, 55, 60, 124, 136, 168, 179; shared, 168

experimental science, 64n

experimenting, 57, 186

explaining, 47, 51

explanation, 68n, 102; degrees of, 151n

explosion, of knowledge, xiii, 19; of the literature, 13, 19, 20

external benefits, 211, 218; costs, 131; diseconomies, 131; economies, 218; effects, 218

extrasensory perception (ESP), 147

fact, as what we correctly believe, 111; logical, 115n; versus proposition, 115
fairy tales, 43
fake, art, 125; evidence, 147
falsifiability, 115-116, 119-120
falsification, 116
falsificationism, 116n
familiarity, 47, 50, 54, 78, 95
Fanny Hill, 131
Faust, 127
fear, 36, 99
feeling, 36, 42, 93, 99-100, 194
Feigl, Herbert, 79n
feminine intuition, 98n
fiction, and true stories, 119; heuristic, 32, 230; in lieu of good data, 222; literary, 118, 119, 210
figure skating, 54
film, annual output of, 171; combining image language, and music, 96n; editor, 16n; pornographic, 134, 138; rating of, 129; shown in cinema or on TV, 16n; types of knowledge conveyed by, 107, 128
filth, 135n
final demand, 196, 232, 238, 240
final product, current knowledge inputs in producing a, 159-160, 196-197, 239; education as, 159, 195, 238; entertainment as, 33, 107n, 108, 176, 180, 290; intermediate versus, xix, 159-160, 196-197, 232, 235; knowledge as, 159, 192, 196, 199-200; may be consumption or investment, 159-160, 196; of publishing industry, 240; radio and television broadcasting as, 200, 238-239; research and development as, 157, 159, 200, 238; value added versus sales of, 240
financial analysis, 158, 159, 196
fine arts, 15, 16n, 24, 90, 92, 94, 120-121
first-person report, 99
five classes of knowledge, 108-109
flash of light, 46, 173
Flexner. Abraham, xxiii
flows of knowledge, 8, 61, 161, 170-173, 176-177; at a rate per unit of time, 161, 171-172; information implies, 175n; internal within a firm, xxviii, 173n, 184, 196, 197, 198, 231-232; internal within a mind, 173; through space,

161, 171, 173; waste or consumption, 176-177
flows versus stocks, 8, 161-177
focal awareness, 45
food, production and consumption, 191
forbidden knowledge, 12, 133-141
Ford Foundation, xiv, xvii, 20
Fordham University, xvii
Fordham University Press, xviii
forecasting, inflation rates, 39-40; the weather, 40, 48; unemployment, 39
foreign languages, knowledge of, 34-35, 41-43, 102; messages in, 132; poetry in, 189; the word "science" in, 30, 67-69
foremen, 191, 229
forgetfulness, 105
form, and contents, 188-189; versus object, 120-122
formal sciences, 31, 66, 69
Fortune Magazine, xxvi
Frank, Judge, 140n
Frankel, Charles, 84
freedom, intellectual, 12, 138; of choice, 9, 155, 156; of research, 141; of speech, 134, 138, 139, 141; of teaching, 141; of the press, 134, 138, 139, 140; preservation of, 12; to be foolish, 149
freight, carrier, 145; forwarder, 104
French, conversing in, 41, 44; grammar, 50; knowing, 34-35, 41, 43; reading, 41; understanding, 44, 50; words for knowing, xiii, 29-30
Friedrich, Carl J., 73
fruit versus light, 11-12
fun of knowing, 23, 174n

Galileo Galilei, 142n
Galis, Leon, 114n
games, 108
gargoyles, 34
Gelehrte, 67
gene, mutations, 134; splicing, 134, 169
General Theory of Relativity, 127
generalizations, abstract, 78; everyday, 179; harmony of, 122; knowledge based on, 64; in the social sciences, 83; scientific, 67n, 102-104
genetic, diversity, 141n; engineering, 142; research, 134, 141, 142
genetics, 134, 141n, 142
geography, 88, 108

geologist, 81
geology, 80
geometry, 90
German, lieder, 132; word for science, 67, 68n; words for knowledge, xiii, 29-30
gestures, 95, 97n, 186
gibberish, 132
Gibbons, Edward, 73, 127
Giddens, Anthony, 168n
giselle, 96
gnoseology, 68n
gnosis, 119n
Gödel, Kurt, 64n
Godkin lectures, xxiii
God, 108, 117, 149
Goethe, Johann Wolfgang, 127
Goldberg Variations, 127
goodness, 122-124
Gore, Daniel, 166-167
gossip, 108, 208-209
government, as supplier, buyer, user, and promoter of knowledge, 157; compelling school attendance, 214; growing role of, 6, 20; paying for broadcasting, 156, 200, 238-239; paying for knowledge production, 10, 33; paying for journals and other print media, 217, 240; paying for R and D, xix, 24, 156, 157, 195, 200, 206, 238-239; paying for schooling, 33, 156, 214, 219, 226, 238; regulating and subsidizing public goods, 218-219, 223; restrictions on knowledge dissemination, 133-143; restrictions on research, 142; university departments of, 88
graduate record examinations, 168
grammar, 35, 50, 70n, 90
Greek, 70n, 71, 108
Gregory, Richard L., 150n
Grey, Zane, 127
Griffin, Donald R., 97n
gross national product (GNP), xx, xxvi, xxvii, xxviii, 171, 180, 240
Grote, John, 29n, 48n
growth, economic, xxii, 4, 10; of computer industry, xiii, xx, 135; of knowledge through maturation, 173; of knowledge occupations, xvii, 232; of knowledge production, xvii, xx, xxvi, xxvii, 10, 235; of number of jour-

nals, 19, 163-165; of productivity, xx, 5, 10, 33, 195-196, 198; population, 4; rates of, xiii, 10, 19, 162, 227
guilt, 36
Gutenberg, Johannes, 166

habits, 45
haircut, 203
hairsplitting, 30
Hall, Judith, 98n
Harbison, Frederick H., 236
harmony, 93, 95, 122, 126
Harvard University, xv, xxiii, 72, 87, 88
hate, 36
Hayek, Friedrich A., 77n, 151, 164n
Head of Medusa, 120
hearing, 49, 92-93, 97, 130, 187
heart-truth, 119
Hebrew, 132
Heilbroner, Robert L., 91n
Hempel, Carl, 79n
Henderson, Robert W., 166n
heretical, 134
Herring, Conyers, 216n, 221n
Herrschaftswissen, 106
Herschel, Sir John, 63, 115n
heuristic, 32, 37n, 222, 230
Hicks, John R., 216n
Hill, Samuel E., 236
Hillman, Donald J., 221n
Hippocrates, 71n
historians, xiv, 11, 62, 64, 65, 67, 74, 81, 147, 204; of science, 162
historical, Cleopatra, 121; sciences, 66n, 67n, 68, 85; statistics, 21; truth, 119
history, ancient, 105; and international relations, 102; and political science, 85, 88; department of, 89; doctrinal, 35; economic, 35, 39, 87; in the humanities, 73, 74, 80, 84, 87; institutional, 23; intellectual, 13, 21, 23, 87; interest in, 121; lessons of, 142n; of astrology, 147; of obsolete knowledge, 145; of past errors, 118; of physics, 145; of science, 65; political, 87; set apart from science, 66n; social, 81, 87; teaching of, 124; truth in, 119
Hogan, Father William T., xvii
Homans, George Casper, 73
home economics, 88-89
homo ludens, 78

Hoover, J. Edgar, 137n
Horace [Horatius Flaccus], 71n
household knowledge, 108, 156, 158, 209
housewife, as domestic servant, 194
how-to knowledge, 8, 22, 32, 44-46, 61, 90
Howell, Wilber Samuel, 63n
Huber, Mary Taylor, xiv
Hughes, Douglas A., 137n, 139n
Hughes, Everett C., xxivn
human capital, improved capacity as, 5, 233; knowledge as, 15, 172, 211, 233
human culture, 70
humane studies, 75-79
humanism, 71
humanities, as a division of academic learning, 60; characteristics of, 50, 81-84; financial support for, 82; in American colleges and universities, 71-72; teaching of, 124; versus arts, 73; versus science, 70, 75-81; versus social science, 73, 86, 87
humanistic, disciplines, 70; education, 84; knowledge, xxiv, 70-84, 85, 109; sciences, 68n, 70, 74, 77, 122; studies, 15, 77
humanists, 15, 18, 74, 87
humming a tune, 39, 42, 54
Hunt, Shane, xxii, xxiii
Hyde, H. Montgomery, 139n
hypostatization, 221-222
hypotheses, alternative, 117, 146; beautiful, 122; competing, 117, 146; disconfirmed, 17, 145; fictitious, 86; fundamental, 32, 62, 66; knowledge of, 118; novel, 9
hypothetico-deductive system, 67n

ice dancing, 54
ideal types, 83, 109, 127
identifying, 54, 98, 118
Iliad, 119
illusions, 150
imagination, 70, 84, 91, 92, 181
imagined introspection, 127
immodesty, 23
imparting, 46, 206
imperatives, 43, 123
imperialism, 22-23
implicit costs, xxii, 233, 240
inactive memory files, 48

incentives to produce knowledge, 183-185
income, distribution, 223; earned by knowledge-producing labor, 17, 240; knowledge flow likened to, 8; psychic, 10
inculcation, 46
individual knowledge, 28
individuation, 73
induction, 63
inductivist error, 118
industry approach, xix, 18, 19, 226-235, 240
ineffable knowledge, 36
infant-industry protection, 5
inferring, 186
inflation of prices, 20, 39-40, 43
information, abortive, 57; acquiring, 60-61, 67n, 120, 133, 178-185, 191-192, 198-201, 209; alternative modes of, 205; as an act, 56; as flow of knowledge, 150; as raw data, 8; as secondary knowledge, 58; contents of, 56-57; demand for, 14, 22, 156, 183-184; economics of knowledge and, 15, 21, 52; goods, 228; knowledge changed through, 57; meanings of, 8-9, 56-58, 203-207; on disconnected events or facts, 8, 58; pieces of, 58, 109, 151; political, 107n; practical, 130; process versus contents of, 9, 56-57, 176n, 205-206; read from instruments, 197; reception of, 14, 57, 158, 161, 181-183, 186-192, 203; scientific and technological, 173, 223; sector, xvii-xxviii, 237-240; sex, 12; systems, 3, 14, 22, 58, 206; transmission of, 7, 14, 28, 57, 186-192; uncertainty of, 14, 22, 55-56; uses of, 203-204, 206-207; value of, 203; versus data, 132n; versus knowledge, 8-9, 56-58, 203-208
information economy, xxvii-xxviii, 21, 237
information machines, xvi, xx, 20, 198-199, 225, 228, 234-235; business expenditures for, 156, 195-196, 199, 200, 235; consumer expenditures for, 156, 199, 235
information science, 14-15, 19, 22, 58, 132n
information scientists, xiv, xxv, 202, 205, 206, 209

information services, xvi, xx, 20, 21, 22, 58, 196, 197, 202, 203, 204, 215, 219, 221, 228; as fast-growing knowledge industry, 234; business expenditures for, 156, 158, 181, 184, 196, 197, 209, 234, 238; consumer expenditures for, 33, 158, 196, 197; government expenditures for, 234, 238; produced for internal use, 237, 239-240; scientific and technical, 173, 234; supply of and demand for, 156, 183-184
information theory, 8-9, 186-187
informing versus knowing, 56
initiative to produce knowledge, 155-158, 183-185
innovation, 157, 181, 236
innovators, headstart of, 157; using received knowledge, 174; with or without search, 182-183
input, as measure of output, 226; of knowledge confused with knowledge as product, 240; of knowledge-labor embodied in knowledge-output, 229
input-output ratios, in education, 10
intraindustry use of knowledge, xxviii, 184, 196, 231-232
Institut de France, 65n
institutional history, 23
institutions, changes in, 13, 20
instructions, 92, 189, 191
instrumental knowledge, 45, 106, 107
intellectual, curiosity, 12, 13, 108, 206, 210; history, 13, 21, 23, 87; immodesty, 23; reading, xvi
intellectual knowledge, xiii, xv, xxiv, 12, 49, 74, 81, 89, 105, 106, 107, 109, 119, 120, 124, 126, 127-128, 133, 171, 206, 207, 210, 239; definition of, 108
intellectuals, 72, 81
intelligence, artificial, 14; military, 55; native, 212; political, 55; reactions dependent on, 136
intentional reception of knowledge, 108-109, 181-183
intercommunication, 168, 179
interdisciplinary, approach, 21; character of this work, xxv, 75n; research, 3, 11
intermediary transmitters of knowledge, 7, 132
intermediate product, broadcasts as, 200, 238-239; final versus, xix, 159-160,

196-197, 235; knowledge as, 159-160, 193-201; versus investment, 159-160, 195-196
internal use of knowledge, xxviii, 173n, 184, 196, 197, 198, 231-232
interpretation, alternative, 150; of message yielding knowledge, 205; of musical composition, 126; subjective, 108-109, 127-128, 179
interpreters of knowledge, 47, 189
interpreting, 50, 186, 205
interrogative pronoun, 38, 41-46
intersubjectivity of knowledge, 168
introspection, 127
intuiting, 28, 57, 63, 92, 186, 189
inventing, 8, 28, 57, 186
inventions, patent protection of, xxii, 5; raw versus developed, 174; secret knowledge and patented, 209; use of patented, 175
inventiveness, 92
inventor, 188, 202
inventory of knowledge, 61, 188
investment, analysis, 158, 196; for knowledge production, 195-196; knowledge production as, 5, 24, 159, 160, 172, 173n, 193, 195-196, 197, 200; in durable goods, 159, 195, 196; in durable knowledge, 172, 195-196, 209; in education, xix, 5, 19, 23, 24, 33, 156, 195-196, 214, 219, 226, 238, 239; in human capital, 5, 172, 195; in intellectual knowledge, 210; in research and development, xix, 5, 19, 23, 24, 156, 157, 158, 181, 195, 196, 197, 200, 206, 208, 238; versus consumption, 159, 193-201; versus current production cost, 159-160, 176, 191-192, 193, 196-198, 209
irreversible processes, 40

James, William, 29, 116n, 179
Japanese, edition, xxv; song, 132; word for science, 67, 68n
Jaws, 127
Jefferson, Thomas, 12, 142
job, description, 190, 229; training-on-the, 227, 233; search, 212
Johns Hopkins University, xvii, 72, 84, 87, 103, 118
Johnson, Virginia E., 139
Jöhr, Walter Adolf, xiv, 178n

joke, 108, 204-205; practical, 44
Jones, Howard Mumford, 73
journalists, xxv, 142, 159, 187
journals, as information goods, 228; as knowledge production, xvi; demand for, 184, 210, 215-217, 221, 222; empirical problems concerning, 234; general-interest, 127; growth of, 19, 163-165; learning from, 60, 167; new data on, xxix; new knowledge in, 162; private and social value of, 215-217; subsidies for, 222; supply of and demand for, 184; uses of, 174; words, pages, and articles in, 171
Joyce, James, 140n
judging, 186
Jupiter Symphony, 105
jurisprudence, 67, 88
justified true belief (JTB), 38, 43, 113; fanatics, 38, 43

Kant, Immanuel, 64, 127
Kaufmann, Felix, 32n, 115n, 148n
Kaufmann, Walter, 61n
Keeney, Barnaby C., 83n
Kennedy, Jessica, xiv
Kennedy, John F., 41
kennen and *wissen*, xiii, 29
Kerr, Clark, xxiii-xxiv
Kerr, Donna H., xiv, 35n, 38n
Kershaw, Joseph A., 129n
Kida, Hiroshi, xxv
King Lear, 119
King Richard II, 119
King Richard III, 121
Kinsey, Alfred Charles, 139
Kirchschläger, Rudolf, 41
Kirzner, Israel, 161n, 173n, 181n
kitsch, 121
knife, 203
Knight, Frank, 144, 151, 152n
Knights of the Range, 127
knowing, a city, 32-33, 34, 36, 42; a feeling, 99-100; a language, 34-35, 43, 45; a literature, 34; a person, 41, 49, 96-97; a tune, 54, 98-99; affective versus cognitive, xxiv, 50, 51, 93, 94; artistic, 15, 54; degrees of, 29, 35, 52-56; elements of, 46-52; emotional, 36, 51; endless fresh, 179; for fun, 23, 174n, 194, 200-201; latent, 43-48; meanings of, 29-58; modes of, 29, 46-52; particle

theory of, 36, 44; procedural, 32; propositional, 22, 31, 34, 35-36, 46, 49; sentimental, 36; state of, 27, 56, 114, 120, 186; strong meaning of, 37-38, 97, 114; types of, 29-52; versus doing, 45, 51; versus informing, 56, 203, 205; weak sense of, 37-38, 117; wide concept of, xiii, 22, 30, 92, 97, 99-100, 117, 118; works of art, 34, 42
knowing how, 8, 22, 30-46, 61; definition of, 44
knowing that, 8, 22, 30-46, 61
knowing, what, 8, 22, 33-46; when or where, 40, 42, 44; who or whom, 36, 41, 42, 44; why, 36
knowledge, a priori, 65; about knowledge, 12; about versus knowledge of, 8, 29, 46, 47, 49, 50, 100; absolutely certain, 63; abstract, 63; academic, 60-61, 105; accepted, 14; accidentally acquired, 60, 108, 130, 173, 181-183; accuracy of, 35, 55-56, 119-120, 148; acquired through study, 60, 61, 67, 69; acquisition of, 60-61, 67n, 120, 133, 178-185, 191-192, 198-201, 209; activities that produce, 16-17, 21, 28, 57, 97, 100, 175, 186-192, 194, 198, 200-201; added, 57, 170; additivity of, 169, 170; aesthetic, 83, 126; affective, xxiv, 50, 51, 93, 94; alternative, 145, 146; analytical, 64, 109, 148; analyzer of, 16, 159, 189; and beauty, 120-122; and goodness, 122-124; and science, 62-70; and truth, 36-38, 43, 59, 113-120; antisocial, 133, 137; application of, 92; applied, 5, 31, 46, 69, 101-102, 106, 109; art as practical, 91; artistic, xvi, 15, 54, 74, 90-96, 98, 109, 118-121, 129n, 234; as a datum, 3-5; as a guide to action, 17, 31, 33, 97, 106, 124, 145, 148, 149, 150, 151-152, 191, 203, 204, 206-207, 209; as a product, 5, 153-241; as an input and an output, 92; as current input for material products, 159, 176, 191-192, 193, 195-198, 209; as endogenous variable, 4; as final output, 159, 192, 196, 199-200; as human capital, 14, 15, 172; as independent variable, 4; as intermediate product, 159-160, 176, 193-201; as interpreted data, 8; as justified true belief, 113; as state of knowing, 27, 114, 120, 186; as that

which is known, 27-28, 114, 120, 125, 186; as warranted or certified belief, 113, 117; as what people know, 105, 150; as what schools teach, 60; assumed as given, 3-4; attributes of, 56; basic, 5, 101-102, 106, 109; basic versus applied, 31, 46, 101-102, 109; belief versus, 32n, 38, 43, 100, 113-114, 117; benefits of, 10, 24, 159, 172, 177, 191, 211-212, 217-224; bits and bites of, 169; boring, 176; business, 55, 104, 108, 156-157, 196, 197, 209; by acquaintance, 29, 43, 47, 50, 119, 179; by study and reflection, 29, 47; carnal, 100; changed by new information, 57, 144-145; classes of, 59-109; classification of, 59-100, 101-109; cognitive, xxiv, 15, 51, 55, 93, 94; common, 91; complete, 43; concrete pieces of, 58; confidence in, 55; confusing, 150; conjectured, 113; consumer expenditures for, 33, 196, 199; consumption of, 159, 176-177, 191-192, 193-194, 196, 200, 209; contents of, 8-9, 29, 56, 58, 120, 122, 128, 203-208; contextual, 8; contradicting, 145; controversial, 147-148; cost of, 178-185, 196-197; costless, 178-180, 182, 201; creation and communication of, 7, 15n, 23, 89, 173-175; currently conveyed, 8; dangerous, 12, 133-134, 140, 141-143; deceptive, 57, 150; deficient, 128-129; demand for, 14, 181-185, 210; descriptive, 32; detailed, 55; dictionary meanings of, 9, 25; direct, 99; diffusion of, 12; disclosure of, 7, 28; disconfirmed, 57, 144-145; discretionary processors, 189; disproved, 145; disseminated below cost, 178; dissemination of, 7, 22, 23, 97, 133, 173-176; division of, 104; divulging new, 7, 28, 173, 175; dormant, 48; double meaning of, 27-29, 114; durability of, 105, 106, 159; economics of, 21; economy, xxvii; embodied in manufactured goods, 157, 181, 230; emotional, 36, 51, 93; empirical, 31, 62-65, 69, 109, 122, 123, 148; enduring, xvi, 57-58, 103-105, 106, 109, 158, 159, 209; entertainment, 33, 107n, 108, 126, 128, 148, 174n, 176, 180, 207; ephemeral, 57-58, 103-105, 106, 109, 126, 158, 159, 170, 209; erotic, 135-

141; erroneous, 117, 144, 147, 149; esoteric, xxiv, 106; ethical, 85, 122-124; everyday, 59-62, 96-97, 167-168; explosion, xiii, 19; explosive, 134, 141-143; factual, 55; false, 57, 145; financed by government, 10, 178, 155-158; five classes of, 108-109; flows of, 8, 61, 150, 161-177; for fun, 23, 174n, 194, 200-201; for future benefits, 6, 159, 161, 172, 173n, 176, 177, 191-192, 210; for immediate practical application, 31, 33, 69, 91, 159, 174; for immediate pleasure of recipient, 6, 156, 174n; for its own sake, 11, 78, 106, 207; for many, 105-106; for only a few, 105-106, 169; forbidden, 12, 18, 133-143; forgotten, 105, 170, 176; form and contents of, 188-189; formal, 31, 66, 69; free of charge, 156, 178, 179, 201; frivolous, 204; fundamental, 206; general-abstract, 105, 119; general-systematic, 103; general versus specific, 102-110; giving immediate satisfaction, 6, 120, 156, 176, 190-192, 193-201; goodness of, 122-124; government expenditures for, 199, 200; gratis, 194; growth of, xxiv-xxv, 16, 162-165, 168-169, 173; having knowledge of, 27; heretical, 134; high-brow, 127-129; highly qualified, 91; historical, 31, 32, 62, 63, 66n, 84, 102-104, 105, 109, 110, 145; household, 108, 156, 158, 209; how-to, 8, 22, 32, 44-46, 61, 90; humanistic, xxiv, 70-84, 85, 109; illusive, 150; imperfect, 22, 115; in intraindustry use, 231-232; in social sciences, 84-90; in the mind, 161, 167-173, 178-180, 186-192; in the strong sense, 37-38, 97, 99, 114; inaccurate, 57; incentives to produce, 14, 183; incomplete, 14, 148; increased by more things known or more brains knowing, 169, 186; individual, 28, 179, 180; industry, 9, 19, 128, 156, 225-231, 232-235, 239-240; ineffable, 36; inexact, 115n; inflammatory, 134, 141-143; information versus, 8-9, 56, 58, 175n, 203-208; instrumental, 45, 106, 107; integrated, 70; intellectual, xiii, xv, xxiv, 12, 49, 74, 81, 89, 105, 106, 107, 109, 119, 120, 124, 126, 127-128, 133, 171, 206, 207, 210, 239; in-knowledge (*cont.*)

tentional search for, 14, 181-183; interesting, 180; intermediary transmitters
of, 7, 132, 174, 188; interpreters of, 47,
189; intersubjective, 168, 180; inventory of, 61, 175, 188; investment in, 5,
24, 159, 160, 172, 173n, 193, 195-196,
197, 200, 209; latent, 43, 48; layman's,
67n, 69, 85; liberal versus useful, xxiii;
life-worldly, 168n, 179; lightweight,
125-128; linguistic, 31; living, 167;
low-brow, 107, 127-129; managerial
processors of, 189; market for, 155,
183-185, 237-238; market value of, 10,
104, 155; maturation of, 173; meanings
of, 29-58, 114; methods of producing,
28-29, 57, 186-191, 198-199; misleading, 57; mission-oriented, 206;
monopoly of, 143; mundane, 59-62,
167-168, 170; musical, 15n, 39, 45, 49,
50, 51-52, 54, 94-96, 98-99, 107;
mutual, 168n; naive, 69; narrow concept of, 22, 38, 43, 114; natural, 62, 63;
negating versus negated, 145; negative, 18, 118, 144-152; new, 10, 57,
133-134, 145, 158-159, 169, 182-184,
229, 233, 234; noncomprehended, 131,
132-133, 170, 176, 180; nonfalsifiable,
99; nonscientific, 79, 81; nontestable,
99; nonverbal, 18, 92-100, 109; nonverifiable, 99; normative, 66, 122, 123;
not measurable, 23-24, 61, 162, 167,
168, 169, 177, 226; not sold in market,
10, 225-226; not yet falsified, 117; objective, 68n; objectivated, 168; objectively true, 22; obscene, 136-141; obsolete, 42, 145-146, 170, 176; of causal
structure, 8, 32; of competing hypotheses, 117, 146; of conjectures and
hypotheses, 118; of ethical values,
122-123; of facts versus propositions,
115; of feelings, 94, 99; of fine arts,
15-16, 90; of foreign language, 34-35,
41, 43; of liberal arts and culture, 90,
119; of light fiction, 108; of literary
works, 119-121; of markets, 3, 22, 145,
157, 181, 209; of observable facts,
115-116; of poetry, 61n, 119; of pronouncements, 118; of propositions
versus facts, 115; of reports, 119, 174n,
189, 204-205; of right and wrong, 124;
of technology, 157, 195-196; of values,

124; *of* versus knowledge *about*, 8, 29,
43, 46, 47, 49, 100, 119, 179; of visual
art, 94, 120-121; of *what, that,* and
how-to, 8, 22; ordered or systematic, 8,
64, 67, 68n, 69; original creators of, 17,
189; painless, 180; partial, 43, 115;
particular-concrete, 103, 105, 109;
pastime, 108, 109, 118-120, 125, 126,
127-129, 133, 170, 192, 196, 199, 204-
205, 207, 208-209, 239; perfect, 63;
perishable, 105, 170; personal, 179,
180; persuasive definition of, 59-60;
philosophical, 68n; piece of, 122, 123,
131, 188-189, 193, 208, 209; political,
108; popular, 68n, 129n; pornographic, 12, 18, 134, 136-141; positive
versus normative, 67, 122, 123; possessed by only one person, 28, 173,
175; potentially usable, 43; practical,
xiii, xxiv, 31, 32, 33, 91, 101, 102, 105,
106, 109, 119-120, 124, 128, 130, 133,
145, 149, 170, 181, 204-205, 209-210,
239; practitioner's, 67n, 69, 85; previously accumulated, 8; private, 61,
167-169, 179; procedural, 32; processors of, 16, 188; produced for profit,
156; production of, xvi-xvii, xx, xxvi,
7, 9, 11, 19, 92, 93, 153-241; production versus distribution of, 7; productive, 5-6, 192; professional, 108; profound, 43; propositional, 22, 34-38, 46,
49; quality of, 111-152; questionable,
148; reactivated, 48; recalled, 43; receiving, 57, 60-61, 95, 188, 190-192,
208; reception of, 14, 57, 158, 161,
181-183, 186-192, 203, 205; recipients
of, 28, 57-58, 93, 94, 105, 108-109, 126,
130-132, 133, 151, 155, 156, 157, 161,
170, 174-175, 177, 178, 181-183, 188-
189, 190-192, 194, 203, 206, 210; reconstructed, 170n; recorded, 145, 161,
167, 170; rejected, 57, 118n, 144, 146;
relevance of, 36, 145; relevant, 170; reliability of, 55-56; religious, 107n, 108;
replacement of lost or obsolete, 176,
177; reproduction of, 159; restricted,
133-143; restrictive definition of,
59-60, 97; retained, 48, 130; retrieved,
48, 170n; romantic, 194; routine processors of, 188-189; satisfying curiosity,
31, 33, 108, 126, 182, 193, 206, 207,
209, 210; scholarly, 89, 170; scientific,

xiii, xvi, 62-70, 74, 81, 85, 89, 92, 102-104, 109, 117, 119, 121-122, 162, 165, 170, 180, 234; scope of, 169; search for new, 14, 157-158, 181-185; secondary, 58; secret, 28, 173, 175, 209; serious, 125-128; shared, 28; shoddy, 128-129; sinful, 135; small-talk, 108, 118, 126, 200-201; social, 28; social stock of, 161-162, 168-170, 176-177; socialization of, 168; socially new, 7, 28, 158-159, 173, 175, 233-234; society, xxvii; sold in interindustry trade, 196, 231-232; specialized, 89; specific versus general, 102; spiritual, 106, 107, 117, 133, 149; stock of, 5, 8, 57, 60, 61, 144-145, 150, 161-177, 178; stored, 48, 61, 167, 176, 188; subjective, 167-168, 179, 180; subjective interpretation of, 107, 108-109; subjectively new, 7, 158-159; subjectively true, 22; subsidiary, 45; subsidized, 178, 210; subversive, 134; superficial, 43; superior, 58, 77, 78, 125-129; supply of, 155, 181-185, 200-201; sure, 146; suspended, 145; synthetic, 109; systematic or ordered, 64, 67, 68n, 69, 91; tacit, 175; technological, xiii, xvi, 4, 5, 10, 133, 145, 157, 158, 181, 196, 209, 234; tested, 117, 144; that has proved its mettle, 148; theoretical, 32, 46, 66n, 102-104, 105, 109; theory of, 18, 111, 153; timely, 145; transfer into new minds of, 7, 124, 132, 133, 143, 159, 170, 173-175, 179-180, 184-192, 198, 200-201, 203, 234; transformers of, 16, 188; transitory, xvi, 57-58, 103-105, 106, 109, 126, 158, 170, 209; transmission of, 7, 14, 28, 57, 131, 159, 161, 170-171, 173, 174-175, 186-192, 203-208; transmitters of, 28, 126, 132, 155, 170, 173, 177, 178, 184, 187-190, 193-194; transporters of, 16, 188; true, 22, 37-38, 97, 114-120, 145, 149; truthful, 12; types of, 12, 25-52, 59-100, 101-109, 171; uncertain, 14, 22, 55-56, 113, 115, 148; undecided, 146; unified, 68n; unintelligible, 132; unintentionally absorbed, 60, 181-183; unproductive, 6; unscientific, 146; unsystematic, 69; unverifiable, 66, 115, 117, 123, 147; unwanted, 108, 129-131, 132, 133, 176, 180, 199; unwholesome, 12, 134-141;

uplifting, 12; use of internally produced, xxviii, 173n, 184, 196, 197, 198, 231-232; useful, 12, 43, 78, 122, 180-181, 202, 206; useless, 23, 149; uses of, 43, 90, 91-92, 109, 155-166, 172-175, 202-224; vague, 148; valid, 149; valuable inputs of, 193-201; value of, 24, 193-194, 207-217; verbalized, 96; verifiable, 116, 117, 123, 147; verified, 99, 116n, 117, 147; versus information, 8-9, 56-58, 203-208; weak sense of, 37-38, 117; wide concept of, xiii, 22, 30, 90, 92, 97, 117, 180; without words, 18, 92-100, 109; workmanlike, 125-128; workman's, 108

knowledge claim, 43, 44, 46, 55, 97, 98, 100, 144, 145, 147-148

Knowledge: Creation, Diffusion, Utilization, xiv, 202n

knowledge economy, xxvii

knowledge factory, xxiii-xxiv

knowledge goods, 215, 228, 240

knowledge industries, definition of, 228; the six major, 232-235; versus knowledge occupations, xix, 18-19, 226-235, 240

knowledge industry, as accepted term, xxiv, xxv, xxvii; as focal point for national growth, xxiii; concept of, xxi, xxiv, xxv, 227, 228; defined by output, 226, 229; operational concept of, xxviiin; universities as, xxiii-xxiv

knowledge occupations, definition of, 228-229; growth of, xvii, 232; versus knowledge industries, xix, 18, 19, 227-235, 240

knowledge-producing, activities, 16-17, 21, 28, 57, 97, 100, 175, 186-191, 194, 198, 200-201; labor, xx, 6, 10, 17, 198, 229, 235-237

knowledge production, as per cent of GNP, xxvii-xxviii; definition of, 92, 175, 186; for consumption, 159, 176-177, 191-195, 196, 200, 209; for intermediate inputs, 159-160, 176, 193-201; for investment, 5, 24, 159, 160, 172, 173n; for use within the firm, xxviii, 173n, 184, 196, 197, 198, 231-232; growth rate of, xxvi; in another mind, 7, 28, 79, 124, 132, 133, 143, 159, 170, 173-175, 179-180, 184-192, 198, 200-201, 203, 234; in one's own mind, 173,

knowledge production (*cont.*)
   175, 178-183, 186, 191; size and
   growth of, xxiv-xxvi, 16, 17, 162-165,
   168-169, 173, 232, 235
knowledge society, xxvii
knowledgeable society, 16, 17
known versus knowing, 18, 27-58
know-nothingism, 24
Küng, Emil, xiv, 178n
Kuzlov, U. I., xxvn
Kyklos, xiv, 161n

labor, "complete" division of, 230; division of, 6, 198, 230, 231; division of artistic, 16n; incomes of knowledge-
   producing, 229; knowledge-
   producing, xx, 10, 17, 198, 229; physical inputs of, 229; productive versus
   nonproductive, 6; ratio of physical to
   knowledge-producing, 6, 10, 198,
   235-237; relations, 102; supply of qual-
   ifed, 10; technological displacement
   of, 236
labor force, composition of, xx, 10, 17,
   190, 198, 235-237; future increase in,
   220; potential, xxvi
laboratory sciences, 78, 80
Ladies' Home Journal, 127
Lady Chatterley's Lover, 139
laetrile, 149
Laidlaw, J. C., 79n
Lalande, André, 63n, 70n
language, analysis, 18, 30, 37; analysts,
   43, 47; knowing a, 34-35, 43, 45; of
   physics, 115n; philosophy, 18, 21, 73,
   80, 97, 111, 114; skills, 61
laser-controlled disease scanner, 234
latent knowing, 43, 48
Latin, 70n, 71, 108, 132
laughter, 204
law, faculty of, 90; study of, 60, 213
laws, and regulation, 20; of nature, 141n
Lawrence, David Herbert, 139
lawyers, 231
laymen, 67n, 69, 85
learning, activities, 45; ambition, 126; as
   knowledge production, 191; branches
   of, 23; effort, 129; intentional, 60-61;
   process, 42; school, 60, 102, 103, 168;
   skills, 42; theory of, 22
Leeson, Kenneth, xxixn, 164-165n
legal, concept of prohibited sexual mate-

rials, 136n; questions, 234; sciences,
   68n; services, 231
Leigh, Vivian, 121
Lekachman, Robert, xxi
Letters and Science, 71-72
Levin, Harry, 79n
Lewis, Clarence Irving, 113n, 123n
liberal arts, 76, 90, 102; education, 108
Libra, 146
librarians, xxv, 185, 202
libraries, xiii, xxix, 14, 15, 16, 23, 162,
   165-167, 171, 228, 234
library science, 14, 22
lieder, 132
life-world versus model-world, 179
light versus fruit, 11-12
linguistic, choices, 30, 62; deficiencies,
   151; knowledge, 31; permissiveness
   versus purism, 205; philosophy, 21, 97
linguistics, 80, 83, 84, 89, 96n, 97
List, Friedrich, 5
listening, 28, 60, 92, 138, 180, 186, 190,
   191, 201, 203, 205
literacy, 167
literary, art, 119; critic, 67; intellectual,
   72, 81; scholarship, 79-80
literature, a part of general education,
   108; explosion of, 13, 19, 20; interest
   in, 121; knowing a, 34, 108; pornographic, 134; teaching of, 124
Little, Ian, M.D., 217n
live shows, 138
living systems, 14
Locke, John, 64n
logic, a part of science, 68n; formal, 65
logical, deduction, 64n, 148; facts, 115n
logical empiricists, 98
London, 104
looking, 180, 203
Louvre, 34
love, 36
love letters, 194
Love Story, 127
lover, 97
Luckmann, Thomas, 168n
Lydian mode, 98

Machlup, Fritz, "Comment," 219n; "The
   Economic Cost of Knowledge," 178n;
   *Information Through the Printed
   Word*, xxixn, 164-165n; *Methodology
   of Economics and Other Social Sci-*

ences, 91n, 109n; "Positive and Normative Economics," 91n; *The Production and Distribution of Knowledge in the United States*, xiii, 233n, 237n, 238; "Professor Hicks' Revision of Demand Theory," 216n; "Stocks and Flows of Knowledge," 161n; "Uses, Value, and Benefits of Knowledge," 202n

Machlup Plan, xxi

MacIver, A. M., 99n

MacKendrick, Paul L., 73

magazines, advertising income lowering price of, 131; and knowledge production, xvi, 6, 19, 60, 231, 234; astrology in, 146; contents of, 127; physical inputs in producing, 232; sex, 134, 138, 185; supply and demand for, 184-185, 210

mail carrier, 188, 203

Main Street, 103

Malcolm, Norman, 114n

management, as an information system, 16, 234; business, 6, 55, 156, 206, 209, 231, 234; consultants, 184, 187, 188, 189, 196, 202, 204, 231; contracts, 231; information services, 204; inseparable from firm, 231; science, 22

managers, 187, 204, 231

Mann, Thomas, 39

map drawing, 41, 42, 44

Marat, Jean Paul, 103

Margenau, Henry, 32n

marginal, changes, 227; effects of small changes, 224; productivity, 214; utility, 207, 214, 215; valuation, 214; versus total benefits, 221

market, demand curve, 213-217, 221-222; knowledge of the market, 3, 22, 145, 157, 181, 209; mechanism, 155, 156, 213, 218; model, 184; prices of goods and services, 181; research, 6, 104, 158, 159, 181, 196, 204, 209; signals, 155; value of knowledge, 10, 104, 180, 216-217, 218

Markle Foundation, xiv

Marschak, Jacob, xxvii, xxviii

Marshall, Alfred, 215n

Marxist investigators, xxv

Masters, William H., 139

masturbation, 135, 139

materialism, 21, 23-24

mathematical derivations, 45

mathematicians, 3, 74

mathematics, 62, 63, 65, 67n, 76, 89, 165, 213

maturation of knowledge, 173

meaning, a function of truth, 116n; verifiability theory of, 116n

meanings, dictionary, 25; of art, 90-92; of knowing, 29-58

measurement, cardinal and ordinal, 53; impossible for stocks of knowledge, 178; not essential to science, 67n; of ambition, diligence, and drive, 212; of benefits and costs, 220; of knowledge flow in physical units, 171; of stocks of recorded knowledge, 162-165; of the nonmeasurable, 177; of total benefits, 223-224; of unemployment, 39; of value of knowledge, 202, 207-217; physical scientists stressing, 80; "science" is, 220

measuring instruments, 197, 199, 234

measuring rod of money, 171n, 178, 180

mechanical arts, 90

media of communication, xvi, xix-xx, 13, 16, 125, 128, 129, 207, 234

medical, cures, 149; doctors, 45, 188

medicine, 60, 90, 149

melody, 54, 93, 95, 121

memory, 48, 60, 61, 96, 99, 105, 131, 132, 145, 146, 161, 176, 188

Memphis, Tennessee, 140

mental, acts, 56; alertness, 180-183; experience, 119; operations, 197; requirements, 190; states, 56, 99, 106

Merz, John Theodore, 65

Mesarovic, Mihajl, 8n

message, addressed, 188; aimlessly retained, 130, 131, 132; carried by knowledge workers, 229; changed in form, 188; comprehension of, 132-133; contents of, 203, 205, 208; conveyed by art, 119; in foreign language, 132; interpreting and processing a, 186; oral, 188; over loudspeaker, 130-131; recorded or remembered, 150; recipient, 130-131, 151, 187; secret, 132; transmitting and receiving a, 187-190, 208; use of, 203-205

messenger, 132

Metalious, Grace, 127

metaphysics, 64n, 87

Metcalf, Keyes D., 166n
methodologists, 32, 81
methodology, 76-77, 85-87, 103, 127-128
Métro, 34
Michelangelo [Buonarroti], 127
Michelson, Peter, 137n
microbes, 134
Middle East, 31
migraine headaches, 39
military, establishment, 206, 233; intelligence, 55; R and D, 233
Mill, John Stuart, 86, 91
Millar, Moorhouse I. X., lectures, xvii, xviii
Miller, Henry, 139
misinformation, 120, 128, 129n
modeling, 93
models, geometric and algebraic, 222; in economics, 35, 155; in science, 122; theoretical, 213
Modern Humanities Research Association, 81-82
Molotov bombs, 12
monetary policy, 102
moral, education, 123-124, 206, 211; judgment, 234; leaders, 12; philosophy, 64, 65, 85, 87; standards, 206, 211; values, 21, 23-24, 83, 124
Morley, Christopher, 149n
Morris, Charles, 66n
Mother Gisson, 119n
motioning, 186
mountain climber, 49
Mozart, Wolfgang Amadeus, 40, 52, 105
Müller-Lyer, Franz, 150n
multigraphing, 198
multi-media, communication, 96n, 138
multiplication table, 57, 105, 169
multiversity, xxiii
mundane, knowledge, 59-62; personal experiences, 38, 96-97
murder, 118
museums, 125; in Paris, 34
music, a part of the quadrivium, 90; and general education, 108; atonal, 95; chamber, 50, 61n, 95, 98, 126, 210; classical, 125-128, 129n; critic, 45, 129; Darwin on, 107; different judgments of, 129; focal attention to, 45; in ballet, 16n, 96, 121; instrumental, 94, 121; knowing a piece of, 54, 98-99; language, image, and, 96n; on radio

and TV, 131; popular, 125-128, 129n; recognizing, 49-50, 95, 98-99; retained in memory, 130; symphonic, 16n, 49, 50, 61n, 95, 121, 210; understanding of, 45, 50, 54, 95; vocal, 94
musician, 45, 50, 92, 98, 201
musicologists, 45, 81
muscle movements, 31
mutual, deterrence, 143; knowledge, 168n

Nagel, Ernest, 66n
National Academy of Science, 65n, 215
national assessment of schools, 168
national defense, 24
National Endowment for the Humanities, xiv, xxviii, xxix, 70, 74, 82, 83
National Foundation for the Arts and the Humanities, 74
national-income accounting, as a special field in economics, 35; conformance with concepts of, 237-238; cost of love letters disregarded in, 194; costless flows of knowledge omitted in, 180; internal flows of information omitted in, 173, 194; radio and TV broadcasting in, 200; treatment of cooking in, 194, 200; treatment of purchases of information machines in, 228; treatment of R and D in, 195, 200; unacceptable concepts of, 239; valuation of knowledge production in, xxviii, 10, 171, 196
National Institute of Education, xiv, 20
National Science Foundation, xiv, xvii, xxvii, xxviii, 20, 70
natural sciences, 60, 65-67, 68n, 78-80, 85, 87, 88, 89, 102, 122, 162, 165
natural scientists, 65-66, 67, 74, 77, 78, 79-80, 81
naúka (Russian word for science), 68n, 69n
necromancy, 146
negative, conclusions, 151-152; knowledge, 18, 118, 144-152; predictions, 151; sentences, 38
negotiating, 198
neighbor, 41, 179
neopositivist, 115n, 123, 147n
Neurath, Otto, 66n
Newman, Cardinal John Henry, xxiii, 78n

New York, 104
New York Yankees, 193
news reporters, 159, 187
newsletters, 19, 164
newspapers, xvi, 6, 19, 60, 118, 127, 128, 131, 146, 228, 231, 232, 234
Newton, Isaac, 118, 142n
Nibelungen Saga, 119
Nightwatch, 48, 127
noise, audial, 131; hearing, 93; mere, 132; semantic versus technical, 151; unpleasant, 131, 176; visual, 131
noneconomists, 18, 22, 23, 180, 183, 215, 216, 241
nonfalsifiable, 99
nonknowledge, 145
nonpecuniary benefits, 10, 24, 194, 211, 212, 218-219
nonproductive labor, 6
nonpropositional knowledge, 36
nonscientific, 81
nonverifiable, 99
nonverbal, art, 93-96, 98-100; knowledge, 92-100, 109; reactions, 93
normative, judgment, 23; propositions, 66, 122, 123; science, 66, 67
note-taking, 198
Notre Dame, 36
novels, 61n, 108, 119, 120, 223
nuclear, devices, 143; physics, 134; technology, 143
nude, 127
nuisance commercials, 130-131
nursery rhymes, 41, 43, 44

object facts, 115n
objective, data, 20; interpretation of knowledge types, 107; versus subjective, 108-109
objectively, observable, 55; true, 22, 99
obscenity, 134, 136-141
observable, 115n
observation, and definition, 148n; casual, 128; knowledge based on, 64, 67n, 147; passive, 179; reports, 122, 147
observer, 37n, 69, 133, 159, 179
observing, 57, 97
obsolescence, 105, 170, 176
obsolete, knowledge, 42, 145-146, 170, 176; textbooks, 128; theories, 42
occupational structure, xx, 10, 17, 190,

198, 235-237; of individual firms, 235-237
occupations approach, xix, 18, 19, 226-235, 240
Office of Telecommunications, xxvii-xxviii
On the Origin of Species, 127
opera, 126, 128, 129, 210
operational, concept, 175, 194; counterpart, 109; definition of science, 147; definition of use of message, 204; proxies, 212; set of data, 222
operations researchers, 3
operettas, 125, 126
ophelimetricians, 220-221, 222
ophelimity, 221n
Oppenheimer, Robert, 143
opportunities, of buying and selling, 3, 6; of innovation, 181; of production, 4
opportunity costs, xxi, xxii, 193, 201, 208, 220
optimizing a search, 55
origin of the universe, 117
original creators of knowledge, 17, 189
Ortéga y Gasset, José, 94
orthology, 27
Osler, William, 118
Oswald, Lee Harvey, 41
other minds, 28, 79, 190, 192
overspecialization, 80
Oxford English Dictionary, 65n, 70n, 135n, 136n, 146
Oxford University, 71

pain, 36, 42, 99
painter, 45, 92, 201
painting, 15n, 52, 61n, 93, 120-121, 186
Panofsky, Erwin, 74
Panthéon, 34
pantomime, 95
paper, for book-printing, 228, 232, 240; newsprint-, 228, 232; writing-, 228
paradigm, 162
parallel lines, 150
parapsychology, 147
parents, 133, 156, 210, 211, 212, 219
Pareto, Vilfredo, 221n
Paris, 34, 36, 39, 42, 44
Parker, William Riley, 82
Parkinson's Law, 10
parochialism, 22
Parrish, Maxfield, 127

particle theory of knowing, 36, 44
pastime, knowledge, 108, 109, 118-120,
    125, 126, 127-129, 133, 170, 192, 196,
    199, 204-205, 207, 208-209, 239; read-
    ing, xvi
Pastoral Symphony, 39, 42, 48
patent, incentive, xv; infringement, 175;
    of invention, xv, 175, 209; protection,
    5; system, xv, 220
peace, 12
Pearson, Karl, 85
peer-group pressures, 210, 214
Peirce, Charles S., 116n
pending matters, 145
performance, as a test of ability, 51; art
    as, 44, 91; artistic, 94-96; attention in,
    32, 42-45; know-how in, 46; musical,
    45, 121; of ballet, 16n, 121; routine or
    semi-automatic, 31; theater, 16n; ver-
    sus precept, 91-92
Persia, 31
persuasive definitions, 59-60
Peyton Place, 127
phenomenological theory of knowledge,
    167
phenomenology, 87
philanthropists, 156, 226
philologists, 29, 81
philology, 73
philosophers, xix, xxiii, 3, 11, 22, 23, 24,
    29, 30, 36, 44, 47, 64, 66, 67, 70, 74, 79,
    97, 101, 104, 111, 113, 149, 179; analyt-
    ic, 37, 43, 113, 123; linguistic, 37, 113;
    neopositivistic, 115n, 123; of knowl-
    edge, 99, 100, 113; of science, 27, 60,
    62
philosophy, analytic, 73, 80; as synonym
    for science, 68n, 85; classical, 71; lan-
    guage, 18, 21, 47, 73, 80, 97, 111, 114;
    moral, 64, 65, 85, 87; natural, 64, 65,
    85; of knowledge, 21, 27, 37, 99, 103,
    111, 114, 117; of science, 62-67, 68-89,
    77-79, 85-87; political, 21; positive, 85;
    professors of, 111; reading in, 13;
    scholastic, 71; schools of, 113, 114;
    teaching of, 124; university depart-
    ments of, 72, 88-89
phlogiston theory, 39
phonograph records, 125, 129n, 199,
    223, 228, 234; classification of, 129n;
    for the blind, 223

physical, abilities, 42; fact, 115; sciences,
    71, 79, 86, 88, 163n; scientist, 80;
    skills, 52; work, 6, 10, 198, 229, 236
physicalism, 78-79, 115n
physicists, 62, 64, 80, 107-108, 143, 162
physics, 22, 62, 76, 78, 107, 108, 145,
    148n, 216, 221, 222
physiologists, 135
physiology, 89
pianist, 45, 50, 51, 54, 98
picture, abstract or realistic, 94; arous-
    ing, 135; artistic or kitsch, 127, 140;
    beauty in, 120-121; of social condi-
    tions, 139; photographic, 199; porno-
    graphic, 133, 138, 140; supposedly
    unwholesome, 133
Pigou, Arthur Cecil, 11, 215n
pioneering, xviii, xxi, xxii
pity, 36
planning and design, 197, 198
Plato, 36
playing, 186
playwright, 15n, 93, 121
pleasure, 6, 36, 78
pneumatics, 87
pneumatology, 87
poetry, 36, 61n, 70n, 80, 93n-94n, 107,
    119, 120, 189, 210
poets, 70, 93
pointing, 186
Polanyi, Michael, 37n, 45, 46
police, 134, 138, 159
political, decisions, 31; economy, 87; in-
    formation, 107n; intelligence, 55;
    knowledge, 108; leaders, 12; maturity,
    211
political science, 17, 63, 68, 81, 85, 88, 89
political scientists, xxv
politicians, 142
Poluninoi, G. V., xxv
Popper, Sir Karl, 32n, 64n, 79n, 115n,
    116n, 118n, 122n, 147n, 148n, 151
Porat, Marc Uri, xxvii-xxviii, 19, 21, 237,
    238-240
pornography, 12, 18, 133-141
Portnoy's Complaint, 140n
positivistic restrictions, 117
possession, double meaning of, 28
postal services, xvi, 234
postulate of subjective interpretation,
    127

postulates, 32, 148

potential, labor force, xxvi; recollecting, 48

practical, action, 31, 33; application in concrete case, 69; joke, 44; knowledge, xiii, xxiv, 31, 32, 33, 91, 101, 102, 105, 106, 109, 119-120, 124, 128, 130, 133, 145, 149, 170, 181, 204-205, 209-210, 239; use of knowledge as art, 91-92

practice, art as, 44, 90; skill acquired by, 32-33

practitioner, and general knowledge, 147; in business, 104; versus scientist, 67n, 69, 85

pragmatic, considerations, 53; insights, 11; reasons, 62; significance, 30-31

pragmatism, 29, 97, 120, 149, 206

prayers, 132

precepts, ethical, 122-124; for practical pursuits, 33, 91-92; versus performance, 91-92

prediction, 40, 102; negative, 151

preferences, consumers', 103, 155, 156; politicians', 169; revealed, 24

prejudice, 38, 77, 129, 133, 137, 141, 211n

prescriptions, 92

price, air available at zero, 216; discrimination, 222; of beef, 106; of knowledge, 155; useful things may have zero, 207

Price, Derek J. de Solla, 162, 163, 164

primary information sector, xxviii, 237, 239

primary-research journal, xiii, 164-165

Princeton University, xvii, xviii, 72, 88

Princeton University Press, xiii, xiv, xviii

printer, 188

printing, 186, 226, 231; presses, 234

Pritchard, Harold Arthur, 113n

probability, estimates, 55-56; theory of meaning, 116n; value, 22, 113, 146, 149

procedural, knowledge, 32; rules, 32, 79

process, in the brain, 95n; information as a, 8-9, 56, 205-206; irreversible, 40; learning, 42; of composing, rehearsing, and performing, 16n

processing, 186, 199

processors of knowledge, 16, 188

production, in economics, 193-194, 201; includes distribution, 7-8

productive versus nonproductive labor, 6, 10

productivity, future, 6, 159, 172, 177, 191-192, 195-196; growth of, xx, 4, 5, 10, 33, 195-196, 198; of different curricula, 213; of education, 24, 195, 211-213, 233

professional knowledge, 108

professor of humanity, 71

propensity to talk, 179, 200-201

property, double meaning of, 28

proposition, analytic, 64, 103; declarative, 36-37; empirical, 67; empirically verified, 147; evaluative, 66; falsifiable, 67; hypothetical, 37; imperative is no, 43; instrumental, 91; mathematical, 115n; meaningful, 116; negative, 38; nonfalsifiable, 66; normative, 66, 123; operational, 67; positive, 67, 91; pseudo, 116n; scientific, 122; synthetic, 103; testable, 98; versus fact, 115

propositional knowledge, 22, 34-38

prurient interest, 139

"pseudo-propositions," 116n

psychic income, 10, 194

psychology, 14, 37, 63, 81, 115n; department of, 87, 88, 89; methodology of, 87; other names for, 87

psychologists, 22, 24, 29, 47, 97n, 135

public, good, 218, 221; health, 24; transportation, 24

public relations, 197, 234; specialists, xxv

publishers, xxv, 190

publishing industry, xxix, 16, 128, 171, 184-185, 226, 231, 240

quadrivium, 90

Quain, Edwin A., xvii, xxiii

quantification, in journal publishing, 171; of knowledge in physical units, 171

quasi, firms, 239-240; industries, 19, 239-240; verbal, 96

R and D, see research and development

racism, 141, 142n

radio, advertising revenue, 131; as knowledge production, xvi, 6, 19, 60, 234; commercials, 129n, 130, 200, 226,

radio (*cont.*)
239; consumers, business, or government paying for, 33, 133, 156, 200, 238, 239; equipment, 171, 199, 232; historical performances on, 131; programs, 127, 128, 156; reproducing knowledge, 159
Radnitzky, Gerard, 69n
ranking of competitors, 54
rape, 118, 137, 140
rating, by referees, 54; of achievement tests, 168-169; of art, 129; of films, 129
Reade, Rolf S. [Alfred Rose],138
reading, a foreign language, 35, 41, 43; as basic skill, 22, 61; as knowing how, 61; as knowledge production, 28, 92, 186, 190, 191, 198, 203, 205; erotic literature, 135, 136-137, 138-141; freedom of, 138; light versus heavy, 125-127; pastime, xvi, 60
recalling, 43
reception of knowledge, 14, 57, 158, 161, 181-183, 186-192, 203, 205
reciting, 41
recognizing, 47, 49, 54, 96-97, 98
recollecting, 47, 48, 49, 53-54
reconstructing, 93, 99
reductivism, 78, 86
reenforcing, 99
referees, 54
refutations, 57, 118
Register Librorum Eroticorum, 138
regression analysis, 41, 43, 44, 50; multiple, 212
regularities, observed, 35, 102
rehearsing, 15n-16n
Reichenbach, Hans, 115n, 116n
reliability, 55
religion, 70, 74, 132, 135n, 149; teaching of, 124
religious, attitudes, 140; authorities, 134-135; congregations, 132; fervor, 141n; knowledge, 107n, 108; leaders, 12; man, 107; restrictions on knowledge dissemination, 133, 137n; values, 83
Rembrandt, [Harmens] van Rijn, 39, 48, 127
remedial education, 169
remembering, 39, 47, 48, 53, 97, 98
reminding, 40
remorse, 36

Rensberger, Boyce, 150n
report, by knowledge provider, 159, 198; not read by decision-maker, 204; on ball game, 193; on value of scientific journal, 215-217, 221-222; rejected or deferred by reader, 174n; to beloved, 194; use of, 204-205
research, academic, 141, 157; applied, 101-102, 206; assistants and associates, xiv, 20, 76; based on old, builds new knowledge, 172; basic, 24, 101-102, 206; dollar value of, 23; empirical, 127, 137; for transitory knowledge, xvi, 104, 158, 209; genetic, 134, 141, 142; grants, 157-158; in the humanities, 76; in the social sciences, 77; laboratory, 226; market, 6, 104, 158, 159, 181, 196, 204, 209; proposals reviewed, 157
research and development, allocating expenditure for, 183n; as a knowledge industry, 227-228, 233-234; as cost of current input or as final product, 195-198, 200; as production of knowledge, 206; business outlays for, xvi, 157, 158, 181, 195, 196, 197, 200, 209, 238; by governments, industries, and universities, 157, 228, 230, 238; complementary with higher education, xv, xix; economics of, 5; evaluation of productivity of, 226; farmed out by firm, 182, 236; for spacecraft, missiles, and weapons, 157; government paying for, xix, 24, 156, 157, 195, 200, 206, 238-239; growth of, xix; in 1962 volume, xix; in universities, 157, 228, 230, 236; induced by patent incentive, xv; industrial, 158; innovation based on, 157, 181; investment in, 195-196, 200; intraindustry use of output of, 238; national-income accounts of, 195, 200; national-income account omitting business investment in, 200, 238; output embodied in material products, 230; producing technology, 157, 200; project selection, 156, 158; scientific and technological, 185, 195; trained personnel needed for, xvi; yielding socially new knowledge, 15, 158, 234
Research and New Knowledge, Cognitive and Artistic, 15
retirement, 176n
retrieval systems, 221

retrieving, 48, 99
revealed preference, 24
revolution, 133
rhetoric, 70n, 90
rhythm, 93, 95, 126
Riccardi, Peggy, xiv
Rich, Robert F., 174n
right to be sure, 37-38, 39, 43, 97, 99, 113, 114
right to foolishness, 149
rock 'n' roll, 126
Roget's Thesaurus, 187
Rome, 105
Romeo and Juliet, 96
Rosental, E. I., xxvn
Ross, William David, 63n
Roth, Michael D., 114n
Roth, Philip, 140n
routine performance, 31
routine processors of knowledge, 188-189
Rowell, Henry, 84n
royalties, 223
Rubin, Michael R., xxviiin
rules, know-how as understanding the, 44; of correspondence, 148; of procedure, 79, 102; of the game, 42; processing, 189
Russell, Bertrand, 28, 29n, 111, 115n, 179
Russian translation, xxv
Rustling of Spring, 127
Ryle, Gilbert, 30, 31n, 42n, 45, 46, 48n

S and T [scientific and technological] information, xvi
Sacramento, 40
Sagittarius, 146
Saint Paul, 137n
Sallo, Denis de, 163
salvation, 106, 108, 117, 135n, 148
Samuelson, Paul, 217n
satisfaction, communicator's, 190, 194, 201; future, 161, 191; immediate, 191, 193-201; intellectual, 148; of curiosity, 31, 33, 126, 207, 209, 210; unpaid and unrecorded, 194
savant, 67
savings function, 4
savoir and connaître, xiii, 29
scales, 199
scent, 96

Schaar, John H., xxiiin
Scheffler, Israel, 32n, 37n
Scheler, Max, 106, 207
Schilpp, Paul A., 148n
scholars, 15, 16n, 67, 72, 102
school, building, 226; expenditures for, xix, 5, 19, 23, 33, 156, 214, 219, 226, 238, 239; learning, 60, 61, 102, 103, 128, 168; of business, 22; producing all types of knowledge, 128, 129; public and private, 226; reform, xxi
schooling, and earnings, 211, 212-215; compulsory, 214; extended and improved, 195, 233; identifying all effects of, 211; investment in, 24, 195-196; longer, 195, 233; private and social returns to, 24, 233; value of, 210-214; years of, 17, 212
Schubert, Franz, 132
Schultz, Theodore W., xxii, xxiii
Schumann, Robert, 132
Schumpeter, Joseph A., 67n
Schutz, Alfred, 168n, 179
science, as highly qualified knowledge, 91; as knowledge a priori, 65; as ordered knowledge, 8; concepts used in, 148n; cosmopolitan meaning of, 67-69, 147; defined, 63-69; defined in non-English languages, 30, 67-69; empirical, 64n; ethics as a, 66n, 122-124; excluding empirical knowledge, 62-64; experimental, 64n; in French, 30, 67n-68n; narrow sense of, 22, 65-67; natural scientists appropriating the term, 65-66, 77; nontranslatable, 69; normative, 67; past errors in, 118, 145; "proper," 64; pseudo-, 146, 147; restricted to natural phenomena, 65; shorthand for natural sciences, 65n, 66n; traditional meaning of, 18, 62-65; versus humanities, 70, 75-81
sciences, academies of, 14, 23, 68; arts and, 90; biological, 82, 85, 88-89, 163n; cultural, 66, 68n, 70-84; demoted, 146-147; empirical, 62-65, 66, 67, 69, 122; formal versus empirical, 31, 66, 69, 122; hard, 165; historical, 66n, 67n, 68, 85; humanistic, 68n, 70, 74, 77, 122; juridical, 68; legal, 68n; mathematical, 82; moral, 67n, 68, 82; natural, 60, 65-67, 68n, 78-80, 85, 87, 88, 89, 102, 122, 162, 165; philological, 68n;

sciences (*cont.*)
philosophical, 68; physical, 22, 71, 79, 86, 88, 163n; psychological, 86; social, 66, 68n, 82, 84-90; theoretical, historical, and technical, 85
scientific, and technical information, xvi; attitude, 117, 148; creation, 16n; information, 173, 221, 223; jargon, 140; journals, 164-165, 215-217, 221-222; knowledge, xiii, xvi, 62-70, 74, 81, 85, 89, 92, 102-104, 109, 117, 119, 121-122, 162, 165, 170, 180, 234; method, 67, 75, 79, 119, 147; modesty, 37; procedure, 115n-116n; propositions, 122; truth, 115n; value, 140; versus humanistic subjects, 70
scientism, 76-81
scientists, 16n, 18, 37, 64, 67, 75-81, 102, 118n, 141n, 146, 188; as artists in communication, 16n, 122; versus laymen and practitioners, 69, 85
scientistic versus scientfic, 77
scientometricians, 162, 165, 171
score, in ball games, 59, 106, 193; musical, 54, 59; test, 54, 76, 81
scriptwriter, 16n
sculptor, 16n, 45, 92, 201
sculpturing, 15n, 61n, 93, 186
sculptures, 120, 138
search, costly, 181; for the unknown, 182; in-house or farmed out, 182
searchers, watchers, and finders, 182-183
secondary information sector, xxviii, 19, 237, 239
secondary knowledge, 58
secret, divulging a, 209; formula, 203; knowledge, 28, 173, 175, 209; message, 132; technical know-how, 209
securities brokers, 196
seeing, 49, 92-93, 96-97, 100, 150, 187
Senior, John L., lectures in American Studies, xvii
Segal, Erich, 127
self-, abuse, 135n; fulfillment, 106; gratification, 135
semantic, change, 162; conversion, 77; distinction between pornography and obscenity, 135n; diversity, 152; noise, 62, 151; positions, 114
semantics, exercise in, 18; historical, 37-38, 62, 85; of information versus knowledge, 8-9, 56-58, 157n, 203-205
semanticists, 32

semiautomatic activity, 31
semiotics, 14, 69n, 96n
sense, impression, 93, 94, 96; objects, 115n; perception, 49, 78, 92-93
September Morn, 127
serendipity, 182-183
serial publications, 164
sermons, 117
service stations, universities as, xxiii
sex, acts, 136, 139; information, 12, 135-141; procreative versus recreative, 135; solitary, 135
sexual intercourse, 100
Shackle, George L. S., 179
Shakespeare, William, 59, 106, 107, 119, 121, 123n
Shaw, Bernard F., 121
Shelley, Percy Bysshe, 93n
shoelaces, 102
show-off, 120, 186, 190
Shterngarts, M. Z., xxvn
sign language, 95
signaling, 186
signals, and data, 132n; by instruments, 197, 199; convertible into knowledge, 191; encoding and decoding, 187; given by knowledge workers, 6, 229; light, 199; market, 155, 218
Sinding, Christian, 127
singer, 50, 92, 94, 98, 132
singing, 186
sinful, conduct, 135n, 137n; knowledge, 135; versus unhealthy, 135n
size constancy, 150
skiing, 41, 42, 44, 45, 50
skills, acquired by doing, 61n; acquired by study, 61n; acquired by training, 49; artistic, 54; and the humanities, 61n; as art of doing, 45; basic, 22, 33, 38, 60, 61, 168, 206; exercise of, 55; hemispheres of brain controlling different, 93n; higher levels of, xxiii, 32; know-how as, 44, 61n; language, 61; learning, 42; musicians' technical, 121
Sleeping Beauty, The, 96
Sloan Foundation, xiv
sloppy speech, 205
small-talk, 108, 118, 126
smelling, 49, 93, 97, 187
Smith, Adam, 5
Smith, B. Othaniel, 34n
Smith, Maggie, 121
smut, 135n

snobbishness, 128, 210
Snow, Charles P., 77n, 79-81
Snow White, 41
social, benefit of education, 210-215, 219; knowledge, 28; priorities, 13; scientists, 11, 55, 64, 65, 67, 68, 74, 87; security, 24; value of scientific journals, 215-217, 221-222; workers, 12
socialization of knowledge, 168
socially new knowledge, 7, 28, 158-159, 173, 175, 233-234
"social physics," 85
social-science knowledge, 84-90
social sciences, and humanities, 73, 74, 86-87; as empirical sciences, 66, 122; books in the, 165; concept of understanding in the, 50, 108-109; divisions and departments of, 60, 87-89, 90; humanistic and scientific elements in, 75n; knowledge of the, 84-90; policy based on, 102; restricted research in the, 134; teaching of, 124
sociologists, xix, xxivn, xxv, 3, 11, 24, 29, 147
sociology, 17, 65n, 81, 88, 89, 147
Sorbonne, 34
soul, 64n, 93, 108
South Carolina College, 87
speaking a foreign language, 35, 41, 43
spectrum, from transitory to enduring knowledge, 109; of knowledge-producing activities, 189; of meanings of benefit-and-cost analysis, 219; of modes of knowing, 46; of quality of art, 127
speculating, 57, 80, 83
spillover effects, 211
Spinoza, Baruch, 66n, 124n
spiritual knowledge, 106, 107, 117, 133, 149
spokesman, 159
spy stories, 132
Sri Lanka, 183n
stage designer, 15n
stained-glass windows, 34
Star Wars, 127
statistical, analysis, 196, 225-233; curiosity, 20; data, 19, 230; disentanglement, 234; estimates, 74; inquiries, 20, 33, 133, 230; mechanics, 117; proxies, 212; records, 212; tables, 75, 140; update, xxvi, xxviii, xxix
statisticians, 180, 194

statistics, economic, 21; historical, 21; imaginary, 230
Stauffer, Robert C., 67n
stenographer, 188
stocks, versus flows, 8, 161-177; yielding flows added to stocks, 172
stocks of knowledge, 5, 8, 57, 60, 61, 144-145, 150, 161-177; in human minds, 167-170; increased by more things known or more brains knowing, 169; not measurable, 178; preexisting, 57; private and social, 167-168; size and growth of, 168; transmitters' and recipients', 170
stories, 108
streets of Paris, 34
structure, occupational, xx, 10, 17, 190, 198, 235-237
styles of living, 211
stylus, 234
subconscious, activity, 31; retention, 170n
subjective, criteria of illegitimate obscenity, 140; evaluation of knowledge quality, 141; interpretation of knowledge type, 107, 108-109, 127-128, 141, 179; judgments, 20, 55; ratings in tests, 54; ratings of art, 129; states of mind, 136; valuation, 211, 212
subjectively, new knowledge, 7, 158-159; true, 22
subscribers, 215-217, 222
subscriptions to periodicals, 165, 171, 222
subsidiary knowledge, 45
subversive communications, 134
Sunday-school classes, 117
sundial, 234
superficial knowledge, 43
superiority complex, 79-80
supernatural phenomena, 146
superstition, 149-150
supply, latent, 184; of information services, 184; of knowledge, 155, 183-185, 200-201; of qualified people, 10
supply and demand, elasticities, 220; for books, 184; for information services, 183-184; for journals, 184; for knowledge, 155; for magazines, 184; law of, 58; theory of, 3
surgeons, 45
survey research, 127, 135n
Susann, Jacqueline, 127

Swan Lake, 96
Swarthmore College, 89
swimming, 31, 32n, 41, 42, 44, 50, 61n
syllogism, 37, 63, 64
symbols, 115-116
sympathy, 36
symphony, 16n, 59, 61n, 95, 121, 126, 129, 210
synthetic versus analytic propositions, 32, 103
systematic or ordered knowledge, 91
systems analysis, 14

Takahashi, Tatsuo, xxv
talent, 43, 46, 49, 76, 128, 169
talking, 179, 186, 187, 200-201; plus listening, 28
tapes, 228
taste, and humanities, 84; artistic, 91; for intellectual knowledge, 210; for poetry and music, 107; of knowledge processor, 189; personal, 126, 128; poor, 128; refined, 107; refining, 70; sense of, 93, 96; standards of, 140; stylistic, 122
tasting, 49, 187
tax law, permitting expensing of R and D outlays, 238
taxi driver, 34
taxonomy of academic subjects, 89
Taylor, Elizabeth, 121
teachers, 128, 171, 187, 188, 190
teaching, 22, 36, 42, 187; good, 128; techniques, 22
technological, innovation displacing clerical or physical labor, 236; journals, 162-165; knowledge, xiii, xvi, 4, 5, 10, 133, 145, 157, 158, 181, 196, 209, 234; progress, xx, 4, 5, 10, 195-196, 198
technology, advance of, 209; as exogenous variable, 4; as trend function, 4; assumed to be given, 4; destructive, 143; financial support for, 75; for producers, 145; future changes in, 220; handbook of, 92; humanized, 83; journals of, 162, 163n, 165; knowledge of, 4, 102, 145, 157; mechanical arts or, 90; new, 10, 133-134, 174, 234; nuclear, 143; of transmission, 131; production of, 10; purchased from the outside, 236; transforming life, 78; up-to-date, 157
tedious exactitude, 47

telephone and telegraph, xvi, 171, 193, 199, 205, 232, 234
telephoning, 198
television, advertising, 129n, 130, 200, 226, 239; as intermediate or final product, 200, 238-239; as knowledge production, 6, 19, 60, 234; commercials, 129n, 130, 239; consumers, business, or government paying for, 33, 131, 156, 200, 238-239; equipment, 199, 232; films for, 16n; programs, 107, 127, 128, 131, 156, 238; receiving sets, 171, 199, 232; reproducing knowledge, 159; sex on, 138; stations' plant and equipment, 196; studio, 226; watching, 60
Terence [Terentius Publius], 71n
terminological proposals, 7-9
terrorist, 133, 143
test, achievement, 53, 168-169; aptitude, 169; of hypotheses, 80; of understanding, 51; performance, 51; recognition, 98; scores, 53, 54, 76, 81
testimony, 63
Teutonic authoritarianism, 27
textbooks, 128
Thatcher, Sanford, xiv, xv
theater, 15n, 16n, 121, 128, 138, 210; in Paris, 34
theologians, 75, 76, 141n
theology, 71, 76, 79, 90
theorizing, 57
theory, beauty of a, 122; never empirically verifiable, 147n; obsolete, 42, 145; of communication, 3, 151, 186; of competition and monopoly, xvii, 3; of relativity, 46; of supply and demand, 3, 58; of the phlogiston, 39; of thermodynamics, 40, 81
therapist, 107
thermodynamics, 40, 81
thermometer, 199, 234
third-party effect, 131
thirteen elements of knowing, 47
thirty-three questions, 39-41, 42-44, 46
Thirty-Years War, 40
Thomson, John Arthur, 65n
thought objects, 115n
toothache, 97n, 99
Toscanini, Arturo, 98
touching, a nettle, 96; a sculpture, 94; a surface, 93; as a sense perception, 49, 93, 97, 187; skin, 97

traffic, 32-33
train schedule, 102, 104, 120
training, capacities built up by, 45, 46;
    for a job, 108; musical, 95; on the job,
    227, 233; skill acquired by, 49; versus
    education, 108; vocational, 102
transdisciplinary research, 21
transformers of knowledge, 16, 188
transitory knowledge, xvii, 57-58, 103-
    105, 106, 109, 126, 158, 170, 209
transitory versus enduring, xvi, 158
translating, 186, 189
translation, of 1962 volume, xxv; of
    poetry, 189; of the word knowledge,
    30; of the word science, 67-68
translator, 189
transmission, by first knower, 159;
    deficiencies in, 151; of knowledge, 7,
    14, 28, 57, 186-192; selective, 131
transmitters of knowledge, 16, 17, 28,
    126, 132, 155, 170, 173, 177, 178, 184,
    187-190, 193-194; main types of, 187-
    190; pleasure of, 190
transporters of knowledge, 16, 188
trend function, 4, 5
Trevor-Roper, Hugh R., 73
trivium, 90
trousers, torn, 40, 43
True Confessions, 127
true or false, 32, 36
truth, and belief, 113-114; and illusion,
    150n; and knowledge, 36-38, 43, 59,
    113-120; as quality of knowledge, 111,
    113-120; confirmed, 119-120;
    demonstrable, 62; historical, 119; in-
    dependent of knowledge, 115; mean-
    ing as a function of, 116n; of ethical
    propositions, 122; of feeling versus
    verbalization, 119; physical versus log-
    ical, 116n; scientific, 115n, 119; test,
    98, 99; theory of, 120; undecided, 36
truth value, 22, 112, 116n, 117, 129n,
    146, 149
Tuileries, 34
tune, humming a, 39, 42, 54; knowing a,
    98; recognizing a, 54
two cultures, 15, 72-73, 75-81
Tyndall, John, 149n
typewriter, 205, 234
typing, 186, 198
typist, 188

ultra-fussy wing, 37, 43

Ulysses, 140n
uncertainty, 9, 55-56, 118
undecidability theorem, 64n
underground press, 134
understanding, a foreign language, 35,
    43, 45; a message, 203; actions and
    thoughts of others, 50; as an element of
    knowing, 45, 47; attaining deeper, 173;
    in the sense of verstehen, 50; levels of,
    53, 173; music, 45, 50, 54; perform-
    ances of skill, 45; requirement of, 55;
    revised, 57; rules of the game, 42; the
    past, 102; the social world, 177; two
    cultures lack mutual, 80; works of art,
    54
unemployment rate, 39
unintentional reception of knowledge,
    60, 181-183
U.S. Bureau of the Census, xxiv
U.S. Congress, 73, 74, 75n, 82, 219
U.S. Department of Commerce, Office of
    Telecommunications, xxviii
U.S. Supreme Court, 139
universal library, 162-167
universals, versus particulars, 103; ver-
    sus unique events, 87, 102
universities, departmentalization in, 14,
    23, 87-89, 90-91; E. S. P. research at,
    147; expenditures for, 156; favoring
    natural sciences, 76; major divisions
    of, 90; promotion policies of, 76
university, as a knowledge factory or in-
    dustry, xxiii-xxiv; buildings in Paris,
    34
University of California, xxiii, 71-72, 88
University of Chicago, 70n, 72, 88
unobservables, 148
unwanted knowledge, 108, 129-131, 132,
    133, 176, 180, 199
unwilling, investors, 210; recipients of
    messages, 130-131; students, 129, 169,
    210
update of statistics, xxvi, xxviii, 13
use of knowledge, 155-166, 202-224; art
    as, 90, 91, 92; by type of knowers, 109;
    includes decisions not to act, 174n; po-
    tential or actual, 43; various meanings
    of, 174-175; versus effects of use, 204

Valley of the Dolls, 127
valuation, as empirical knowledge, 123;
    future, 210; in terms of money, 212; ob-

valuation (*cont.*)
  jective versus subjective, 211; of inputs
  and outputs, 193-201
value, antimony of, 207; cultural, 21,
  23-24, 78, 126, 210; economic, 24; exchange value versus use, 207; judgment, 12, 20, 55, 123, 128; market
  value and social, 218-219, 220; money,
  23-24, 171-172; nonmaterial, 12; of air,
  216, 222; of information, 203; of information machines, 199; of knowledge, 207, 217; of schooling, 210; private versus social, 5, 10, 210-215; scarcity, 208; theory of social, 221; total
  versus marginal, 216; truth, 22, 112,
  116n, 117, 129n, 146, 149; unpaid part
  of, 214, 215-217, 222; versus usefulness, 202
value added, xxviii, 28, 238, 240
values, aesthetic, 120-122, 129n; held by
  knowledge recipients, 109; in humanistic studies, 70, 83; moral and
  cultural, 21, 23-24, 124
valuing, 23-24
verifiability, of knowledge, 99, 116, 117;
  requirement of, 115-116, 119-120;
  theory of meaning, 116n
verifiable, in principle, 116n; knowledge, 99, 116, 123, 147; theories never
  empirically, 147n
verification requirement retracted, 148n
verisimilitude, 116
verstehen, 50
Veysey, Lawrence, R., 65n
violence, 133
Violin Concerto, 127
Virgil [Publius Vergilius Maro], 71n
Virgo, 146
vocational curriculum, 102

Walpole, Horace, 183n
Walsh, Raymond J., 5n
warranted belief, 117
Warren Commission, 41

Washington, 104
watches and clocks, 40, 199, 234
watching, 60, 92, 186, 190, 191
Watson, James D., 142n
weather forecast, 40, 48, 209
Weaver, Warren, 9n, 186
Weber, Max, 69n, 109
Webster's Dictionary, 9, 146
weighting, different attributes of knowl-
  edge, 56; in tests, 53
Weisbrod, Burton A., 219n
Weiss, Carol, 174n
Weisskopf, Victor F., 95n
welfare, economics, 10, 35, 217n; na-
  tional, 180; social, 222
Whitehead, Alfred North, 78, 111n,
  115n, 119
William and Mary College, 87
Williams, John, 127
Willig, Robert D., 217n
wine tasting, 41, 42, 44, 45
wisdom, 58
wissen, kennen, and *können*, xiii, 29
Wissenschaft, 30, 68n, 69n
Wittgenstein, Ludwig, 116n
Wolff, Christian, 63
Wolin, Sheldon S., xxiiin
Woodward, C. Vann, 84n
Wordsworth, William, 93n
World List of Scientific Periodicals, 163n
Wright, Edmond L., 150n
writer, 92, 190
writing, a foreign language, 35, 41, 43; as
  an act producing knowledge, 186, 198,
  205; as basic skill, 22, 61; plus reading,
  22, 28
Wythe, George, 12n

Yale University, 72, 87
youth unemployment, 20

Zaner, Richard M., 168n
zoology, 88

LIBRARY OF CONGRESS CATALOGING IN PUBLICATION DATA

Machlup, Fritz, 1902-
    Knowledge, its creation, distribution, and economic
significance.

    Includes index.
    1.   CONTENTS: v. 1. Knowledge and knowledge production.
    1.   Learning and scholarship—United States.
2.   Knowledge, Theory of.   I.   Title.
AZ505.M3   1980   001   80-7544
ISBN 0-691-04226-8 (v. 1)

FRITZ MACHLUP was Walker Professor of Economics and International Finance at Princeton University until his retirement in 1971. He is at present Professor of Economics at New York University.